The Spirit
Poured Out
on All Flesh

The Spirit
Poured Out
on All Flesh

Pentecostalism and the Possibility of Global Theology

AMOS YONG

Baker Academic
Grand Rapids, Michigan

Published by Baker Academic
a division of Baker Publishing Group
P.O. Box 6287, Grand Rapids, MI 49516-6287
www.bakeracademic.com

Printed in the United States of America

Library of Congress Cataloging-in-Publication Data

Yong, Amos.
    The Spirit poured out on all flesh : Pentecostalism and the possibility of global theology / Amos Yong.
        p.   cm.
    Includes bibliographical references and index.
    ISBN 0-8010-2770-5 (pbk.)
    1. Pentecostalism. 2. Theology, Doctrinal. I. Title.
BR1644.Y66 2005
230′.994—dc22   2005007055

To
Rick Howard,
Dan Albrecht,
and
Frank Macchia,
my teachers in Pentecostal faith

Contents

Preface

At least four contexts frame the ideas in the following pages. First, there is the variety of pentecostal contexts. This book has arisen out of my experience growing up as a "pentecostal preacher's kid," attending a pentecostal Bible college (Bethany College of the Assemblies of God, Santa Cruz, California), affiliating with a classical pentecostal denomination (the Assemblies of God), and teaching courses on the Holy Spirit at a pentecostal institution of higher education (North Central University of the Assemblies of God, Minneapolis). It reflects my attempts to think through my own pentecostal experience and the pentecostal "tradition" toward a pentecostal theology that is authentically, thoroughly, and unabashedly pentecostal from beginning to end. Still, this volume presents only my one pentecostal perspective and voice. And though attempting to re-present the pentecostal experience in all its diversity, I am limited by my reliance on secondary resources and English-language accounts. Pentecostal readers of this book can and should weigh in both on whether their experiences are captured in the following pages and on whether this kind of theological text can help us "think pentecostally."

Second, there is the variety of ecumenical contexts, including the church catholic. This book concerns not only pentecostal theology but also, as the subtitle indicates, what, if anything, pentecostalism can contribute to a Christian theology for the world of the twenty-first century. Since Azusa Street, pentecostalism has contributed an "experience"; here I not only reflect on the theological content of the experience but also attempt to rethink entirely the Christian theological enterprise from that perspective. The result, I hope, is a new type of systematic theology that also furthers the conversation in the theological academy.

But more, the ecumenical context in our time includes the encounter between the world religions. Although I have written other books on this topic, here I reflect explicitly on the full range of the Christian experience. This book thus provides a kind of initial and very provisional summa of the broad range of my theological thinking, hinted at in my previous publications. The provisionality of the book you hold in your hands, however, derives not only from the unfinished nature of all theological reflection but also from my conviction that Christian theology in our time cannot occur in isolation from the world religious traditions; yet the necessary crossover and return with at least the major religions of the world is not done here (even if there is a start in ch. 6). Much more dialogical work needs to occur with Judaism, Islam, Hinduism, and the Chinese religious traditions—at least—before I will be ready to reengage (God willing) the task of Christian systematic theology as a whole.

Third, there is the eschatological context of the already-but-not-yet, which the Christian theological tradition calls the "age of the Spirit." The outpouring of the Spirit on the day of Pentecost inaugurated the "last days" (Acts 2:17); yet the last day remains ahead of us. Now we live in a time of betwixt and between, after Jesus but before the return of Christ. The chapters in this book reflect the tensions caused by this eschatological context: of theology as particular and yet aspiring toward the universal; of theology as local and yet claiming to be global; of theology as occasional and yet handed down once for all; of theology as narrativistic and yet also metanarrativistic; of theology as conservative and yet novel; of theology as modern and yet postmodern; and so on. This is a theology pursuing after the Spirit, reflecting the attempt to "live in" and "walk according to" the Spirit. I call this a *pneumatology of quest*—a dynamic, dialectical, and discerning theology of the question, driven by a "pneumatological imagination." (I should say that the original proposal for the book included two chapters, 8 and 9, devoted to the hermeneutical and methodological underpinnings of this pneumatological imagination. They had to be left out because the first seven chapters grew beyond their originally anticipated length. I hope that there are sufficient clues throughout the text for readers to discern the method in my madness. Those who desire a more explicit articulation can consult my more lengthy argument in *Spirit–Word–Community: Theological Hermeneutics in Trinitarian Perspective* [Burlington, VT: Ashgate, 2002] or the more succinct version in "The Hermeneutical Trialectic: Notes toward Consensual Hermeneutic and Theological Method," *HeyJ* 44, no. 1 [2004]: 22–39.) Thus the following ideas are fallible and subject to correction, perhaps to the point of being relegated finally to the dustbin of history as it anticipates the day when prophecies and tongues will cease and even knowledge shall come to an end (1 Cor. 13:8).

Fourth and most important is the immediate context of my life. My wife, Alma, has walked with me these last almost seventeen years, helping me discern the Spirit. Without her, this context, which holds the other contexts together, dissolves. Words cannot express my gratefulness to God for her. Our children are the greatest blessing of the Spirit, even as they have been taught by the Spirit beyond their years (and their peers): Aizaiah is a first-year teenager but going into high school, and Alyssa is in her first year in double digits but going into middle school. Anna, our youngest daughter, asked one day, a few weeks before her ninth birthday, "Dad, what book are you writing now?" "A book on pentecostal theology." "What does pentecostal mean?" (We have been attending a Baptist General Conference church here in the Twin Cities for the last five years since I began teaching at Bethel.) My prayer is that one day Anna and her siblings will come to experience pentecostal faith for themselves.

Crystal, Minnesota
June 2004

Acknowledgments

Books are always the product of individuals in community. My thanks are to the following:

- David Parker, editor of the *Evangelical Review of Theology*, for permission to revise portions of my article "The Marks of the Church: A Pentecostal Re-reading," *ERT* 26, no. 1 (2002): 45–67, for inclusion in §3.2;
- Jacques Matthey, editor of the *International Review of Mission*, for permission to revise my essay "'As the Spirit Gives Utterance . . .': Pentecost, Intra-Christian Ecumenism, and the Wider *Oekumene*," *IRM* 92, no. 366 (2003): 299–314, for use in §4.1.1 and §4.3.3;
- Frank Macchia, editor of *Pneuma: The Journal of the Society for Pentecostal Studies*, for permission to use sections of both my "Oneness and the Trinity: The Theological and Ecumenical Implications of 'Creation *ex nihilo*' for an Intra-Pentecostal Dispute," *PNEUMA* 19, no. 1 (1997): 81–107, in §4.1 and §4.3.3, and my "To See or Not to See: A Review Essay of Michael Palmer's *Elements of a Christian Worldview*," *PNEUMA* 21, no. 2 (1999): 305–27, in §7.1.3;
- Peter Sherry, Betty Bond, and the interlibrary loan staff at Bethel University for helping me find and obtain some of the research material for this volume;
- Bethel University, St. Paul, Minnesota, where I teach, for providing paid leave for interim (January) term 2004, during which I finished the initial draft of the book, and to Provost Jay Barnes for approving a stipend during summer term 2004, when I completed the final draft;

- Cecil M. Robeck Jr. for his encouragement over the years; for critical comments that helped me rethink the structure of the book and especially the rhetoric of the chapter, section, and subsection titles; and for sharing with me unpublished and forthcoming essays;
- my sisters and brothers on the Afropentecostal list serve for helping me wrestle with the difficult questions related to naming and understanding world pentecostalism in general and the African, African American, Afro-Caribbean, and African diaspora pentecostal experiences in particular;
- Louis (Bill) Oliverio Jr. for offering critical reflections on chapters 1, 2, and 6; Allan Anderson for providing valuable feedback on chapter 1; Paul Lewis for saving me from making some embarrassing mistakes in §1.2.2; Paulson Pulikottil and Roger Hedlund for commenting on §1.2.3, and Paulson for going the extra mile to read chapter 6 from his Asian Indian Pentecostal perspective; Eric Williams for assuaging my doubts on §1.3; Gregory Zuschlag for assisting the clarification of my ideas in §2.2.3 and chapters 5 and 7; Michael Lodahl for checking over my dialogue with the Wesleyan tradition in §2.2.3 and §6.2.1; Thorsten Moritz for challenging questions and perceptive suggestions on chapter 3; Jeffrey Gros for rendering insightful comments on chapters 3 and 4; Jim Beilby for nuancing my arguments in §3.3 and §7.3.2; F. LeRon Shults and Barry Linney for assessing my discussion in chapter 5; Paul R. Eddy for helping me be more specific about some of my claims in chapter 6; and Dennis W. Cheek for reading over chapter 7;
- Elizabeth Groppe, Glen Menzies, Timothy Berkley, and Frank Macchia for reading over the entire manuscript and giving me invaluable suggestions for how to improve it in terms of both form and content;
- the North Central University Honor Society for responding to my presentation on §6.1;
- my North Central University students in Current Pentecostal Issues, spring semester 2004, for persevering through, and providing feedback on, the manuscript;
- all my pentecostal and nonpentecostal teachers and friends from whom I have learned over the years and whose ideas have blended in with my own; I try to acknowledge my sources in the footnotes of this book when I can remember them (although, in the case of revisions of previously published material, notes are streamlined because of space constraints), but in too many cases to tell, I have internalized your ideas and cannot recall where they originated.

- Brian Bolger, editor at Baker Academic, with whom I have been blessed to work a second time.

This said, my friends and colleagues should not be held responsible for the views presented in this book. Indeed, the book would have been better if I had heeded all you have said. My ignorance, shortsightedness, stubbornness, and fallibility prevented me, however, from following all your suggestions. I release it with all of its flaws, hoping it will spur theologians to correct and improve upon it as the Spirit leads.

There are many I have learned from, yet three of my teachers in pentecostal faith stand out, to whom I dedicate this book. Rick Howard inspired and initiated me into the scholarly reading of the Bible in exegesis courses on Hebrews and Revelation during my sophomore and junior years at Bethany College. Dan Albrecht showed me during my college years how to integrate heart and mind "pentecostally" and later modeled how to be both loyal to, and critical of, the tradition that nurtured me in Christian faith. Frank Macchia has been at the vanguard of the first generation of pentecostal theology in the academy and from the beginning of our friendship has encouraged me in my "thinking in, through, and beyond the (pentecostal) box." If there are any virtues in these pages, these mentors of mine deserve to receive at least some of the credit. All of the many foibles that remain are my own responsibility.

Abbreviations

AJPS	*Asian Journal of Pentecostal Studies*
AusPS	*Australasian Pentecostal Studies*
BHS	Yves Congar, *I Believe in the Holy Spirit*, trans. David Smith, 3 vols. (New York: Seabury; London: Geoffrey Chapman, 1983)
CP	*The Collected Papers of Charles Sanders Peirce*, ed. Charles Hartshorne and Paul Weiss, 6 vols. (Cambridge, MA: Harvard University Press, 1931–1935)
CPCR	*Cyberjournal for Pentecostal/Charismatic Research*
CSR	*Christian Scholar's Review*
DD	*Dharma Deepika: A Journal of South Indian Missiological Research*
EPTA	*European Pentecostal Theological Association Bulletin*
ER	*Ecumenical Review*
ERT	*Evangelical Review of Theology*
FD	John Fletcher, "The Language of the Father's Dispensation," ed. Laurence W. Wood, *Asbury Theological Journal* 53, no. 1 (1998): 65–78
HeyJ	*Heythrop Journal*
IRM	*International Review of Mission*
JAAR	*Journal of the American Academy of Religion*
JAM	*Journal of Asian Mission*
JEPTA	*Journal of the European Pentecostal Theological Association*
JES	*Journal of Ecumenical Studies*
JETS	*Journal of the Evangelical Theological Society*
JPT	*Journal of Pentecostal Theology*
JPTSup	Journal of Pentecostal Theology Supplement Series
NIDPCM	*The New International Dictionary of Pentecostal and Charismatic Movements*, ed. Stanley M. Burgess and Eduard M. van der Maas, rev. and exp. ed. (Grand Rapids: Zondervan, 2002)
PNEUMA	*Pneuma: The Journal of the Society for Pentecostal Studies*

PPP	*Presence, Power, Praise: Documents on the Charismatic Renewal,* ed. Kilian McDonnell, 3 vols. (Collegeville, MN: Liturgical Press, 1980)
PR	*The Pneuma Review*
S&C	*The Spirit and the Church*
SIHC	Studies in the Intercultural History of Christianity
SJT	*Scottish Journal of Theology*
TCSPS	*Transactions of the Charles S. Peirce Society*
WCC	World Council of Churches
WesTJ	*Wesleyan Theological Journal*

Introduction

Emerging Global Issues for Pentecostalism and Christian Theology

The Christian theological task at the dawn of the twenty-first century—what I call our late modern world—is no less complex than it has been historically.[1] It has been further complicated, however, by several factors arising over the last few centuries. These include the challenges raised by modern science, by our increasing awareness of the diversity of religions, and by our present transitional situation between modernity and its aftermath (postmodernity, postcolonialism, postpatriarchalism, post-Christendom, etc.).[2] The questions are legion. Can theology keep up with the ever-shifting framework of modern science? Can theology bear witness to the essentials of Christian faith even while learning from the world's religions? Can theology proceed to recognize the limits of reason without capitulating to relativism? Can theology continue to make universal truth claims, given the particularistic nature of theological reflection? Can theology speak to the postcolonial situation, and can it be relevant to persons and groups seeking liberation

---

1. Following here, among others, Robert Cummings Neville, *Religion in Late Modernity* (Albany: State University of New York Press, 2002). *Late modern* is to be preferred over *postmodern* for at least two reasons: it is less reactionary in its connotations and better captures the sense that life in our time is still driven by the forces of modernity.

2. For elaboration, see Amos Yong and Peter G. Heltzel, "Robert Cummings Neville and the Global Future of Theology," in *Theology in Global Context: Essays in Honor of Robert Cummings Neville*, ed. Amos Yong and Peter G. Heltzel (New York: T & T Clark, 2004), 29–42, esp. 30–34.

from colonialist Christian ideologies? Can the sacred and major texts of the Christian tradition be retrieved and reappropriated, originating as they do from patriarchal contexts? Can theology speak publicly and authoritatively in a situation where Christianity is no longer a dominant political and cultural force?

The hypothesis of this book is not only that Christian theology can continue to speak in this new global context but also that pentecostal theology in particular can do so—a bolder and more ambitious claim. Two caveats are appropriate. First, because there are many skeptics who doubt that theology can speak globally, this emerging theology will need to be *aspired toward* and argued for. Second, because I suspect that the forces of globalization will tempt "global theology" toward homogeneity, I will consciously attempt instead a "world theology" that enables us to emphasize the particularities of local discourses and perspectives.

This introduction is divided into three parts: defining world pentecostalism, identifying the promise and challenge of pentecostal theology in world context, and sketching our distinctive theological method.

I.1 WORLD PENTECOSTALISM: WORKING DEFINITIONS

My thesis is that pentecostalism as a worldwide movement provides an emerging theological tradition through which to explore the possibilities and challenges confronting the development of Christian theology for our late modern world. But for starters, what is "pentecostalism as a worldwide movement"?

Pentecostalism is, has been, and will be a contested idea. As problematic as it may be, I wish to cast my lot here with the *New International Dictionary of Pentecostal and Charismatic Movements,* which identifies three types of pentecostalisms in the twentieth century: the classical Pentecostal movement, connected to the Azusa Street revival in Los Angeles in 1906–1909; the charismatic-renewal movement in the mainline Protestant, Orthodox, and Roman Catholic churches beginning in the 1960s; and a neocharismatic "catch-all category that comprises 18,810 independent, indigenous, postdenominational groups that cannot be classified as either pentecostal or charismatic but share a common emphasis on the Holy Spirit, spiritual gifts, pentecostal-like experiences . . . , signs and wonders, and power encounters."[3] In this book, I use "Pentecostal" and "Pentecostalism" (capitalized) to refer to the classical expression, and "pentecostal" and "pentecostalism" (uncapitalized) to refer to the movement in general or to all three types inclusively. Rather than attempt to defend in the

3. *NIDPCM* xviii–xxi; quotation, xx.

abstract my choice to define pentecostalism inclusively, I proceed in the hope that the rationale for thinking pentecostalism broadly will emerge over the course of this volume.

Pentecostalism inclusively defined is a worldwide movement both numerically and geographically. Statisticians estimate about 525 million adherents in the year 2000, representing 28 percent of the total Christian population and about 8.65 percent of the world population. There are 65 million classical Pentecostals, 175 million charismatics, and 295 million neocharismatics. Of these, 400-plus million, or more than 76 percent, are located in Latin America, Africa, and Asia.[4] Clearly, the most vibrant pentecostal communities are now in the Southern and Eastern Hemispheres,[5] although traffic from South to North, from East to West, and vice versa is now busier than ever before, especially given the telecommunication revolution.

The explosion of pentecostalism, broadly considered, in the twentieth century has been of perennial interest not only to pentecostals themselves but also to outside scholars. Recently it caught the attention of the prominent historian Philip Jenkins.[6] Jenkins's *Next Christendom* brings to mind Philip's first-century CE experiences in Samaria (Acts 8). This first Philip preached the gospel, accomplished signs and wonders, cast out demons, healed the sick, and engaged in power encounters. The present Philip sees the emerging Christendom as featuring essentially the same pentecostal-type phenomena, orientations, and commitments. The first Philip stepped aside when the then powers that be—Peter and John—came from Jerusalem because they had heard of all the commotion taking place in Samaria. The present Philip describes the present Christendom as transitioning from deferring to the powers that be—the Euroamerican and Latin Western churches—to taking responsibility for the shape, beliefs, and practices of the new Christianity according to criteria measured by their indigenous Southern and Eastern experiences and contexts. The first Philip found himself ministering to Samaritans the one day and to the Ethiopian eunuch from the prophet Isaiah the next, truly a microcosm of the plurality of tongues and languages called

4. *NIDPCM*, part 2, "Global Statistics," esp. 286–89.

5. For more on the collapse of Euroamerican hegemony, see Eduardo Mendieta, "From Christendom to Polycentric Oikonumé: Modernity, Postmodernity, and Liberation Theology," in *Liberation Theologies, Postmodernity, and the Americas*, ed. David Batstone et al. (New York: Routledge, 1997), 253–72; Pablo Richard, *Death of Christendoms, Birth of the Church*, trans. Phillip Berryman (Maryknoll, NY: Orbis, 1987); and Winston Crawley, *World Christianity, 1970–2000: Toward a New Millennium* (Pasadena, CA: William Carey Library, 2001).

6. Philip Jenkins, *The Next Christendom: The Coming of Global Christianity* (Oxford: Oxford University Press, 2002).

forth by the Spirit's outpouring on the day of Pentecost. The present Philip suggests that the coming Christendom will be radically pluralistic, centered not in Rome or Canterbury but variously in Seoul, Beijing, Singapore, Bombay, Lagos, Rio, São Paulo, and Mexico City. The "next Christendom" will be dominated by new developments in the pentecostal and, Jenkins suggests, Roman Catholic churches. Everything points to the increasing attractiveness of pentecostal religion: salvation understood especially in terms of present healing and concrete spiritual experiences that also serve to initiate membership into a worldwide community.[7]

How will this affect Christian theology in the twenty-first century? The Asian bishops of the Roman Catholic Church have been anticipating this question in light of the changing face of the Catholic Church in Asia. Thomas Fox suggests that the emergence of Catholic Christianity in Asia is characterized by a "Triple Dialogue": with the poor, with the various cultures of Asia, and with the diversity of Asian religious traditions.[8] The emphases are clearly on:

- a postmodern theology that makes heard the cries of the poor, the victim, and the marginalized rather than the voices of the powerful;
- a postpatriarchal theology focused on youth and women;
- a postfoundationalist theology that values methodological pluralism;
- a postcolonial theology in which indigenous and local traditions, languages, and practices are privileged;
- a posthierarchical theology that embraces dialogical and democratic processes;
- a post-Cartesian theology that gives recognition to the inductive, existential, lived, and nondual character of reflection alongside deductive, propositional, more abstract, and dualistic forms of theologizing;
- and a post-Western and post-European theology open to engaging the multiple religious, cultural, and philosophical voices of Asian traditions and spiritualities.

7. See André Droogers, "Globalisation and Pentecostal Success," in *Between Babel and Pentecost: Transnational Pentecostalism in Africa and Latin America*, ed. André Corten and Ruth Marshall-Fratani (Bloomington: Indiana University Press, 2001), 41–61, esp. 54–59; and Harvey Cox, *Fire from Heaven: The Rise of Pentecostal Spirituality and the Reshaping of Religion in the Twenty-First Century* (Reading, MA: Addison-Wesley, 1995).

8. Thomas C. Fox, *Pentecost in Asia: A New Way of Being Church* (Maryknoll, NY: Orbis, 2002).

In the Catholic Church, of course, such new directions have to be developed in dialogue with both the dogmatic tradition of the Latin Church and the papal hierarchy.

But if Jenkins is correct that the growing churches of the East and South will be predominantly Catholic and pentecostal, how will the latter respond theologically to this new situation? Herein lies the promise and the challenge for pentecostal theology. On the one hand, academic pentecostal theology is coming of age in time to take its place in this new theological conversation, and to do so unencumbered by either a fully developed (dogmatic) theological tradition or a magisterium. On the other hand, this lack of a developed theological tradition means that the way forward is by no means clear. But to lack a *developed* tradition is not the same as to lack a theological tradition altogether. In fact, there may be many more theological resources in the pentecostal tradition than one might think. Walter Hollenweger's analysis of the fivefold roots of pentecostalism, for example, suggests what is available:

- The "black oral root" connects with not only the slave religious experience of the late nineteenth century but also the contemporary explosion of independent pentecostal and charismatic-type churches in western and sub-Saharan Africa.
- The "Catholic root" refers to what has taken place in the Roman Catholic Church since the charismatic-renewal movements of the late 1960s.
- The "evangelical root" is the entire trajectory from Wesley through the nineteenth-century Holiness movement and the complex present relationship between pentecostals, Wesleyan-Holiness, and conservative evangelicalism.
- The "critical root" points to the kind of countercultural identity exemplified in the feminist, pacifist, signs-and-wonders, and academic strains of pentecostalism.
- The "ecumenical root" includes those in the tradition of Boddy, Dallière, Du Plessis, and others leading pentecostals into involvement with, and membership in, the World Council of Churches, among other formally organized ecumenical bodies.[9]

In this account, pentecostalism's roots have established trajectories not only for its future developments but also for its theological reflections. The sources that fed into the early-twentieth-century pentecostal

9. Walter Hollenweger, *Pentecostalism: Origins and Developments Worldwide* (Peabody, MA: Hendrickson, 1997).

revivals have developed into major tributaries and streams. These have now brought world pentecostalism, in all its diversity, into contact with a wide range of dialogue partners. And what may be most challenging is also perhaps what is most exciting about the present and future prospects of pentecostal theology: these dialogue partners are similar to, and congenial with, the voices that anticipate the new theology relevant to the churches of the East and the South in the twenty-first century.

1.2 Pentecostalism: The Possibilities and Challenges of World Theology

The promise of, and the challenge for, pentecostal theology in world context thus come into clearer focus, along three lines: the ecumenical, the interreligious, and the relationship between religion and science. Let me briefly explicate each to set up the late modern context for pentecostal theology today.

To begin, pentecostalism as a global reality is already an ecumenical force, the latter defined, according to the Greek *oikoumenē*, as referring to the worldwide or catholic household of God. As such, pentecostal theology has been, and will need to continue to be, ecumenically engaged, receiving from the past and present traditions of the church catholic even as it attempts to bring gifts to the church catholic. At the same time, worldwide pentecostalism poses all kinds of ecumenical questions to the church catholic, not the least of them being the overall antiecumenical postures adopted by most pentecostal churches and denominations. Most challenging, however, may be the presence of Oneness pentecostalism, which has to be confronted at the beginning of any attempt to do pentecostal theology in world perspective.[10] The Oneness rejection of the traditional doctrine of the Trinity as tritheistic has been particularly divisive, not to mention its doctrine of salvation by water (baptism) and Spirit (reception). For many, especially orthodox trinitarians and conservative evangelicals, Oneness pentecostals are sectarians at best and theological and doctrinal heretics at worst.[11]

10. Oneness constitutes as much as 25 percent of all U.S. classical Pentecostals (*NIDPCM* 294) and perhaps totals twenty million worldwide; Talmadge L. French, *Our God Is One: The Story of the Oneness Pentecostals* (Indianapolis: Voice & Vision, 2001), 17. See also James C. Richardson Jr., *With Water and Spirit: A History of Black Apostolic Denominations in the U.S.* (Washington, DC: Spirit, 1980).

11. See, e.g., Gregory A. Boyd, *Oneness Pentecostals and the Trinity* (Grand Rapids: Baker, 1992); E. Calvin Beisner, *"Jesus Only" Churches* (Grand Rapids: Zondervan, 1998); H. Wayne House, *Charts of Cults, Sects, and Religious Movements* (Grand Rapids: Zondervan, 2000),

Recently, however, Kenneth Gill has reframed the Oneness-trinitarian dispute as a matter of theological contextualization.[12] His study, focusing on the Iglesia Apostólica as an indigenous pentecostal church in Mexico, suggests that this young church is more orthodox than not, even in its theology. Gill defends this proposal along five lines.[13] First, Oneness christology is neither Arian nor unitarian (Christ considered as being fully divine). Second, Mexican Apostolics embrace a legitimate Bible-centered piety that contextualizes the gospel in plain, narrative, and nonphilosophically oriented terms. Third, trinitarian theology is difficult to understand, perennially threatened by subordinationism on the one side and tritheism on the other, and the Oneness understanding is vigilant against the latter.[14] Fourth, Gill observes the Apostolic understanding of Father, Son, and Spirit as modes of God to be much closer to the more recent (especially Barthian) "modal view," wherein God exists eternally in a threefold manner objectively apart from human experience, than to ancient modalism, which renders the triune character of God only apparent rather than real. Finally, Gill suggests that according to a fivefold criteriology for any orthodox (he uses "evangelical") formulation of the doctrine of God—(a) Jesus Christ is divine; (b) God has internal consistency (as in having one center of consciousness, will, etc.); (c) the three modes function simultaneously; (d) each mode is divine rather than only appearing to be divine; and (e) God exists eternally as Father, Son, and Spirit—Mexican Apostolic theology meets all these criteria except the last, and this because it has not really had time to address it. Gill concludes that these Apostolics should "not be rejected as heretical or unitarian, but be accepted as a sincere group of believers who are attempting to be faithful to the Christian scriptures."[15]

Over time, however, the Oneness argument may solidify rather than "grow up" as implied by Gill's suggestion (see ch. 5 below). For the moment, insofar as Gill's proposal hinges, to some extent, on Apostolic theology as part of the contextualization of the gospel in Mexico, this

---

ch. 17; and Ron Rhodes, *The Challenge of the Cults and New Religions* (Grand Rapids: Zondervan, 2001), ch. 12.

12. Kenneth D. Gill, *Toward a Contextualized Theology for the Third World: The Emergence and Development of Jesus' Name Pentecostalism in Mexico*, SIHC 90 (Frankfurt, Ger.: Peter Lang, 1994).

13. Ibid., ch. 8.

14. Gill notes for the benefit of his evangelical readers that even the Lausanne Covenant (1974) stays away from *Trinity* and *persons* as difficult patristic categories for contemporary understanding: "We affirm our belief in the one eternal God, Creator and Lord of the world, Father, Son and Holy Spirit, who governs all things according to the purpose of his will" (ibid., 236 n. 16).

15. Ibid., 233.

raises further questions about the contextualization of pentecostalism around the world. One element of the promise of pentecostal theology is its capacity to nurture an "intercultural theology" that is global and multicultural, inclusive of voices from the Eastern and especially Southern Hemispheres, and emergent from a genuine dialogue between Western pentecostal missions churches and the indigenous pentecostal movements in the two-thirds world.[16] But although pentecostalism has so far shown great adaptability and flexibility in effectively contextualizing the pentecostal witness to the gospel in very diverse situations, there remain two distinct but related issues: that regarding the indigenous expressions of the gospel and that regarding the gospel's encounter with other faith traditions. The former concerns the capacity of the gospel to be enculturated or incarnated in foreign wineskins, whereas the latter concerns what happens when the gospel encounters other faiths and not just other cultures.

This leads to discussion of the second promise of, and challenge for, world pentecostal theology, that regarding the relationship of Christianity and other religions. The interreligious question is intimately related to the intercultural one, since, especially in the Eastern and Southern Hemispheres, religion and culture are only very arbitrarily distinguishable from each other. Two brief examples, one more extreme and the other more mainstream, will suffice. Take, first, the case of the Bible Mission in India founded by Mungamuri Devadas (1875–1960).[17] Although the central doctrines of the Bible Mission—emphases on Spirit baptism, tongues, visions and dreams, divine healing, exorcisms, the imminent return of Christ, and "waiting in the presence of God" or tarrying—appear straightforwardly pentecostal, followers of Devadas "claim that they have nothing to do with the Pentecostals."[18] Further, the congruence of Bible Mission praxis with the popular religiosity of the Indian subcontinent includes several questionable features, including the singing of hymns in the bhakti tradition; the heavy emphasis on ongoing revelation through dreams and visions (perhaps explicable in light of the high illiteracy of Bible Mission followers); an understanding of the realm of the demonic and of exorcism that has as much continuity as discontinuity with the background Indian cosmology; the similarity between Bible Mission tarrying and the Hindu yogic spirituality of silent

16. The nomenclature *intercultural theology* is Hollenweger's; for an overview, see Lynne Price, *Theology out of Place: A Theological Autobiography of Walter J. Hollenweger*, JPTSup 23 (Sheffield, Eng.: Sheffield Academic Press, 2002), ch. 4.

17. P. Solomon Raj, *A Christian Folk-Religion in India: A Study of the Small Church Movement in Andhra Pradesh, with a Special Reference to the Bible Mission of Devadas*, SIHC 40 (New York: Peter Lang, 1986).

18. Ibid., 78.

meditation; and the understanding of Devadas as a guru whose spirit continues to speak to the faithful and guide the church even after his demise (or "translation," as Bible Mission devotees see it). The result is characterizations of the Bible Mission as non-Christian, as a heretical sect, as a healing cult, as an exotic new movement, perhaps even as a legitimate expression of pentecostal Christianity contextualized in India, all depending on one's viewpoint.[19]

The second example, the West African Celestial Church of Christ (CCC), founded by Samuel B. J. Oschoffa (1909–1985), raises more pointedly the challenge of culture *and* religion even if the movement is becoming increasingly mainstream.[20] In this case, the question is whether the CCC, perhaps like other West African Aladura churches, has laid Christian terminology over an essentially unchanged Yoruba worldview, so that "God and the Holy Spirit became the new *Orisha* [Yoruba deities] and Christianity became the new 'cult' system."[21] In many obvious ways, the CCC is charismatic (not only in terms of its founding personality) and pentecostal (especially the centrality of the Holy Spirit in all aspects of the life of the church; the pervasiveness of visions, dreams, and prophecies; and the presence of glossolalia, etc.), even Christian (in its affirmation of the Nicene Creed). But those arguing in favor of reading the CCC as a syncretism of Christianity and Yoruba religiosity would point to the parallels between CCC beliefs in indiscernible incorporeal forces and Yoruba cosmology; between CCC liturgy and rituals (even that of the Eucharist) and Yoruba rites of passage; between CCC use of water, color, and other ritual symbols and objects found also in Yoruba symbolism; and between Oschoffa's elevation (practically speaking, at least) to the status of CCC ancestor after his demise/translation in 1985 and Yoruba ancestorology, among other correspondences. Even though CCC leadership has consistently, adamantly, and publicly rejected any affiliation with Yoruba traditions, these observations raise the difficult questions about religious syncretism versus religious contextualization, on the one side, and the relationship between Christianity and other faith traditions, on the other side. The latter issue impinges on the former, even though it poses its own distinctive challenges especially when the world religious traditions are involved and not just indigenous worldviews. One could respond that charges of syncretism reflect the perspective of those "who stand outside [the CCC] circle of faith and

19. As reported by Roger Hedlund, a specialist on indigenous Christianity in India, email to author, November 21, 2003.

20. Afeosemime U. Adogame, *Celestial Church of Christ: The Politics of Cultural Identity in a West African Prophetic-Charismatic Movement*, SIHC 115 (Frankfurt, Ger.: Peter Lang, 1999).

21. Ibid., 4.

hence fail to see or to experience its inner unity."[22] Although I appreciate this distinction regarding insider and outsider perspectives, I think
it necessary to develop this not just as a methodological issue but as a
biblical and pneumatological one in terms of the metaphor of the plurality of tongues giving witness to the one God. My claim is that precisely
because of these challenges, pentecostalism needs to give much more
thought to both theology of culture and theology of religion if it is to
fulfill its task of developing a world theology.

Finally, the promise of, and challenge for, pentecostal theology as
world theology in the late modern world concerns the relationship between religion and science. On this front, pentecostal practitioners of
the sciences are only currently emerging. This means that pentecostals
have yet to contribute their own critical perspectives on the scientific
enterprise. But herein lies pentecostalism's ambivalence: On the one
hand, pentecostalism has rejected modernity's homogenizing forces and
has participated in postmodernity's celebration of plurality and difference. On the other hand, pentecostalism certainly remains a child of
modernity, given its own globalizing propensies and its participation
in the forces of globalization.

A new study by Simon Coleman (a cultural anthropologist) focuses
this ambivalence for world pentecostal theology. His research employs
the recently established (1983) Swedish charismatic denomination Livets
Ord (Word of Life) as a lens through which to explore what he calls
"the globalisation of charismatic Christianity."[23] The forces of globalization are illuminated in the highly advanced use of modern technology
(multimedia communications, television, the Internet, etc.), in the com-
modification of material culture (art, architecture, consumer products,
etc.), and in the transportable worship experience that utilizes a vernacular language but standardizes a liturgy with a clearly recognizable
environmental background and phenomenology. This study calls attention to additional lacunae in pentecostal theological reflection, namely,
regarding the social processes undergirding pentecostal experience
and regarding the nature of the material world, which bends to human
technological instrumentalization. Such reflections require a theology
of culture and a theological anthropology that engage in a sustained
dialogue with the broad range of the human sciences, and a theology
of creation that takes seriously the natural sciences.

Clearly, pentecostal theology for the late modern world needs to engage
discussions on all of these fronts: the ecumenical, the interreligious,

22. Ibid., 213.
23. Simon Coleman, *The Globalisation of Charismatic Christianity: Spreading the Gospel of Prosperity* (Cambridge: Cambridge University Press, 2000).

and the religion-science interfaces (chs. 5–7 below). But what would be distinctive about the *theological* perspective enabling a specifically pentecostal contribution to these matters?

I.3 Pentecostal Distinctives for a World Christian Theology

I suggest that a distinctive pentecostal perspective would highlight a Lukan hermeneutical approach, a pneumatological framework and orientation, and an experiential base. Let me elaborate briefly on each.

First, a distinctive pentecostal theology would be biblically grounded. Yet its approach to Scripture may be through a hermeneutical and exegetical perspective informed explicitly by Luke-Acts. If the genius of pentecostalism is its yearning to experience afresh the power of the Holy Spirit manifest in the first-century church and if Luke is the author most concerned with, and interested in, the operations of the Spirit,[24] then this convergence should not be surprising. This pentecostal vision of original Christianity is animated by the conviction that the accounts in the book of Acts (especially) are not merely of historical interest but an invitation to participate in the ongoing work of the Holy Spirit.[25] Thus, for pentecostals, Luke-Acts has served somewhat as a template allowing readers to enter into the world of the early church. In this volume, a Lukan hermeneutic will be deployed both in order to establish the biblical credentials of world pentecostal theology and in order to provide a point of entry into the diversity of biblical texts (see §2.1.1). I see as unavoidable such an open acknowledgment of approaching the whole of Scripture through a part of the whole: no one can be merely and fully biblical in the exhaustive sense of the term. Better to concede one's perspective up front, since this better protects against a naïve biblicism that often results in aspirations to be "biblical."[26]

24. See G. W. H. Lampe, "The Holy Spirit in the Writings of St. Luke," in *Studies in the Gospels: Essays in Memory of R. H. Lightfoot,* ed. D. E. Nineham (Oxford: Basil Blackwell, 1957), 159–200.

25. The motto of the Anabaptist theologian James William McClendon Jr., "This is that," reflects the congruence between "this world" and "that" experience of the earliest Christians; see his *Systematic Theology,* vol. 1, *Ethics* (Nashville: Abingdon, 1986), esp. 32–35.

26. This I do "without wishing to absolutize the Acts of the Apostles" ("Statement of the Theological Basis of the Catholic Charismatic Renewal," *PPP* 3:1–10; quotation, 2), even while proceeding with the conviction that Theophilus (whom Luke addressed) was not any less deprived of the inspired word of God by having access only to these two writings.

Second, a distinctive pentecostal theology would be theologically guided, specifically through the core thematic motif of Jesus the Christ (the anointed one) and the core orienting motif of pneumatology. The heartbeat of pentecostal spirituality is the dynamic experience of the Holy Spirit. The theological gift of pentecostalism to the church catholic, I suggest, is to contribute to the recent renaissance in pneumatology more specifically and in pneumatological theology in general. Although this pneumatological orientation—what I have elsewhere called a pneumatological imagination[27]—derives in large part from the late-nineteenth-century Holiness movement's quest for understanding sanctification and its relationship to the baptism of the Holy Spirit, the last generation has witnessed a remarkable explosion of what might be called pneumatological theology. Perhaps coinciding with the emergence of the charismatic-renewal movement among the mainline and Roman Catholic churches since the 1950s, theologians have not only been reflecting more about the Spirit (pneumatology) but also rethinking traditional theological loci from the starting point of pneumatology.[28] This volume is intended as a modest pentecostal contribution to the contemporary discussion in pneumatological theology. More precisely, my wager is that this pneumatological orientation and dynamic open up space for the Spirit of God to redeem the perspectives and contributions of all flesh (Acts 2:17b)—including those engaged in ecumenical, multifaith, and religion-science dialogues and discourses—in order to orchestrate this plurality of voices and to hasten the coming reign of God.

But whereas pneumatology provides the orienting dynamic for this theology, christology provides its thematic focus. Although this book wrestles with the complex issues surrounding the relationship between Christ and the Spirit, it is nevertheless the case that the Holy Spirit is at least the Spirit of Jesus. Pentecostal piety has therefore always been a Jesus-centered piety, and not only among the Oneness or "Jesus-only" churches (see *PPP* 1:xxvii–xxviii). Concerned after all with Jesus the Christ, Christian theology will therefore be christocentric in some sense. The quest in this volume can therefore be understood to be pneumatologically driven and christologically centered, and each element would be understood to illuminate the other. The goal is to find a third way between or beyond the subordination of the Spirit to Christ (or vice

27. On the pneumatological imagination, see Amos Yong, *Spirit–Word–Community: Theological Hermeneutics in Trinitarian Perspective* (Burlington, VT: Ashgate, 2002), part 2.

28. Representative are Clark Pinnock, *Flame of Love: A Theology of the Holy Spirit* (Downers Grove, IL: InterVarsity, 1996); and D. Lyle Dabney, "Otherwise Engaged in the Spirit: A First Theology for the Twenty-First Century," in *The Future of Theology: Essays in Honor of Jürgen Moltmann*, ed. Miroslav Volf, Carmen Krieg, and Thomas Kucharz (Grand Rapids: Eerdmans, 1996), 154–63.

versa) and the displacement of the Spirit from Christ (or vice versa), toward a robustly trinitarian theology of mutuality, reciprocity, and perichoresis (see §5.2).

Finally, a distinctive pentecostal theology would also be confessionally located, in the sense of emerging from the matrix of the pentecostal experience of the Spirit of God. In the case of world pentecostalism, confessional location cannot be doctrinally delineated as would be the case in creedal denominations and churches. Nevertheless, pentecostals are also confessors, not only with regard to their faith in the Lord Jesus Christ but also in terms of their testimonies about what the Lord has done. By confessional location, then, I refer specifically to the realities of pentecostal life "on the ground." In this way, as I hope to show, pentecostal theology cannot be merely abstract but is intensely practical. More important, this allows retrieval of pentecostal perspectives far from the center, in what Allan Anderson calls "voices from the margins."[29] And last but not least, only such a theology holds forth the promise of bridging theological reflection with the present actualities of pentecostal worship, life, and practice (thereby following the ancient dictum linking prayer and theology: *lex orandi lex credendi*).

Needless to say, the kind of world pentecostal theology aspired to cannot be individually produced. Rather, it has to emerge from the convergence of ecumenical and pentecostal reflection, negotiating all along the tension between the universal and the particular, the global and the local, the church catholic and the pentecostal churches. Further, any argument toward world theology needs to be fallibilistic (reflecting the limitations of reason recognized by our post-Enlightenment situation), multiperspectival (reflecting our postcolonial situation), and self-critical and dialogical (reflecting our post-Christendom situation). As fallibilistic, the argument will need to continually traverse the hermeneutical circle from theory and ethics to the missionary and ministry experience of the church and vice versa. In the argument as multiperspectival, insights will need to be gained not only from marginalized voices and locations but also from the various academic disciplines both in the hard sciences and the humanities. And in the argument as self-critical and dialogical, issues in theological hermeneutics and theological method cannot be avoided.

The following are, in some respects, no more than programmatic essays toward a world pentecostal theology. Yet pentecostals can no longer put off providing their own apologetic and systematic theology: apologetic in the sense of engaging anyone interested in these matters

29. Allan Anderson, "The 'Fury' and 'Wonder'? Pentecostal-Charismatic Spirituality in Theological Education," *PNEUMA* 23, no. 2 (2001): 287–302; quotation, 299.

on our own terms even as those terms are translated into appropriate public discourses, and systematic in the sense of rethinking the content *and* structure of theology in terms of the pneumatological dynamic of pentecostal experience. So pentecostal apologetics in the late modern world will have to acknowledge the cautions of the anti-intellectualism of its ancestors but move beyond that and come of age by engaging the existing conversations with humility and yet conviction. Similarly, pentecostal theology in the twenty-first century will need to build on developments made during its scholastic phase[30] but also move beyond them and come of age by engaging the broad spectrum of conversations as a full dialogue partner seeking to learn but also able to contribute something fresh. In these senses, the road is wide open for the development of a world pentecostal theology that is *in via* (along the way); more aptly put, it will be a pneumatological theology of quest.

The hypothesis of this volume will be prosecuted as follows. Chapter 1 introduces worldwide pentecostalism, focused especially on the pentecostal experience of the Holy Spirit on the ground. The next two chapters elaborate on the pentecostal experience of the Spirit in terms of a pneumatological soteriology (ch. 2) and a pneumatological ecclesiology (ch. 3). Chapter 4 explores intra-Christian and multifaith ecumenical implications, and chapter 5 takes up the specific theological challenges posed by Oneness pentecostalism's doctrine of God. The last two chapters pursue the kind of public theology required of world theology by engaging theology of culture and theology of religions (ch. 6) and theology of creation (ch. 7). Come Holy Spirit, lead us into all truth . . .

---

30. See Douglas Jacobsen, "Knowing the Doctrines of Pentecostals: The Scholastic Theology of the Assemblies of God, 1930–1955," in *Pentecostal Currents in American Protestantism*, ed. Edith L. Blumhofer, Russell P. Spittler, and Grant A. Wacker (Urbana: University of Illinois Press, 1999), 90–107; cf. Gary B. McGee, "'More Than Evangelical': The Challenge of the Evolving Theological Identity of the Assemblies of God," *PNEUMA* 25, no. 2 (2003): 289–300; and Simon Chan, "The Renewal of Pentecostalism: A Response to John Carpenter," *AJPS* 7, no. 1 (2004): 315–25.

1

"Poured Out upon All Flesh"

Salvation, the Spirit, and World Pentecostalism

On the day of Pentecost, the crowd asked, "What does this mean?" Peter answered that this was the last days' outpouring of God's Spirit upon all flesh. Today our theological question is, What does it mean that God did so then and continues to pour out the Spirit on men and women, young and old, slave and free (Acts 2:17–18; cf. Joel 2:28–29)? The beginnings of a response to this question will take us toward a pentecostal theology for the late modern world along at least three lines. First, insofar as theology is doxology, then pentecostal theology will be reflection on the prayers, praises, worship, and liturgies of those upon whom the Spirit has been poured out. Second, insofar as theology is theodicy, then pentecostal theology will be reflection on the fallenness of the human condition and on the divine response of the outpouring of the Spirit. Finally, insofar as theology is second-order reflection on lived experience, then pentecostal theology will be reflection on the triumphs over sin, sickness, and Satan that are enjoyed by those visited by the Spirit. In short, the beginnings of a pentecostal theology will be the saving works of God accomplished through the Spirit's being poured out on all flesh. For this reason we begin this exploration of a world pentecostal theology by focusing on the phenomenology of pentecostalisms in Latin America, Asia, and Africa.

Such a phenomenology of world pentecostalisms is important also since my own pentecostal experience is, by and large, limited to the North American context. Because the biases that inevitably inform my discussion are derived from this context, they will need to be checked, expanded, and corrected by the worldwide pentecostal experience. Further, the upward social mobility and increasing institutionalization of classical Pentecostal denominations in North America have resulted in churches almost indistinguishable from evangelical churches on any given Sunday morning.[1] Arguably, such a convergence has produced an increasing openness of North American evangelicalism to the movement of the Spirit in the church and the development of a more Bible-centered piety among pentecostals influenced by evangelical spirituality. At the same time, it may have also resulted in the loss of a distinctive pentecostal witness. Finally, a case can be made that North American pentecostalism is no longer at the vanguard of what God is doing through this movement in the world. "Classical Pentecostalism is unlikely to be a major power in the developed world because it represents the mobilization of a minority of people at the varied margins of that world, whereas in the developing world it represents the mobilization of large masses."[2] For all of these reasons and more, any attempt to develop a pentecostal theology today needs to attend to the world pentecostal phenomenon.

My coverage of world pentecostalism is, however, necessarily limited. Not only am I reliant on mostly secondary sources; my selections are also shaped by my theological agenda, especially insofar as theology not only derives from experience (and hence is descriptive) but also informs experience (and hence is prescriptive). At the same time, I submit the following phenomenological overview to be representative of world pentecostalism as actually occurring on the ground. In each section, I begin with an introductory overview of the literature, then move on to thematic and case study analyses of the Spirit's being poured out on all flesh.

1. Thus Margaret M. Poloma, *The Assemblies of God at the Crossroads: Charisma and Institutional Dilemmas* (Knoxville: University of Tennessee Press, 1989); Edith L. Blumhofer, *Restoring the Faith: The Assemblies of God, Pentecostalism, and American Culture* (Urbana: University of Illinois Press, 1993), ch. 11; and Mickey Crews, *The Church of God: A Social History* (Knoxville: University of Tennessee Press, 1990).

2. David Martin, *Pentecostalism: The World Their Parish* (Oxford: Blackwell, 2002), 67.

1.1 ON YOUR SONS AND DAUGHTERS: LATIN AMERICAN PENTECOSTALISMS

The three types of pentecostalism in Latin America combined to number more than 141 million by the year 2000, approximately 27 percent of world pentecostalism (*NIDPCM* 287). The literature on the explosion of pentecostalism in this region is itself staggering and resists summary statements.[3] Several notable elements, however, should be highlighted, beginning with the diversity of Latin American pentecostalisms. It is composed of autochthonous churches, some antedating Azusa Street; churches founded by classical Pentecostal missions organizations; Oneness or Apostolic churches; and a wide spectrum of Latino/a churches in North America.[4]

Second, the Latin American pentecostal experience can also be understood to provide an alternative to "popular Latino Catholicism, the occult, and mainline Protestantism."[5] Regarding the Catholic Church, pentecostalism provides an experiential, emotional, nonritualistic, and dualistic (in church-state relations and church-world relations) alternative.[6] From the Catholic perspective, pentecostalism is considered to be sectarian and cultic, and its activities illegitimate proselytism. Relations between Catholics and pentecostals remain tense in many areas, given the predominantly Catholic history of many Latin American nations and regions.[7] Regarding the occult, pentecostal polemics are often directed against the "demonic" manifestations of Candomblé and Umbanda (Brazil), Santeria (Cuba), voodoo (Haiti), and so on. Yet it is sometimes difficult to categorize the complex reality on the ground as pentecostalism blends into spiritist/animist versions of Christianity.[8] Regarding mainline Protestantism, it should be noted that the conservative-liberal divide in North America is much less noticeable in the Latin American context,

---

3. For a rich bibliography (by André Droogers), see Barbara Boudewijnse, André Droogers, and Frans Kamsteeg, eds., *More than Opium: An Anthropological Approach to Latin American and Caribbean Pentecostal Praxis*, Studies in Evangelicalism 14 (Lanham, MD: Scarecrow, 1998), 249–312.

4. See Manuel J. Gaxiola-Gaxiola, "Latin American Pentecostalism: A Mosaic within a Mosaic," *PNEUMA* 13, no. 2 (1991): 107–29.

5. Gastón Espinosa, "*El Azteca*: Francisco Olazábal and Latino Pentecostal Charisma, Power, and Faith Healing in the Borderlands," *JAAR* 67, no. 3 (1999): 597–616; quotation, 614.

6. See the analysis by David Lehmann, *Struggle for the Spirit: Religious Transformation and Popular Culture in Brazil and Latin America* (Cambridge, MA: Polity, 1996).

7. See Brian H. Smith, *Religious Politics in Latin America: Pentecostal vs. Catholic* (Notre Dame, IN: University of Notre Dame Press, 1998).

8. As observed by Mike Berg and Paul Pretiz, *Spontaneous Combustion: Grass-Roots Christianity, Latin American Style* (Pasadena, CA: William Carey Library, 1996).

including the Latino/a pentecostal experience of North America.[9] But the situation is more complex across Latin America especially when the definitions of political conservatism or political liberalism differ from region to region and when the Latin American world features various types of Protestantism and pentecostalism and the interchangeability of *evangélicos* and *pentecostales*.[10]

Third, whereas earlier analysts emphasized functionalist explanations of Latin American pentecostal growth related to rapid social change since the 1950s, more recent interpreters have highlighted a complex of social, political, economic, ideological, psychological, and even moral-ethical factors at work.[11] Yet the religious draw of pentecostalism should not be underestimated: physical, emotional, and spiritual healing; access to the supernatural; tongues as a sign; the centrality of music and song; oral, narrative, and vernacular modes of communication; the empowerment of women; networks of support, solidarity, and skill development—each of these is either essentially religious or includes a specifically religious dimension.[12]

This section explores further the phenomenon of Latin American pentecostalism both thematically and through a case study. It provides observations regarding the political dimension of Latin American pentecostalism, then analyzes a distinctive type of feminism in the Latin American pentecostal experience, and concludes with an overview of the Misión Iglesia Pentecostal in Chile. The questions throughout are these: what has salvation meant in Latin American pentecostalism, and how has this been manifested and experienced?

1.1.1 *The Sons of Latin American Pentecostalism: Toward a Pentecostal Politics of the Spirit*. In a recent study, Timothy Steigenga has devoted

9. Preliminary findings show that the 28 percent of U.S. Latinos who are Pentecostal or charismatic are generally religiously and theologically conservative but socially and politically liberal; see Gastón Espinosa, Virgilio Elizondo, and Jesse Miranda, "Hispanic Churches in American Public Life: Summary of Findings," *Interim Reports*, 2nd ed. (March 2003), http://www.hcapl.org/resources.html; and Samuel Cruz, "A Rereading of Latino(a) Pentecostalism," in *New Horizons in Hispanic/Latino(a) Theology*, ed. Benjamín Valentín (Cleveland: Pilgrim, 2003), 201–16. For snapshots of Latino pentecostals in the United States, see Arlene M. Sanchez-Walsh, *Latino Pentecostal Identity: Evangelical Faith, Self, and Society* (New York: Columbia University Press, 2003).

10. Karl-Wilhelm Westmeier, *Protestant Pentecostalism in Latin America: A Study in the Dynamics of Missions* (Cranbury, NJ: Associated University Presses / Fairleigh Dickinson University Press, 1999), 15–21.

11. Summarized by Daniel R. Miller, "Introduction," in *Coming of Age: Protestantism in Contemporary Latin America*, ed. Daniel R. Miller (Lanham, MD: University Press of America, 1994), esp. xiv–xvii.

12. See David Martin, *Tongues of Fire: The Explosion of Protestantism in Latin America* (Cambridge, MA: Blackwell, 1990), ch. 9.

extended attention to a topic that has gained increasing notice among students of Latin American religion: pentecostalism and politics.[13] While recognizing that no generalizations about pentecostal politics should be made without factoring in region, political context, and religious beliefs and practices, Steigenga illuminates how, as a result of the explosion of the charismatic movement (also known as neopentecostalism) in Guatemala during the 1960s and 1970s, more than 80 percent of Protestants (*evangélicos*) and perhaps 50 percent of the entire population were pentecostals by 1980.[14] This provides the context for two especially interesting events. The first case was an army coup in March 1982 that "called to power" the retired general Efraín Ríos Montt. Under the Christian Democratic ticket (and as a member of the Catholic Church), Montt had run for and probably won the presidency in 1974, but was cheated by his fellow army officers, who installed their favored candidate. After failing to win a second nomination from the Christian Democrats in 1977, Montt retired. Disillusioned, he showed up in 1978 at the doorsteps of the newly established neopentecostal church El Verbo and came into his born-again experience under the guidance of El Verbo leadership. Over the next four years, Montt was discipled by El Verbo elders and lay leaders. In the weeks preceding the election date, March 7, 1982, El Verbo elders fasted and prayed over Montt's aspirations for making a third run at the presidency, but resulting prophecies indicated that his time was not yet. The coup d'état on March 23 by young army officers and their invitation to the (allegedly) surprised Montt to assume command was understood by El Verbo elders (who believed Montt's claim to innocence) as confirmation of prophecy. The general proceeded to retain two El Verbo elders as spiritual advisors to the president.

Montt's brief tenure was thoroughly ambiguous.[15] On the one hand, he was touted as the nation's first evangelical leader, who would cleanse the nation from its corruption and injustice. Toward that end, Montt articulated (over national television) and implemented a "Victory 82" vision for a new Guatemala based on morality, order/discipline, and national unity. The morality represented (arguably) a convergence of

13. Timothy J. Steigenga, *The Politics of the Spirit: The Political Implications of Pentecostalized Religion in Costa Rica and Guatemala* (Lanham, MD: Lexington, 2001).

14. The 50 percent figure, ibid., 81; the 80 percent figure is from Virginia Garrard-Burnett, *Protestantism in Guatemala: Living in the New Jerusalem* (Austin: University of Texas Press, 1998), 119. For more on pentecostal growth in Guatemala during this period, see Dennis A. Smith, "Coming of Age: A Reflection on Pentecostals, Politics, and Popular Religion in Guatemala," *PNEUMA* 13, no. 2 (1991): 131–40.

15. For a sympathetic North American evangelical perspective on Montt, see Joseph Anfuso and David Sczepanski, *Efrain Rios Montt: Servant or Dictator?* (Ventura, CA: Vision House, 1983).

conservative Catholic mores and neopentecostal legalism (symbolized concretely by the presence of El Verbo elders in the president's cabinet). The discipline included new policies of "no robo, no miento, no abuso" (no stealing, no lying, no abuse of government authority and resources) for governmental employees and attempts to restore law and order (against the guerrilla resistance movements). Finally, Montt sought to build a unified state from the variegated indigenous populations. On the other hand, Montt's vision quickly alienated him from various constituencies. The officers who put him in power came to see his moralism as motivated by religious fundamentalism, and the Catholic hierarchy reacted against his Protestant dispositions and spiritual advisors. Further, the indigenous peoples were massacred, relocated, or forced into exile by an army thought to be either authorized by Montt or out of his control altogether.[16] For these reasons, the army ended Montt's presidency in August 1983.

But this was not all for pentecostal politics in Guatemala. The second case concerned Jorge Serrano, Montt's former president of the council of state and member first of the neopentecostal Elim Church and then of the Catholic charismatic-renewal organization El Shaddai. While running for president in 1990, Serrano promoted "a 'spiritual warfare' project of national exorcism known as 'Jesus is Lord of Guatemala,' to free the country from a curse relating to pre-Christian religion."[17] Serrano's victory in the election was a first for pentecostal politics. As with Montt, however, Serrano's tenure was also ambiguous. Questions were raised not only about his human-rights policies and practices but also about his personal morality. In June 1993, he was exiled to Panama.

These cases are not glowing examples of pentecostal engagement with politics. Further, although El Verbo elders served as Montt's spiritual advisors, it appears that neither they nor the two neopentecostal presidents operated in the public political sphere on the basis of a distinctive pentecostal identity. In fact, politicians such as Montt and Serrano may

16. I am grateful to John Sniegocki for pointing me to some of the evidence regarding Montt's culpability, e.g., *Guatemala: Massive Extrajudicial Executions in Rural Areas under the Government of General Efraín Ríos Montt* (London: Amnesty International, 1982). A fair analysis is David Stoll, "Evangelicals, Guerrillas, and the Army: The Ixil Triangle under Ríos Montt," in *Harvest of Violence: The Maya Indians and the Guatemalan Crisis*, ed. Robert M. Carmack (Norman: University of Oklahoma Press, 1988), 90–116.

17. Paul Freston, *Evangelicals and Politics in Asia, Africa, and Latin America* (Cambridge: Cambridge University Press, 2001), 274; see also David Stoll, "'Jesus is Lord of Guatemala': Evangelical Reform in a Death-Squad State," in *Accounting for Fundamentalisms: The Dynamic Character of Movements*, ed. Martin E. Marty and R. Scott Appleby (Chicago: University of Chicago Press, 1994), 99–123.

have used their pentecostal affiliations rather than been useful to their pentecostal constituencies or to the nation.[18]

These events are important, however, because they anticipate central developments of the twenty-first-century pentecostal experience along four lines. First, Montt and Serrano are representative of the increasing number of pentecostals who will aspire to and even run for public office. Second, not only will there be more pentecostal candidates; some have been, and many more will indeed be, elected to office. Serrano's election, "the first of a Protestant as president, represents the coming of age of Protestants in public life."[19] Third, not only are pentecostals voting; their voting is evidence of an emerging sociopolitical consciousness. In the case of Guatemala, in addition to individual members being involved in guerrilla warfare against the repressive government, pentecostal churches are increasingly engaging in emergency relief work (in response to the civil war), addressing racism regarding the Indian population so that *ladinos* (those of mixed Spanish and Indian blood) no longer exploit the *indígenas* (pure Indians), and developing social and community services.[20] Finally, even for pentecostals who retain the strict apolitical stance prevalent in twentieth-century pentecostal history, such a stance is more rhetorical than real. As demonstrated by the indigenous peoples in the Guatemalan mountains, apolitical orientations are actually discourses that reorder and restructure an alternative way of life—an alternative politics, in this case between the army, on the one side, and the guerrillas, on the other—resulting in new educational, economic, social, and political realities.[21]

What is taking place in Guatemala is representative of Latin American pentecostalism. In Brazil, for example, the "politics of the Spirit" has also been increasingly manifest, with pentecostal entry into politics as far back as 1962, when one of the leaders of the pentecostal church Brasil para Cristo ran for and was elected to the federal congress. From 1979 to 1982, the newly founded Workers' Party attracted sizable numbers of pentecostals (*crentes*), many of whom were very active, even providing leadership.

18. See Everett Wilson, "Guatemalan Pentecostals: Something of Their Own," in *Power, Politics, and Pentecostals in Latin America*, ed. Edward L. Cleary and Hannah W. Stewart-Gambino (Boulder, CO: Westview, 1997), 139–62, esp. 154.

19. Edward L. Cleary, "Evangelicals and Competition in Guatemala," in *Conflict and Competition: The Latin American Church in a Changing Environment*, ed. Edward L. Cleary and Hannah W. Stewart-Gambino (Boulder, CO: Lynne Rienner, 1992), 167–95; quotation, 189.

20. Richard E. Waldrop, "The Social Consciousness and Involvement of the Full Gospel Church of God in Guatemala," *CPCR* 2 (1997), http://www.pctii.org/cyberj/cyber2.html.

21. As argued by David Stoll, *Between Two Armies in the Ixil Towns of Guatemala* (New York: Columbia University Press, 1993), ch. 6.

Then in 1986, a breakthrough year, thirty-three *evangélicos* were elected to the constituent assembly charged with rewriting the constitution after twenty-one years of military rule; of these, eighteen were pentecostals, thirteen of whom were members of the Asamblea de Dios.[22]

But this is not all.[23] Pentecostals are increasingly involved in neighborhood organizations focused on improving the material living conditions of the wider communities in which they live, especially in more diverse neighborhoods that are less dominated by Catholic leadership and a Catholic population. In the latter contexts, pentecostals have shown the capacity to work with Catholics and even spiritists. Although involvement in labor struggles is much more difficult to track, especially because of the nonviolent modes of resistance insisted upon by *crentes*, their participation often makes a significant difference because of their large numbers. Further, the Brazilian pentecostal experience has also provided a distinctive, powerful counterdiscourse to racism, in that God is no respecter of persons and the Holy Spirit is seen to be given to all persons regardless of the color of their skin. Finally, some pentecostals have resisted unjust structures, policies, and conditions and aligned themselves against the immoral perpetrators of injustice.

Space constraints do not allow comment on pentecostal politics in Nicaragua (where pentecostals were engaged on both sides of the Sandinista-Contra civil war), Colombia, Venezuela, Peru, or Argentina.[24] The preceding facts, however, support the following summary statements. First, pentecostals in Latin America are becoming increasingly engaged in social and political activities. Second, such engagement shows an emerging awareness that salvation is not only an otherworldly anticipation but also a this-worldly experience, manifest in the material,

22. See Paul Freston, "Brother Votes for Brother: The New Politics of Protestantism in Brazil," in *Rethinking Protestantism in Latin America*, ed. Virginia Garrard-Burnett and David Stoll (Philadelphia: Temple University Press, 1993), 66–110; and R. Andrew Chestnut, *Born Again in Brazil: The Pentecostal Boom and the Pathogens of Poverty* (New Brunswick, NJ: Rutgers University Press, 1997), ch. 7.

23. Material from this paragraph derives from John Burdick, *Looking for God in Brazil: The Progressive Catholic Church in Urban Brazil's Religious Arena* (Berkeley: University of California Press, 1993), chs. 6 and 7, esp. 206–20; Rowan Ireland, "The *Crentes* of Campo Alegre and the Religious Reconstruction of Brazilian Politics," in Garrard-Burnett and Stoll, eds., *Rethinking Protestantism in Latin America*, 45–65; and idem, "Pentecostalism, Conversions, and Politics in Brazil," in Cleary and Stewart-Gambino, eds., *Power, Politics, and Pentecostals in Latin America*, 123–37. See also Cecília Loreto Mariz, *Coping with Poverty: Pentecostals and Christian Base Communities in Brazil* (Philadelphia: Temple University Press, 1994), for discussion of similar developments in Catholic pentecostalism in Brazil.

24. On the Nicaraguan situation, see David Stoll, *Is Latin America Turning Protestant? The Politics of Evangelical Growth* (Berkeley: University of California Press, 1990), ch. 8.

economic, social, and political dimensions of human existence. Third, pentecostal leaders and laypersons are realizing more than ever that the outpouring of the Spirit and the saving work of God do not preclude but include these various dimensions. Here the early modern pentecostal conviction that the presence and activity of the Spirit meant the healing of the body or the provision of the material needs of the believer is extended to encompass the sociopolitical sphere.

Certainly, I am not claiming that Latin American pentecostalism as a whole is becoming a politicized faith. In general, pentecostals remain focused on either eschatological salvation or, if they have been introduced to such, the prosperity gospel of individual blessings in this life. Yet it is also undeniable that pentecostal experience, like all religious experience, is inherently political and that pentecostals are becoming more intentionally political. Pentecostals continue to lack a well-thought-out sociopolitical vision, and, because of their decentralized nature, cannot be expected to produce anytime soon such a distinctive pentecostal perspective. In any case, I would argue that Latin American pentecostals need to build on the factors that currently motivate them: "Fervent moralism, a conviction that God punishes the unjust in this world as well as in the next, and Old Testament images of a people struggling against injustice may motivate *crentes* to denounce and resist the unjust patron or the compromised bureaucrat."[25] And if pentecostals respond from these convictions, this would be one of the many essential starting points toward a world pentecostal theology.

1.1.2 *The Daughters of Latin American Pentecostalism: Toward a Pentecostal Egalitarianism*. If the sons of Latin American pentecostalism are becoming more sociopolitically engaged, what about its daughters? Elizabeth Brusco's study of pentecostal women in Colombia provides a point of entry into the broader Latin American pentecostal context.[26] Given the patriarchal and machismo context of Latin America, Brusco's research suggests that pentecostalism enables a distinctive and strategic form of female collective action that benefits women and transforms their lives. These transformations, however, are unlike those aspired to and, in some cases, experienced by Euroamerican white feminists. Rather, they are consistent with Latin American women's views and aspirations of well-being in the home, at church, and in society.

In the home, Brusco delineates the powerful transformation effected by pentecostal conversion. For starters, it refocuses the husband's atten-

---

25. Rowan Ireland, *Kingdoms Come: Religion and Politics in Brazil* (Pittsburgh: University of Pittsburgh Press, 1991), 107.

26. See Elizabeth E. Brusco, *The Reformation of Machismo: Evangelical Conversion and Gender in Colombia* (Austin: University of Texas Press, 1995).

tion away from the machismo role performed in the public sphere with other women. Instead, the truly converted husband becomes not only a faithful spouse but also one whose reputation no longer depends on abusing his wife. Further, pentecostal conversion undermines machismo behaviors such as drinking and gambling. Instead of squandering wages, the truly converted husband is now a breadwinner, bringing home the paycheck and providing for the needs of the household. Finally, pentecostal conversion transforms gender roles and relationships over the long haul. Instead of being an absent parent, the truly converted male is present and active in the home as parent and husband.

In the church, pentecostal conversion gives women public voice, authority, and leadership. Because the Spirit has been poured out also upon the maidservants (*hermanas*), they have now been empowered to at least testify, if not prophesy. Oftentimes manifestations of the charismatic gifts of the Spirit bring an increased recognition of the woman's authority in things spiritual and ecclesial. Finally, positions of leadership open up, even if they begin with the children's, youth, or women's ministries. And although most pastoral and elder positions remain with men, the gains made should not be underestimated. *Hermanas* often emerge with new roles in the pentecostal worship service and liturgy. They have found a voice as the Spirit has given utterance, and in the process have also found recognition of their gifts and identities. For both married and especially unmarried women, *hermanas* find in the church a new community and network of support. Particularly where missionary monies have enabled the establishment of health care ministries, orphanages, child care organizations, schools, and rescue missions, women have been empowered to serve in these various contexts.[27]

Combined, these factors enable a certain kind of upward mobility resulting in the transition of pentecostal families from the peasant to the professional classes. Wives are no longer sexual objects but partners. The family economic capacity has increased, and its consumption patterns are now much more clearly identifiable (e.g., in the children's clothing, the decor of the home, and even an upgraded family automobile). Not only wives, mothers, or homemakers, many have found and fulfilled a higher calling in the Lord's work as ministers of the gospel in church settings and in a variety of parachurch and secular contexts. In short, the family's social status has been significantly elevated through conversion and nurture in pentecostal faith and practice.

27. See Everett A. Wilson, *Strategy of the Spirit: J. Philip Hogan and the Growth of the Assemblies of God Worldwide, 1960–1990* (Carlisle, Eng.: Paternoster and Regnum, 1997), esp. ch. 9.

The trade-off in most instances is that this newfound social status still locates women in spheres under male domination. This is true not only at home, where the wife is under the headship of the husband, and at church, where the woman is under the authority of a (usually) male pastor, but also in the public domain. But converted pentecostal women, both married and single, have been healed (from maladies and sicknesses indicative of sin), delivered (from the devil and his ways), and set apart (sanctified) as the brides of Christ. They are now empowered to fulfill their roles at home, in the church, and in society and released to do the work of the Lord as appropriate within these various spheres of life.

Brusco's findings in Colombia are representative of what is taking place among Latin American pentecostal women.[28] Pentecostalism creates moral space and autonomy for women in the domestic sphere by transforming spousal relationships, leveling out patriarchalism, and tempering *machismo* even as it empowers women and provides opportunities for them in the public spheres. This has led some commentators to talk about pentecostalism in Latin America as a "preferential option for women."[29] I find this language about the Latin American situation appropriate especially since the benefits of pentecostalized religion cut across the spectrum from classical Pentecostal churches to the indigenous churches, including Catholic charismatic congregations in between. As Steigenga's empirical data makes plain, "it is religious beliefs, rather than religious affiliation, that are the primary religious factors influencing attitudes toward gender equality"—and women in Catholic charismatic parishes are just as likely to experience similar transformations.[30]

In sum, the daughters of Latin American pentecostalism are finding salvation in the here and now. Granted, many of the redemptive aspects discussed here apply to Christian conversion in general and not only to pentecostal conversion. Yet the pentecostal conviction that the Spirit is poured out indiscriminately upon sons and daughters has brought about a certain kind of "egalitarian patriarchalism," if I may coin a new term. The patriarchalism certainly is sustained by the Latin American cultural ethos but also reinforced by literal readings of certain passages in the

---

28. These results can be followed all across the Western Hemisphere; see Anna Adams, "Perception Matters: Pentecostal Latinas in Allentown, Pennsylvania," in *A Reader in Latina Feminist Theology: Religion and Justice*, ed. María Pilar Aquino, Daisy L. Machado, and Jeanette Rodriguez (Austin: University of Texas Press, 2002), 98–113; and Hannake Slootweg, "Pentecostal Women in Chile: A Case Study in Iquique," in Boudewijnse, Droogers, and Kamsteeg, eds., *More than Opium*, 53–71.

29. R. Andrew Chestnut, *Competitive Spirits: Latin America's New Religious Economy* (Oxford: Oxford University Press, 2003), 158–59.

30. Steigenga, *The Politics of the Spirit*, 131, 135.

New Testament. The egalitarian impulse is equally forceful, however, from other parts of the New Testament and especially in the wake of the pentecostal experience of the Spirit. And this, I suggest, is another of the essential starting points toward a world pentecostal theology.

Yet the question posed by Cornelia Butler Flora years ago remains: although pentecostal conversion has enabled women to fulfill many of their personal needs, why has pentecostalism failed to effect social transformation on the issue of sexism?[31] I suggest it is not too late for the revolutionary nature of the pentecostal experience to effect just such a transformation. The righting of the nation, however, requires the righting of the home. Pentecostalism has begun the latter and now needs to set its sights on the former. The Misión Iglesia Pentecostal in Chile is one pentecostal church that has begun to move in this direction.

1.1.3 *The Misión Iglesia Pentecostal in Chile*. This small denomination may be one of pentecostalism's best-kept secrets because it breaks the stereotype about what it means to be pentecostal in so many ways. On the one side, in contrast to classical Pentecostalism's general sectarianism, focus on eschatological salvation, and apolitical orientation, the Misión Iglesia Pentecostal (MIP) is ecumenical, socially engaged, and consciously and prophetically political. On the other side, in contrast to the theological illiteracy and unconscious syncretism of the numerous indigenous pentecostal churches of Chile, especially those in the Andean highlands,[32] the MIP approves of and encourages theological education and is conscious of the processes of contextualizing pentecostal beliefs and practices in Chile. How did this come about?

The MIP emerged from an unintended schism in the Iglesia Evangélica Pentecostal in 1952, during the heyday of pentecostal growth resulting from rapid social change and anomie experienced in the context of urbanization and modernization.[33] Several features of the MIP from

31. Cornelia Butler Flora, *Pentecostalism in Colombia: Baptism by Fire and Spirit* (Cranbury, NJ: Associated University Presses / Fairleigh Dickinson University Press, 1976), esp. ch. 6.

32. For indigenous pentecostalism in Chile, see Juan Sepúlveda, *The Andean Highlands: An Encounter with Two Forms of Christianity* (Geneva: WCC Publications, 1997), esp. ch. 4; and "Indigenous Pentecostalism and the Chilean Experience," in *Pentecostals after a Century: Global Perspectives on a Movement in Transition*, ed. Allan H. Anderson and Walter J. Hollenweger, JPTSup 15 (Sheffield, Eng.: Sheffield Academic Press, 1999), 111–34.

33. This is the standard thesis on the pentecostal explosion in Chile. See Christian Lalive d'Epinay, *Haven of the Masses: A Study of the Pentecostal Movement in Chile*, trans. Marjorie Sandle (London: Lutterworth, 1969); and Emilio Willems, *Followers of the New Faith: Culture, Change, and the Rise of Protestantism in Brazil and Chile* (Nashville: Vanderbilt University Press, 1967). For MIP origins, see Frans H. Kamsteeg, *Prophetic Pentecostalism in Chile: A Case Study on Religion and Development Policy* (Lanham, MD: Scarecrow, 1998), 94–103.

its early years have portended later history: (1) its more open attitude toward other pentecostal and even nonpentecostal churches; (2) its egalitarianism, allowing and encouraging women pastors; and (3) its commitment to theological education. This ecumenical, social, and theological vision was nurtured through the first decade of the MIP's existence and has blossomed in concrete ways.

First, with the Iglesia Pentecostal de Chile—which also broke off from the Iglesia Evangélica Pentecostal, but earlier, in 1946—the MIP joined the World Council of Churches in 1961. They remain two of the very few pentecostal denominations affiliated with the WCC even today, as most pentecostals continue to insist that the WCC is representative of the apostate "last-days super church" as derived from a dispensationalist hermeneutic. Second, with the Iglesia Pentecostal de Chile and other Protestant churches, the MIP established the Communidad Teológica Evangélica in 1966 as the first interchurch and interdenominational theological training center in Santiago.

Third, beginning with the implementation of the socialist Christian Democratic program of participatory democracy in the 1960s and continuing through the military coup of Augusto Pinochet in September 1973, the social consciousness of the MIP was transformed into sociopolitical action. Emphases on meeting basic needs and providing education were broadened, and the church's social commitment and witness became institutionalized in various ways: in the Comisión Técnica Asesora (CTA) in 1975, which handled foreign aid for social projects, and in the Servicio Evangélico para el Desarrollo, or Evangelical Service for Development (SEPADE), in 1978, which focused more comprehensively on the church's social witness. Efforts at community development in both the CTA and the SEPADE included the development of soup kitchens, the formation of nutrition and food distribution programs, the provision of scholarships and education, attention to health and housing needs, the establishment of community centers, and the creation of neighborhood projects and workshops designed not only to raise public consciousness but also to empower transformative action.[34]

Last but not least, nongovernmental organizations such as the CTA and the SEPADE functioned in some ways as the social and political conscience and voice of the (at least MIP and associated sister) churches to society and to the government.[35] This role became all the

34. Kamsteeg, *Prophetic Pentecostalism in Chile*, ch. 5, discusses the CTA and the SEPADE.
35. See Frans Kamsteeg, "Pentecostalism and Political Awakening in Pinochet's Chile and Beyond," in *Latin American Religion in Motion*, ed. Christian Smith and Joshua Prokopy (New York: Routledge, 1999), 187–204.

more prominent during the Pinochet regime. Although many of the churches—conservative pentecostal and Protestant churches as well as some quarters of the Catholic Church—hailed Pinochet's ascent to power as overturning the (demonic) Marxist rule of the previous government, and while even the Iglesia Metodista Pentecostal publicly demonstrated its support for Pinochet in holding the annual Te Deum celebration in its new Jotabecche Cathedral in December 1974, the MIP in conjunction with other affiliated churches was quick to voice criticism of the new government through various channels. First MIP officials expressed solidarity with the Comité Pro-Paz (Ecumenical Committee for Peace), founded in October 1973, which included Catholics and mainline Protestant denominations besides a few pentecostals. Then the MIP joined with the Asociación de Iglesias Evangélicas de Chile, formed in November 1974, which worked closely with the WCC to make numerous public statements providing an alternative Christian perspective to the public rhetoric of the conservative churches. Finally, through SEPADE and, in the 1980s, the Confraternidad Cristiana de Iglesias, the MIP denounced the military for continuing the social degeneration of the nation.

In this framework it is not surprising to see attempts by MIP theologians such as Juan Sepúlveda to dialogue with liberation theology.[36] Sepúlveda suggests four convergences between the kind of pentecostal theology advocated by the MIP and liberation theology: (1) their common origins in the world of the poor; (2) acknowledgment of the role of their experiences of God for the two theological self-understandings; (3) the centrality of popular and yet critical Bible reading such that readers are empowered by the Spirit to engage with the harsh realities of lower-socioeconomic-class life; and (4) an understanding of the church as community.

Yet it is also for these reasons perhaps that the MIP has struggled for survival amidst the plethora of pentecostal options available in Chile. The figures of approximately two thousand members and seventeen churches by the early 1990s are evidence of the consistent loss of adherents to other more classically pentecostal churches that are not reticent about voicing criticism using the familiar sectarian rhetoric.[37] As a leader-driven

36. Juan Sepúlveda, "Pentecostalism and Liberation Theology: Two Manifestations of the Work of the Holy Spirit for the Renewal of the Church," in *All Together in One Place: Theological Papers from the Brighton Conference on World Evangelization*, ed. Harold D. Hunter and Peter D. Hocken, JPTSup 4 (Sheffield, Eng.: Sheffield Academic Press, 1993), 51–64; and "Pentecostal Theology in the Context of the Struggle for Life," in *Faith Born in the Struggle for Life: A Rereading of Protestant Faith in Latin America Today*, ed. Dow Kirkpatrick, trans. Lewistine McCoy (Grand Rapids: Eerdmans, 1988), 298–318, esp. 303–4 and 315–16.

37. The figures are from Kamsteeg, *Prophetic Pentecostalism in Chile*, 102–3.

initiative, the church's ecumenical, social, and political vision is only minimally engaged by the laity even if they have benefited from its programs. And especially after the end of the Pinochet regime in 1989, the desire of the laity has been to return to classical pentecostal expressions with emphases on missions and evangelism.

Yet MIP theologians such as Sepúlveda argue that the future of pentecostalism in Chile depends on how her churches respond to contemporary challenges, for example, the increasing secularization associated with continual upward social mobility and the emergence of the pentecostal middle class.[38] Pentecostalism in urban Chile is in some sense at a crossroads, with more and more children growing up and rejecting the social sectarianism, moral perfectionism, and anti-intellectualism of previous generations. Street preaching and other revivalist strategies and approaches no longer accomplish what they used to, and the lack of formal education, theological and otherwise, is increasingly felt in our technological global village.

The MIP appears to be a church ahead of its "pentecostal time." Its sociopolitical vision is a sign that pentecostals around the world recognize that the encounter with, and experience of, the Spirit of God are not merely an individualistic or private matter. Thus the salvation brought by the Spirit includes not only the classical pentecostal emphasis on the empowerment to bear verbal witness to Jesus but also the capacity to do so in concrete social and political ways. Are these emphases peculiar to the Latin American pentecostal context, perhaps a reflection of the people opting out of traditional Catholicism for a variant of the Protestant alternative?

1.2 On Your Young and Old: Asian Pentecostalisms

In view of the preceding, I suggest that pentecostalism in Asia provides distinct but complementary insights toward a world pentecostal theology. The three types of pentecostalism in Asia combined to number almost 135 million in the year 2000, approximately 26 percent of world pentecostalism (*NIDPCM* 287). But the numbers may be deceiving, given the vast regions of Asia, the disparate languages, cultures, and people groups, and the uneven distribution of pentecostal growth. For instance, there are countries, such as the Philippines, that are largely Catholicized and, in that sense, Christianized, even as there are countries, such as

38. Edward L. Cleary and Juan Sepúlveda, "Chilean Pentecostalism Coming of Age," in Cleary and Stewart-Gambino, eds., *Power, Politics, and Pentecostals in Latin America*, 97–121.

Tibet or Japan, with barely a Christian presence. To mention Japan is to be drawn to the strange situation of East Asia, where, in contrast, neighboring South Korea serves as a hub of world pentecostalism in Asia, perhaps second only to North America and Brazil in terms of pentecostal growth. Then there are also Islamic nations, such as Malaysia and Indonesia in Southeast Asia—the latter's dominant Muslim majority presenting a very different environment for pentecostalism in contrast to the former's 52–48 percent Muslim population—and Pakistan and its neighbors in western Asia with their own distinctive set of challenges for pentecostalism. And last, but certainly not least, there are the populous nations of China and India, each featuring ancient histories, well-developed intellectual and cultural traditions, powerful religious visions with increasingly worldwide influence, and yet, interestingly, vibrant *indigenous* pentecostal communities, churches, and movements within their borders that constitute almost half of Asian pentecostalism.[39] Thus Asian pentecostalism defies easy characterization.

This section, conscious of the underlying theological concerns of this volume, focuses on selected aspects of indigenous pentecostalism in Asia, highlighting three types of pentecostal movements and experiences. In the Philippines, the section explores the challenges that younger indigenous pentecostal churches pose to classical Pentecostalism. It then compares Korean and autochthonous Chinese Oneness pentecostal traditions. It concludes with a survey of the "pentecostal preferential option for the poor" among the Dalits of Kerala, South India. As in the discussion on Latin American pentecostalism, the questions throughout remain: what has salvation meant in Asian pentecostalism, and how has this been manifested and experienced?

1.2.1 *Seeing Visions and Dreaming Dreams: Pentecostalisms in the Philippines*. The more than seven thousand islands constituting the Philippines have meant that incoming Christian traditions since the sixteenth century have never been able to propagate a homogeneous faith. Although almost 80 percent of Filipinos today are baptized Roman Catholics, perhaps no more than 5 percent of these are regular church attendees, and many of the rest practice a form of piety that is deeply marked by animistic features.[40] Similarly, Pentecostal missionaries who began arriving in the mid-1920s today face an analogous phenomenon. Certainly, the classical Pentecostal denominations have exhibited steady growth, and even

39. Barrett and Johnson's (*NIDPCM* 286) statistics of as many as 50 million indigenous pentecostals in inland China—perhaps conservative, given claims of as many as 80–100 million in some sources—plus 16.5 million indigenous pentecostals in India give a total of about 67 million in these two countries alone.

40. George W. Harper, "Philippine Tongues of Fire? Latin American Pentecostalism and the Future of Filipino Christianity," *JAM* 2, no. 2 (2000): 225–59, esp. 230–33.

the autochthonous urban pentecostal movements, such as the Jesus Is Lord Church, have quickly matured if such maturity is measured by sociopolitical activity and engagement.[41] Yet churches and movements in the remote islands and the more inaccessible mountain regions have developed their own distinctive brand of pentecostalism.

Pentecostalism in the Cordillera Mountains of the northern Luzon area is a case in point. The Cordilleran inhabitants are known as Igorot, literally, "mountaineers." Cordilleran religiosity is basically animistic.[42] The Igorot believe in various levels of spirit beings, including the creator spirit, the spirits of the dead, and the spirits of the underworld. Their priests or shamans negotiate the relationship between these spirit beings and the people: counseling, performing thanksgiving or healing rituals (the latter diagnosing the causes of illness or misfortune and prescribing cures), and interpreting omens, dreams, and visions, among other functions. Liminal occasions such as births, weddings, preparing for hunting or harvest seasons, moving into a new house, and funerals often require shamanic expertise.

It is in this context that Assemblies of God missionaries began working in 1947 especially among the Kankana-ey, the largest Igorot tribe of the northern Luzon.[43] Growth factors over the decades have included many of the typical pentecostal features: miraculous signs and wonders and divine healing; lay empowerment through the Holy Spirit; and mobilization of the laity for ministry and evangelism. Kankana-ey pentecostals have, in the process, adapted their Cordilleran religiosity to their new faith.[44] Instead of offering ritual sacrifices to the various spirit beings in order to attain needed blessings, Kankana-ey pentecostals look to God as the faithful provider and wait on God ritually through prayer and fasting. Instead of thinking of misfortunes or calamities as either originating from curses inflicted by enemies or resulting from the activities of unhappy spirit beings, Kankana-ey pentecostals practice their own forms of spiritual warfare in response, which often include blessing those who curse them. Instead of looking to the shaman when members of the

41. See Bishop Dr. Eddie C. Villanueva, "Jesus Is Lord Church," in *The New Apostolic Churches*, ed. C. Peter Wagner (Ventura, CA: Regal, 1998), 257–70; and Joseph R. Suico, "Pentecostalism: Towards a Movement of Social Transformation in the Philippines," *JAM* 1, no. 1 (1999): 7–19.

42. William R. Filson, "A Pentecostal Response to Cordilleran Religions," *AJPS* 2, no. 1 (1999): 35–45.

43. Julie C. Ma, "A Pentecostal Woman Missionary in a Tribal Mission: A Case Study," *CPCR* 3 (1998), http://www.pctii.org/cyberj/cyber3.html.

44. For what follows, see Julie C. Ma, *When the Spirit Meets the Spirits: Pentecostal Ministry among the Kankana-ey Tribe in the Philippines*, SIHC 118 (Frankfurt, Ger.: Peter Lang, 2000), esp. ch. 8.

community are sick, Kankana-ey pentecostals look to the healing power of the Holy Spirit. Further, while retaining the Cordilleran worldview that sees dreams, visions, and omens as meaningful, Kankana-ey pentecostals have come to see the Holy Spirit as the source of comforting and edifying dreams and visions (according to Acts 2:17),[45] even while recognizing and overcoming fearful dreams as derivative from evil spirits. Most significantly, the complex spirit world of Cordilleran religiosity is slowly replaced with a world of rulers, authorities, cosmic powers, and "spiritual forces of evil in the heavenly places" (Eph. 6:12).

Pentecostalism in the neighboring Ibaloi tribe, however, appears to remain much closer to Cordilleran religiosity. Perhaps because the Assemblies mission focused on the Kankana-ey to the neglect of the Ibaloi, an indigenous form of pentecostalism, known also as Santuala, has emerged among the latter. The origins of pentecostal influence on this group of churches remain shrouded in obscurity.[46] A woman named Maura Balagsa, who was miraculously healed through the ministry of an unnamed "Christian pastor," established Santuala in 1950. Its worship services today feature undeniable pentecostal characteristics: emotional and affective singing, dancing, and hand clapping; belief in dreams and visions, including the ritual practice of seeing visions, accompanied by interpretations of these visions by Santuala elders; and prayers for divine favor and blessing, including the laying on of hands for divine healing.

Upon closer inspection, however, Julie Ma, a Korean Assemblies of God missionary to the northern Luzon, suggests that Santuala religiosity has resulted in a syncretistic amalgamation of pentecostal and Cordilleran beliefs and practices.[47] Most blatantly Cordilleran are the religious slaughtering of animals at weddings and funerals and the prayers for the deceased during the latter half of prolonged funeral rites. More nuanced forms of syncretism include ritual dancing as a means of inviting and engaging the Holy Spirit; member chest tapping, which shows love and affection; repetitious hand shaking as a form of religious greeting; eating together during the latter portions of the service as a mode of fellowship and of sharing community life; and seeing visions for lengthy portions of the service, representing attempts to discern God's will (neglecting the Bible). This mixture of Cordilleran and pentecostal

45. Note that visions and dreams are obvious modes of engaging the divine both in pentecostalism and in non- or semiliterate societies; see, e.g., Lionel Caplan, *Power and Religion: Essays on the Christian Community in Madras* (Madras, India: Christian Literature Society, 1989), esp. ch. 4.

46. Julie C. Ma, "Santuala: A Case of Pentecostal Syncretism," *AJPS* 3, no. 1 (2000): 61–82.

47. Ibid., 69–76.

forms and meanings was unchecked, Ma suggests, because of a lack of proper Christian and biblical teaching. She concludes, "Even though the *Santuala* acknowledge the work of the Holy Spirit and, thus, call on the Spirit in prayer and healing, it is sometimes doubtful if healing takes place by the Spirit because of their syncretistic practices."[48]

Questions I have raised elsewhere about Ma's understanding and usage of the idea of syncretism as applied to Kankana-ey pentecostalism are pertinent also to her treatment of Santuala.[49] Ma is certainly right to be concerned about an improper fusion of biblical Christianity and Filipino animism. At the same time, her reliance on North American conservative Protestant definitions of syncretism is questionable in this context. In none of the instances of the "more nuanced forms of syncretism" that Ma describes are the meanings deployed antithetical to biblical Christianity. Further, the Santuala prayers for the dead have been influenced by Catholic piety and should be understood within that framework or as a variant of the ambiguous Corinthian practice of baptism for the dead (1 Cor. 15:29). Finally, might not the ritual sacrifice of animals be understood as a tithe, given not in monies but in goods (in this case, animals)? And how would this practice differ in essence from the widespread practice among neopentecostal televangelists of encouraging their viewers to "sow a seed" financially in order to reap the blessings that God has for them? Certainly, I am not advocating these practices as valid expressions of Christian faith. Further, I am also interpreting these realities without the kind of firsthand experience of Santuala that Ma possesses. My point is to call attention to syncretism as a complex phenomenon, one that sits not in contrast to, but across a fluid spectrum from, the kind of indigenization that Ma as an evangelical-pentecostal missionary seeks.

For our purposes, note first that Kankana-ey and Santuala pentecostalisms seek, through ritual practices, to engage God, who blesses and heals by the power of the Holy Spirit; in these instances, salvation is material, concrete, and experienced, not abstract or doctrinal. Second, the Igorot are not exceptional in their desire for health rather than sickness, for success in mining or farming rather than disaster, for abundant life rather than tragedy; for them, the Holy Spirit is not merely an idea but an essential aspect of lived and existential reality. Finally, since these are primarily oral, not written, cultures, they engage the divine primarily through narrative means such as dreams or visions.

---

48. Ibid., 80.
49. Amos Yong, "Going Where the Spirit Goes: Engaging the Spirit(s) in J. C. Ma's Pneumatological Missiology," *JPT* 10, no. 2 (2002): 110–28.

For all these reasons, Filipino pentecostalism presents both promises and challenges for world pentecostal theology.

1.2.2 *And They Shall Be Healed: East Asian Pentecostalisms*. Similar promises and challenges hold forth for pentecostalism in East Asia. Here it would be helpful to compare and contrast South Korean and Chinese forms of pentecostalism. Both cases include phenomenal growth over the course of the last half of the twentieth century. In the Korean case, this growth has come through established classical Pentecostal churches, whereas in the Chinese case, this growth has come through indigenous, independent churches.

The Korean case is especially intriguing, given the explosion of pentecostal Christianity such that even mainline Protestant denominations and churches have taken on a noticeably pentecostal cast.[50] Factors identified as playing key roles in Korean pentecostal expansion include the following: Protestant preparation through conservative biblicism in Sunday schools, which created a fertile ground for pentecostal adaptation; prayer meetings, including all-night prayer services and the establishment of "prayer mountain" retreat centers; exorcisms, healings, miracles, signs, and wonders; authoritarian but charismatic leadership; lay training and empowering for ministry and evangelism; establishment of smaller home groups providing fellowship and a context for discipleship; and clearly established goals for congregational and individual growth.[51] Although many of the usual elements associated with pentecostal development are found in this list, there are also noteworthy features, such as the place of the Bible and conscientious targeting and strategic planning for growth.

Partly because of its tremendous size, visibility, and influence, the ministries and leadership of the 700,000-member Yoido Full Gospel Church (Assemblies of God), the largest congregation in the world, have come under increasing scrutiny. Some have even suggested that Yoido's success should be attributed, at least in part, to the adoption of Korean shamanistic practices by its leadership, including its founding pastor, Yonggi Cho.[52] Critics note the correlations between pentecostal cosmology and the indigenous Korean spirit worldview; between the

---

50. For a history from an outsider's perspective, see Yoo Boo-Woong, *Korean Pentecostalism: Its History and Theology*, SIHC 52 (Frankfurt, Ger.: Peter Lang, 1988); see also Wonsuk Ma, "The Korean Pentecostal Movement: Retrospect and Prospect for the New Century," *AusPS* 5–6 (2001): 63–94.

51. Lee Jae Bum, "Pentecostal Type Distinctives and Korean Protestant Church Growth" (Ph.D. diss., Fuller Theological Seminary, 1986), 251–52, cited in David Martin, *Tongues of Fire*, 147.

52. Yoo Boo-Woong, "Response to Korean Shamanism by the Pentecostal Church," *IRM* 75 (1986): 70–74; and Lee Hong Jung, "*Minjung* and Pentecostal Movements in Korea," in Anderson and Hollenweger, eds., *Pentecostals after a Century*, 138–60, esp. 146–47.

phenomenology of pentecostal infilling or baptism in the Holy Spirit and that of shamanic spirit possession and between pentecostal exorcism and folk religiosity's appeasement of spirits; between pentecostal prayer mountain retreat sites and the prominence of mountains in shamanism; and between Cho's message of positive thinking, material prosperity, good health, and bodily healing and shamanic ritual activity directed toward similar if not identical objectives.[53] Given these parallels, are pentecostals restorationists of New Testament Christianity, or are they accommodationists to the indigenous traditions of Asia?

Certainly, shamanism has influenced Korean pentecostalism: it has enabled Koreans to accept the Christian God and the spiritual world; the Korean concept of *han* has focused the gospel message as one of healing in material, personal, and family dimensions; and its emphasis on material blessings has resulted in the marginalization of social concerns and the prevalence of an individualistic orientation. But defenders of Cho and Korean pentecostalism see pentecostal success as evidence not of syncretism but of the successful contextualization of the gospel in a shamanistic environment.[54] Further, they have also noted Cho's attempt to derive his theology from biblical principles, his adoption of classical Pentecostal theology on every major doctrine, and his collaborative networking not with local Korean shamans but with international pentecostal and charismatic ministries.[55] Finally, they point out that Cho's gospel is not limited to individual prosperity; rather, alongside Yoido's healing ministries are social services such as care for the elderly, vocational training, medical and financial aid, and youth and family outreaches. Anderson concludes, "There is an enormous difference between

53. Doongsoo Kim, "The Healing of *Han* in Korean Pentecostalism," *JPT* 15 (1999): 123–39, suggests that pentecostalism is similar to shamanism in the dealing with *han* through a theology of material blessings, in the roles of pastors compared with those of shamans, and in healing rituals, even if pentecostals such as Cho are not consciously influenced by shamanism. Cf. David Chung, *Syncretism: The Religious Context of Christian Beginnings in Korea*, ed. Kang-nam Oh (Albany: State University of New York Press, 2001), 178. For an overview of the consumers of shamanism in Korea and why it remains attractive in an industrial society, see Chongho Kim, *Korean Shamanism: The Cultural Paradox* (Burlington, VT: Ashgate, 2003).

54. See Allan Anderson, "The Contribution of Cho Yonggi to a Contextual Theology in Korea," *JPT* 12, no. 1 (2003): 85–105. Anderson comes to his own conclusions, albeit in dialogue with Cho's writings and Korean theologians such as Lee Young Hoon and Jeong Chong Hee. See also Ig-Jin Kim, *History and Theology of Korean Pentecostalism: Sunbogeum (Pure Gospel) Pentecostalism* (Zoetermeer, Neth.: Uitgeverij Boekencentrum, 2003); and Wonsuk Ma, William W. Menzies, and Hyeon Sung Bae, *David Yonggi Cho: A Close Look at His Theology and Ministry* (Goonpo, Kor.: Hansei University Press; Baguio City, Phil.: Asia Pacific Theological Seminary Press, 2004).

55. Myung Soo Park, "David Yonggi Cho and International Pentecostal/Charismatic Movements," *JPT* 12, no. 1 (2003): 107–28, discusses specifically Cho's networking.

interacting with shamanism and *becoming* shamanistic. . . . Although the Korean liberation theology known as *Minjung* theology has espoused the concerns of the poor and oppressed, it is to the Pentecostal churches that the poor and oppressed (the *minjung*) flock for relief."[56]

Chinese pentecostalism compares and contrasts with the Korean version in a number of important points.[57] Both feature the prominence of the material and physical dimensions of salvation. In the Chinese case, the rural poor often do not have access to either health insurance or health care, and pentecostal healing provides an alternative or complementary source of health and well-being to traditional Chinese alchemic and medicinal practices. Further, both pentecostalisms see no gap between the Bible and the day-to-day lives and needs of the people, and personal testimonies "prove" the self-explanatory nature of (at least certain relevant passages of) the Bible. In the Chinese case, this is especially important, since the ministry of healing is experienced through the "priesthood of all believers" during home or hospital visits and not through the special services of itinerant healing evangelists. Finally, both Chinese and Korean pentecostalism are grassroots movements. As such, they have been and remain oral traditions, feature a predominance of women, and emphasize charismatic, change-oriented, and action-motivated mentalities.[58]

Yet the contrasts between the two pentecostalisms are also important. Whereas Korean pentecostalism remains much more connected with Western denominations, Chinese pentecostalism is largely indigenous, reflecting the political situation under the Communist regime since the 1950s, when churches and religious bodies were required to register with the government to operate officially.[59] Whereas Korean

56. Anderson, "The Contribution of Cho Yonggi," 97, 103. But cf. Jong Chun Park, *Crawl with God, Dance in the Spirit: A Creative Formation of Korean Theology of the Spirit* (Nashville: Abingdon, 1998), who confesses to having had the pentecostal experience of glossolalia (see 154–55), while continuing to work out of the more liberal Methodist tradition in seeking not only the kind of indigenous and enculturated Korean Christianity characteristic of the Yoido Full Gospel Church but also the *minjung*-liberation and interfaith theology intentionally attendant to the lived realities of Asia.

57. For an overview, see Luke Wesley, "Is the Chinese Church Predominantly Pentecostal?" *AJPS* 7, no. 1 (2004): 225–54.

58. Daniel H. Bays, "Christian Revival in China, 1900–1937," in *Modern Christian Revivals*, ed. Edith L. Blumhofer and Randall Balmer (Urbana: University of Illinois Press, 1993), 161–79.

59. Perhaps for this reason, Chinese pentecostalism is mainly focused on the miraculous and otherworldly aspects of Christianity, since any political involvement is thought to be a selling out to the agenda of the government-registered churches; see Edmond Tang, "'Yellers' and Healers: Pentecostalism and the Study of Grassroots Christianity in China," in *Asian and Pentecostal: The Charismatic Face of Christianity in Asia*, ed. Allan Anderson and Edmond Tang (Oxford: Regnum; Baguio City, Phil.: Asia Pacific Theological Seminary Press, 2005), 467–86, esp. 472.

pentecostalism's success stories are by and large documented, Chinese pentecostalism remains shrouded in obscurity, located primarily in the rural inland as underground or isolated house churches. Whereas Korean pentecostalism is increasingly institutionalized, Chinese pentecostalism remains egalitarian, theologically untrained, focused on spiritual piety, and intertwined with popular religiosity. And finally, whereas Korean pentecostalism has remained predominantly trinitarian, Chinese pentecostalism features a noticeable Oneness contingent.

The most prominent strand of Oneness pentecostalism in China is the True Jesus Church (TJC).[60] Founded between 1917 and 1919 by (Paul) Wei Enbo, Zhang Pin, and Barnabas Zhang (Tung),[61] the TJC is millenarian, communal, and exclusivistic/sectarian, with the expected emphasis on divine healing. Its central doctrines include the oneness or unity of God; baptism in Jesus' name only and by immersion in natural/running water; and baptism in the Holy Spirit with the evidence of tongues speech. These certainly reflect the influence of U.S. Oneness pentecostal teachings. The TJC's indigenous features, however, may have enabled its flourishing in East Asia: a supernaturalistic cosmology connecting with classical Pentecostal angelology and demonology; the emphasis on filial piety transferred to a Jesus piety; and the spirit possession of folk religiosity taken over by the baptism in the Spirit.[62] And if success is measured by missionary ventures, the TJC is well established in Taiwan—in fact, with headquarters now on that island—and growing also in Japan.[63]

Certain features of the East Asian pentecostal experience stand out. First, the pentecostal gospel adapted to the East Asian context has resulted in salvation understood as deliverance from evil spirits and as the healing of the body, in the empowerment of the Holy Spirit manifest in miracles and Christian witness, and in emphases on prayer and

60. See Daniel H. Bays, "Indigenous Protestant Churches in China, 1900–1937: A Pentecostal Case Study," in *Indigenous Responses to Western Christianity,* ed. Stephen Kaplan (New York: New York University Press, 1995), 124–43, esp. 132–37.

61. Tung is the name given in Yamamoto Sumiko, *History of Protestantism in China: The Indigenization of Christianity* (Tokyo: Toho Gakkai and Institute of Eastern Culture, 2000), 45.

62. See Murray A. Rubinstein, *The Protestant Community on Modern Taiwan: Mission, Seminary, and Church* (Armonk, NY: M. E. Sharpe, 1991), 130–39, for some of these convergences. On the last point, connecting shamanistic spirit mediumship and pentecostal Spirit baptism, see Alan Hunter and Kim-Kwong Chan, *Protestantism in Contemporary China* (Cambridge: Cambridge University Press, 1993), 152–55.

63. For the TJC in Taiwan, see Rubinstein, *The Protestant Community on Modern Taiwan,* ch. 4. For the influence of the TJC in Japanese pentecostalism, particularly the Spirit of Jesus Church, see Mark R. Mullins, *Christianity Made in Japan: A Study of Indigenous Movements* (Honolulu: University of Hawai'i Press, 1998), 97–104, 150–53.

revival services.[64] Second, despite the Oneness doctrinal matrix of the TJC, East Asian pentecostalisms evince distinctive Jesus and Spirit pieties. Arguably, leaning upon the Holy Spirit in prayer and awaiting the Spirit's visitation have resulted in the Spirit of Jesus empowering Chinese pentecostals to follow the way of the cross.[65] Third, pentecostal successes are clearly connected to the greater Sinification of Christianity in China, the empowering of Chinese personnel and leadership, and the adoption of Chinese idiom.[66] Questions persist about why pentecostal Christianity has flourished among the mission churches in South Korea and among the indigenous churches in China but not at all in Japan. Was this because of Japan's humiliation at the end of World War II? Is it because of the staunch Buddhist ethos of the Japanese people in contrast to the more loosely developed Buddhist-Confucianist-Daoist matrix of Korea and China? If so, how might that compare with the dominant Hindu environment of South India?

1.2.3 *From Dreams and Visions to Reality? Dalit Pentecostalism in India*. Like China, pentecostalism in India consists mainly of indigenous expressions (more than 80 percent), some of which predate the arrival of Azusa Street missionaries to its shores.[67] The Indian case, however, presents its own distinctive challenges for pentecostalism.[68] First, pentecostal mission has proceeded not in an ecclesial vacuum but amidst the Orthodox (Syrian) presence, which traces its lineage back to the apostolic ministry of Saint Thomas. Further, pentecostal growth has persisted in the context of widespread unemployment and abject poverty. Finally, popular forms of Hinduism that feature a thaumaturgical worldview, renunciant gurus, and enlightened sages form the dominant cultural

64. Allan H. Anderson, "Pentecostalism in East Asia: Indigenous Oriental Christianity?" *PNEUMA* 22, no. 1 (2000): 115–32.

65. For an overview of the persecution of the Chinese churches under the Communist regime, see Paul Marshall, with Lela Gilbert, *Their Blood Cries Out: The Worldwide Tragedy of Modern Christians Who Are Dying for Their Faith* (Dallas: Word, 1997), 75–83.

66. See John K. Fairbank, "Introduction: The Place of Protestant Writings in China's Cultural History," in *Christianity in China: Early Protestant Missionary Writings*, ed. Suzanne Wilson Barnett and John King Fairbank (Cambridge, MA: Harvard University Press, 1985), 1–18, esp. 9–10; and Daniel Bays, "The Protestant Missionary Establishment and the Pentecostal Movement," in *Pentecostal Currents in American Protestantism*, ed. Edith L. Blumhofer, Russell P. Spittler, and Grant A. Wacker (Urbana: University of Illinois Press, 1999), 50–67, esp. 63.

67. The 80 percent figure derives from G. B. McGee and S. M. Burgess, "India," *NIDPCM* 118–26, esp. 125.

68. For an introduction to pentecostalism in India, see Ivan Satyavrata, "Contextual Perspectives on Pentecostalism as Global Culture: A South Asian View," in *The Globalization of Pentecostalism: A Religion Made to Travel*, ed. Murray W. Dempster, Byron D. Klaus, and Douglas Petersen (Irvine, CA: Regnum International; Carlisle, Eng.: Paternoster, 1999), 203–21.

and religious world of India. Nevertheless, pentecostals in India have experienced the saving and empowering work of God in ways similar to other pentecostals around the world. This is certainly the case among the Dalit pentecostals.

Although Dalit pentecostals can be found throughout the Indian subcontinent, sociopolitical circumstances in South India have led to the segregation and thereby the distinctive identification of Dalit pentecostalism in that region.[69] The Dalits—from *dal*, "to crack," "open," "split," thus meaning "broken," "crushed," or "destroyed"—who are considered polluted and therefore untouchable, are one of the endless subcastes at the bottom of the four-caste system composed of Brahmins, Kshartiyas (warriors), Vaisyas, and Sudras (menial serfs). By the mid–nineteenth century, the Sudras were literally bound to slavery. Truly untouchable, they were thought to be barely (if at all) human and were even put to death if they did not stay clear of upper-caste paths. Even after slavery was legally outlawed in the 1850s, Dalits had no means of upward mobility, and many became bonded laborers. The plight of the Dalit, who constitute almost one-fourth (up to 200 million) of the population of India, remains abysmal.

Modernization since the early twentieth century has led to Dalit conscientization, empowerment, and activism. Many have converted to either Buddhism or Christianity in order to escape their fate.[70] The obstacles to Dalit liberation, however, have been nigh insurmountable for various reasons.[71] First, the cultural system of Indian identity makes it almost impossible to escape untouchability even through religious conversion. So, for example, the Indian government has denied scheduled-caste benefits to Dalits who are Christians on the grounds that original Christianity did not have caste distinctions. Second, upper-caste Hindus have a vested interest in preserving Dalitness not only for social and political reasons but perhaps also for religious ones. The particular form of Brahmanic Hinduism prevalent among the elite assumes the existence of a class of untouchables. Third, Dalits who convert to other religions confront even further alienation. Their conversions are assumed to be nonreligiously motivated. Further, Christian converts are assumed to be

69. For an overview of Indian pentecostalism against the backdrop of Indian Christianity, see Roger E. Hedlund, *Quest for Identity: The "Little Traditions" in Indian Christianity* (Delhi: Mylapore Institute for Indigenous Studies and ISPCK, 2000).

70. John C. B. Webster, *Religion and Dalit Liberation: An Examination of Perspectives*, 2nd ed. (Delhi: Manohar, 2002), ch. 3, describes the midcentury movements toward Buddhism under the leadership of Ambedkar.

71. The essays in James Massey, ed., *Indigenous People: Dalits—Dalit Issues in Today's Theological Debate* (Delhi: ISPCK, 1994), explicate the difficulties confronted by the Dalit quest for liberation.

already uplifted by missionary patronage and therefore not in further need. And finally, prejudice and class distinctions have persisted even in the churches. The institutional structures of the churches have not been as liberative as Dalits expected. Indeed, many Dalits converted to pentecostalism from other churches when pentecostalism became an option in the 1920s because they realized that insufficient progress had been made regarding their lot among the mainline denominations and because the egalitarian understanding of Spirit-filled and baptized Christians promised the liberation they sought.

Certainly in the beginning (the 1920s through the 1940s) there were mutual cooperation and shared table fellowship between Dalit and Syrian Christians in the pentecostal churches.[72] Because the reception of Spirit baptism as evidenced by tongues affirmed that God is no respecter of castes, Dalits were "brothers and sisters" instead of being addressed by their caste names (as they were in mainline congregations). Pentecostal missionaries went the extra mile in identifying with the Dalits among whom they ministered—for example, Robert Cook, a former Assemblies of God missionary turned Church of God, Cleveland (in 1936), once baptized a leper and laid hands in prayer upon him.[73] Indeed, pentecostal polemics against other "churches" nurtured a sense of self-worth among Dalits, functioning even "to create a sense of superiority."[74] Higher standards of holiness, such as decreased polygamy, sorcery, or adultery, were achieved among Dalit pentecostals than were accomplished in the mainline churches. This nurtured Dalit self-understanding and enabled a heightened sense of belonging. Following from this, indigenous Dalit preachers and leaders exhibited divinely sanctioned and humanly acknowledged authority and power in their ministries. Women, the "outcasts among the outcasts," were given public roles in the churches and worship services. The Spirit-filled, celebrative pentecostal worship provided a this-worldly uplift for Dalits even as it cultivated an eschatological sense of hope. In sum, a sense of solidarity was created in Dalit pentecostal churches that enabled the ongoing efforts of Dalit resistance and the development of a countercaste discourse.

Yet at the end of the day, the dreams and visions of liberation have not been fully actualized in the pentecostal churches. Even in Cook's

---

72. T. S. Samuel Kutty, *The Place and Contribution of Dalits in Select Pentecostal Churches in Central Kerala from 1922 to 1972* (Delhi: ISPCK, 2000), esp. ch. 3.

73. Ibid., 84. See Robert F. Cook, *Half a Century of Divine Leading and 37 Years of Apostolic Achievements in South India* (Cleveland, Tenn.: Church of God Foreign Missions Department, 1955). To its credit, the Church of God supported Cook's ministry to the Dalits; this is more than can be said of the Assemblies of God, which did not substantially pick up the challenge.

74. Kutty, *The Place and Contribution of Dalits*, 88.

Church of God there emerged, during the 1950s and 1960s, the gradual realization that the initial integration did not abolish caste discrimination, since Syrians retained access to education, jobs, out-of-state and even foreign support system networks, and so on. Unable even to pass their educational exams, Dalits were increasingly bypassed for leadership positions. By the late 1960s, not only were Dalits a minority among leaders; Syrian Christians were clearly leery of having Dalit pastors because they feared hindering the growth of the church and losing societal status. Further, intermarriage between Dalits and Syrians declined considerably over the years, as did the personal forms of address. Worse, segregation grew, resulting in some instances in outright racism. Thus, "a veteran Dalit Pentecostal evangelist in the Church of God says that the Pentecostals preached equality but practised inequality."[75] Put more harshly, Dalits were "exploited because of their enthusiastic and otherworldly spirituality with the promise that all their sacrificial services will be rewarded one day when they reach heaven. . . . The Syrian leadership wanted Dalit participation when they wanted cheap labour but did not like to share power with Dalit leaders."[76]

In the state of Kerala with its ancient tradition of Orthodox churches, Dalit pentecostals in the Church of God began to formally organize their call for redress in 1968 as the socioeconomic gap between Syrians and Dalits widened and as disharmony and resentment grew. In June 1970, Dalits submitted a memorandum pleading for equal privileges, requesting that at least 60 percent of Bible college candidates be admitted from Dalit backgrounds; that Bible college directors include one Syrian and one Dalit; that there be greater representation in the churches; that a Dalit be appointed to assist the denomination's state secretary; that more serious consideration be given to church construction requests; and that all Dalit pastors be promoted upon completing their five years of service in the denomination. In May 1971, the Syrian majority decided upon the segregation of Dalits. The attempt by Dalits to negotiate an amicable settlement failed, and in 1972, the Church of God was divided into the Church of God (Division) in Kerala for Dalits—sixty churches, which through Dalit leadership grew to more than two hundred by 1994—and the Church of God in India (State) for Syrian and upper-caste pentecostals. But even here there was unequal distribution of properties and resources.[77]

75. Ibid., 119. For a Dalit account, see J. Yesu Natha Das, "An Evaluation of the History of Pentecostal Dalits in Kerala" (Th.M. thesis, South Asian Institute of Advanced Christian Studies, Bangalore, 2001), esp. 92–102.
76. Kutty, *The Place and Contribution of Dalits*, 147, 149.
77. Ibid., 119–33; Das, "An Evaluation," 103–6.

Yet the Dalit contribution to pentecostalism in South India should not be ignored.[78] Their pioneering charismatic ministries, sacrificial giving, establishment of schools and Bible colleges for Dalits, and even founding of pentecostal denominations exemplify their Christian commitment. "Pentecostal spirituality, characterised by extended prayer meetings, zealous witnessing, and self-venting aggressive worship through song and dance, has often proved useful in bringing people out of the clutches of depression, worthlessness, aimlessness in life, fear and anxiety—to a life of immense activity for the cause of Christ."[79] Undoubtedly, the pentecostal baptism of the Spirit empowered the Dalit persistence against all odds, "helped to overcome the walls of caste prejudice and discrimination and invited all members in the Church to have this experience hoping to constitute a community without caste discriminations."[80]

Dalit pentecostals continue to seek the abundance of life promised by Jesus. They have suffered loss on all sides: with their Hindu relatives for converting to Christ; with the government for scheduled-caste benefits; and with their fellow Syrian Christians for being too emotional, for being Communists, or for being Christian converts expecting financial gain or other benefits.[81] As pentecostal Dalits become more ecumenically aware, they will surely contribute to the wider Christian resistance against caste prejudice in India. "Jesus the Dalit"—the friend of the outcast, who spoke about the last being first and emptied himself as a lowly slave and died (godforsaken) outside the gate—is also the one who sends the Spirit to constitute a new people of God in which the vision of there being neither slave nor free will finally become a reality.[82]

Clearly, a world pentecostal theology will need to take account of the experiences of Asian pentecostals across the continent.[83] The preceding coverage has been selective to the extreme. Yet patterns of the pentecostal experience of God are emerging: salvation as material, concrete, and social; the dialectic between divine revelation and human reception; and the emphasis on the Holy Spirit. Will we find further confirmation of these themes in the African pentecostal experience?

78. Kutty, *The Place and Contribution of Dalits*, ch. 5; Das, "An Evaluation," ch. 5; and Paulson Pulikottil, "Ramankutty Paul: A Dalit Contribution to Pentecostalism," in Anderson and Tang, eds., *Asian and Pentecostal*, 245–57.

79. Reuben Louis Gabriel, "Reflections on Indian Pentecostalism: Trends and Issues," *DD* 6, no. 2 (2002): 67–76; quotation, 69.

80. Kutty, *The Place and Contribution of Dalits*, 153.

81. Das, "An Evaluation," ch. 6.

82. Samuel Rayan, "Outside the Gate, Sharing the Insult," in *Leave the Temple: Indian Paths to Human Liberation*, ed. Felix Wilfred (Maryknoll, NY: Orbis, 1992), 125–45.

83. Wonsuk Ma, "Toward an Asian Pentecostal Theology," *AJPS* 1, no. 1 (1998): 15–41.

1.3 On My Men- and Maidservants and on the Cosmos: Pentecostalisms in Africa and the African Diaspora

Pentecostalism is as complex in Africa as it is in Asia and Latin America, if not more so. Although typological constructs by social scientists, religious-studies scholars, and theologians have evolved over the last generation, there is general agreement that the three kinds of pentecostalism are well represented on the African continent.[84] Yet even here categorization of the situation in Africa is contested. There are classical Pentecostal denominations in Africa alongside Ethiopian (nonpentecostal) churches that have seceded from mainline missionary churches; older churches (dating back to the first half of the twentieth century) established by Africans for Africans and categorized variously as African-initiated, indigenous, or independent churches (AICs), prophet-healing churches, or, in specific regions, Spirit churches (East Africa), Aladura churches (West Africa), the Kimbanguist Church (Central Africa), and Zionist and/or Apostolic churches (South Africa); and newer indigenous churches (since the 1970s) that are nevertheless deeply connected with the charismatic-renewal and "prosperity" movements of Western pentecostal churches. Further, these geographical references underscore the extremely diverse historical, social, and political characteristics of the continent. The North African environment is predominantly Muslim and somewhat lacking in pentecostal Christian presence. West and East Africa, however, have strong pockets of Christian and Islamic influence, the former featuring especially vibrant neopentecostal or charismatic expressions.[85] The sub-Saharan region offers its own distinctive topographical environments that have perennially challenged mission-sending agencies and resulted in the emergence of a unique brand of pentecostalism in the heart of the con-

---

84. See Allan Anderson, *African Reformation: African Initiated Christianity in the 20th Century* (Trenton, NJ: Africa World Press, 2001), ch. 1.

85. The standard introduction to West African pentecostalism remains Harold W. Turner, *History of an African Independent Church*, 2 vols. (Oxford: Clarendon, 1967). More recently, for classical, charismatic, and independent streams of pentecostalism in West Africa, see, respectively, E. Kingsley Larbi, *Pentecostalism: The Eddies of Ghanaian Christianity* (Accra, Ghana: Centre for Pentecostal and Charismatic Studies and Blessed Publications, 2001); Cephas N. Omenyo, *Pentecost outside Pentecostalism: A Study of the Development of the Charismatic Renewal in the Mainline Churches in Ghana* (Zoetermeer, Neth.: Uitgeverij Boekencentrum, 2002); and Afeosemime U. Adogame, *Celestial Church of Christ: The Politics of Cultural Identity in a West African Prophetic-Charismatic Movement*, SIHC 115 (Frankfurt, Ger.: Peter Lang, 1998). For an overview of the East African pentecostal situation, especially in Kenya, see Francis Kimani Githieya, *The Freedom of the Spirit: African Indigenous Churches in Kenya* (Atlanta: Scholars Press, 1997).

tinent.[86] And the South African situation has posed its own challenges in terms of the history of apartheid in the twentieth century.[87]

The result is a wide range of pentecostal-type expressions—churches featuring emphasis on the Holy Spirit, divine healing, exorcism, prophecy, revelation, speaking in tongues, and other charismatic gifts—apart from any connections to classical Pentecostal churches or missionary organizations, especially in the sub-Saharan region of the continent. In most of these cases, there is no agreement about the criteria for pentecostal classification. Although more than half of the 126-plus million pentecostals in the African continent derive from the indigenous or independent churches, many of these do not identify themselves explicitly as "pentecostal."

The situation is even more complex when the African diaspora is factored in. Black Africans were dispersed across Latin America, where there are various histories remaining to be written. My interests lie, however, in the distinctive Caribbean experience and, from there, the emerging phenomenon of black European and British pentecostalism. And to come back to the entire stream of black pentecostalism in North America is to return to the putative origins of modern pentecostalism.

The following overview can be no more than a sketch directed by our quest for a world pentecostal theology. When the question of how Africans have experienced and encountered the outpouring of the Spirit is posed, my attention is directed toward the prophecy referring to menservants and maidservants and to signs in the heavens above and on the earth below (Acts 2:18–19). There God embraces the servants (doulous/doulas, literally, "slaves") as God's own in contrast to "your" sons and daughters, old and young (2:17). This signifies the marvelousness and miraculousness of the gift of the Spirit to even the most despised category of persons in the first century. The early modern pentecostal movement was similarly reviled partly because of the claim that the Spirit had been poured out upon the black man and woman. Pentecostal theology as a postcolonial, countercultural, and prophetic discourse cannot but take advantage of this analogy—even if the analogy breaks down along the way—when dealing with pentecostal liberationist movements both in South Africa and in the African diaspora. But first, what about the signs on the earth below resulting from the Spirit's

---

86. Dated but still useful are G. C. Oosthuizen, *Post-Christianity in Africa: A Theological and Anthropological Study* (Grand Rapids: Eerdmans, 1968); and Martinus Daneel, *Old and New in Southern Shona Independent Churches*, 2 vols. (The Hague: Mouton, 1971–1974).

87. An older work is Bengt Sundkler, *Bantu Prophets in South Africa* (London: Oxford University Press, 1961). Newer research is Gerald Pillay, *Religion at the Limits: Pentecostalism among Indian South Africans* (Pretoria: University of South Africa Press, 1994).

outpouring on all flesh? Might this be a cue for us to look more closely at the pentecostal phenomenon of the environmentally conscious and tree-planting indigenous Spirit churches of Zimbabwe?

1.3.1 *Signs on the Earth Below: The Movement of the Spirit in Zimbabwe.* AICs in South Africa and Zimbabwe are predominantly pneumatocentric: oriented toward the Holy Spirit and featuring prominently charismatic manifestations and forms of worship, such as prophecy, faith healing, exorcism, glossolalia, and dreams and visions.[88] This phenomenology qualified their designation as "neo-charismatic" in the *NIDPCM* and justifies our including them in this book. Although most of the churches are typically sectarian and exclusivistic (e.g., Johane Maranke's African Apostolic Church and Samuel Mutendi's Zion Christian Church), a few have been open to what might be called an ecumenism of the Spirit. Since the early 1970s, two such ecumenical organizations that have emerged in Zimbabwe have included AICs: the Fambidzano yemaKereke avaTema (Cooperative of Black Churches) in 1972 and the Association of African Earthkeeping Churches (AAEC) in 1991.[89] Although these churches are certainly not representative of Zimbabwean and South African pentecostalism on the whole, the particular charism of the Spirit manifest in them is invaluable to the development of a world pentecostal theology.

The AAEC was formed because the Fambidzano cooperative had pulled back from the invitation to affiliate with the Zimbabwean Institute of Religious Research and Ecological Conservation (ZIRRCON), founded in 1988, primarily because of ZIRRCON's prior association with the Association of Zimbabwean Traditional Ecologists (AZTREC). ZIRRCON and AZTREC were founded to respond to the environmental crisis precipitated by the civil war of the 1960s and 1970s, rapid social change, and prolonged ecological irresponsibility. Their primary initiatives included combating deforestation and desertification, planting trees, conserving wildlife, and protecting water resources. The AAEC saw the objectives of ZIRRCON (and AZTREC) as sufficiently worthwhile and urgent to overcome existing barriers to working with traditional religionists. Although there was justifiable concern about, and even challenges to, alliances with ZIRRCON, there was also the clear recognition that the destruction of the environment not only jeopardized

88. Here I rely on the work of my former teacher, Martinus L. (Inus) Daneel, e.g., M. L. Daneel, *Quest for Belonging: Introduction to a Study of African Independent Churches* (Gweru, Zimbabwe: Mambo, 1987); and "African Independent Church Pneumatology and the Salvation of All Creation," in Hunter and Hocken, eds., *All Together in One Place,* 96–126.

89. M. L. Daneel, *Fambidzano: Ecumenical Movement of Zimbabwean Independent Churches* (Gweru, Zimbabwe: Mambo, 1989), gives the early history of Fambidzano.

human life but also signified the human failure to care for the earth (Gen. 1:26). Over time, differences were resolved through dialogue and the establishment of proper boundaries within the alliance to ensure the Christian integrity of AAEC involvement.

In this wider ecumenical framework, the Holy Spirit of the AICs has become the "earthkeeping and earth-healing Spirit" of the AAEC. The Holy Spirit is understood to inspire appropriate socioeconomic processes through development, agricultural projects, and education. More important, the Spirit who convicts humans of their sins enables confession of ecological sins: chopping down and not replanting; overgrazing; destroying river banks; neglecting the construction of contour ridges; and causing soil erosion through irresponsible farming. Proper repentance leads to specific reparative actions focused on restoring and renewing the earth. Here the central activity is the AAEC tree-planting ceremony.

Whereas AZTREC has its own tree-planting ceremonies within a traditional religious setting and most ceremonies are conducted by multireligious congregations, the AAEC proceeds solidly within a Christian framework of the cosmic Christ (cf. Col. 1:15–20). A typical ceremony consists of these elements: the confession of ecological sins that cause "firewood shortage, soil erosion, poor crops and the absence of wildlife";[90] the exorcism of the destroyer (Satan) of the earth; a homily focused on Christ as Savior of the world, including its environment; a tree-planting rite intended "to pacify the aggrieved land and its creator [as] 'the only way we can seek forgiveness for having caused the nakedness of the land'";[91] the planting of a new seedling, representing the bread broken and buried in order to birth new life; and a cup of water poured out on the new seedling, representing the water of purification and fertility. Typical also is an exhortation by Bishop Wapendama of the Signs of the Apostles Church, given at a tree-planting ceremony to a multireligious audience:

> We, deliverers of the stricken land, were sent by Mwari [the supreme creator being of African traditional religiosity] on a divine mission. Deliverance, Mwari says, lies in the trees. Jesus said: "I leave you, my followers, to complete my work." And that task is the one of healing! We, the followers of Jesus, have to continue with this healing ministry. So let us all fight, clothing, healing the earth with trees! It is our task to strengthen this mission

90. M. L. Daneel, *African Earthkeepers: Wholistic Interfaith Mission* (Maryknoll, NY: Orbis, 2001), 165.

91. Ibid., 170. The significance of this act should not be underestimated, since tree planting was a prominent symbol of colonial Christianization, especially the ritual planting of the Christian cross; see David Chidester, *Christianity: A Global History* (San Francisco: HarperSanFrancisco, 2000), 354.

with our numbers of people. We shall clothe and heal the entire land with trees and drive off affliction. I believe we can do it.[92]

Participation in the liturgy assumes responsible aftercare by the community to nurture the soil. Divinely sent rain is understood as God's response. Conscious and persistent offenders against the environment are barred from tree-planting ceremonies and the Eucharist, with the hope of encouraging repentance, forgiveness, and full restoration to the community. The centrality of the Holy Spirit in the AIC/AAEC approach should not be missed. This is clearly seen in the tree-planting ceremony, which functions analogously to the Eucharist. The epiclesis, which invites the Spirit to give life through the eucharistic elements, occurs also in the invitation to the Spirit to give life, through the implanted seedlings, to the earth and to the human communities that depend upon their environments. An ecological theology thus emerges wherein God is understood as creator, Christ as earthkeeper, and the Holy Spirit as earth healer and the source of life. This work of the Spirit as life giver includes opposition to the destroyer (accomplished through convicting human beings of the sin of environmental destruction and inspiring acts of resistance) and deliverance from the destroyer (through the exorcism of the demonic and the expulsion of offenders). From this a holistic cosmology arises whereby the divine, natural, and human realms are integrated through the presence and activity of the Spirit. Here the Spirit represents the immanence of God, a corrective to the transcendence of the supreme creator (e.g., Mwari) of African traditions. This leads, finally, to a pneumatological ecclesiology whereby the church is understood to be empowered by the Spirit as a sociopolitical and environmental healer and liberator. The work of the Spirit integrates theory and praxis and is rooted in the ecumenical reality of the wider church, motivated by the missionary mandate of Christ as empowered by the Spirit, directed toward liturgical enactment and the transformation of ecclesial structures and activities, and informed by ecological awareness and the responsible use of scientific technology.

Over the past fifteen years, ZIRRCON initiatives have led to the development of nurseries and the planting of trees to reforest the land. An estimated eight to nine million seedlings have been planted through AIC involvement in ZIRRCON's efforts. This is certainly not the only thing that some pentecostal-type churches in Zimbabwe are doing, but

92. Quoted in M. L. Daneel, "Liberative Ecumenism at the African Grassroots," in *Full of Life for All: Challenges for Mission in Early 21st Century*, ed. [M. L.] Inus Daneel, Charles Van Engen, and Henrik Vroom (New York: Rodopi, 2003), 295–327, at 322.

its significance should not be underplayed. Amidst providing new communities of fellowship, belonging, and social aid for those displaced by civil war and rapid urbanization, AICs have also hearkened the call of the Spirit, who long ago "hovered over the waters" and whose outpouring even in these last days continues to articulate the groanings of creation (cf. Rom. 8:19–23). In short, Zimbabwean AICs recognize that the saving work of the Spirit includes the restoration, renewal, and sanctification of the environment. The gifts of the Spirit therefore empower this healing work.[93] This work touches not only the environment but also human communities and relationships. Yet the African pentecostal experience of the liberative Spirit is still an ambiguous one, as when viewed in light of pentecostalism in South Africa.

1.3.2 *On My Men- and Maidservants: South African Pentecostalisms.* The recent history of apartheid has with few exceptions divided white from black pentecostalism in South Africa.[94] About 40 percent (ten million) of the black population is within the orbit of the indigenous Spirit-, prophet-, and pentecostal-type AICs (usually Zionist or Apostolic, or their offshoots), and a smaller, mostly white population is within the more strictly defined (classical) Pentecostal churches, such as the Apostolic Faith Mission (AFM) and the Full Gospel Church of God.[95] As with AICs in other parts of Africa, these churches feature holistic soteriologies replete with physical healing, deliverance from trouble, exorcisms, prophecies, dreams, visions, and other pentecostal manifestations. Yet there is a spectrum of opinions and attitudes within these AICs toward traditional African religious beliefs and practices—such as those regarding ancestors, the spirit world, and burial rituals—that range from outright rejection to ongoing participation.[96]

---

93. See Daneel, *Quest for Belonging*, ch. 6.

94. For an introduction to apartheid, see Paul Maylam, *South Africa's Racial Past: The History and Historiography of Racism, Segregation, and Apartheid* (Burlington, VT: Ashgate, 2001). One of the exceptions is the Assemblies of God, begun by white Pentecostal missionaries but from the beginning and continuing to the present thoroughly interracial and even with a majority of black members. See Peter Watt, *From Africa's Soil: The Story of the Assemblies of God in Southern Africa* (Cape Town: Struik Christian Books, 1992).

95. Allan H. Anderson and Gerald J. Pillay, "The Segregated Spirit: The Pentecostals," in *Christianity in South Africa: A Political, Social, and Cultural History,* ed. Richard Elphick and Rodney Davenport (Berkeley: University of California Press, 1997), 227–41.

96. The researcher who has explored many of these South African pentecostal issues in depth is Allan H. Anderson; see A. H. Anderson, *Bazalwane: African Pentecostalism in South Africa* (Pretoria: University of South Africa Press, 1992); A. H. Anderson, with Samuel Otwang, *Tumelo: The Faith of African Pentecostals in South Africa* (Pretoria: University of South Africa Press, 1993); and A. H. Anderson, *Zion and Pentecost: The Spirituality and Experience of Pentecostal and Zionist/Apostolic Churches in South Africa* (Pretoria: University of South Africa Press, 2000).

The focus here, however, is on the racial divide in South African pentecostalism. The South African situation of oppression under whites may be the exception in Africa, since many of the impoverished African nations have experienced oppression most recently "at the hands of their own [black] élite."[97] Within months after the founding of the AFM in 1908, segregation was already occurring, especially in Western Pentecostal missions churches. By the 1950s, the heyday of apartheid, AFM leaders were defending the "mental, emotional and spiritual superiority of the white race, all based on the Scriptures."[98] White pentecostals not only acquiesced in the apartheid ideology; they also actively defended it. In keeping with the traditional apolitical stance of classical Pentecostalism, involvement in politics was considered sinful and advocated only by liberal Christians (if they were considered Christians at all). At best, individuals had to resign from pastoral church ministry to engage in the struggle against apartheid; at worst, such persons were considered "backslidden" in pursuing these kinds of activities. In accordance with the government's official position, African nationalism and black political movements were considered to be inspired by Communism and hence representative of the evil system of the antichrist.[99] What is striking is that the worldwide pentecostal community exerted comparatively little pressure on the South African pentecostal denominations that supported apartheid, in contrast to other Protestant denominations that did respond to and, in some cases, cut off affiliation with South African churches that defended apartheid policies.[100]

Yet there have always been pentecostal voices, both white and black, resistant to apartheid. Among blacks, Nicholas Bhengu (1909–1985) confronted apartheid by fighting crime, strengthening black self-confidence, developing black independence from white Afrikaners, and establishing village and communal settlements for the rural poor Pentecostals, even as he railed against the demons of the AICs.[101] Among whites,

97. Paul Gifford, *African Christianity: Its Public Role* (Bloomington: Indiana University Press, 1998), 324.

98. Anderson and Pillay, "The Segregated Spirit," 238.

99. Thus did the state president, P. W. Botha, accuse pentecostal activist Frank Chikane: "You love and praise the African National Congress with its Marxist and atheistic ideology, landmines, bombs and necklaces perpetrating the most horrendous atrocities imaginable; and you embrace and participate in their call for violence, hatred, sanctions, insurrection and revolution." Letter from P. W. Botha to Frank Chikane, March 24, 1988, in Frank Chikane, *The Church's Prophetic Witness against the Apartheid System in South Africa* (Johannesburg: Thorold's Africana Books, 1988), 60–64; quotation, 62.

100. See Nico Horn, "Crossing Racial Borders in Southern Africa: A Lesson From History," *CPCR* 3 (1998), http://www.pctii.org/cyberj/cyber3.html.

101. On Bhengu, see Walter J. Hollenweger, *The Pentecostals: The Charismatic Movement in the Churches*, trans. R. A. Wilson (Minneapolis: Augsburg, 1972), ch. 10; and Anderson, *Zion and Pentecost*, 89–93.

Ray McCauley of the "faith churches" network of the International Fellowship of Christian Churches (IFCC) called for a "unity of witness in the faith" that included pentecostals' recognition of their complicity in apartheid, confession of their silence, and repentance from, and rejection of, racism.[102] By the 1980s—finally—the tide was beginning to turn. Students at white pentecostal Bible colleges protested against racism, and in a show of solidarity, one pentecostal school received those expelled for these activities.[103] Pentecostal scholars were still critical of the use of Marxist philosophy but now rejected apartheid as unbiblical and "contrary to the gospel."[104]

Undeniably, this new situation among pentecostal churches owed a great deal to the life and work of Frank Chikane.[105] Growing up in the AFM, Chikane was ordained a minister by the church in 1980. He had already been repeatedly detained by the government for his subversive activity, undergoing six weeks of torture from June to July 1977. Chikane was suspended from ministry for twelve months in 1981 for persisting in "political" activity—engaging in activity directed toward undermining the apartheid laws of the government—after which his ordination certificate was completely withdrawn. Undaunted, he continued to oppose apartheid and was arrested again in 1985 on charges of treason. Although released on bail, he was placed under house arrest from dusk to dawn, and his house was attacked with fire bombs, among other assassination plans that were discovered. Chikane was formally acquitted of the treason charges, yet he continued the resistance. He was elected general secretary of the South African Council of Churches in July 1987. In 1990, the AFM decision was reversed, and he was reinstated as minister with an apology from the church. For his work, Chikane was then elected vice-president of the AFM in 1996, becoming director general in the Office of the President of South Africa in 1999.

Chikane was motivated by his experience in the township of Soweto. As mediator, he saw the violence against an entire generation of children and youth evidenced in their malnutrition, poverty, housing rot,

102. Rev. Ray McCauley, "Epilogue," in *The Road to Rustenburg: The Church Looking Forward to a New South Africa*, ed. Louw Alberts and Frank Chikane (Cape Town: Struik Christian Books, 1991), 198–204; and Japie LaPoorta, "Unity or Division: A Case Study of the Apostolic Faith Mission of South Africa," in Dempster, Klaus, and Petersen, eds., *The Globalization of Pentecostalism*, 151–69, esp. 164–65.

103. Allan Anderson, "Dangerous Memories for South African Pentecostals," in Anderson and Hollenweger, eds., *Pentecostals after a Century*, 89–107, esp. 105.

104. F. P. Möller, *Church and Politics: A Pentecostal View of the South African Situation* (Braamfontein, South Africa: Gospel Publishers, [1990]), 34.

105. See Frank Chikane, *No Life of My Own: An Autobiography* (Maryknoll, NY: Orbis, 1989).

and ideological education. He also experienced the violent repression and imprisonment of nonviolent resisters without trial on suspicion of "noncooperation with the government."[106] In such situations, where war is present and the alleged space for debate is either created by violent means or completely eliminated, the Christian task is to discern legitimate from illegitimate authorities.[107] Spirit-filled Christians cannot be neutral in these cases but are required to take sides with the oppressed and to work toward the liberation of both the oppressed and their oppressors.[108] Throughout, Chikane's pentecostal commitments were never in doubt: "My entire life has been a deeply devotional struggle both against faith and for faith. This, in a sense, is what the Pentecostal tradition is all about. It is a quest to understand and make spiritual sense of one's life experience."[109]

Partly because of Chikane's increasing influence, pentecostal presence in the South African sociopolitical situation became more noticeable. The 1985 *Kairos Document* included a few pentecostal theologians, and the 1986 *Evangelical Witness* drawn up by Concerned Evangelicals featured more than half of its signatories as pentecostals.[110] This was followed by the *Relevant Pentecostal Witness* in 1988. Signatories repented for Pentecostal complicity with apartheid on both the level of doctrine and that of practice. They recognized that the liberation of the black South African is simultaneously the liberation of the white South African from the ideology of superiority. Most significantly, the document retrieved and reappropriated resources from the pentecostal tradition—from the black experience at Azusa Street as a model for a

106. Frank Chikane, "Children in Turmoil: The Effects of the Unrest on Township Children," in *Growing Up in a Divided Society: The Contexts of Childhood in South Africa*, ed. Sandra Burman and Pamela Reynolds (Evanston, IL: Northwestern University Press, 1986), 333–44; and *The African Churches and the South African Crisis* (London: Catholic Institute for International Relations [CIIR], 1988).

107. Frank Chikane, "Where the Debate Ends," in *Theology and Violence: The South African Debate*, ed. Charles Villa-Vicencio (Grand Rapids: Eerdmans, 1988), 301–9.

108. Frank Chikane, "Doing Theology in a Situation of Conflict," in *Resistance and Hope: South African Essays in Honour of Beyers Naudé*, ed. Charles Villa-Vicencio and John W. De Gruchy (Grand Rapids: Eerdmans; Claremont, South Africa: David Philip, 1985), 98–102; and "EATWOT and Third World Theologies: An Evaluation of the Past and Present," in *Third World Theologies: Commonalities and Divergences*, ed. K. C. Abraham (Maryknoll, NY: Orbis, 1990), 147–69.

109. Frank Chikane, interview, in Charles Villa-Vicencio, *The Spirit of Freedom: South African Leaders on Religion and Politics* (Berkeley: University of California Press, 1996), 60–73; quotation, 63.

110. See Kairos Theologians, *The Kairos Document: Challenge to the Church* (Grand Rapids: Eerdmans, 1986); Concerned Evangelicals, Soweto, *Evangelical Witness in South Africa: A Critique of Evangelical Theology and Practice by South African Evangelicals* (Grand Rapids: Eerdmans, 1986).

nonracist and nonsexist church, the reevaluation of the black roots of Pentecostalism, the tradition of pentecostalism's prophetic witness, and the experiences of pentecostal Spirit baptism as restoring human dignity—toward this end.[111]

The end of apartheid in the 1990s also featured increased pentecostal consciousness of the need to participate in the liberation of South Africa. The Rustenburg Conference represented almost the entire spectrum of Christian churches, including a significant number of pentecostal/AIC representatives, affirming the need for justice, for the church to make restitution, and for Christian action. Marginalized from the power structures of South Africa for most of the twentieth century, pentecostals are no longer political outsiders. A survey in 1992 noted that almost 50 percent of pentecostals, including Zionist and Apostolic church members, have supported the African National Congress: what was once denounced as evil (African nationalism) is now championed as good. In 1994, Kenneth Meshoe, a Pentecostal pastor in Vosloorus, a black township in East Gauteng, was elected to the national parliament from the new pentecostal-dominated African Christian Democratic Party (ACDP). The United Christian Democratic Party is even smaller, but it had been led by a pentecostal, Lucas Mangope.[112] Will the black and white pentecostals who were once segregated work together to contribute to the development of a new South Africa?

1.3.3 *On My Men- and Maidservants: Pentecostalism and the African Diaspora*. The same question pertains to the churches of the African diaspora. At least two aspects to the African diaspora concern this study: the theological, on the one side, and the geographical and sociohistorical, on the other. Regarding the latter, we will look at the black experience in the Caribbean, in the United Kingdom, and in the United States, all with a history of slavery from the earliest days. Theologically, the "African diaspora" calls attention to the "consistent patterns of African 'survivals' or retentions, even when family-bonds, language and religion

---

111. For an exposition, see Japie LaPoorta, "The Necessity for a Relevant Pentecostal Witness in South Africa," *EPTA* 10, no. 1 (1991): 25–33, esp. 30–32; also "A Declaration of Solidarity with the Relevant Pentecostal Witness in South Africa," *EPTA* 10, no. 1 (1991): 34–35; and J. Nico Horn, "The Experience of the Spirit in Apartheid: The Possibilities of the Rediscovery of the Black Roots of Pentecostalism for South African Theology," in *Experiences of the Spirit: Conference on Pentecostal and Charismatic Research in Europe at Utrecht University, 1989*, ed. Jan A. B. Jongeneel, SIHC 68 (Frankfurt, Ger.: Peter Lang, 1991), 117–39, esp. 130–36.

112. Allan Anderson, "Pentecostals and Apartheid in South Africa during Ninety Years, 1908–1998," *CPCR* 9 (2001), http://www.pctii.org/cyberj/cyber9.html. For an overview of the increasingly political engagement of African pentecostals, see Ogbu U. Kalu, *Power, Poverty, and Prayer: The Challenges of Poverty and Pluralism in African Christianity, 1960–1996*, SIHC 122 (Frankfurt, Ger.: Peter Lang, 2000), ch. 5, esp. 126–32.

were ruthlessly broken up. This continuum refers to belief in a spiritual reality, narrativity of theology, empowerment by the spirit, music and rhythms, dreams and visions, or healing in belonging which were not destroyed but rather began to influence the 'host-societies.'"[113] Clearly, the two are connected: blacks in these regions have survived slavery and its children—segregation, discrimination, and racism—mainly through accommodating their religious traditions to new environments and new challenges.[114] Our question is this: how did the emergence of pentecostalism in the African diaspora contribute to the black resistance against oppression?

Caribbean pentecostalism has always been transcontinentalistic and transnationalistic, not quite African, nor quite American, nor even Latin American.[115] There is much about Caribbean pentecostalism that we do not know, especially since the pentecostal experience on the smaller islands has not been adequately studied. Nevertheless, several features of pentecostalism in this region stand out. First is the diversity of pentecostalisms in the Caribbean, ranging from the Cuban experience under Communist rule in the past generation to the Puerto Rican experience as a U.S. territory under the influence of North American pentecostal missionary ventures and encompassing everything in between. Second, as with Puerto Rico, there remains the widespread presence of North American missions churches, especially from the Holiness wing of pentecostalism, such as the Church of God, Cleveland, and the Church of God of Prophecy. Third, as part of the larger African diaspora, Caribbean pentecostalism often competes against, and on occasion is phenomenologically comparable with, other new religious expressions of the African diaspora, such as voodoo (Haiti), Santeria (Cuba), or Rastafarianism (Jamaica). Fourth, as is the case in Latin America and China, there is a strong Oneness presence, even if represented in the Caribbean by the tradition of black Apostolic churches.[116] In all cases, pentecostalism in the Caribbean has provided an alternative countercultural discourse that is in some respects rooted in Christianity but in other respects

113. Roswith Gerloff, "Pentecostals in the African Diaspora," in Anderson and Hollenweger, eds., *Pentecostals after a Century*, 67–86; quotation, 69.

114. The standard account remains Albert J. Raboteau, *Slave Religion* (New York: Oxford University Press, 1978).

115. See the essays by Hurbon, Austin-Broos, Bastian, Oro and Semán, and Freston in André Corten and Ruth Marshall-Fratani, eds., *Between Babel and Pentecost: Transnational Pentecostalism in African and Latin America* (Bloomington: Indiana University Press, 2001), part 2.

116. See, e.g., Roswith Gerloff, "Hope of Redemption: The Religious, Cultural, and Socio-political Significance of Oneness (Apostolic) Pentecostalism in Jamaica," in Jongeneel, ed., *Experiences of the Spirit*, 141–74.

marginal to, and indicting of, the dominant Christian traditions. The attractiveness of pentecostalism no doubt resides, in part, in its openness to the life of the spirit, in its providing space for and cultivating communal and ritual expressions of that life, and in the adaptability of the pentecostal worldview and cosmology to that of African religious traditions and vice versa.[117]

The influence of Caribbean pentecostalism, however, has extended far beyond the islands, primarily by way of immigration to the United Kingdom beginning in the 1950s.[118] The black pentecostal experience in Britain clearly provides members with "an alternative basis for identity and difference, not as Blacks in a White society, but as 'Christians' in an imperfect society and world."[119] This is also the case for Apostolic women: quadruply marginalized as blacks, as pentecostals, as Oneness, and as female, women are nevertheless "saints" with newly constituted identities valued by God and their Spirit-filled communities. As significant has been the shift from a "theology of prohibitives," with its emphases on interior spiritualities and otherworldly transcendence, to a "theology of possibilities" as pentecostals now actively seek out ways to retain and reshape their identities as blacks in a multicultural Britain.[120] Black pentecostalism has thus afforded the opportunity for an interstitial and transboundaried identity to emerge, one that is culturally British, Caribbean, and African; that is religiously Christian, pentecostal, and syncretistic (of African and Caribbean elements); and that is fully engaged in the tensions between a private and a public spirituality, between an otherworldly and a this-worldly focus, between the concerns for personal faith and those for social justice.

Roswith Gerloff suggests several distinctive theological contributions of the black pentecostal experience in Britain through these processes.[121]

117. E.g., Diane J. Austin-Broos, *Jamaica Genesis: Religion and the Politics of Moral Orders* (Chicago: University of Chicago Press, 1997), part 3.

118. E.g., Malcolm J. C. Calley, *God's People: West Indian Pentecostal Sects in England* (New York: Oxford University Press, 1965); and Roswith Gerloff, guest ed., "The African Christian Diaspora in Europe and the Quest for Human Community," special issue, *IRM* 89, no. 354 (2000).

119. Nicole Rodriguez Toulis, *Believing Identity: Pentecostalism and the Mediation of Jamaican Ethnicity and Gender in England* (New York: Berg, 1997), 274.

120. Joel Edwards, "Afro-Caribbean Pentecostalism in Britain," *JEPTA* 17 (1997): 37–48, esp. 45–47.

121. Roswith I. H. Gerloff, *A Plea for British Black Theologies: The Black Church Movement in Britain in Its Transatlantic Cultural and Theological Interaction with Special Reference to the Pentecostal (Oneness) and Sabbatarian Movements*, 2 vols., SIHC 77 (Frankfurt, Ger.: Peter Lang, 1992), 1:255–70, 388–90; see also Roswith I. H. Gerloff, "The Holy Spirit and the African Diaspora: Spiritual, Cultural, and Social Roots of Black Pentecostal Churches," *JEPTA* 14 (1995): 85–100, esp. 89–90; and "'Africa as the Laboratory of the

First, black British pentecostalism may provide a model for both the unconscious and the conscious struggle of blacks against white oppression and for the development of an intercultural theology that combats racism, builds empathy, and reconciles black and white.[122] Second, black British pentecostalism emphasizes God's activity in history instead of focusing only on God's eschatological redemption or on the transcendent nature of God. Third, the Apostolic churches may provide insights into narrative reconstruals of Christian doctrines, such as the doctrine of God (Trinity) and the incarnation, relevant to twenty-first-century Christianity dominated by the Eastern and Southern churches. Fourth, because of increased awareness of Britain's multireligious society, bridges are being built not only between trinitarian and Oneness pentecostals but also with those of other faiths. Pentecostals' multifaith ecumenism can be seen in their involvement in the Centre for the Study of Islam and Christian-Muslim Relations at the Selly Oak Colleges (now part of the University of Birmingham) and in discussions with Muslims, Sikhs, and Buddhists on "the dilemma of interfaith dialogue for Pentecostal Christians," held at the First United Church of Jesus Christ Apostolic in Wolverhampton.[123] In light of these developments, Gerloff poses the question whether pentecostalism can be understood as Africa's gift to the church catholic:

> In a genuine Pentecostal theology which is not borrowed language from alien traditions, God and the Holy Spirit are experienced and articulated (if only by oral modes of communication) as life-enhancing power, as a cosmological energy not only in church but in the world which awakens people, reforms their liturgies, helps them to act both prayerfully and politically, offers them healing and wholeness, guides them into the future and creates unity in diversity . . . which, as in the Epiclesis of the ancient Church, "renews the face of the earth."[124]

This question about whether pentecostalism is the gift of black Africa to the church is as old as the debate on whether to attribute the origins of classical Pentecostalism in the United States to the leadership of

---

World': The African Christian Diaspora in Europe as Challenge to Missions and Ecumenical Relations," in *Mission Is Crossing Frontiers: Essays in Honor of the Late Bongani A. Mazibuko*, ed. Roswith I. H. Gerloff (Pietermaritzburg, South Africa: Cluster, 2003), 401–42, esp. 427–34.

122. Robert Beckford, "Jesus Is Dread: Black Cultures, Liberation, and Mission," in *Mission Matters*, ed. Lynne Price, Juan Sepúlveda, and Graeme Smith, SIHC 103 (Frankfurt, Ger.: Peter Lang, 1997), 121–34; and "Black Pentecostals and Black Politics," in Anderson and Hollenweger, eds., *Pentecostals after a Century*, 48–59.

123. Gerloff, *A Plea for British Black Theologies*, 1:255–58.

124. Gerloff, "The Holy Spirit and the African Diaspora," 88.

the white Charles Fox Parham (1873–1929) at Bethel Bible College in Topeka, Kansas, in 1901 or to that of the black William J. Seymour (1870–1922) at Azusa Street in Los Angeles in 1906.[125] Without denying Parham's important contributions, it can be maintained that the Azusa Street experience launched pentecostalism as a national (if not international) phenomenon. For Seymour, of central significance was not the charismatic phenomenology of the revival but the fact that in the outpouring of the Spirit at Azusa Street, "the 'color line' was washed away in the blood."[126] Because of the importance of the black North American experience for world pentecostal theology, here we will explore further the significance of the African diaspora in the United States.

1.3.4 *On My Men- and Maidservants: Black Pentecostalism in the United States*.[127] Seymour understood the reconciliation of races as made possible by the cross of Christ but actualized through the outpouring of the Spirit. In the words of Ithiel Clemmons (1921–1999), a Church of God in Christ pastor, bishop, and scholar: "Seymour championed one doctrine above all others: There must be no color line or any other division of the Church of Jesus Christ because God is no respecter of persons. . . . This inclusive fellowship is not a human construct but a divine glossalalic community of human equality. Spiritual power sprang more from interracial equality than from glossolalia."[128] It should therefore come as no surprise that the earliest pentecostals influenced by Azusa Street embodied this vision and that the first pentecostal denominations emerging from the revival were biracial in character. Southern pentecostals such as those belonging to the Church of God of Prophecy "frequently transgressed racial and gender hierarchies in a region dominated by

---

125. See Iain MacRobert, *The Black Roots and White Racism of Early Pentecostalism in the USA* (New York: St. Martin's, 1988).

126. Frank Bartleman, *Azusa Street: The Roots of Modern-Day Pentecost* (1925; repr., Plainfield, NJ: Logos International, 1980), 54; also Dale T. Irvin, "'Drawing All Together in One Bond of Love': The Ecumenical Vision of William J. Seymour and the Azusa Street Revival," *JPT* 6 (1995): 25–53; and Douglas J. Nelson, "The Black Face of Church Renewal: The Meaning of a Charismatic Explosion, 1901–1985," in *Faces of Renewal: Studies in Honor of Stanley M. Horton Presented on His 70th Birthday*, ed. Paul Elbert (Peabody, MA: Hendrickson, 1988), 172–91.

127. For introductions, see Charles Edwin Jones, *Black Holiness: A Guide to the Study of Black Participation in Wesleyan Perfectionist and Glossolalic Pentecostal Movements* (Metuchen, NJ: American Theological Library Association and Scarecrow, 1987); and Sherry Sherrod DuPree, *African-American Holiness Pentecostal Movement: An Annotated Bibliography* (New York: Garland, 1996).

128. Marlon Millner, "We've Come This Far by Faith: Pentecostalism and Political and Social Upward Mobility among African-Americans," *CPCR* 9 (2001), http://www.pctii.org/cyberj/cyber9.html.

Jim Crow and intense patriarchalism."[129] Nevertheless, the social forces of segregation and racism were too strong even for those filled with the Spirit. By the mid-1920s, segregated denominations were emerging: most whites found that the "three strikes" of being black, poor, and pentecostal were too much to handle.[130] By the time of the Great Depression, the fires of early pentecostal social concern had fizzled as the churches, both white and black, combated severe poverty either by focusing on achieving minimal personal comforts or by emphasizing otherworldly and eschatological solutions.[131]

But what also happened was that the black pentecostal resistance to racism, segregation, and oppression shifted from being primarily an articulated discourse to being an embodied ecclesiology.[132] By this I mean the various ways in which the Sanctified Church tradition of North America participated in and accomplished the transformation of Afro-Caribbean and African "survivals": folklore, popular mythology, music, and so forth.[133]

129. Randall J. Stephens, "'There is Magic in Print': The Holiness-Pentecostal Press and the Origins of Southern Pentecostalism," *Journal of Southern Religion* 5 (2002), http://jsr.as.wvu.edu/2002/jsrlink5.htm. An excellent sociocultural history of southern black pentecostalism is Karen Lynell Kossie, "The Move Is On: African American Pentecostal-Charismatics in the Southwest" (Ph.D. diss., Rice University, 1998).

130. Leonard Lovett, "Aspects of the Spiritual Legacy of the Church of God in Christ: Ecumenical Implications," in *Black Witness to the Apostolic Faith*, ed. David T. Shannon and Gayraud S. Wilmore (Grand Rapids: Eerdmans, 1988), 41–49, esp. 49, mentions this in terms of "triple jeopardy." I would add a fourth strike: being a poor, black, pentecostal *woman*!

131. See Brian K. Blount, *Go Preach! Mark's Kingdom Message and the Black Church Today* (Maryknoll, NY: Orbis, 1998), 242. On the eschatological orientation of black spirituality, see George C. L. Cummings, "The Slave Narratives as a Source of Black Theological Discourse: The Spirit and Eschatology," in *Cut Loose Your Stammering Tongue: Black Theology in the Slave Narratives*, ed. Dwight N. Hopkins and George C. L. Cummings (Maryknoll, NY: Orbis, 1991), 46–66.

132. See, e.g., Zora Neale Hurston, *The Sanctified Church* (Berkeley, CA: Turtle Island, 1983), esp. 79–107; Cheryl J. Sanders, *Saints in Exile: The Holiness-Pentecostal Experience in African American Religion and Culture* (New York: Oxford University Press, 1996); and Sherry Sherrod Dupree, "In the Sanctified Holiness Pentecostal Charismatic Movement," *PNEUMA* 23, no. 1 (2001): 97–114.

133. James S. Tinney, "A Theoretical and Historical Comparison of Black Political and Religious Movements" (Ph.D. diss., Howard University, 1978), 221, calls attention to Seymour's background growing up on a slave plantation and his familiarity with Louisiana Creole religion, including Haitian voodoo. For more on the retention of African and Afro-Caribbean religiosity in black American slave religion, see James A. Forbes Jr., "A Pentecostal Approach to Empowerment for Black Liberation" (D.Min. thesis, Crozer Theological Seminary, 1975), 73:

It was a great surprise to the author to get a more balanced picture of the true nature of Voodoo in Haiti. I expected to see the instruments of witchcraft. I had been taught to think of Voodoo almost totally in terms of the use of destructive power. But

Instead of being considered merely "primitive" expressions of power set within an otherworldly orientation, these were resources that black pentecostals ritualized in their Christian worship in order to empower themselves against the challenges posed by racism, sexism, and classism. For these reasons, the black pentecostal worship experience has always included not only the aesthetic dimension but also the ethical: the Spirit's descent, resulting in dancing, clapping, shouting, chanting, the testimony, the sermon, the applause, glossolalia, and even ecstatic possession, works alongside the spirituals, blues, jazz, rhythm, rap, gospel music, and instrumentalizations to empower black communities from week to week in the acts of resistance, rebellion, and reform demanded in their day-to-day existence.[134] Further, there are the "tarrying," the "seasons of prayer," revivals, special fasts, regional/national convocations and conventions, and so on, which contribute to the formation of an entire way of life, a spirituality of resistance.[135] And not to be overlooked is black female agency: black women in the Sanctified Church were "pro-black, pro-women, and pro-uplift"; as "prophets in this tradition," black women (womanists) contributed to the survival of their sons and daughters and to the transformation of their churches, communities, and workplaces.[136] In sum, "black women in the Holiness-Pentecostal churches spoke with authority, leading congregations, interpreting the Bible, and dealing with financial matters and other organizational concerns. Like women in the

observation of a Voodoo ceremony and an unbiased or positive presentation of its meaning revealed that Voodoo is the form of Afro-American religion which supplied cohesion and strength for the black people of Haiti. I also learned that while witchcraft is practiced in the area it cannot be lumped in with the religious ceremonies which center around the effort to make contact with the spirit world. It became very clear why Voodoo had to be discredited. It was largely due to the unifying power of Voodoo that the Haitian peasants were able to throw off the yoke of bondage.

134. See Robert A. Mills, "Musical Prayers: Reflections on the African Roots of Pentecostal Music," *JPT* 12 (1998): 109–26; Paul McIntyre, *Black Pentecostal Music in Windsor* (Ottawa: National Museums of Canada, 1976); and Michael Spencer, *Protest and Praise: Sacred Music of Black Religion* (Minneapolis: Fortress, 1990), chs. 7–8. For more on black church worship, ritual, and liturgy, see Arthur E. Paris, *Black Pentecostalism: Southern Religion in an Urban World* (Amherst: University of Massachusetts Press, 1982), ch. 3; and William Clair Turner Jr., "The United Holy Church of America: A Study in Black Holiness-Pentecostalism" (Ph.D. diss., Duke University, 1984), ch. 5. A constructive black theology of the spirituals is Donald H. Matthews, *Honoring the Ancestors: An African Cultural Interpretation of Black Religion and Literature* (New York: Oxford University Press, 1998).

135. David D. Daniels III, "'Until the Power of the Lord Comes Down': African American Pentecostal Spirituality and Tarrying," in *Contemporary Spiritualities: Social and Religious Contexts*, ed. Clive Erricker and Jane Erricker (New York: Continuum, 2001), 173–91.

136. Cheryl Townsend Gilkes, *If It Wasn't for the Women: Black Women's Experience and Womanist Culture in Church and Community* (Maryknoll, NY: Orbis, 2001), chs. 3, 5; quoted phrases, 46, 91.

mainline black churches, they were role models, confronting the dominant society's stereotypical images of black women."[137]

These elements are all clearly present in the largest and best-known denomination of the Sanctified Church tradition: the Church of God in Christ (COGIC).[138] Founded initially by Charles Harrison Mason (1866–1961) and Charles Price Jones (1865–1949) in 1897 after they were expelled by the National Baptist Convention for preaching sanctification as a second work of grace, COGIC eventually split into two wings: Mason's, which accepted the pentecostal experience and message after encountering it at Azusa Street under Seymour's ministry, and Jones's, which rejected it.[139] Set against the backdrop of Southern slavery complete with lynching mobs and violence against blacks, Mason adapted African religiosity—including the use of herbs and animal entrails, following the biblical tradition of the Urim and Thummin and the casting of lots, for which he was accused (by blacks and whites) of superstitious activities at best and magical practices at worst[140]—to the black church tradition, which in turn enabled COGIC churches to "conjure" up an alternative existence in the black pentecostal community as manifest through the dance, the shout, and so on, all representative means of resistance to, and survival in, a hostile environment. Whereas it had been previously suggested that "'spirit possession' in some African cultures was descriptive of the same religious experience transposed in western culture as the baptism of the Holy Ghost," Mason and the COGIC understood this experience as "one which empowers us to change the world. . . . To 'dance in the Spirit' is to participate in a celebrated victory that has already been won in history in preparation for a future 'yet to be,' and at the same time, recognize the power of God as the demonic is confronted

---

137. Clarence Taylor, *The Black Churches of Brooklyn* (New York: Columbia University Press, 1994), 188.

138. See Ithiel C. Clemmons, *Bishop C. H. Mason and the Roots of the Church of God in Christ* (Bakersfield, CA: Pneuma Life, 1996). For an overview of COGIC, see Anne H. Pinn and Anthony B. Pinn, *Fortress Introduction to Black Church History* (Minneapolis: Fortress, 2002), ch. 3; and C. Eric Lincoln and Lawrence H. Mamiya, *The Black Church in the African American Experience* (Durham, NC: Duke University Press, 1990), ch. 4.

139. On the break between Jones and Mason, see David Douglas Daniels, "The Cultural Renewal of Slave Religion: Charles Price Jones and the Emergence of the Holiness Movement in Mississippi" (Ph.D. diss., Union Theological Seminary, 1992), 271–76.

140. Clarence E. Hardy, "'Take the Bible Way': Charles Harrison Mason and the Development of Black Pentecostalism as Biblical Magic" (paper presented at the annual meeting of the Society of Pentecostal Studies, Southeastern College, Lakeland, FL, March 14–16, 2002). Hardy here follows, among others, Theophus H. Smith, *Conjuring Culture: Biblical Formation of Black America* (New York: Oxford University Press, 1994), who explores both black spirituality as a means of transforming/creating (conjuring) reality and the African American diasporic use of the Bible as a healing (magical) sourcebook.

in the *eternal now*."[141] Most important, the black pentecostal quest for embodying divine power was captured in the ritual reception of the Holy Spirit and confirmed through reinforced and sustained holiness codes of purity and through social, political, and cultural activism.

In all this, Mason can be understood as a prophetic figure in the Sanctified Church tradition who was followed by others in the black pentecostal and Apostolic movement. Elder Robert Clarence Lawson (1883–1961) was mentored by the Apostolic preacher Garfield T. Haywood (1880–1931), but he left Haywood's Pentecostal Assemblies of the World to found the Church of Our Lord Jesus Christ of the Apostolic Faith in 1919.[142] In 1925, Lawson self-published *The Anthropology of Jesus Christ Our Kinsman* while pastoring the Refuge Church of Christ in New York City.[143] In this important work, he boldly and creatively addressed the problem of racism against blacks by arguing from the patristic soteriological principle "What the Lord did not take on he did not redeem" to the conclusion that Jesus is the universal Savior and kinsman Redeemer "to all having their blood in his veins."[144] And who is Jesus not a relative to if all are descendants of Noah through Shem, Japheth, and Ham? But more significantly, human beings participate in this redeeming work of Christ insofar as they are united with him by the original pentecostal Spirit. Here Lawson showed himself to be squarely in the pentecostal and African American Christian traditions instead of merely mimicking the emerging Afrocentrist arguments of the liberal academy with which he was familiar. Because the churches have betrayed this rule of redemption over the centuries, the last-days pentecostal revival of the Spirit is intended to breathe new life into the churches on precisely this point, enabling the churches to rise above prejudice and overcome racism. Lawson's hope is "that the Pentecostal people would teach to these [mainline churches] a wonderful lesson by example in showing that the true people of God are one regardless of what nationality or race they may belong; by abiding together in the bonds of fellowship, love, and organization. . . . We trusted that the Pentecostal people would rise to redeem man by example and precept. It is alright to sing and shout and pray and preach loud, but what this poor world is longing for is the real love of God, lived."[145]

---

141. Lovett, "Aspects of the Spiritual Legacy of the Church of God in Christ," 46, 49; italics Lovett's.

142. On Lawson, see Douglas Jacobsen, *Thinking in the Spirit: Theologies of the Early Pentecostal Movement* (Bloomington: Indiana University Press, 2003), ch. 5.

143. Elder R. C. Lawson, *The Anthropology of Jesus Christ Our Kinsman* (1925; repr., New York: Church of Christ, 1969). My thanks to Marlon Millner for bringing this book to my attention.

144. Ibid., 41.

145. Ibid., 29.

More recently, others such as James Forbes and Leonard Lovett have also seen the pentecostal experience of the Spirit as having sociopolitical implications. Forbes, now senior pastor of the famous Riverside Church in New York City, in "A Pentecostal Approach to Empowerment for Black Liberation," his thesis for the doctor of ministry degree, argued for a pneumatology of liberation that joined spirituality and social justice. The church is empowered by the Spirit to work beyond its borders—for example, in poverty; racial, class, and religious injustices; community strife; and situations of war.[146]

Building on this approach, Leonard Lovett, president of the Society for Pentecostal Studies in 1976, has also proposed for black Holiness pentecostalism a "pneumatological liberation theology" that notes that "liberation is not the product of human ideology but divine 'new creation.'"[147] This work of the Spirit is directed to the spiritualization and the humanization of all peoples, especially blacks. The spiritualization of blacks refers to the awakening of consciousness that empowers the self to be a change agent of the socioeconomic-political structures of oppression. Lovett has gone on to address directly "The Problem of God as Holy Spirit in a Niggerized World" in order to convey the conviction that racism and social injustice can be dismantled by the power of the pentecostal Spirit.[148] Yet the transformation of such a world must occur among whites as well. While distinguishing between personal racism, group racism, and sociostructural/institutional racism, Lovett is clear that for whites the struggle against racism must include confronting the sins of idolatry, self-deification, and complacency: "Racism is pervasive and exists when one group intentionally or unintentionally refuses to share power and resources with another group, thus resulting in oppression. Racism exists when persons are subjugated on the basis of the pigmentation of their skin."[149]

A younger generation of black intellectuals has arisen to translate the pentecostal message for the black church and for North American theology as a whole. Donald Wheelock and Robert Franklin (both COGIC)

---

146. Forbes, "A Pentecostal Approach to Empowerment for Black Liberation," chs. 4–5.

147. Leonard Lovett, "Black Holiness-Pentecostalism: Implications for Ethics and Social Transformation" (Ph.D. diss., Emory University, 1978), ch. 5, esp. 161–72; quotation, 162.

148. Leonard Lovett, "Liberation: A Dual-Edged Sword," *PNEUMA* 9, no. 2 (1987): 155–71, esp. 156–60.

149. Leonard Lovett, "Racism: Death of the Gods," in *The African Cultural Heritage Topical Bible* (Bakersfield, CA: Pneuma Life, 1995), 73–79; quotation, 75. See also idem, *Kingdom Beyond Color: Re-examining the Phenomenon of Racism* (Orlando, FL: Higher Standard Publishers, 2004).

connect a pneumatological theology of black worship with sociopolitical transformation.[150] For Wheelock, Spirit baptism is both personal and communal, linking the mission of the church to the world. For Franklin, if the prophetic and rhetorical dimensions of worship are heeded, the worship experience should empower worshipers to engagement with the world as partners of the Spirit of God. William Clair Turner Jr.'s study of the United Holy Church of America highlights black pentecostalism as marked by social consciousness, holiness, and prophetic empowerment.[151] Yet by and large, the theological tradition of the Sanctified Church has remained marginalized in attempts to develop pentecostal theology, perhaps for the following reasons.[152] First, blacks do not seem to be as concerned about embracing their identity as pentecostal as they are about their finding meaning to life as blacks in a white world. Second, black Christian identity seems to be defined more denominationally—that is, COGIC or African Methodist Episcopal—than it is by movements such as pentecostalism. Third, much of the black church tradition may already be "pentecostal" in the loose sense of exhibiting pentecostal-style features in worship.[153] Fourth, in contrast to white pentecostal denominations with their own network of educational institutions, black pentecostals have been less successful in converting their educational institutions to accredited four-year colleges; and even their theological seminaries are staffed by black Christian faculty in general rather than black pentecostals specifically.[154] Finally, whereas white pentecostal theology has become increasingly connected to the broader discourse of evangelical theology, black pentecostal theologians have not been interested in what they have considered to be the racist ideology of North American evangelical thought; they have been drawn instead to sociopolitical and liberation theologies.

Nonetheless, the previous neglect of black theological reflection for the development of pentecostal theology is beginning to be remedied,

150. Donald Ray Wheelock, "Spirit Baptism in American Pentecostal Thought" (Ph.D. diss., Emory University, 1983), esp. 331–50; and Robert Franklin, *Another Day's Journey* (Minneapolis: Fortress, 1997). Franklin's book advances previous arguments toward a black North American liberation theology forged in dialogue with black intellectuals such as Booker T. Washington, W. E. B. DuBois, Malcolm X, and Martin Luther King Jr.; see Robert Franklin, *Liberating Visions: Human Fulfillment and Social Justice in African-American Thought* (Minneapolis: Fortress, 1990).

151. Turner, "The United Holy Church of America," esp. ch. 6.

152. I acknowledge help on this issue from especially Marlon Millner and David D. Daniels of the Afro-pentecostal list serve.

153. See Adrienne Gaines, "Revive Us, Precious Lord," *Charisma* 28, no. 10 (May 2003): 36–44.

154. David D. Daniels III, "'Live So Can Use Me Anytime, Lord, Anywhere': Theological Education in the Church of God in Christ, 1970–1997," *AJPS* 3, no. 2 (2000): 295–310.

and this study is meant to take seriously this theological tradition and its contributions. At its core, black pentecostalism is much less about believing in biblical testimonies of divine power as doctrinal propositions than it is about experiencing the divine power that liberates black churches and communities. "Black pentecostalism affirms with dogmatic insistence that liberation is always the consequence of the presence of the Spirit."[155] This study is motivated by what Ithiel Clemmons wrote a few months before his death:

> In April 1960, the Holy Spirit surprisingly broke through the structures and theologies of the historic Protestant traditions with a charismatic outpouring. . . . African-Americans in that period of the 60s were focusing on the Civil Rights movement. The connection should have been, but never has been made. The connection between the quest for righteousness and justice and the surprising charismatic irruptions is yet to be followed to its providential conclusion.[156]

Can we follow the providential breeze of the Spirit, which blows where it wills?

This chapter has surveyed various aspects of selected pentecostal groups, movements, and individuals around the world. The guiding question throughout has been the nature of the pentecostal experience of salvation and of the Spirit of God. Although the preceding does not assume that all aspects of the pentecostal churches, movements, and even individual pentecostal lives discussed are theologically valid, this overview is necessary to highlight several ideas. First, our discussion will need to proceed in light of the vast diversity of world pentecostalisms; discernment will thus be important to weed out what is unhelpful from what is crucial. Second, pentecostal theology cannot be constructed in the abstract, apart from the lived realities of pentecostalism on the ground; following the conviction that orthodoxy is first and foremost right worship—as in the classical theological dictum *lex orandi lex credendi*—pentecostal theology should be rooted in the experiences of the worshiping community. Third, the foregoing has called attention to pentecostalism's holistic soteriology: the encounter with the Spirit of God brings about spiritual life; bodily healing; communal koinonia;

155. Leonard Lovett, "Black Origins of the Pentecostal Movement," in *Aspects of Pentecostal-Charismatic Origins*, ed. Vinson Synan (Plainfield, NJ: Logos International, 1975), 120–41; quotation, 140.

156. Quoted in Millner, "We've Come This Far by Faith"; cf. Walter J. Hollenweger, *Pentecost between Black and White: Five Case Studies on Pentecost and Politics* (Belfast, Northern Ireland: Christian Journals, 1974), ch. 1.

the transformation of material, social, political, and historical circumstances; and responsible ecological living. Last, there is already the clear
connection between pentecostalism and the poor, disenfranchised, and
marginalized of the world;[157] pentecostal theology thus will be liberative
in the holistic senses indicated above. The remaining chapters expand
the theological reflections already begun in this chapter toward the reconstruction of a world pentecostal theology for the late modern world.
Come Holy Spirit, upon all flesh . . .

157. So as not to miss the challenge repeatedly thrown by Walter Hollenweger, repre-
sentative of which is his essay "The Pentecostal Elites and the Pentecostal Poor: A Missed
Dialogue?" in *Charismatic Christianity as a Global Culture,* ed. Karla Poewe (Columbia:
University of South Carolina Press, 1994), 200–214.

2

"And You Shall Receive the Gift of the Holy Spirit"

Toward a Pneumatological Soteriology

The previous chapter suggested that the pentecostal experience of the Spirit is the experience of the transformation of lives and communities as confronted by the living God. In this chapter, we begin to reflect on how these experiences inform a world pentecostal theology. Most tangible from the preceding has been the idea that the pentecostal experience is not merely charismatic but soteriological. The beginning thematic locus of any world pentecostal theology, I suggest, is the doctrine of salvation.

To ask about the doctrine of salvation is to follow the precedent established by the crowd on the day of Pentecost. In response to the day's events and Peter's sermon, they asked, "What should we do?" Peter's response remains pertinent: "Repent, and be baptized every one of you in the name of Jesus Christ so that your sins may be forgiven; and you will receive the gift of the Holy Spirit. For the promise is for you, for your children, and for all who are far away, everyone whom the Lord our God calls to him" (Acts 2:37–39). These words of Peter anticipate the central features of a world pentecostal soteriology. Minimally, it will be centered on Jesus Christ and enabled by the Holy Spirit; be dynamic, featuring distinctive experiences (e.g., repentance and baptism) yet set within a broader process; include theological (the forgiveness of sins) and social/intergenerational (children) dimensions; be historical and social (the promise for Jews and those Gentiles "far away"); and involve human response (repentance) to divine initiative (God's call). What is noteworthy here is that salvation in Christ and in his name is thoroughly pneumatological from beginning to end.

A world pentecostal perspective on the doctrine of salvation therefore leads to a pneumatological soteriology. This would be in contrast to soteriologies that tend to bifurcate the work of Christ and of the Spirit, such as those articulated by Protestant scholasticism. In that framework, Christ provides salvation objectively (e.g., in justification) and the Spirit accomplishes salvation subjectively (e.g., in sanctification). Hence the soteriological work of the Spirit is subsequent to and subordinated to the work of Christ.[1] In response, a pneumatological soteriology understands salvation to be the work of both Christ and the Spirit from beginning to end. To use Pauline language: the Holy Spirit enables the proclamation, hearing, and understanding of the gospel, justifies through the resurrection of Christ, provides for the adoption of believers, accomplishes rebirth and renewal, sanctifies hearts and lives, and provides the down payment for eschatological transformation.[2] In all of this, the Spirit is not an appendage to Christ in the process of salvation but saves with Christ throughout.

The goal of this chapter is to develop especially the central biblical (§2.1) and theological (§2.2) features of a world pentecostal and pneumatological soteriology. This exploration will assume the experiential dimension of the pentecostal encounter with the Spirit of God discussed in the preceding chapter and make explicit references to that discussion only on occasion. It will also look ahead by assessing the merits and demerits of pneumatological soteriology in light of the Christian theological tradition (§2.3). Although theological construction should take into account the biblical data and contemporary experience, it should also locate its proposals in dialogue with the historical tradition. The pentecostal and pneumatological soteriology developed here features both continuities and discontinuities with previous understandings.

1. This is argued in detail by Steven M. Studebaker, "Pentecostal Soteriology and Pneumatology," *JPT* 11, no. 2 (2003): 248–70, esp. 252–66, building on the work of Frank Macchia (whose writings are cited below).
2. On the Spirit and salvation in Paul, see Gordon D. Fee, *God's Empowering Presence: The Holy Spirit in the Letters of Paul* (Peabody, MA: Hendrickson, 1994), ch. 14.

2.1 SPIRIT SOTERIOLOGY AND SPIRIT CHRISTOLOGY: LUKAN AND PENTECOSTAL PERSPECTIVES

If a world pentecostal theology is Christ centered and Spirit driven, it will feature both a Spirit christology and a Spirit soteriology. This section surveys the biblical bases for these notions by employing Luke-Acts as a lens through which to focus on these ideas in the rest of the New Testament. Before proceeding with the exegetical task, however, much more needs to be said about the centrality of Luke-Acts to the pentecostal biblical imagination.

2.1.1 *Luke-Acts: Toward a Pentecostal Hermeneutic.* From the days of Azusa Street onward, pentecostals have understood the modern outpouring of the Holy Spirit as a fulfillment of prophecy. If the original day of Pentecost was foretold by Joel, it was only the "early rain" awaiting the abundant showers of a "later rain" (Joel 2:23). Insofar as modern pentecostalism was understood to fulfill this prophecy of a "latter rain" revival anticipating the last days,[3] the template for organizing and explaining this later experience has been drawn from the early Christian experiences recorded in the book of Acts.

Acts itself is suggestive for this pentecostal reading. Not only does Luke record the promise of the pentecostal gift of the Spirit to all succeeding generations (Acts 2:39), but the open-endedness of the early Christian story (Acts 28:23–31) also seems to point to the ongoing development of the pentecostal story, especially in the "latter rain" revival. In addition, since the promise of the Spirit is specifically connected to the empowerment for Christian witness to the ends of the earth (Acts 1:8), the missionary dimension of the Spirit's outpouring was considered especially urgent by eschatologically minded pentecostals for precipitating the final events of the last days (cf. Matt. 24:14). Further, the return to "biblical Christianity" could be realized only if its defining features were discernible, and where else would this be clearly found except in the book of Acts? Finally, pentecostals understood their experience of speaking in tongues to be the sign

---

3. See D. William Faupel, *The Everlasting Gospel: The Significance of Eschatology in the Development of Pentecostal Thought,* JPTSup 10 (Sheffield, Eng.: Sheffield Academic Press, 1996), esp. ch. 6; and Larry McQueen, *Joel and the Spirit: The Cry of a Prophetic Hermeneutic,* JPTSup 8 (Sheffield, Eng.: Sheffield Academic Press, 1995), ch. 4. This is to be distinguished from the mid-twentieth-century Latter Rain Movement, which understood itself also in terms of Joel 2:23 but with reference to fulfilling the prophecy about "abundant rain"; see Richard M. Riss, *A Survey of 20th-Century Revival Movements in North America* (Peabody, MA: Hendrickson, 1988), 112–24.

of the Spirit's outpouring according to the pattern of Acts (2:1–4; 10:44–46; 19:1–7).[4] Classical Pentecostals defended this doctrine of tongues as the initial physical evidence of Spirit baptism by arguing that the historical narrative of Acts should be read theologically as a normative account of what happens when an individual receives the Holy Spirit.

But here we arrive at the central question for pentecostal theology. It touches on not only the initial-evidence doctrine but also the issues surrounding pentecostal hermeneutics in general: how legitimate is it to rely upon the book of Acts for theological and doctrinal formulation? North American pentecostal theologians have been criticized on these matters by conservative Protestants and evangelicals with whom they have been in closest dialogue.[5] The debate concerns three separate but interconnected questions. First, from a Protestant theological perspective, what is the material outcome of the pentecostal choice to have Luke-Acts provide the organizing framework for theology? Second, how viable is the pentecostal reliance upon the narrative genre of Luke-Acts for theological and doctrinal reflection rather than upon the more didactic genres of the New Testament? Finally, is not Luke's interest primarily historical rather than theological or doctrinal, and if so, is not the notion of Luke-Acts as a "pentecostal canon within the canon" bound to shipwreck the project for a world pentecostal theology?

Yet the tide had begun to turn in favor of pentecostal hermeneutics by the mid–twentieth century. Hans Conzelmann's *Die Mitte der Zeit* (1953) was one of the first to argue that Luke was a theologian in his own right. More specifically, Luke and Acts tell the redemptive plan of God in history—in Jesus and in the church—as part of a theological response to the question regarding the delay of the parousia.[6] Although Conzelmann's specific thesis has been subjected to rigorous criticism,

4. For an illuminating study of the emergence of this doctrine and of how early pentecostal preachers came to understand the Acts narrative, see James R. Goff Jr., *Fields White unto Harvest: Charles F. Parham and the Missionary Origins of Pentecostalism* (Fayetteville: University of Arkansas Press, 1988), esp. ch. 3.

5. Pentecostal text-critical scholar and exegete Gordon Fee discusses the issues in Gordon Fee and Douglas Stuart, *How to Read the Bible for All Its Worth* (Grand Rapids: Zondervan, 1982), ch. 6; and Gordon Fee, *Gospel and Spirit: Issues in New Testament Hermeneutics* (Peabody, MA: Hendrickson, 1991).

6. Hans Conzelmann, *The Theology of St. Luke*, trans. Geoffrey Buswell (Philadelphia: Fortress, 1982). Cf. also Eric Franklin, *Christ the Lord: A Study of the Purpose and Theology of Luke-Acts* (Philadelphia: Westminster, 1975), who attempts to move the emphasis from Luke as *Heilsgeschichte* theologian to Luke as eschatological theologian, who reinterprets history in what might be called a realized-eschatological direction in light of the delay of the parousia.

he gave impetus to the study of Luke as a theologian, which has continued unabated.[7]

Pentecostal scholars have picked up on this emergent tradition of Luke the theologian and responded to their critics by pointing out that the conservative Protestant view assumed a Pauline theological and doctrinal framework that subordinated other New Testament authors and perspectives. Canadian pentecostal Roger Stronstad has been especially vocal on this point.[8] He has argued at length both the general thesis that the Lukan writings have their own theological integrity and the more specific thesis that this integrity is to be found in the Lukan understanding of the Spirit of God's empowering Jesus (resulting in the charismatic Christ) and the church (resulting in the charismatic community). In addition, Luke's charismatic theology leads toward a more robust trinitarian theology in acknowledging the distinctiveness of the Spirit's mission to empower believers to bear charismatic and vocational witness to the risen Christ.[9] The result is that pentecostals are justified in reading the narratives of Luke-Acts theologically and doctrinally not over and against Paul but alongside Paul (and the other New Testament authors).

This chapter will later take issue with Stronstad's limitation of Lukan theology to that of charismatic empowerment. I stand solidly with him and others, however, in affirming that Luke has a theological perspective with its own integrity that not only has inspired and should continue to inform pentecostal theologizing but also should be accounted for in any attempt to develop a world theology for the twenty-first century. Hence, Luke provides world pentecostal theology a perspective on the remainder of the Scriptures, just as Paul provided the dominant

7. See, e.g., I. Howard Marshall, *Luke: Historian and Theologian* (Exeter, Eng.: Paternoster, 1970); I. Howard Marshall and David Peterson, eds., *Witness to the Gospel: The Theology of Acts* (Grand Rapids: Eerdmans, 1998); W. Ward Gasque, *A History of the Interpretation of the Acts of the Apostles* (Grand Rapids: Eerdmans, 1975), ch. 10; and François Bovon, *Luke the Theologian: Thirty-Three Years of Research (1950–1983)*, trans. Ken McKinney (Allison Park, PA: Pickwick Papers, 1987).

8. See Roger Stronstad, *The Charismatic Theology of St. Luke* (Peabody, MA: Hendrickson, 1984); and *Spirit, Scripture, and Theology: A Pentecostal Perspective* (Baguio City, Phil.: Asia Pacific Theological Seminary Press, 1995).

9. Other pentecostal exegetes who defend one or another version of the latter thesis are James B. Shelton and, more extensively, Robert P. Menzies. See James B. Shelton, *Mighty in Word and Deed: The Role of the Holy Spirit in Luke-Acts* (Peabody, MA: Hendrickson, 1991); and Robert P. Menzies, *The Development of Early Christian Pneumatology: With Special Reference to Luke-Acts* (Sheffield, Eng.: JSOT, 1991); *Empowered for Witness: The Spirit in Luke-Acts*, JPTSup 6 (Sheffield, Eng.: Sheffield Academic Press, 1994); and Robert P. Menzies and William W. Menzies, *Spirit and Power: Foundations of Pentecostal Experience* (Grand Rapids: Zondervan, 2000), passim, but esp. ch. 6.

theological categories for Protestant theology during and since the sixteenth century. This "Lukan privilege" is significant because it not only overcomes the divide between narrative and didactic genres of Scripture, especially regarding theological and doctrinal value, but also enables us to recognize that all narratives are didactic in some respect and that all didactic writings are set within some sort of narrative framework. Further, Lukan narratives are now read alongside, not instead of, other biblical narratives—John's, Matthew's, Paul's, and so on—so as to enable a more fully biblical theology to emerge for our new world situation. Finally, proceeding with this plain admission of Luke-Acts as the pentecostal lens through which to read the Bible acknowledges the particularity of the scriptural starting point for pentecostal theologizing even while it exposes the misguidedness of the claim that there is any purely biblical theology apart from experiential traditions of interpretation that approach the canon from some standpoint.[10]

2.1.2 *Spirit Christology in Luke-Acts.* Now for a theological understanding of the good news for humankind: the person and work of Jesus Christ. Given the experiential dimension of pentecostal theology (ch. 1 above) and the exegetical privileging of Luke-Acts in pentecostal hermeneutics, I suggest a form of Spirit christology: Jesus is the revelation of God precisely as the man anointed by the Spirit of God to herald and usher in the reign of God.[11] This Spirit christology proposal is not meant, however, to replace the dominant Logos christology of the theological tradition. The two christologies are complementary (see further §2.3.1); Spirit christology is a fully biblical but marginalized theological perspective that can speak to, and needs to be reappropriated for, our time.

The conviction regarding Spirit christology derives from explicitly Lukan material. For starters, there is Jesus' own explicit self-understanding: "The Spirit of the Lord is upon me, because he has anointed me to bring good news to the poor. He has sent me to proclaim release to the captives and recovery of sight to the blind, to let the oppressed go free, to proclaim the year of the Lord's favor" (Luke 4:18–19, quoting Isa. 61:1–2). Building on this, there are the early Christian kerygmatic claims regarding Jesus of Nazareth as "a man attested to you by God with deeds of power, wonders, and signs that God did through him among you, as you yourselves know—this man, handed over to you according

10. I long ago learned this from William W. Menzies, "Synoptic Theology: An Essay in Pentecostal Hermeneutics," *Paraclete* 13, no. 1 (1979): 14–21, who argues that *all* scriptural interpretation is inherently informed by experience, even if this means biased by the lack of particular experiences, such as glossolalia or the *charismata*.

11. Here and in §2.1.3 are elaborated ideas about Spirit christology and Spirit soteriology previously sketched in Amos Yong, *Spirit-Word-Community: Theological Hermeneutics in Trinitarian Perspective* (Burlington, VT: Ashgate, 2002), 28–34.

to the definite plan and foreknowledge of God, you crucified and killed by the hands of those outside the law" (Acts 2:22b–23), and as the one "that God has made . . . both Lord and Messiah, this Jesus whom you crucified" (2:36).[12] Thus the earliest Christians prayed to God about "your holy servant Jesus, whom you anointed" (4:27), and spoke about "how God anointed Jesus of Nazareth with the Holy Spirit and with power, how he went about doing good and healing all who were oppressed by the devil, for God was with him" (Acts 10:38).

The emerging picture of Jesus as the Christ, the Spirit-anointed revelation of God, needs to be understood in terms of his person and work. Spirit christology sees Jesus not only as one anointed by the Spirit to do the mighty works of God but as a fully anointed one whose life from beginning to end was of the Spirit.[13] Luke records that Jesus was conceived by the Spirit in the womb of Mary (Luke 1:35; cf. Matt. 1:18); that his dedication as a baby was presided over by the Spirit (2:25–32); that he grew strong in spirit and in wisdom (the latter associated with the Spirit; 1:80; 2:52; cf. Isa. 11:2); that the Spirit descended upon him "in bodily form" at his baptism (3:21–22); that he was then led by the Spirit into the wilderness (4:1); that he overcame the temptations of the devil and returned to Galilee "filled with the power of the Spirit" (4:14); that his public ministry, inaugurated in the synagogue of Nazareth, was anointed by the Spirit from beginning to end (4:18–19); and that his death was a matter of his commending his spirit to the Father (23:46). The author of Hebrews makes explicit further details about the life and death of Christ, details consistent with Luke's portrait. Besides confirming the humanity of Jesus in no uncertain terms—that Jesus was "like his brothers and sisters in every respect" (Heb. 2:17) and that he "offered up prayers and supplications, with loud cries and tears, to the one who was able to save him from death, and . . . he learned obedience through what he suffered" (5:7–8)—Hebrews also notes that Jesus offered himself up on the cross "through the eternal Spirit" (9:14). Finally, the life of Jesus ends not in death but in resurrection. Whereas Luke simply records Peter's proclamation that God raised Jesus from the dead (Acts 2:24, 32), Paul is much more specific about "the gospel concerning his Son, who was descended from David according to the flesh and was declared to be the Son of God with power according to

12. Arguably, these references are at the heart of Luke's own original christology; see Richard F. Zehnle, *Peter's Pentecost Discourse: Tradition and Lukan Reinterpretation in Peter's Speeches of Acts 2 and 3* (Nashville: Abingdon, 1971), esp. 66–70.

13. See Gerald F. Hawthorne, *The Presence and the Power: The Significance of the Holy Spirit in the Life of Jesus* (Dallas: Word, 1991); and Jürgen Moltmann, *The Way of Jesus Christ: Christology in Messianic Dimensions*, trans. Margaret Kohl (New York: HarperSanFrancisco, 1990), esp. ch. 3.

the spirit of holiness by resurrection from the dead" (Rom. 1:3–4; cf. 1 Tim. 3:16; cf. 1 Pet. 3:18).

This last Pauline claim is precisely Luke's thesis except that Luke applies it to the life and ministry of Jesus: if the Spirit of God who anointed Jesus dwells in you, the Spirit will empower you to do the same works (Acts) that Jesus did under the same anointing (Luke). Important here is the question concerning the works of Jesus. Luke's Gospel is about Jesus the messianic Christ, the anointed one, who fulfills the prophets (Luke 4:18–19; cf. Isa. 61:1–2). His ministry throughout is to the poor, the downtrodden, the marginalized: witness his ministry to the lame, lepers, sinners, tax collectors, and so forth.[14] He releases the captives, literally freeing those oppressed by demons (4:32–34; 8:1–3, 26–40; 9:37–43; 11:13–15). He opens the eyes of the blind (e.g., 7:21–22; 18:35–43).[15] He sets the oppressed free, for example, the sinner woman (7:36–50), the family with the boy suffering from epileptic seizures (9:37–43), and women in general, especially in terms of their being valued as full human beings (e.g., 8:1–3; 10:38–42). Last, he proclaims the favorable year of the Lord, the liberative Day of Jubilee.[16] This refers not only to the cancellation of debts both literal (as in the Zacchaeus story; 19:1–10) and spiritual (as in the forgiveness of sins imparted by Jesus; e.g., 7:47–50) but also to the granting of a second chance at life, as was given to the widow of Nain, who, having lost her only son, would have been henceforth without voice, representation, or means in society (7:11–17).[17] Luke's Spirit christology is thus intimately tied in with the life and ministry of Jesus.

2.1.3 *Spirit Soteriology in Luke-Acts*. But also the Spirit's anointing of Jesus is promised to his followers (Luke 24:49). Hence the transition from Luke to Acts is the transition from Spirit christology to Spirit soteriology.[18]

14. Walter E. Pilgrim, *Good News to the Poor: Wealth and Poverty in Luke-Acts* (Minneapolis: Augsburg, 1981); and S. John Roth, *The Blind, the Lame, and the Poor: Character Types in Luke-Acts* (Sheffield, Eng.: Sheffield Academic Press, 1997).

15. On these various aspects of Jesus' ministry, see Graham H. Twelftree, *Jesus the Miracle Worker: A Historical and Theological Study* (Downers Grove, IL: InterVarsity, 1999).

16. Robert B. Sloan Jr., *The Favorable Year of the Lord: A Study of Jubilary Theology in the Gospel of Luke* (Austin, TX: Scholars Press, 1977); and Helen R. Graham, *There Shall Be No Poor among You: Essays in Lukan Theology* (Quezon City, Phil.: JMC Press, 1978), ch. 1.

17. One of the few sources I have found that sees this miracle to be as much for the widow as for the son raised from the dead is John Linskens, *Christ Liberator of the Poor: Secularity, Wealth, and Poverty in the Gospel of Luke* (San Antonio, TX: Mexican American Cultural Center, 1976), 18.

18. See Richard Shaull and Waldo Cesar, *Pentecostalism and the Future of the Christian Churches: Promises, Limitations, Challenges* (Grand Rapids: Eerdmans, 2000), part 2, ch. 6; and Ralph Del Colle, "Incarnation and the Holy Spirit," *S&C* 2, no. 2 (2000): 199–229, esp. 224–26.

For Luke, the gift of the Spirit to the followers of Jesus empowers them to overcome sin, temptation, and the devil; authorizes them to cast out demons and heal the sick; and enables them to do the works of the ministry on behalf of the poor, the captives, and the oppressed—all as Jesus did. These themes need to be explicated briefly.

First, the gospel (as good news) includes the forgiveness of sins. This was a feature of Jesus' ministry and repeatedly evidenced in early Christian proclamation (e.g., Acts 3:19; 5:31; 10:43; 13:38–39; 26:18; cf. Luke 24:47).[19] It is consistent with the Pauline claim that Christ enables the forgiveness of sins. Further, it heralds the day of the Lord's favor, when all sins and debts are canceled (cf. Matt. 18:23–27). Most important, the forgiveness of sins is linked with the gift of the Holy Spirit (Acts 2:38; cf. John 20:22–23), a connection we will return to momentarily (§2.2.2).

Second, the gospel includes deliverance from the devil and his demons in realizing the eschatological reign of God. Jesus not only exorcised demons[20] but also declared that "if it is by the finger of God ['Spirit of God'; see Matt. 12:28] that I cast out the demons, then the kingdom of God has come to you" (Luke 11:20).[21] The Twelve were given authority over demons and diseases even as they were commissioned to proclaim the kingdom of God (9:1–2), and the seventy returned rejoicing, "Lord, in your name even the demons submit to us" (10:17). The early church continued this ministry of deliverance as empowered by the Spirit (Acts 5:16; 8:6–7; 13:6–12; 16:16–18).[22]

Third, the gospel includes the healing of the sick. The Spirit who empowered Jesus to heal also empowered the early Christians to minister healing to the sick (Acts 5:16; 8:6–7; 9:32–35; 14:8–10; 28:8–9). But note that the ancients understood salvation as healing from disease followed by the restoration of the individual to the community.[23] This is subtly

---

19. I am helped here by Larry W. Hurtado, *Lord Jesus Christ: Devotion to Jesus in Earliest Christianity* (Grand Rapids: Eerdmans, 2003), 185–88.

20. See the charismatic scholar Graham H. Twelftree, *Jesus the Exorcist: A Contribution to the Study of the Historical Jesus* (Tübingen: J. C. B. Mohr; Peabody, MA: Hendrickson, 1993).

21. Edward J. Woods, *The "Finger of God" and Pneumatology in Luke-Acts* (Sheffield, Eng.: Sheffield Academic Press, 2001), argues that in this pericope (Luke 11:14–26) Luke's redactive preference for the "finger of God" rather than the "Holy Spirit" (Matt. 12:28) signifies reference to God the Father as actor against Beelzebub. At the level of Lukan studies, Woods's argument has plenty going for it. But at the canonical level, the Matthean version justifies a pneumatological understanding of Luke's text.

22. Susan R. Garrett, *The Demise of the Devil: Magic and the Demonic in Luke's Writings* (Minneapolis: Fortress, 1989).

23. See Ben Witherington III, "Salvation and Health in Christian Antiquity: The Soteriology of Luke-Acts in Its First-Century Setting," in Witherington, *The Acts of the Apostles: A Socio-rhetorical Commentary* (Carlisle, Eng.: Paternoster; Grand Rapids: Eerdmans, 1998), appendix 2.

communicated in Jesus' giving back to his father the boy freed of the epileptic spirit (Luke 9:42) and in the return of the lame man at the Beautiful Gate to his community (Acts 3:1–10). But healing as a communal experience is most evident in the case of cured lepers (cf. Luke 5:12–14; 17:11–19) and demoniacs who were allowed to return to their homes and communities. In these instances, the Gospel healing accounts can be understood as processes of social transformation engaging the unbelieving community and breaking social taboos rather than merely in individualistic senses.[24] Salvation is now understood in terms of "hospitality": being reconstituted into the divine community, the new people of God. The needy are best able to appreciate the divine hospitality given through Jesus and the Spirit (the affluent need a conversion of heart), and the saved then become instruments of divine hospitality heralding the eschatological kingdom.[25]

This leads, fourth, to the gospel as directed toward the needs of the poor, the freeing of captives, and the liberation of the oppressed, precisely through calling into reality a new community and social order wherein there is neither rich nor poor, slave nor free, oppressed nor oppressor (Gal. 3:28; Col. 3:11).[26] This is most clearly seen in the communalism of the early church, "All who believed were together and had all things in common" (Acts 2:44); in God's empowering and using uneducated and ordinary persons (Acts 4:13), including women (e.g., 21:8–9); and in the leaders of the early church as servants of all (Acts 6:1–6; cf. Luke 9:48), among other manifestations. These are essential features of the new community of God brought about by the outpouring of the Holy Spirit on the day of Pentecost (see §2.2.1).

Last but not least, the gospel also has an eschatological dimension that is both realized and future. Jesus himself notes that the reign of God is not merely coming: "For in fact, the kingdom of God is among you" (Luke 17:21). Further, the promised outpouring of the Spirit makes present the "last days" (Acts 2:17), which Jesus was anointed to proclaim and inaugurate (Luke 4:19). Certainly the church continues to anticipate the return of Jesus (Acts 1:11), and he "must remain in heaven until the time of universal restoration that God announced long ago through his holy prophets" (Acts 3:21). But in the meanwhile, the church lives betwixt and between; in the now and yet anticipating the not-yet; as saved, as

24. Martyn Percy, *Power and the Church: Ecclesiology in an Age of Transition* (Washington, DC: Cassell, 1998), ch. 2.

25. Brendan Byrne, *The Hospitality of God: A Reading of Luke's Gospel* (Collegeville, MN: Liturgical Press, 2000).

26. Richard J. Cassidy, *Jesus, Politics, and Society: A Study of Luke's Gospel* (Maryknoll, NY: Orbis, 1978); and Matthias Wenk, *Community-Forming Power: The Socio-ethical Role of the Spirit in Luke-Acts*, JPTSup 19 (Sheffield, Eng.: Sheffield Academic Press, 2000).

being saved, and yet looking to full salvation. It looks to be saved from the wrath to come (Rom. 5:9) even while believing that "salvation is nearer to us now than when we became believers" (Rom. 13:11b).

These dimensions—the forgiveness of sins, the deliverance from evil powers, the healing of the body, the liberation of the poor and oppressed, the establishment of the new people of God, and the eschatological salvation of God—identify constitutive elements for a pentecostal understanding of salvation informed throughout by pneumatology. Here follows the sketch of a pneumatological soteriology that integrates these biblical themes and insights with the pentecostal experiences of the Spirit delineated in the preceding chapter.

2.2 Sketching a Pneumatological Soteriology

My main thesis is that Christian salvation includes both the transformation of human beings into the image of Jesus by the power of the Holy Spirit and the transformation of all creation into the new heaven and new earth by the triune God. Hence the main components of a christologically directed and pneumatologically driven soteriology entail fleshing out what I call the multidimensionality of salvation given through the Spirit; elaborating on the eschatological and pneumatological dynamic of the experience of salvation; and articulating a phenomenology of conversion by the power of the Spirit commensurate with this view.

2.2.1 *The Multidimensionality of Salvation.* The early-twentieth-century pentecostals talked about a "four-fold" gospel of Jesus as Savior, baptizer, healer, and coming king (which became the basis of Aimee Semple McPherson's [1890–1944] International Church of the Foursquare Gospel in 1923) and a "five-fold" gospel adding Jesus as sanctifier (prominent among the Holiness wing of the tradition).[27] The preceding analysis of Luke-Acts shows how the soteriological imagination of the early pentecostals was informed by their experiences of Jesus and the Spirit of God, experiences that were told about in the Bible. The fivefold gospel is expanded here in light of the foregoing Lukan Spirit soteriology by discussing the seven dimensions of salvation.

Personal salvation refers to the traditional understanding: individuals encountering and being transformed into the image of Jesus Christ by the Spirit. This includes, in part, deliverance from oppressive situations and conditions and, in part, release from spiritual captivity and the exorcism

27. See Donald W. Dayton, *Theological Roots of Pentecostalism* (Peabody, MA: Hendrickson, 1987), esp. 21–23; and Steven J. Land, *Pentecostal Spirituality: A Passion for the Kingdom*, JPTSup 1 (Sheffield, Eng.: Sheffield Academic Press, 1993), 18–20.

of demonic forces. It also includes, minimally, individual repentance, baptism, the forgiveness of sins, and the reception of the gift of the Holy Spirit (Acts 2:38; cf. also, in Paul's case, 9:17–18; 22:16). Already it is clear that personal salvation is never merely individualized, insofar as baptism involves the believing community. Yet the individual aspect of salvation cannot be neglected: there are (or should be) identifiable moments in human lives when the awareness of the need for repentance comes to the fore and lives are turned in the opposite direction from which they were headed. Shortly we will unpack the meaning of personal salvation in terms of moral, intellectual, affective, sociopolitical, and religious conversion (§2.2.3).

Family salvation calls attention not only to the promise of the gift of the Spirit "for your children" (Acts 2:39) but also to the fact that individuals are who they are precisely as members of families. The salvation of the individual is thus intimately connected with the salvation of his or her family. This was declared to Cornelius (Acts 11:14), and proved to be the case for the households of Lydia (16:14–15), the Philippian jailer (16:31–33), and Crispus (18:8a). Some might argue that although family conversions were the norm for ancient societies, which followed the head of the household as a rule of thumb, individual conversion is the norm for modern societies. In light of the fact that "family" in the ancient world refers not to the nuclear family of modernity but to households, clans, and tribes,[28] I prefer to see the modern situation as an exception to the rule. Individuals still often come to repentance following after their family members, and many a fervent prayer has been offered up (and answered by God) on behalf of an unbelieving spouse by the believing spouse or on behalf of rebellious children by believing parents. This makes at least some sense of the otherwise enigmatic statement by Paul that families are made holy through believing spouses/parents (1 Cor. 7:14).

Ecclesial salvation expands on the notion of family salvation and uses family metaphors (cf. Luke 8:19–21; Mark 3:31–35) to point to the communal dimension of what it means to be saved. Thus the connection between ecclesiology and soteriology that sees salvation effected through baptism: the death and burial of the unbelieving individual in and with Christ and his or her resurrection into a new life, existence, and community, the living body of Christ (cf. Rom. 6:3–4; 1 Cor. 12:13; Eph. 4:15–16). Believing the good news of Jesus Christ leads to baptism (e.g., Acts 8:12, 36–38; 10:47–48). Salvation as ecclesial means being baptized into a new relationship with Jesus and his body by the power of the Spirit. Read another way, the outpouring of the Spirit (the book of Acts) not only made

28. Stephen C. Barton, *Life Together: Family, Sexuality, and Community in the New Testament and Today* (New York: T & T Clark, 2001), ch. 3, esp. 41.

possible individual reception of the saving grace of God but also made real and actual the new people of God and a communal way of life. *Material salvation* refers to the embodied nature of human beings (cf. §1.2.2). This includes the healing—of mind, soul, and body; mental, emotional, and physical—ministered by Jesus and made possible by the power of the Spirit. Material salvation is directed primarily to the poor, the marginalized, and the oppressed, perhaps because they experience their diseased and deprived conditions in palpable ways.[29] The good news is specified as being for the poor, who are lifted up by the gospel; the hungry are fed while the rich are sent away (Luke 1:52–53). Unlike Matthew, who sees Jesus blessing the "poor *in spirit*" and those who "hunger and thirst *for righteousness*" (Matt. 5:3, 6; italics added), Luke sees Jesus blessing the poor and the hungry *as such* and admonishing the rich and the full *as such* (Luke 6:20–21, 24–25). For these reasons, the early church ministered to the sick, the impoverished, the naked, the stranger, and those in prison (cf. Matt. 25:31–46) and sought to care for widows and children, the most vulnerable members of society (Acts 6:1–6; cf. James 1:27).[30]

Social salvation is an extension of, and yet complementary to, ecclesial salvation.[31] It refers, on the one hand, to the healing and reconciliation of interpersonal relationships, most tangibly experienced in the church and to which the church is called to bear witness. It also refers, on the other hand, to the redemption of the socioeconomic and political structures—including fallen and destructive public structures, what Walter Wink calls the public and social manifestations of the demonic[32]—a redemption that, when accomplished in society at large, is also transformative for ecclesial relations (cf. §1.1.1; §1.1.3). These notions take some explication. This is most efficiently accomplished by following out the consequences of the

29. Miroslav Volf, "Materiality of Salvation: An Investigation of the Soteriologies of Liberation and Pentecostal Theologies," *JES* 26 (1989): 447–67.

30. For these reasons, David Peter Seccombe's thesis in *Possessions and the Poor in Luke-Acts* (Linz, Austria: Studien zum Neuen Testament und seiner Umwelt, 1982), esp. 24–43, is correct in what it affirms (that "the poor" refers to Israel under Roman oppression) but not in what it denies (that "the poor" therefore does not necessarily refer to poor in a literal sense).

31. Pentecostal reflection on social salvation is emerging; see, e.g., Frank D. Macchia, *Spirituality and Social Liberation: The Message of the Blumhardts in the Light of Wuerttemberg Pietism* (Metuchen, NJ: Scarecrow, 1993), esp. ch. 5; Eldin Villafañe, *The Liberating Spirit: Toward an Hispanic American Pentecostal Social Ethic* (Lanham, MD: University Press of America, 1992); and Douglas Petersen, *Not by Might nor by Power: A Pentecostal Theology of Social Concern in Latin America* (Oxford: Regnum, 1996).

32. See Walter Wink's trilogy: *Naming the Powers: The Language and Power of the New Testament*; *Unmasking the Powers: The Invisible Forces That Determine Human Existence*; and *Engaging the Powers: Discernment and Resistance in a World of Domination* (Philadelphia: Fortress, 1984, 1986, 1992).

outpouring of the Spirit on the day of Pentecost for what St. Paul refers to in terms of there being neither Jew nor Greek, neither slave nor free, neither male nor female (Gal. 3:28),[33] and for what contemporary discourse refers to in terms of racial, class, and gender reconciliation.

Racial reconciliation: Seymour's reading of the Azusa Street outpouring of the Spirit as washing away the color line (§1.3.3) finds concrete justification in the Pentecost narrative. Included among the ethnicities and languages brought together at Pentecost were the Egyptians (this includes Africans, representative of the black race), Cretans (see the famous saying "Cretans are always liars, vicious brutes, lazy gluttons"; Titus 1:12), and the Arabs (Acts 2:9–11). From this group, three thousand were saved, the new work of God was inaugurated, and the new people of God was established. Imagine the reconciling power of the pentecostal gospel, which includes Semites alongside Africans (later specified in terms of the Ethiopian eunuch; Acts 8:26–40) and Arabs (all the more important given the more recent Arab-Israeli conflicts) and which breaks down and overcomes negative stereotypes of ethnic nationalities (such as that of Cretans). In retrospect, Acts 2 describes the worldwide church of the twenty-first century and anticipates the eschatological gathering of all peoples, tongues, tribes, and nations in the reign of God (Rev. 5:9; 7:9; 13:7; cf. 21:22–26). Early modern pentecostalism captured this biblical vision through Seymour's leadership, but this did not last. An honest assessment of the current situation is that personal and sociostructural racism is still very much a present sin and manifestation of demonic power that needs to be confessed and dismantled by the church (see §4.2.3).

Class reconciliation: The outpouring of the Spirit upon all flesh not only reconciles ethnicities and races but also heals divisions erected by class. A new people of God emerged who had "all things in common" (cf. Acts 2:40–47; 4:32–37). The church brought together those otherwise socially segregated: the unschooled (4:13) and the well educated (e.g., Paul and Apollos; cf. 18:24); the disenfranchised and those in religious or political power (e.g., Cornelius in Acts 10, Sergius Paulus in 13:7–12, Crispus in 18:8, Sosthenes in 18:17, and Publius of Malta in 28:7–10); and the socially marginalized and differently abled (e.g., the Ethiopian of Acts 8, who was a foreigner and a eunuch). No wonder modern pentecostalism, in providing space for and nurturing the poor, the sick, the social outcasts and misfits, the economically destitute, the spiritually impoverished, and the politically marginalized or invisible, has been called a

---

33. E.g., Norman E. Thomas, "The Church at Antioch: Crossing Racial, Cultural, and Class Barriers," in *Mission in Acts: Ancient Narratives in Contemporary Context*, ed. Robert L. Gallagher and Paul Hertig (Maryknoll, NY: Orbis, 2004), 144–56.

"haven for the masses" and understood as representing the "vision of the disinherited."[34] Much work needs to be done to address inner-city slum conditions, violence on all scales, and economic structures of injustice that are demonically inspired to exploit mass labor for the gain of the rich, just to name three of the present challenges. But the church cannot ignore these matters if, as black pentecostal theologian Alonzo Johnson notes, "oppression is understood to include economic, political, cultural, as well as psychological and spiritual realities" (see §4.3.1).[35]

Gender reconciliation: The outpouring of the Spirit has been from the beginning also upon both male and female: sons *and* daughters would prophesy (Acts 2:17–18). The value and ministry of women are affirmed not only in Luke (e.g., 1:40; 2:36–38; 8:1–4; 11:27–28) but throughout Acts (e.g., Dorcas, Lydia, Damaris, Priscilla, Philip's evangelist-prophetess daughters, and other unnamed women). Modern pentecostalism has featured numerous women evangelists, pastors, church planters, missionaries, and leaders.[36] Nevertheless, sexism remains widespread not only in societies around the world but also in churches, including pentecostal churches. Full salvation includes the redemption of women and of the fallen social structures that have conspired to prohibit women's full realization of the image and calling of God in their lives (see §4.3.2).

Cosmic salvation refers not only to the interconnectedness of human beings and their environment (cf. Acts 2:19–20) but also to the redemption of all creation (perhaps not excluding the fallen principalities, spiritual authorities, and powers; cf. Eph. 6:12).[37] In fact, Paul explicitly connects the cosmic salvation of all creation and the human redemption of the body with the work and groanings of the Spirit of God (Rom. 8:19–23). Meanwhile the Spirit not only heralds the day of the Lord through the Messiah (Luke 4:19) but also works to bring it about. Indeed, the arrival of the day of the Lord is a thoroughly pneumatological event that transforms all creation (Isa. 32:15–16) and effects even relationships

34. See Christian Lalive d'Epinay, *Haven of the Masses: A Study of the Pentecostal Movement in Chile*, trans. Marjorie Sandle (London: Lutterworth, 1969); and Robert Mapes Anderson, *Vision of the Disinherited: The Making of American Pentecostalism* (New York: Oxford University Press, 1979), even if the sociological theories undergirding these arguments need to be scrutinized. See Albert G. Miller, "Pentecostalism as a Social Movement: Beyond the Theory of Deprivation," *JPT* 9 (1996): 97–114.

35. Alonzo Johnson, *Good News for the Disinherited: Howard Thurman on Jesus of Nazareth and Human Liberation* (Lanham, MD: University Press of America, 1997), ch. 4; quotation, 150. Also Hyeon Sung Bae, "Full Gospel Theology as a Distinctive Theological Practice for Korean Pentecostal Theology," *S&C* 2, no. 2 (2000): 169–81, esp. 175–77, 179–80.

36. See "Women, Role of," *NIDPCM* 1203–9; cf. §1.1.2.

37. Wink, *Engaging the Powers*, 73–85.

between the wolf and the lamb, the leopard and the kid, the calf and the lion (cf. Isa. 11:6-9; 65:25). For contemporary society, cosmic salvation is especially urgent given the pollution of the environment and bodies of water, the destruction of our ecosystems, the degradation of our rain forests, the erosion of our soils, and the greenhouse effect, among other concerns. Along with our tree-planting AICs in Zimbabwe (§1.3.1), recent "environmental spiritualities" are also drawing on pneumatological themes in their commitment to the greening of cities, the purifying of water and air systems, and the renewal of the natural environment (see §7.3.3).

Last but not least is *eschatological salvation*. Traditionally, this has been construed in individualistic terms related to one's final abode in either heaven or hell. These are the categories of the Apocalypse—the presence of God or the bottomless pit; the heavenly Jerusalem or the lake of fire; inside the city or outside the gates—and the full force of these powerful symbols should not be overlooked. Nevertheless, the foregoing analysis of Pentecost as signifying the eschatological outpouring of the Spirit indicates that eschatological salvation is experienced now *and* awaited. Thus salvation is both historical and directed toward the future transformation of all creation into the new heavens and new earth.[38] Against the fundamentalist view, prevalent in many pentecostal circles, that sees all creation as apocalyptically destroyed, this transformational perspective suggests that (a) apocalyptic texts that on the surface imply the destruction of the world are better understood in terms of the eschatological purification of God; (b) the specific Christian hope for the resurrection of the body suggests both that there is a greater continuity than discontinuity between this and the next world and that God values the embodied nature of created things sufficiently to preserve them; and (c) God will finally save and vindicate the people of God, who yearn for divine intervention into their experiences of persecution, oppression, and alienation, and God will finally redeem the world, which was created good.[39] The apocalyptic elements of the New Testament anticipate the critique and judgment of the present sociopolitical and historical

38. Bonaventure Kloppenburg, OFM, *Christian Salvation and Human Temporal Progress*, trans. Paul Burns (Chicago: Franciscan Herald Press, 1979). See also Peter Althouse, *Spirit of the Last Days: Pentecostal Eschatology in Conversation with Jürgen Moltmann*, JPTSup 25 (New York: T & T Clark, 2003); and Jürgen Moltmann, *The Coming of God: Christian Eschatology*, trans. Margaret Kohl (Minneapolis: Fortress, 1996), esp. 267-74.

39. The connections between (b) and (c) are argued explicitly in Joel B. Green, "'Witnesses to His Resurrection': Resurrection, Salvation, Discipleship, and Mission in the Acts of the Apostles," in *Life in the Face of Death: The Resurrection Message of the New Testament*, ed. Richard N. Longenecker (Grand Rapids: Eerdmans, 1998), 227-46.

order. Jesus' exorcisms thereby overturn the reigning forces of this world and inaugurate the new order of the reign of God.[40]

The "not yet" aspect of eschatological salvation will include the saving work of the Spirit in the personal, familial, social, and cosmic dimensions as well. More specifically, as Miroslav Volf puts it, the final reconciliation is not only between God and human beings but also between humans themselves, including the reconciliation between victims and victimizers.[41] Hence it must necessarily accomplish the forgiveness of all sins, bring about justice, vindicate the oppressed, and yet reveal the mercy of God. Divine grace is manifest precisely in the eschatological redemption of sinners and those sinned against. In anticipation of this final redemption, the Spirit continues to issue an open-ended invitation to "anyone who wishes [to] take the water of life as a gift" (Rev. 22:17), even as the Spirit blows forth the winds of refreshing preceding the return of the Messiah and the universal restoration of God (Acts 3:19–21). And although this cosmic salvation may not be a literal universalism,[42] it certainly will entail the submission of all things under Jesus, the exaltation of his name (Phil. 2:9–11), and the final subjection of both the Son and all things under God "so that God may be all in all" (1 Cor. 15:28). Because of the continuity between the present historical work of the Spirit of God and the final redemptive act of the triune God, the eschatological motif runs as a thread woven throughout the entirety of this pentecostal theology instead of being set off as its own separate topic (or chapter) for discussion.

Salvation considered in these personal, familial, ecclesial, material, social, cosmic, and eschatological terms does not necessarily mean that individuals experience the saving work of God in this sequence or that these are updated categories for the older idea of the history of salvation. The point, rather, is that full salvation as concretely historical includes all of these dimensions and that to individualize salvation is to arbitrarily abstract one dimension from a much more complex and complicated process of relationships. This needs to be kept in mind as

40. Here I follow the argument of N. T. Wright regarding the apocalyptic eschatology of first-century Judaism as expecting a new world order rather than looking for the destruction of the present space-time cosmos. See N. T. Wright, *The New Testament and the People of God* (Minneapolis: Fortress, 1992), ch. 10; and *Jesus and the Victory of God* (Minneapolis: Fortress, 1996), ch. 6.

41. See Miroslav Volf, "The Final Reconciliation: Reflections on a Social Dimension of the Eschatological Transition," *Modern Theology* 16, no. 1 (2000): 91–113. For background discussion, see Miroslav Volf, *Exclusion and Embrace: A Theological Exploration of Identity, Otherness, and Reconciliation* (Nashville: Abingdon, 1996), ch. 5.

42. See the most recent debate on this in Robin Parry and Chris Partridge, eds., *Universal Salvation? The Current Debate* (Carlisle, Eng.: Paternoster, 2003).

we work our way through what has traditionally been understood as the personal *ordo salutis* ("order of salvation") in the remainder of this chapter, before returning to the larger ecclesial and social pictures in the next two chapters.

2.2.2 *Dynamic Salvation and Baptism in the Holy Spirit*. Solidly rooted in the Wesleyan Holiness tradition as they are, classical Pentecostals have traditionally debated the question whether there are one, two, or even three "works of grace." Early Pentecostals such as William H. Durham (d. 1912) came to be convinced that the work of Christ on Calvary accomplished both the justifying forgiveness of sins and the sanctification of the believer, with the latter then being appropriated gradually over the remaining course of life.[43] At one level, Durham was simply championing the centrality of the person and work of Christ, prominent among turn-of-the-century Holiness, revivalist, and pietistic circles long before the fivefold gospel of Jesus became a pentecostal shibboleth. At another level, however, Durham's "finished work of Calvary" position was clearly a rejection of the Holiness understanding of sanctification as a second crisis experience following initial salvation. Pentecostals who were influenced by Durham came to define the baptism of the Spirit not in soteriological terms but as the endowment of power for witness (cf. Acts 1:8). Some of those who remained in the Holiness tradition but came into the pentecostal experience retained sanctification as a second work of grace and equated it with the baptism of the Holy Spirit. Other Holiness pentecostals posited a three-stage experience of Christian salvation: conversion (justification), sanctification (entire), and the baptism of the Holy Spirit (for power to witness).

More recently the debate has shifted as a result of pentecostals' engagement in dialogue with especially evangelical Protestants and Roman Catholic charismatics about (to simplify the complex issues) whether the baptism of the Holy Spirit is an experience equivalent to or subsequent to that of salvation.[44] Those who defend the former position tend to see initial conversion as including the full bestowal of the Spirit and

---

43. See D. William Faupel, "William H. Durham and the Finished Work of Calvary," in *Pentecost, Mission, and Ecumenism: Essays on Intercultural Theology*, ed. J. A. B. Jongeneel, SIHC 75 (Frankfurt, Ger.: Peter Lang, 1992), 85–95; and Edith L. Blumhofer, "William H. Durham: Years of Creativity, Years of Dissent," in *Portraits of a Generation: Early Pentecostal Leaders*, ed. James R. Goff Jr. and Grant Wacker (Fayetteville: University of Arkansas Press, 2002), 123–42.

44. See Henry I. Elderly, *Treasures Old and New: Interpretations of "Spirit-Baptism" in the Charismatic Renewal Movement* (Peabody, MA: Hendrickson, 1988); and Koo Dong Yun, *Baptism in the Holy Spirit: An Ecumenical Theology of Spirit Baptism* (Lanham, MD: University Press of America, 2003).

later experiences of Spirit baptism as releases of the Spirit and gifts of the Spirit in the life of the believer. Advocates for the latter position are usually classical Pentecostals who agree that the Spirit is given at conversion but continue to define the later Spirit baptism in terms of charismatic empowerment to witness.[45]

My own view attempts to affirm the tension between Durham's once-for-all reception of salvation and the gradualist tradition that sees salvation as a dynamic process of experiencing the "increasing fullness" of the Spirit. In so doing, I acknowledge the possibility of subsequent crisis experiences not only of "Spirit baptism" empowering the believer for Christian service but also of what I would call sanctifying intensification drawing the believer more consciously into ever deeper intimacy with Christ.[46] This proposal is pneumatologically motivated and understands salvation in dynamic and eschatological terms. The remainder of this section (§2.2) will develop this idea in four steps by moving away from the intricacies of pentecostal debates to explicate pneumatological soteriology in dialogue with the Christian theological tradition.

The first step toward a robust pneumatological doctrine of salvation retrieves the early church's understanding of Christian initiation.[47] Catholic charismatic theologian Kilian McDonnell has suggested that this entails

- initial contact with Christians and the Christian faith, followed by repentance and the decision to enter the conversion process;
- a period of catechetical instruction and moral (re)formation, varying in length (partly because of the extenuating circumstances confronting the oft persecuted early church) but usually between two and three years;

45. For an overview of the debate generated by his work, see James D. G. Dunn, "Baptism in the Spirit: A Response to Pentecostal Scholarship on Luke-Acts," *JPT* 3 (1993): 3–27; and William Atkinson, "Pentecostal Responses to Dunn's *Baptism in the Holy Spirit*," *JPT* 6 (1995): 87–131.

46. The idea of increasing fullness goes back to pentecostal pioneer David Wesley Myland (1858–1943); see Douglas Jacobsen, *Thinking in the Spirit: Theologies of the Early Pentecostal Movement* (Bloomington: Indiana University Press, 2003), 117–20. The language of "intensification" is from my colleague F. LeRon Shults, *Reforming Theological Anthropology: After the Philosophical Turn to Relationality* (Grand Rapids: Eerdmans, 2003), 186–88, but used here for my purposes.

47. The following derives from Kilian McDonnell and George T. Montague, *Christian Initiation and Baptism in the Holy Spirit: Evidence from the First Eight Centuries*, 2nd rev. ed. (Collegeville, MN: Liturgical Press, 1994).

- a culminating rite of Christian initiation including water baptism, anointing—the reception of the Holy Spirit (later known as confirmation)—and celebration of the Eucharist (the Lord's Supper).

Baptism for the forgiveness of sins consists of renunciation of the devil and his works; taking off one's old clothes (signifying putting off the old person); confession of faith in Father, Son, and Holy Spirit; immersion in water (signifying identification with the death, burial, and resurrection of Jesus); and putting on new white robes (signifying putting on Christ). Anointing or confirmation includes the laying of hands on the catechumens by the bishop; the invocation of the Holy Spirit; the anointing with oil (signifying the initial giving and receiving of the Spirit after the model of Jesus' baptism); and the expectation that the charisms, including speaking in tongues, will be manifest.[48] The catechumens proceed to celebrate the Eucharist for the first time with the congregation. As they gather around the Lord's Table, the body of Christ celebrates the unity and fellowship of the Spirit. John Chrysostom (ca. 347–407) says, "Let us learn the wonder of this sacrament. . . . We become a single body . . . members of his flesh and bone of his bones. That is what is brought about by the food that he gives us. He blends himself with us so that we may all become one single entity in the way the body is joined to the head."[49]

To this, some respond that the charisms operate outside baptism and that the Holy Spirit's work is not confined to the baptized.[50] But this misses the point of the patristic understanding, which grants both matters. As McDonnell summarizes, the patristic view of Christian initiation sees the giving and receiving of the Holy Spirit as central and normative for all the baptized. Along the way, classical pentecostals who affirm the doctrine of tongues as the initial evidence of Spirit baptism would be happy to see that the church fathers also understood tongues as a normal—if not normative—manifestation following the reception of the Spirit.[51] The

48. On the centrality of confirmation to the patristic understanding of Christian initiation, see G. W. H. Lampe, *The Seal of the Spirit: A Study in the Doctrine of Baptism and Confirmation in the New Testament and the Fathers* (New York: Longmans, Green, 1951). Harold D. Hunter, *Spirit-Baptism: A Pentecostal Alternative* (Lanham, MD: University Press of America, 1983), ch. 5, traces out developments in the rite of confirmation after the patristic period and observes structural parallels between this and the classical pentecostal understanding of Spirit baptism.

49. John Chrysostom, *Homilies on John* 46, quoted in Kilian McDonnell, "Does the Theology and Practice of the Early Church Confirm the Classical Pentecostal Understanding of Baptism in the Holy Spirit?" *PNEUMA* 21, no. 1 (1999): 115–34; quotation, 124.

50. Martin Parmentier, "Water Baptism and Spirit Baptism in the Church Fathers," *CPCR* 3 (1998), http://www.pctii.org/cyberj/cyber3.html.

51. Kilian McDonnell, "Response to Martin Parmentier on Water Baptism and Spirit Baptism in the Church Fathers," *CPCR* 3 (1998), http://www.pctii.org/cyberj/cyber3.html.

patristic process of Christian initiation may have emerged following the template established by Peter on the day of Pentecost: repentance, baptism for the forgiveness of sins, and reception of the Holy Spirit. (This has always been the claim of Oneness or Apostolic pentecostals, with the added clarification that water baptism has to be "in Jesus' name"—following the pattern of the early church; cf. Acts 2:38; 8:16; 10:48; 19:5—and that Spirit baptism is evidenced by glossolalia.)[52] So, when we trace back the gift of the Spirit to Jesus himself (Luke 24:49; cf. John 20:22) and notice that Jesus the giver of the Spirit is also the Christ anointed by the Spirit, we see a Lukan pneumatological soteriology taking shape: Jesus the Christ, anointed by the Spirit to do the works of the reign of God, pours out that same Spirit upon all flesh in order that his followers also may accomplish perhaps even greater works than he did (cf. John 14:12).

Herein lies the significance of the proclamation of John the Baptist, preserved by all four Gospel writers and repeated by Jesus himself: "I baptize you with water; but one who is more powerful than I . . . will baptize you with the Holy Spirit and fire" (Luke 3:16; see Mark 1:8; Matt. 3:11; John 1:33; cf. Acts 1:5; 11:16).[53] I suggest that this baptism of (or in) the Holy Spirit relates to neither merely the classical pentecostal emphasis of the endowment for power to witness (although it includes this as well) nor merely the idea of Christian initiation into the body of Christ (although, again, it includes this also). Rather, I propose that we retrieve this metaphor of baptism of the Holy Spirit to capture the dynamic and full experience of Christian salvation not only in terms of dying with Christ but also in terms of being raised with him to do the things that he did. In this way, the baptism of the Holy Spirit denotes Christian salvation, broadly considered, as nothing less than the gift of Jesus Christ himself to us in the totality of his Spirit-anointed life, death, and resurrection.[54]

52. See Andrew Urshan, *The Doctrine of the New Birth* (Cochrane, WI: Witness of God, 1921), repr. in *Seven "Jesus Only" Tracts*, ed. Donald W. Dayton (New York: Garland, 1985).

53. Although I was initially led by D. Lyle Dabney to reconceive soteriology in terms of the baptism of the Holy Spirit—see his "The Justification of the Spirit: Soteriological Reflections on the Resurrection," in *Starting with the Spirit, II: Task of Theology Today*, ed. Gordon Preece and Stephen Pickard (Adelaide: Australia Theological Forum and Openbook, 2001), 59–82—I have since been reminded that this has been one of the dominant understandings among theologians in the Catholic charismatic-renewal movement.

54. Initially, the parallel with the Oneness pentecostal understanding of the baptism of the Holy Spirit in soteriological terms will seem obvious. As will be clear in this and the next chapter, however, my proposal has affinities with the Oneness soteriology in spirit, not in letter—certainly not in the Oneness emphasis on the evidential tongues having salvific significance—even if I hope that the possibilities for further dialogue are aided in what follows. For a representative Oneness discussion of baptism in the Holy Spirit as essential to salvation, see David Bernard, *The New Birth* (Hazelwood, MO: Word Aflame, 1984), esp. ch. 8.

This proposal—our second step toward a robust pneumatological soteriology—leads to the following theological insights, utilizing at this juncture the traditional *ordo salutis* of classical Protestantism. First, baptism in the Holy Spirit is anticipated and precipitated by Jesus' offer of the Spirit to all humankind in order to draw all persons to himself (cf. John 16:7–8). Second, baptism in the Holy Spirit is the culmination of the rite of Christian initiation, which includes repentance and baptism for the forgiveness of sins (Acts 2:38; cf. John 3:5–6; Titus 3:5), into the body of Christ (1 Cor. 12:13). Third, the metaphor of baptism in the Holy Spirit makes the connection between the fact that Jesus "was raised for our justification" (Rom. 4:25) and Jesus' arising from the dead by the power of the Spirit and concludes that the justification of sinners is also a pneumatologically accomplished reality that includes, but is not limited to, the forgiveness of sins (understood in forensic terms).[55] This means, fourth, that baptism in the Holy Spirit understands justification as intimately related to sanctification, not in order to advocate any kind of works righteousness but in order to see that God both *declares* sinners righteous through Jesus Christ and *makes* sinners righteous through the purifying fire of the Spirit, restoring them to the full image of God as revealed in the life of Jesus.[56] Fifth, baptism in the Holy Spirit unites believers with Christ in his resurrection power—"If the Spirit of him who raised Jesus from the dead dwells in you, he who raised Christ from the dead will give life to your mortal bodies also through his Spirit that dwells in you" (Rom. 8:11)—and thereby empowers and releases them for ministry in and for the church, and through the church to the world. And finally, baptism in the Holy Spirit is the down payment for the eschatological redemption of God (Eph. 1:13–14; 2 Cor. 1:21–22), which could also be understood in terms of what the Orthodox call *theōsis* ("deification"): being made participants in the divine nature and in the life of God (cf. 2 Pet. 1:4; see also §5.2.1).[57]

Nevertheless, it must also be conceded that the foregoing narrative exegesis of Luke-Acts delivers neither a systematically developed soteriology nor a rigid *ordo salutis* because the "pattern" of Acts, if one exists

---

55. Frank D. Macchia, "Justification and the Spirit: A Pentecostal Reflection on the Doctrine by Which the Church Stands or Falls," *PNEUMA* 22, no. 1 (2000): 3–21; and Veli-Matti Kärkkäinen, "The Holy Spirit and Justification: The Ecumenical Significance of Luther's Doctrine of Salvation," *PNEUMA* 24, no. 1 (2002): 26–39.

56. Wesley was not willing to concede this in any doctrine of salvation; see John Wesley, *A Plain Account of Christian Perfection* (Kansas City, MO: Beacon Hill, 1966).

57. See Veli-Matti Kärkkäinen, "Grace and the Ecumenical Potential of Theosis," ch. 11 in *Toward a Pneumatological Theology: Pentecostal and Ecumenical Perspectives on Ecclesiology, Soteriology, and Theology of Mission*, ed. Amos Yong (Lanham, MD: University Press of America, 2002).

at all, "is the absence of uniformity in sequence."[58] How, then, are we to understand afresh the traditional *ordo salutis* for our time?

2.2.3 *A Pneumatological Theology of Conversion.* This leads, in the third step toward a pneumatological soteriology, to a dialogue with the Wesleyan theological tradition as precursor of modern pentecostalism. This includes a retrieval of the ideas of both John Wesley himself, particularly the notion of *via salutis* (the "scripture way of salvation," as Wesley put it), and his designated successor, John Fletcher.[59]

To begin with Wesley (1703–1791) is to recognize the doctrine of grace that permeates his soteriology.[60] Wesley understood all creation as sustained by the prevenient grace of God. This prevenient grace both makes salvation possible and also undergirds the actual experience of salvation by human beings. With this basic presupposition in place, Wesley spoke of the "scripture way of salvation" in various places in terms of

- convicting or initially repenting grace;
- regenerating or awakening grace;
- convincing, converting, or practically repenting grace;
- justifying, forgiving, or adopting grace;
- initially assuring grace;
- sanctifying, growing, and ongoing repenting grace;
- entirely sanctifying or perfecting grace;
- ultimately assuring (glorifying) grace.[61]

Note that Wesley was practically motivated. He intentionally structured the various means of grace to correlate with his understanding of the *via salutis*, expecting real changes to occur in the lives of his parishioners as they engaged the way of Jesus.[62] Hence, divine grace did not preclude

---

58. Hunter, *Spirit-Baptism*, 90.

59. As Wesley was not a systematic theologian and as I am not a Wesley expert, I rely on the many excellent studies by recognized Wesley scholars. On Fletcher, see Laurence W. Wood, *The Meaning of Pentecost in Early Methodism: Rediscovering John Fletcher as John Wesley's Vindicator and Designated Successor* (Lanham, MD: Scarecrow, 2002).

60. See Kenneth J. Collins, *The Scripture Way of Salvation: The Heart of John Wesley's Theology* (Nashville: Abingdon, 1997); and Randy L. Maddox, *Responsible Grace: John Wesley's Practical Theology* (Nashville: Kingswood, 1994).

61. My list draws from the chapter and section divisions of Collins, *The Scripture Way of Salvation;* and from Maddox, *Responsible Grace*, ch. 7.

62. The general means of grace include attitudes, virtues, watchings, self-denial, taking up the cross daily, exercising the presence of God—in brief, the practices of obedience that pervade the Christian life. Particular means include acts of worship, discipline, prayer, fasting, the Lord's Supper, Christian fellowship/conferencing, the devotional reading of Scripture, and so forth. The prudential means of grace include works of piety, works of

human response. An important point is that Wesley's discussion implicitly acknowledges the difficulty of articulating a systematic *ordo salutis* from the biblical materials. Not only do regenerating, converting, adopting, and assuring grace combine to constitute for Wesley what the broader Protestant tradition recognizes as justifying grace; converting, assuring, growing, and perfecting grace also combine to constitute for Wesley what that same broader tradition recognizes as sanctifying grace—hence, for Wesley, justification was understood as initial sanctification. It is less important to draw from this that the categories overlap (even if they do) than to follow Wesley's insight into the dynamic processes of human salvation. There are not only movement—hence the emphasis on the *way* of salvation, which should caution us against reifying these concepts into a rigid order of salvation—but also possibly reversals (testifying here to Wesley's conviction that one could indeed fall from grace). The attractiveness of Wesley's *via salutis* is that it preserves space for the possibility of crisis moments (as in the conversion or perfection experiences) that serve to move persons from one to another phase in their spiritual lives even while it recognizes the fluidity (e.g., which of the many times I said the "sinner's prayer" during my childhood years was "it"?) of all spiritual journeys.

The importance of John Fletcher (1729–1785) for our purposes is his association of the Lukan baptism in the Holy Spirit with perfecting grace. Fletcher had come over time to see the pentecostal language and imagery in the book of Acts as having significance for understanding sanctification (cf. Acts 15:8–9). Although certainly later Methodist and Holiness thinkers followed Fletcher in this regard, whether the later Wesley aligned himself with Fletcher's views is still heavily debated.[63]

---

mercy, particular acts/rules for holy living, class/band meetings, prayer meetings, covenant services, watch night services, love feasts, visiting the sick, doing all the good we can and doing no harm, reading devotional classics and edifying literature, and so forth. These are all fully discussed in Henry H. Knight III, *The Presence of God in the Christian Life: John Wesley and the Means of Grace* (Metuchen, NJ: Scarecrow, 1992).

63. For the nineteenth-century developments, see Roland Wessels, "The Spirit Baptism, Nineteenth Century Roots," *PNEUMA* 14, no. 2 (1992): 127–57; and Donald W. Dayton, "From Christian Perfection to the 'Baptism in the Holy Ghost,'" in *Aspects of Pentecostal-Charismatic Origins*, ed. Vinson Synan (Plainfield, NJ: Logos International, 1975), 39–54; and *Theological Roots of Pentecostalism* (Peabody, MA: Hendrickson, 1987), chs. 2–4.

The debate concerning Wesley and Fletcher has been conducted between Laurence Wood and Randy Maddox. See Laurence Wood, "Pentecostal Sanctification in Wesley and Early Methodism," *PNEUMA* 21, no. 2 (1999): 251–87; Randy Maddox, "Wesley's Understanding of Christian Perfection: In What Sense Pentecostal?" *WesTJ* 34, no. 2 (1999): 78–110; Laurence Wood, "Historiographical Criticisms of Randy Maddox's Response," *WesTJ* 34, no. 2 (1999): 111–35; and Wood, *The Meaning of Pentecost in Early Methodism*, which continues his running conversation with Maddox. Wood's familiarity with the primary-source literature does not mean that his interpretations are conclusive—on this, see

Clearly, Fletcher connected the pentecostal baptism of the Holy Spirit with full sanctification. This emphasizes the divine initiative accomplishing the perfection of the believer even as it made Wesley nervous that such a passive understanding of sanctification undercuts the responsive role of human beings in the process of sanctification.[64] Both theologians' insistence on avoiding any kind of works righteousness underscores the importance of the doctrine of prevenient grace in their soteriologies, even as our observing this difference between Wesley and Fletcher reminds us that it may be more beneficial to preserve rather than resolve this tension. But whereas the earlier Wesley understood the baptism of the Holy Spirit to refer to the conversion experience, Fletcher's view of such baptism as a second work of sanctifying or perfecting grace may have led the later Wesley at least to broaden his understanding to include the entirety of the Christian salvation experience.[65] Thus the mature Wesley may have seen Christian conversion as synonymous with sanctification. And so Christian salvation is defined as "a thorough change of heart and life from sin to holiness."[66] This background illuminates the nineteenth-century Holiness references to many "anointings" and "baptisms" throughout the individual believer's salvation and sanctification experiences.[67]

What emerges is consistent with the dynamic pneumatological soteriology advocated here.[68] Baptism in the Holy Spirit as a metaphor for Christian salvation calls attention to the process of humans experiencing the saving graces of God along with the presence of crisis moments when such grace is palpably felt as radically transformative. Thus we can say that a dynamic pneumatological soteriology emphasizes three logical moments of the baptism of the Holy Spirit: "I was saved" reflects the initial experience(s) of receiving the Holy Spirit, traditionally called

Melvin Dieter, review of *The Meaning of Pentecost in Early Methodism*, by Laurence Wood, *WesTJ* 38, no. 1 (2003): 242–46. Because I remain unconvinced that the evidence demands the later Wesley to be understood solely in Fletcherian terms, I continue to advocate the plausibility of the following reading of the earlier Wesley for our constructive purposes.

64. See Maddox, "Wesley's Understanding of Christian Perfection," esp. 90–91.

65. See Laurence W. Wood, *Truly Ourselves, Truly the Spirit's: Reflections on Life in the Spirit* (Grand Rapids: Francis Asbury, 1989), 202–8.

66. John Wesley, *Notes on the Bible* to Matt. 18:3 and Acts 3:19, quoted in Maddox, *Responsible Grace*, 152.

67. Donald Dayton, "The Doctrine of the Baptism of the Holy Spirit: Its Emergence and Significance," *WesTJ* 13 (1978): 114–26, esp. 117.

68. Thus Laurence W. Wood, *Pentecostal Grace* (Wilmore, KY: Francis Asbury, 1980), ch. 4, esp. 115–24, defends a dynamic soteriology that is not as rigid as either a Reformed doctrine of divine decrees or a dispensationalist interpretation of salvation history. I would underscore this dynamism in order to nuance the crisis-oriented moments that are present in the remainder of Wood's argument.

repentance, conversion, regeneration, or justification; "I am being saved" reflects the ongoing experiences of being filled with the Spirit, traditionally called sanctification; "I will be saved" reflects the long-anticipated day when we shall "see him as he is" (1 John 3:2) and experience the full baptism of the eschatological Spirit resulting in union with the triune God.

This kind of dynamic pneumatological soteriology requires a theology of conversion commensurate with the complexity of the human encounter with God. Fortunately, the Catholic charismatic theologian Donald Gelpi, SJ, has developed just what the doctor ordered.[69] While constructed for the Catholic Church's Rite for Christian Initiation of Adults (RCIA), Gelpi's insights have solid interdisciplinary credentials even as they are set within a robust pneumatological framework informed by the Catholic charismatic renewal. In brief, conversion is defined as "a turning from and a turning to. . . . One turns from irresponsible to responsible living in some realm of experience."[70] Several features of Gelpi's model of conversion are important. To begin, conversion is a personal experience that occurs within a matrix of social processes. From this, and building on the work of Bernard Lonergan, there are different domains wherein conversion is experienced besides the religious one, and these include the intellectual, the affective, the moral, and the sociopolitical. Intellectual conversion results in our taking responsibility for the truth or falsity of our beliefs and for the explanatory frameworks within which our beliefs sit. Affective conversion results in our taking responsibility for our emotional health and maturation. Moral conversion results in our taking responsibility for our practical deliberations and our choice of actions in interpersonal relations. Sociopolitical conversion enlarges the sphere of moral conversion, resulting in our taking responsibility for the institutional structures of our lives, which inform and shape the common good. It follows that religious conversion results in our taking responsibility for our encounter with the transcendent, or with God, whereas specifically Christian conversion results in our taking responsibility for our life of faith in light of the particular incarnational and pentecostal gifts of God.[71] This is suggestive of the normative nature of conversion: our taking responsibility in any particular domain emerges as a result of a series of self-conscious reflections measuring our perspectives and

69. Donald L. Gelpi, *The Conversion Experience: A Reflective Process for RCIA Participants and Others* (New York: Paulist, 1998).

70. Ibid., 26.

71. The distinction between religious conversion in general and Christian conversion in particular is important; for a discussion of the former in comparing different types of conversions in the world's religious traditions, see Alfred Clair Underwood, *Conversion: Christian and Non-Christian* (New York: Macmillan, 1925).

choices against the realities, values, ideals, and principles that have been interiorized through the conversion process.

The foregoing leads, finally, to the observation that conversion in any domain is dynamically related to those in other domains.[72] Affective conversion, for example, reorders our emotions so that other domains of life are engaged more healthily. Intellectual conversion informs the other four forms of conversion. Moral conversion understands the other forms of conversion to have practical and interpersonal consequences. Sociopolitical conversion deprivatizes the other conversions. Religious conversion in general, and Christian conversion more specifically, trans-values—by which Gelpi means relocates within a new frame of reference—the conversion experiences in the other domains.[73] Of course, even as conversion in one realm impacts conversion in the others, the lack of conversion in any one realm—what Gelpi calls the "counter-dynamics of conversion"—negatively impacts, either by prohibiting or distorting, conversion in the other realms.

As a Jesuit, Gelpi notes that Christian conversion is the reorientation of the totality of our intellectual, affective, moral, and sociopolitical lives according to the revelation of God in Jesus Christ as nurtured by our participation in the sacraments (see further §7.3.1). But note that he also shows how such reorientation is accomplished by the divine Breath's (Gelpi's neologism for the Holy Spirit) assimilation of ourselves with Jesus and by the Breath's charismatic gifts to individual members within and for the benefit of the larger church.[74] So Christian conversion provides the impetus for the renewal of the mind, the healing of the heart, the sanctification of human activities, and the reconciliation of human relationships, all as the Spirit of God assimilates the believer with the mind, heart, and life of Jesus.[75] At the same time, as Gelpi insists, the dynamics and counterdynamics of the various natural conversion experiences—for example, intellectual, affective, and both forms of moral conversion—prior to religious or Christian conversion

---

72. Gelpi, *The Conversion Experience*, 42–57.

73. These Gelpian insights are consistent with the findings of New Testament exegesis, which highlight conversion in narrative terms as a dynamic process of transformation that resists rigid patterns of conceptualization, classification, and categorization; see Beverly Roberts Gaventa, *From Darkness to Light: Aspects of Conversion in the New Testament* (Philadelphia: Fortress, 1986), esp. chs. 2–3 on Luke-Acts; and Joel Green, "'To Turn from Darkness to Light' (Acts 26:18): Conversion in the Narrative of Luke-Acts," in *Conversion in the Wesleyan Tradition*, ed. Kenneth J. Collins and John H. Tyson (Nashville: Abingdon, 2001), 103–18.

74. Gelpi, *The Conversion Experience*, ch. 8.

75. Gelpi writes most powerfully about these processes of transformation throughout Donald L. Gelpi, *The Firstborn of Many: A Christology for Converting Christians*, 3 vols. (Milwaukee: Marquette University Press, 2001).

are not inessential to it, oftentimes precipitating Christian conversion and giving it its distinctive and qualitative shape.

But enough has been said of Gelpi's theology of conversion for now to indicate why it serves as the fourth ingredient for a robust pneumatological soteriology. Having relocated Christian initiation within the broader communal and liturgical life of the church (step one), understood Christian salvation within the framework of the Lukan narrative and in terms of the metaphor of the baptism of the Holy Spirit (step two), and reconceived the *ordo salutis* toward a more dynamic *via salutis* (step three), we can utilize Gelpi's multidimensional and interactive theory of conversion (step four) to bring all of these insights together in a coherent fashion. Note the following gains. First, Gelpi's theory is able to account for the holistic nature of Christian conversion seen in the New Testament and captured in the gospel metaphor of baptism in the Holy Spirit. Salvation as a multidimensional reality—in relationship to God, to others, to the world, and so forth—is preserved in the various domains in which conversion is experienced. Second, Gelpi's theory of conversion articulates the complex processes of repentance experienced by early Christian catechumens. Crisis moments of conversion are identifiable—when transformation from irresponsibility to responsibility occurs—but set against a fluid backdrop of ecclesial, interpersonal, and sociopolitical relationships. The traditional impasse between conversion understood as a crisis event and conversion as a dynamic process is hereby overcome.[76] Finally, the dynamic, complex, and interactive series of conversion processes mean not only that any theology of conversion will resist systematic definition[77] but also that every conversion experience in any domain serves as a divinely gracious prompt for deeper conversion in other domains and that finite human beings will never completely convert in this life.[78] In this case,

---

76. Thus "Malines Document I" puts this in terms of "Experience as Growth or Crisis"; see *PPP* 3:33–34.

77. Matthias Wenk, "Conversion and Initiation: A Pentecostal View of Biblical and Patristic Perspectives," *JPT* 17 (2000): 56–80.

78. Here I wish to correct what I wrote about Gelpi in Amos Yong, *Beyond the Impasse: Toward a Pneumatological Theology of Religions* (Grand Rapids: Baker, 2003), 60–61—both where I questioned his insistence "on Christian conversion as a prerequisite for pneumatological understanding" and where I argued as insufficiently dialectical his claim that "only those who have experienced some level of Christian conversion . . . can adequately undertake the task of doing Christian theology." I was wrong on two counts. First, factually, I misread Gelpi as claiming that Christian conversion was a prerequisite to engaging the Spirit of God and reflecting on that experience. His theological system allows for a non-Christian encounter of, and reflection on, the divine Breath (see further §7.2.3). Second, the underlying criticism in the second charge is simply wrongheaded, since Christian conversion is necessary for *Christian* theology. My thanks to Gregory Zuschlag for calling attention to these matters.

a *via media* is found in the ancient argument about whether salvation depends on divine initiation or human responsibility.

2.3 PNEUMATOLOGICAL SOTERIOLOGY AND THE CHRISTIAN THEOLOGICAL TRADITION

It remains to be clarified how the constructive proposal developed here compares with the understanding of the Christian theological tradition. This section first compares Spirit christology with the dominant historical christologies, proceeds to analyze pneumatological soteriology in light of traditional theories of the atonement, and concludes with a discussion on pentecostal theology as a "traditioning" enterprise.

2.3.1 *Spirit Christology and the Tradition.* The following should not be construed as an attempt to canvass the entire history of christological reflections. My modest intention is to locate the Spirit christology proposed here within the theological tradition and to argue for its full inclusion as a legitimate model for contemporary christology. Toward these ends, let me make two general historical remarks before dealing with the important but challenging issue of the relationship between the Spirit and the Son.

First, the Spirit christology of the Synoptics in general and of Luke in particular has always sat alongside the Logos christology of the Johannine Gospel. The former emphasized Jesus' humanity, the latter his deity. The latter may have emerged naturally from the former insofar as the former could not adequately account for a number of features—for example, Jesus' dispensing forgiveness of sins (the prerogative of God alone) or the dynamics surrounding the "messianic secret." It should come as no surprise that early Christian reflection on Jesus preserved both perspectives. The Antiochene school's preference for a literal and historical reading of Scripture led its proponents to champion what is now known as a "Logos-anthropos" understanding of Jesus, emphasizing the joining of the Logos with a human being, whereas the Alexandrian school's preference for an allegorical hermeneutic led its members to advocate a "Logos-sarx" christology, emphasizing the union of the Logos and human flesh.[79]

Second, the challenges confronted by the early church inevitably focused on explicating the nature of Jesus and his relationship to the Father. The emergent Nicene and Chalcedonian confessions therefore

---

79. On Alexandria and Antioch as hermeneutical traditions, see David S. Dockery, *Biblical Interpretation Then and Now: Contemporary Hermeneutics in the Light of the Early Church* (Grand Rapids: Baker, 1992), chs. 3–4.

declared Jesus as being of the same substance (*homoousios*) with the Father, his divine and human natures united in his person. The mystery of Christ was preserved in the apophatic "four fences" of Chalcedon: without confusion, without change, without division, without separation. Still, declaring Jesus unequivocally divine led to a diminished emphasis on his humanity in the later tradition, especially in the popular consciousness. As a result, the Antiochene voice became muted whereas the Alexandrian perspective became dominant. The Synoptic Gospels were reduced to present what Jesus did, even as John's Gospel was understood to provide the definitive account of who Jesus really was.

The details of the Chalcedonian definition were never universally accepted, especially in the Christian East, and vibrant Monophysite and Nestorian traditions remain today, reminding us of various points of dispute.[80] Further, the tension for most Protestant theologies is to overcome the temptation to separate completely the scriptural dimension of the apostolic traditions from the ecumenical consensus of the postapostolic traditions, and to take seriously the priority and normativity of the biblical witness for theological reflection. Finally, the attempt to articulate a world pentecostal theology will inevitably need to engage the theology and christology of Oneness pentecostalism.

The rationale for retrieving and reappropriating Spirit christology for world pentecostal theology should be clear. First, it reengages the complex question Jesus posed through the entirety of the gospel witness, "Who do you say that I am?" and results in a new appreciation for his humanity. Second, it requires us to locate the patristic consensus in specific Hellenistic contexts even while it enables us to approach the christological question afresh using contemporary anthropological and existential categories. Third, it participates in the renaissance of pneumatology in contemporary theology even as it contributes to the quest for a robustly trinitarian theology. Fourth, it provides bridges to the practical relevance and the implications for Christian living—Jesus as the man of the Spirit models our lives as anointed by the Spirit—not as well afforded by traditional christological accounts. Finally, it redirects Oneness theologians toward the underlying narrative base more appropriate to their Jewish "theology of the name" than their current attempts to rehabilitate the Logos category for theological and christological purposes (see §5.3.3).

This said, my Spirit christology proposal is certainly not meant to displace the Johannine Logos account. In fact, although Spirit christology provides a more plausible contemporary account of the divine-human interface in the life of Jesus than the incarnational model, John's

---

80. Paul R. Fries and Tiran Nersoyan, eds., *Christ in East and West* (Macon, GA: Mercer University Press, 1987).

perspective—"And the Word became flesh and lived among us, and we have seen his glory, the glory as of a father's only son, full of grace and truth" (John 1:14)—is crucial to protect Spirit christology from lapsing into adoptionism. Further, "In the beginning was the Word, and the Word was with God, and the Word was God" (John 1:1) preserves the mystery of the incarnation and the innertrinitarian relations that Spirit christology on its own terms loses. Finally, and most important, even granted that the Spirit has historically been subordinated to the Son, thereby prohibiting a fully perichoretic trinitarian theology from emerging, Logos christology protects Spirit christology from the reverse subordinationist tendency: that of subjecting the person and work of Jesus to the Spirit. A robustly trinitarian theology will need to avoid both pitfalls by articulating a fully relational, mutual, and reciprocal understanding of the Son and the Spirit (§5.3.1).

Thus the primary challenge for pneumatological theology is to preserve, without disengaging the Spirit from the Son altogether, the integrity of the Spirit's mission against the theological tradition's tendency to subordinate the Spirit to the Son.[81] Is it possible that pentecostalism's emphasis on the Spirit might lead to a neglect of both the person and the work of the Son?[82] Possibly, yes; necessarily, no. Although Logos christology may protect the theologian against this neglect, Spirit christology is not completely without its own resources.

It is here that the recent work of D. Lyle Dabney on a pneumatology of the cross—what he calls a *pneumatologia crucis*—is helpful.[83] Dabney is

81. My attempts to engage this challenge in earlier work—in Yong, *Beyond the Impasse*, and, before that, in Amos Yong, *Discerning the Spirit(s): A Pentecostal-Charismatic Contribution to Christian Theology of Religions*, JPTSup 20 (Sheffield, Eng.: Sheffield Academic Press, 2000)—consciously erred on the side of distinguishing the mission of the Spirit from that of the Son in order to purchase theological space for understanding the distinctiveness of the mission of the Spirit. In many ways, the proposals in this volume are meant to return to a more centrist position.

82. This is the argument of Thomas A. Fudge, *Christianity without the Cross: A History of Salvation in Oneness Pentecostalism* (Parkland, FL: Universal, 2003)—that Oneness pentecostal churches such as the United Pentecostal Church have shifted the gateway to salvation from the cross of Christ to water and Spirit baptism according to Acts 2:38. Although there are methodological difficulties with the way in which Fudge prosecutes his thesis, it nonetheless captures the concerns of many regarding pneumatological and pentecostal theology.

83. D. Lyle Dabney, "*Pneumatologia crucis*: Reclaiming *theologia crucis* for a Theology of the Spirit Today," *Scottish Journal of Theology* 53, no. 4 (2000): 511–24. For an overview of Dabney's important and emerging project in pneumatological theology, see Amos Yong, "A Theology of the Third Article? Hegel and the Contemporary Enterprise in First Philosophy and First Theology," in *Semper reformandum: Studies in Honour of Clark H. Pinnock*, ed. Stanley E. Porter and Anthony R. Cross (Carlisle, Eng.: Paternoster, 2003), 208–31, esp. 226–30.

very concerned with the identity of the Spirit and indeed sees the Spirit's presence and activity in the Gospel of Mark (as we have previously in Luke) in the life, work, death, and resurrection of Jesus. What Dabney highlights, however, is that the Spirit not only enables Jesus' offering of himself on the cross (Heb. 9:14) but also remains present with Jesus through the passion, which ultimately separates the Father from the Son. Jesus' cry, "Abba, Father" (Mark 14:36a), is enabled, as Paul elsewhere notes, only by the Spirit (cf. Rom. 8:15; Gal. 4:6).

> The Holy Spirit is the Spirit of the self-sacrifice and resurrection of Jesus Christ made manifest in the Trinitarian kenosis of God on the cross, the possibility of God even in the midst of every impossibility that God could be present and active, the divine possibility that the living God might be found even in the midst of chaos and death, indeed, precisely in the midst of chaos and death, the possibility that God might yet be for us and we might yet be for God, and thus the possibility that even those who suffer that deadly estrangement might beyond death be raised to new life, transformed life, a life in which the crushed and broken and incoherent bits and pieces of a life are taken up anew and made whole.[84]

Thus the Spirit of the cross also leads the followers of Jesus to their crosses, explaining in part why those who bear witness to the gospel are oftentimes also martyrs for the cause of Christ (the Greek for "witnesses" in Acts 1:8 is *martyres*).[85] Why not, if the way of the cross is a "way of negation"?[86] The Spirit who is always hidden and points to the Son also leads followers of Jesus to empty themselves in the service of the Son. Hence salvation understood as baptism in the Holy Spirit is nothing less than receiving the gift of the Spirit of God, which enables human participation in the self-sacrificing death and resurrection life of Jesus the Christ.

    2.3.2 Spirit Soteriology and Traditional Theories of the Atonement. Dabney's proposal for identifying the Spirit in terms of the cross of Christ raises the question about the relationship between Spirit christology and the work of Christ, also known traditionally as the atonement. As Spirit christology complements Logos christology, so also does pneumatological

84. D. Lyle Dabney, "Naming the Spirit: Towards a Pneumatology of the Cross," in Preece and Pickard, eds., *Starting with the Spirit, II,* 28–58; quotation, 58. See also Tom [Thomas A.] Smail, "The Cross and the Spirit: Towards a Theology of Renewal," in Tom [Thomas A.] Smail, Andrew Walker, and Nigel Wright, *Charismatic Renewal: The Search for a Theology* (London: SPCK, 1995), ch. 4.

85. See Thomas A. Smail, *Reflected Glory: The Spirit in Christ and Christians* (London: Hodder & Stoughton, 1975), ch. 8.

86. See Mark J. Cartledge, *Charismatic Glossolalia: An Empirical-Theological Study* (Burlington, VT: Ashgate, 2002), 200–203.

soteriology complement the traditional theories of the atonement. This can be seen by refocusing the ransom, satisfaction, penal substitutionary, and moral-influence theories of the saving work of Christ in pneumatological perspective.[87]

The ransom or dramatic theory of the atonement was dominant during the first Christian millennium.[88] Building on Jesus' own words—that "the Son of Man came . . . to give his life a ransom for many" (Mark 10:45; cf. Matt. 20:28)—the basic elements include an original owner (God), a lost possession (creation in general and humankind in particular), a usurper (the devil; cf. 1 John 5:19), and a ransom (the Son of Man in exchange for the rightful owner's recovery of what was lost). In the patristic understanding, the unfolding of the plot results in the devil being deceived by God insofar as the ransom does not remain under the power of death (cf. Acts 2:23–28; 1 Cor. 15:54–57). Critical questions have always followed this theory—such as the following: How is the devil in the position to demand payment of a ransom from God? Is it fair that God deceives the devil by raising up the ransom from the dead? Is redemption purely a cosmic affair or transaction between God and the devil, so that the primary problematic is framed in terms of the demonic? How can the ransom theory remain plausible to the modern mindset, which has demythologized the idea of the devil?

The pneumatological soteriology defended here not only reinvigorates the idea of the demonic (itself a pneumatological category; see §6.2.2) but reorients it according to contemporary sensibilities. Insofar as Satan represents the sum total of all evil and sin is thereby understood in cosmic and social terms, the ransom theory empowers a redemptive, nonviolent resistance against evil, following the example of Jesus (reliant on cunning and ingenuity).[89] And insofar as the liberation of the captives accomplished by Jesus included the exorcism of demons from those held in bondage by destructive forces, so also does full salvation need to account for the triumph of Christ over the rulers and authorities of this present world (cf. Col. 2:15).

The satisfaction theory has been dominant since Anselm's articulation of it in the eleventh century. For Anselm, human beings had dishonored

---

87. Atonement theories are legion—e.g., H. D. McDonald, *The Atonement of the Death of Christ* (Grand Rapids: Baker, 1985), part 3—but these four theories have been the most prominent historically. See also Jonathan R. Wilson, *God So Loved the World: A Christology for Disciples* (Grand Rapids: Baker, 2001), part 2, for a contemporary attempt to retrieve these atonement theories for our time.

88. See the classic Gustaf Aulén, *Christus Victor: An Historical Study of the Three Main Types of the Idea of the Atonement*, trans. A. G. Hebert (London: SPCK, 1970).

89. Darby Kathleen Ray, *Deceiving the Devil: Atonement, Abuse, and Ransom* (Cleveland: Pilgrim, 1998), ch. 7.

God in their fall into sin, thereby incurring the divine wrath. How could that wrath be appeased by human beings who had already failed in their obligations? For this reason, God became a man in Jesus Christ: his sinless life restored to God the honor due to God, and his sacrificial death satisfied and appeased the wrath of God. Critical questions have also followed this theory, including these: Is redemption purely a cosmic affair or transaction between God the Father and God the Son, so that the primary problematic is framed in terms of the demands of God manifest in the divine wrath? What about more recent "divine violence" criticisms, suggesting that the theory relies on violent images of the Father exacting the payment for sin from the Son through death (e.g., Isa. 53:4), images that in turn sanction human violence and, more abhorrently, acts of child abuse in particular?[90]

Though related to Anselm's satisfaction theory, the penal-substitution theory was developed primarily by the Reformers who understood human disobedience not only as insulting God's honor but also as breaching God's law. If the breaking of the divine law incurs the penalty of death, how can this penalty be satisfied by those under its condemnation? Hence the proposal that the death of Christ and the shedding of his blood on the cross in place of guilty human beings atone for—propitiate or expiate (cf. Rom. 3:25)—all sin. In addition to the critical questions posed to the satisfaction theory, others more pertinent to the penal-substitution theory include these: If Jesus' life and death pay the penalty for all sin, how can further punishment be exacted on sinners—for example, in an eternal hell—without resulting in "double jeopardy" and undermining the efficacy of Jesus' substitutionary atonement? (Later Reformed theology developed the idea of limited atonement—Christ died only for the elect—precisely in order to deal with this issue; but this proposal does not adequately account for the claim that Jesus is "the atoning sacrifice for our sins, and not for ours only but also for the sins of the whole world"; cf. 1 John 2:2; 1 Tim. 4:10.) Building on this, does not Jesus' atonement for sin define salvation as a forensic matter to the neglect or undermining of the ethical dimension?

Instead of being an outmoded notion limited to the feudal and penitential context of Anselm's medieval period or a piece of legalistic speculation amidst the emerging Protestant city-states, I suggest that the satisfaction and substitutionary theories remain pertinent for our time. Given our increasing awareness of the web of interconnectedness that binds all life forms together to the point that human survival

90. J. Denny Weaver, *The Nonviolent Atonement* (Grand Rapids: Eerdmans, 2001), chs. 5–6; and John Howard Yoder, *Preface to Theology: Christology and Theological Method* (Grand Rapids: Brazos, 2002), 299–305.

is always at the expense of other forms of life, including other human life, the blood guilt that is upon our own heads as survivors requires the atoning sacrifice of Jesus in order for us to engage each other, the earth, and the divine in good conscience.[91] The pneumatological framework defended here provides the broader multidimensional soteriology making rehabilitation of these biblical images possible. The Spirit who empowers Jesus' sacrificial offering (cf. Heb. 9:13–14) also makes possible its application through the resurrection of Jesus from the dead (cf. Rom. 4:25). This makes genuine not only the proclamation of good news offering the forgiveness of sins (see §2.1.3) but also the experience of the gift of the Spirit, which enables the giving and receiving of this forgiveness (cf. John 20:22–23). Most important, insofar as the Spirit, who raised Jesus for our justification, also gives life to us (Rom. 8:11), the experience of forgiveness of sins deals not merely with the covering of our past failures but also with the empowering of our future actions so that they retain their full moral and ethical significance. This more dynamic understanding of the satisfaction and substitutionary theories effectively sidesteps both the divine-violence and double-jeopardy criticisms, since the former is now a trinitarian rather than binitarian affair and the latter applies only within a static framework.

The moral influence of the atonement was first proposed by Abelard in response to Anselm and then developed into a much more subjectivistic theory by modern Protestant liberalism. For Abelard, the problem was neither the devil (as in the ransom theory) nor God's wrath (as in the satisfaction theory). Rather, the problem lay in the human heart, estranged and alienated from God by shame, guilt, and self-condemnation (cf. Gen. 3:8; Rom. 8:1). How can human beings be brought to the realization that the devil is no more than a false accuser, that the Father awaits the return home of his prodigal children with open arms (cf. Luke 15:20–24), and that nothing can separate us from the love of God (Rom. 8:31–39)? Through the gift of divine love by the Holy Spirit (Rom. 5:5): the death of Christ reveals the accomplished reconciliation between God and human beings, which illuminates, heals, and transforms the human heart (2 Cor. 5:14–20). Later versions of this theory, especially among liberal Protestant thinkers, tended to emphasize much more than Abelard did the subjective work of Christ at the expense of any objective dimension.

91. Robert Cummings Neville, *Symbols of Jesus: A Christology of Symbolic Engagement* (Cambridge: Cambridge University Press, 2001), esp. ch. 2, argues this point. I include the earth in light of the realization, among African independent churches, "of a common guilt which, in a sense, makes all of us 'varoyi'—earth destroyers"; see Marthinus L. Daneel, *African Earthkeepers: Wholistic Interfaith Mission* (Maryknoll, NY: Orbis, 2001), 166.

A pneumatological reappropriation of the moral-influence theory preserves its central insights regarding both the necessary transformation of soul and the healing of moral character even while it locates these realities within the interpersonal, ecclesial, and sociopolitical matrices wherein Christian salvation is experienced and played out. Further, it provides a norm to measure the transformation of heart according to the image of Jesus, so that one is converted over and over again by the power of the Spirit so as to put on the mind of Christ, embody the virtues of Jesus, and accomplish the things he did. In this way, the existential and experiential dimensions of the atoning work of Christ are retained as accomplished by the Spirit.[92]

2.3.3 *Pneumatological Soteriology and the Tradition: Retrieving, Reconstructing, Reappropriating.* Although the preceding represents only a preliminary effort to redeem the history of the Christian theological tradition for world pentecostal theology, it is important, given especially early modern pentecostalism's ambivalence toward the history of the postapostolic church. Let me make explicit a pentecostal theology of the tradition and summarize how a world pentecostal and pneumatological soteriology retrieves, reconstructs, and reappropriates this theology.

Pentecostals have been historically more interested in the apostolic experience than in its subsequent history. More recently, however, this has begun to change with the appearance both of full-scale historical theology[93] and of an attempt to reconceive pentecostal spirituality in full dialogue with the Christian spiritual tradition. The latter is especially pertinent here because of Simon Chan's insights about not only the content and legacy of the theological tradition but also the processes of "traditioning."[94] Pentecostals now realize that traditions are generally not static entities—although they could become so and remain only antiquarian objects of interest to posterity—but are living, dynamic, and self-perpetuating realities.[95] Granted, there are particular challenges for pentecostal traditioning, including pentecostal emphases on the direct vertical experience of God rather

92. See Richard Shaull and Waldo Cesar, *Pentecostalism and the Future of the Christian Churches: Promises, Limitations, Challenges* (Grand Rapids: Eerdmans, 2000), esp. 144–47.

93. David Bernard, *A History of Christian Doctrine*, 3 vols. (Hazelwood, MO: Word Aflame, 1995–1999)—written, no doubt, to validate Oneness theology against the "aberrations" of the tradition.

94. Simon Chan, *Pentecostal Theology and the Christian Spiritual Tradition*, JPTSup 21 (Sheffield, Eng.: Sheffield Academic Press, 2000), esp. ch. 1.

95. See Dale T. Irvin, *Christian Histories, Christian Traditioning: Rendering Accounts* (Maryknoll, NY: Orbis, 1998).

than on the mediated horizontal experience of divine activity, on oral transmission as opposed to having a well-developed written culture, and on personal piety versus "dead orthodoxy." Yet pentecostalism's oral mode of communication and narrative framework are conducive to the task of traditioning, and the pentecostal orientation is a further aid to the process of traditioning precisely because such traditioning is pneumatologically accomplished. As Philip Thompson reminds us, the Holy Spirit not only enables the memory of the church (John 14:25–26) but also empowers the appropriation of such memory (activity) in a way that reenacts the covenant relationship between God and God's people.[96]

At the same time, any reenactment is not merely a repetition of the tradition but a fresh experience of the tradition in a new time and place. So the pneumatological dynamic of the traditioning process ensures its vitality and relevance. In addition, it is precisely the responsibility of the eschatological Spirit of God not only to bring renewal but also to accomplish new things. For this reason, pentecostals should be open to the development of doctrine. This would not be a case of the Spirit's "revelation" as going "beyond Christ" but rather "a matter of drawing ever more deeply upon the treasury of God's reality and grace as it is found in Jesus Christ."[97] I would further say that included in this journey into the depths of God's grace in Jesus Christ would be new realizations of the truth appropriate to new situations and circumstances.

So what can we say about pneumatological soteriology in world pentecostal perspective? The advantage of understanding soteriology in terms of the baptism in the Holy Spirit is its dynamism in characterizing full salvation as a holistic and eschatological experience. This characterization in turn enables pentecostal theology to avoid a number of impasses in the classical debates.

First, salvation is a *holistic* and multidimensional process of the transformation of individuals in their spiritual, natural, and social environments; this gives meaning to the experience of the forgiveness of sins and to the deliverance from the principalities and powers of this age. The saving work of the Spirit transforms human persons precisely by reconciling them to God, to each other, and to their natural habitats. There is no necessary antagonism either between the salvation of the

---

96. Philip Edward Thompson, "Toward a Baptist Ecclesiology in Pneumatological Perspective" (Ph.D. diss., Emory University, 1995), esp. ch. 5. From a Catholic perspective, see Jerome M. Hall, *We Have the Mind of Christ: The Holy Spirit and Liturgical Memory in the Thought of Edward J. Kilmartin* (Collegeville, MN: Liturgical Press, 2001), esp. 109–22.

97. Daniel A. Tappeiner, "A Theology of Church History as *apologia* for the Pentecostal/Charismatic Movement," *AJPS* 2, no. 1 (1999): 63–75; quotation, 74.

spirit and the salvation of the body or between the new birth and the social or "green" gospels.[98]

Second, salvation is a holistic and dynamic process: I was saved, I am being saved, and I will be saved. The saving work of the Spirit reconceived in this way sidesteps three perennial questions. Initially, it inextricably links what is traditionally known as justification, sanctification, and glorification. This is especially important for pentecostals who understand Spirit baptism in terms of an endowment of power for witness, to the neglect of the call to holiness, since it requires ongoing emphasis on the ethical dimension of salvation.[99] Yet insofar as Wesley's doctrine of prevenient grace is seen to undergird the entire process, salvation includes both God's initiative and human response (Phil. 2:12b–13).[100] There is no necessary antagonism between justification and sanctification, in salvation understood as a gift from God and yet requiring some human response as enabled by the Spirit.

Further, the saving work of the Spirit understood as dynamic process overcomes the ongoing debate about whether the baptism in the Holy Spirit is understood as a conversion-initiation experience or as a second (sanctifying) or even third (empowering) work of grace. Although a few classical Pentecostal exegetes have persisted valiantly in distinguishing between the initial salvific gift of the Spirit and the later experience of Spirit baptism and in defending the latter idea as Luke's distinctive theological contribution, most see both as gifts of

98. Thus LeRon Shults redefines salvation as "embodied relations of peace and justice in community" even while he moves away from an individualistic notion of *ordo salutis* to the idea of "salutary ordering in community"; see F. LeRon Shults and Steven J. Sandage, *The Faces of Forgiveness: Searching for Wholeness and Salvation* (Grand Rapids: Baker, 2003), esp. 104, 156–61.

99. J. Denny Weaver, *Keeping Salvation Ethical: Mennonite and Amish Atonement Theology in the Late Nineteenth Century* (Scottsdale, PA: Herald, 1997), captures the traditional Anabaptist and Mennonite understandings that were threatened during the nineteenth-century "evangelicalization" of the traditions, when the displacement of *Christus victor* atonement images by penal substitutionary views of the work of Christ resulted in the disassociation of salvation from the ethical life, from commitment to nonviolent resistance, from loving one's enemies, and from forsaking vengeance—all normal expectations among the earliest Christians.

100. The African American "Pray's House" ritual, which provides structures for pursuing holiness at various crisis moments throughout life, from childhood through adulthood, has been adapted by black pentecostals, most evidently in the liturgical context of "tarrying" and the "ring-shout." Together they signify a posture of active expectation that recognizes God's sovereignty in dispensing the gifts of grace and the Spirit. See Alonzo Johnson, "'Pray's House Spirit': The Institutional Structure and Spiritual Case of an African American Folk Tradition," in *Ain't Gonna Lay My Ligion Down: African American Religion in the South*, ed. Alonzo Johnson and Paul Jersild (Columbia: University of South Carolina Press, 1996), 8–38, esp. 16–25.

the Spirit.[101] In my view, the one baptism in the Holy Spirit, taken as a New Testament metaphor for the full salvific work of God, in fact demands a variety of experiences, each of which could be significant of conversion in different areas or at deeper levels, including that of being redirected toward bearing more focused and intensive witness to the gospel.[102] In this case, the experience of being filled with the Holy Spirit occurs "at *any* point in the Christian pilgrimage," reflecting various stages of the free work of God that accomplishes different things in the life of the believer.[103] Although this understanding of Spirit baptism includes the process of conversion-initiation, it does not exclude—in fact, it expects—the crisis experience(s) defended by the classical Pentecostal understanding of baptism of the Holy Spirit as a second (or third) work of grace related to charismatic endowment and vocational empowerment. Put succinctly, the baptism in the Holy Spirit refers both to Christian initiation (but understands salvation in a dynamic Wesleyan rather than a forensic Lutheran/Reformed sense) *and* to empowerment for service (but understands this as holding out the possibility of multiple deepening and intensifying experiences of the Spirit rather than only as "second" or "third" works of grace). Thus there is no necessary antagonism between Spirit baptism understood as Christian initiation, on the one hand, and Spirit baptism understood as a later empowering of the Spirit, on the other.[104]

101. Exegetes who see Luke's "gift of the Holy Spirit" in terms of charismatic empowerment include Roger Stronstad, James Shelton, and Robert Menzies (see nn. 8–9 above). Those who see the Spirit given both at conversion-initiation and for vocational empowerment include Gordon Fee, Howard Ervin, Max Turner, Harold Hunter, J. R. Williams, and French Arrington. See esp. Max Turner, *Power from on High: The Spirit in Israel's Restoration and Witness in Luke-Acts*, JPTSup 9 (Sheffield, Eng.: Sheffield Academic Press, 1996), esp. part 1; and Howard Ervin, *Conversion-Initiation and the Baptism in the Holy Spirit: An Engaging Critique of James D. G. Dunn's Baptism in the Holy Spirit* (Peabody, MA: Hendrickson, 1984); and idem, *Spirit Baptism: A Biblical Investigation* (Peabody, MA: Hendrickson, 1987).

102. I initially argued this in terms of understanding Spirit baptism in three stages—those of innocence, growth, and the adept—which I now wish to complexify by seeing the stages themselves as nonlinear processes; see Amos Yong, "Tongues of Fire in the Pentecostal Imagination: The Truth of Glossolalia in Light of R. C. Neville's Theory of Religious Symbolism," *JPT* 12 (1998): 39–65.

103. Donald Ray Wheelock, "Spirit Baptism in American Pentecostal Thought" (Ph.D. diss., Emory University, 1983), 342–43; italics original.

104. Does this lead to a kind of pentecostal elitism for those who have the pentecostal experience? No, because there is no hierarchy of conversion experiences with pentecostal empowerment at the top. Rather, following out the logic of our pneumatological theology of conversion, one who is more converted intellectually or morally, and so forth, is no more filled with the Spirit or superior as a Christian than one who is less converted. This goes also for those with the conversion experience of charismatic empowerment for witness.

Finally, the saving work of the Spirit understood as dynamic process bypasses the question whether saints are eternally secure or can apostatize. Both sides of this debate assume salvation to be a discrete experience. The view defended here affirms the power of crisis experiences to grant confidence regarding the eschatological salvation of God even as it locates those conversion experiences as ever deeper intensifications of being turned and oriented toward God in the various domains of life. There is therefore no necessary antagonism between the assuring witness of the Spirit, on the one hand, and the capacity to grieve and even fall away from the Holy Spirit (cf. Heb. 6:4–6), on the other.

In sum, salvation is a gift from God to the world, not just a transaction between divine persons or occurring only within the inner trinitarian life of God. Hence the dichotomy between salvation as being of God and salvation as demanding human response is a false one. We do better to see salvation as human participation in the saving work of God through Christ by the Holy Spirit. In this way, salvation is not some abstract or speculative deal but the concrete experiences of embodied, social, political, economic, and spiritual beings as the Holy Spirit is poured out on them.

This chapter has correlated the pentecostal experiences of the saving power of God, described in chapter 1, with soteriological themes in the Bible viewed specifically through a Lukan lens. Jesus is the Christ, the one anointed by the Spirit to save, and salvation is baptism of the Holy Spirit into the life, death, and resurrection of Christ. The result is a pneumatological soteriology with three emphases: a multidimensional understanding of the domains in which salvation is experienced; a dynamic view of the various processes and levels through which conversion occurs; and an alertness and sensitivity to both retrieving and reappropriating the previous formulations of the Christian theological tradition. In this way, we can give preliminary systematic articulation to the pentecostal intuition of the fivefold gospel: Jesus is Savior precisely as healer, sanctifier, and baptizer, all in anticipation of the full salvation to be brought with the coming kingdom. The next chapter continues to engage the demands of the theological tradition by picking up on a theme already broached: salvation understood in ecclesial terms (§2.2.1). This raises a complex question: what is the church? Come Holy Spirit, in your community-forming power . . .

3

The Acts of the Apostles and of the Holy Spirit

Toward a Pneumatological Ecclesiology

As we have now seen, the Christian tradition has long understood salvation in terms of receiving the Spirit and being baptized into Jesus Christ. But baptism into Jesus entails becoming a member of the body of Christ. As such, soteriology includes and even presupposes ecclesiology and vice versa.[1] Yet over the course of time, and especially with the emergence of the free-church and pietist traditions after the Reformation, soteriology has been privatized in terms of the individual's personal relationship with Jesus, resulting in the separation of soteriology from ecclesiology. Standing within both the free-church and pietist traditions for the most part, pentecostals have also tended to talk about soteriology apart from ecclesiology; if they have talked about ecclesiology at all, it is usually as an afterthought.

The preceding pneumatological soteriology has sought to begin the reconciliation of pentecostal understandings of salvation and the church.

---

1. For this reason, Clark Pinnock treats ecclesiology before soteriology in *Flame of Love: A Theology of the Holy Spirit* (Downers Grove, IL: InterVarsity, 1996).

121

If we take the Lukan narrative seriously, we cannot talk about salvation, the church, or the Spirit apart from each other. For good reason, Luke's second volume has been variously called the Acts of the Apostles and the Acts of the Holy Spirit. The outpouring of the Spirit on the day of Pentecost made the grace of God available to all precisely through the establishment of a new people of God. This leads to the thesis central to pneumatological ecclesiology: the church is an organic, dynamic, and eschatological people of God called after the name of Jesus and constituted in the fellowship of the Holy Spirit.[2]

This chapter therefore not only assumes but also informs and explicates essentially the pneumatological soteriology of the previous chapter. Further, it continues to explore the question concerning the relationship between pentecostal theology and the Christian theological tradition, with the presumption that any understanding of the church as an organic reality will need to confront the various historical forms and self-understandings of the church. We proceed to locate this discussion of the doctrine of the church amidst the current debates (§3.1); retrieve and reappropriate the doctrine of the church understood historically in terms of the marks of unity, holiness, catholicity, and apostolicity (§3.2); and conclude with a sketch of what a pneumatological theology of the sacraments and of sacramentality might look like (§3.3). Woven together throughout are both more strictly soteriological and more strictly ecclesiological matters, both historical and contemporary concerns, and the experiences of both the church catholic and the church pentecostal.

3.1 The Doctrine of the Church: Whither Ecclesiology?

The question "What is the church?" has become a central concern with the emergence of the ecumenical movement in the twentieth century. The divisions between East and West, between Catholic and Protestant, and between the innumerable Protestant denominations and congregations mean, however, that we are far from agreement on even what the right questions are for ecclesiology. This section explores the issues currently debated, beginning first within pentecostalism, then moving

2. Among the growing ecumenical literature, see Jürgen Moltmann, *The Church in the Power of the Spirit: A Contribution to Messianic Ecclesiology*, trans. Margaret Kohl (London: SCM, 1977); William R. Barr and Rena M. Yocom, eds., *The Church in the Movement of the Spirit* (Grand Rapids: Eerdmans, 1994); Philip Edward Thompson, "Toward a Baptist Ecclesiology in Pneumatological Perspective" (Ph.D. diss., Emory University, 1995); and John J. Markey, OP, *Creating Communion: The Theology of the Constitutions of the Church* (Hyde Park, NY: New City, 2003).

to the contemporary scene, and finally setting both within the broader historical context of the Christian theological tradition.

3.1.1 *The Pentecostal Question: What Ecclesiology?* Pentecostals have not generally given sustained thought to ecclesiology.[3] When pentecostals have said anything, the result has been that pentecostal ecclesiology has gone the way of free-church ecclesiology in general and its evangelical forms more specifically.[4] The basic New Testament images are recalled—for example, the church as the people of God, as the body of Christ, as the temple of the Spirit—and the church's fourfold mission of worship, instruction, fellowship, and evangelism is usually delineated. Issues related to the proper biblical form of church government are also normally discussed, with congregationalism favored but various forms of presbyterianism and episcopalianism operative, along with the doctrine of the priesthood of all believers. The *ordinances* (rather than sacraments) of baptism and the Lord's Supper (rather than Eucharist) often conclude these treatments. Most pentecostals have subordinated these matters to the more pressing task of world mission and evangelization.

This linkage of ecclesiology with the Christian mission goes back to one of the few pentecostals who have produced book-length treatments of the doctrine of the church, the Assemblies of God missiologist Melvin Hodges.[5] Hodges's pentecostal experience leads him to take his ecclesiological cues from the book of Acts. From this he discerns not only that the church is God's missionary agency to the ends of the earth but also that the Spirit empowers the church for the ministries of the gospel in various contexts. At the level of the individual, all persons, including nominal Christians, are to be brought into an experiential knowledge of the gospel and "into the fellowship of the life in the Holy Spirit."[6] At the corporate level, the Christian mission is to establish

---

3. Veli-Matti Kärkkäinen, *An Introduction to Ecclesiology: Ecumenical, Historical, and Global Perspectives* (Downers Grove, IL: InterVarsity, 2002), 72–74, asks whether there is any pentecostal ecclesiology.

4. This is seen in published systematic theology textbooks, e.g., Michael L. Dusing, "The New Testament Church," in *Systematic Theology: A Pentecostal Perspective*, ed. Stanley M. Horton, rev. ed. (Springfield, MO: Logion, 1995), 525–66; Guy P. Duffield and Nathaniel M. Van Cleave, *Foundations of Pentecostal Theology* (Los Angeles: L.I.F.E. Bible College Press, 1983), ch. 8; and J. Rodman Williams, *Renewal Theology*, vol. 3, *The Church, the Kingdom, and Last Things* (Grand Rapids: Zondervan, 1992), part 1.

5. Melvin L. Hodges, *The Indigenous Church*, rev. and enl. ed. (Springfield, MO: Gospel Publishing House, 1976); and *Build My Church* (Springfield, MO: Gospel Publishing House, 1957). For a contemporary reconstruction of the idea of the church as a missionary fellowship, see Steven J. Land, *Pentecostal Spirituality: A Passion for the Kingdom*, JPTSup 1 (Sheffield, Eng.: Sheffield Academic Press, 1993), ch. 3.

6. Melvin Hodges, *A Theology of the Church and Its Mission: A Pentecostal Perspective* (Springfield, MO: Gospel Publishing House, 1977), 95.

self-propagating, self-governing, and self-supporting local congregations and ministries. These would be the dominant features of what Hodges calls "the indigenous church": established, overseen, and developed by local (i.e., "native") leadership with (Western) missionaries serving only the role of consultants. Although Hodges's definition of the indigenous church is congruent with the pentecostal narrative of the diversity of tongues, which gave testimony to the mighty works of God on the day of Pentecost (see §4.1.2), Hodges nowhere makes this explicit connection, nor does he develop fully the ecclesiological implications of his pentecostal perspective. So, while Hodges's understanding of the church is practical (motivated as it is by the church's missionary mandate) and realistic (emergent as it is from the actual missionary experiences of the church), it assumes uncritically the free-church ecclesiology and inherits thereby all the problems that go along with it.

One of the challenging issues for free-church ecclesiology, especially when wedded to pentecostal missionary zeal, is that of proselytism. Hodges's missionary ecclesiology, which targets all "nominal Christians," has, by and large, become standard for most pentecostal evangelists. As the Finnish pentecostal systematician Veli-Matti Kärkkäinen has noted, however, this has resulted in alienating pentecostals from other Christian traditions,[7] thus highlighting the inner-Christian divisions for the unbelieving world, precisely because these attempts to evangelize those baptized in other churches are seen as illegitimate acts of "sheep stealing" by those churches. This is the issue of proselytism as a theological and ecclesiological matter, not just a practical one. If certain pentecostals consider certain baptized persons to be non-Christian, then these are appropriate evangelistic targets. The formal ecclesiological question has therefore emerged as urgent for pentecostals.

Not surprisingly, two pentecostals involved in ecumenical work have led the way in recent ecclesiological reflection: Simon Chan and Miroslav Volf. Chan has urged pentecostals to rethink their understanding of the church in dialogue with the great tradition of the church as a whole and the Christian spiritual tradition more particularly.[8] Central to his proposal is that pentecostals replace their individualized pneumatologies with an *ecclesial* pneumatology. Instead of prioritizing the believer's personal relationship with God, this relationship should be seen as mediated and constituted variously by the Spirit through the body of Christ. If the

---

7. Veli-Matti Kärkkäinen, *Toward a Pneumatological Theology: Pentecostal and Ecumenical Perspectives on Ecclesiology, Soteriology, and Theology of Mission*, ed. Amos Yong (Lanham, MD: University Press of America, 2002), ch. 14; cf. *PPP* 2:505; 3:144–46.

8. Simon Chan, *Pentecostal Theology and the Christian Spiritual Tradition*, JPTSup 21 (Sheffield, Eng.: Sheffield Academic Press, 2000), esp. ch. 4; and "Mother Church: Toward a Pentecostal Ecclesiology," *PNEUMA* 22, no. 2 (2000): 177–208, esp. 184–96.

church is thereby constituted by the Spirit, then, Chan suggests, there are corollaries. First, the church is thereby a dynamic and eschatological reality. Second, there is only one catholic church—there being only one Spirit—most evidently realized in the Eucharist (Chan does not shy away from this term given his conviction that pentecostals need to engage the historic ecclesiological traditions of "mother church"; I also will use "Eucharist" and "Supper" interchangeably in what follows). Third, the church is graced by the healing gifts of the Spirit, both in the Eucharist and in the charismata. Fourth, the church is a "truth-traditioning community" guided by the Spirit in its proclamation of the word. Fifth, the church is the means through which the Spirit is made present and active in the world; thus the concept of the universal Creator Spirit is carefully circumscribed, precisely in order to safeguard the identity of the Spirit as the Spirit of God and the Spirit of Jesus Christ.[9] Finally, the church constituted by the Spirit is a worshiping community whose liturgical play is intimately intertwined with, and made relevant by, the Spirit to the realities of everyday life. Throughout it is evident that Chan's ecclesial pneumatology signals the important ecclesiological questions for pentecostal theology.

Although Miroslav Volf's doctrine of the church is less distinctively pentecostal, his pentecostal upbringing and ongoing affiliation with pentecostalism have informed his deeply pneumatological ecclesiology.[10] His avowed purpose is to counter the individualistic tendencies in the free-church tradition by dialoguing with Catholic and Orthodox visions of the church. Volf hence traces the correlations between the doctrines of the church and the Trinity in the ecclesiology of Cardinal Joseph Ratzinger. In the Catholic hierarchical and sacramental ecclesiology as developed by Ratzinger, the individual stands in faith insofar as he or she participates in the local congregation, symbolized by the figure of the priests and bishops, and the local congregation does the same insofar as it participates in the church universal, symbolized by the union of bishops and cardinals under the pope. Salvation is understood in terms of moving from self-standing and self-centeredness toward being in communion with Christ as represented by the church. This ecclesial structure is illuminated by the light of Ratzinger's doctrine of the Trinity, which, following the tendency of Western trinitarian theology, locates the union of the triune God not at the level of persons, as in Eastern

9. Chan, *Pentecostal Theology and the Christian Spiritual Tradition*, 110–16. Chan's call to be circumspect about these matters is very important, even if I disagree with him about the importance of the *Creator Spirit* (see chs. 6–7 below).

10. Miroslav Volf, *After Our Likeness: The Church as the Image of the Trinity* (Grand Rapids: Eerdmans, 1998).

theology, but at the level of the one divine substance. Ratzinger's view thus reconceives personhood as activity but in the process dissolves the trinitarian persons into pure relations. At the same time, given the acceptance of the *Filioque*, there remains an implicit subordination even within the Godhead. These aspects of Ratzinger's understanding of the Trinity combine to ground an ecclesiology that subsumes the individual under the whole, the latter most perfectly and visibly manifest through the papacy, even as the trinitarian relations find their unity in the one divine substance.

Volf goes on to observe that the ontological personalism that equates being and personhood allows the Eastern Orthodox theologian John Zizioulas to retain the identities of the divine persons and develop a theological anthropology that maintains personal identity even while defining personality in terms of relations. Orthodox salvation—deification or *theōsis*—is the movement from isolated individuality to personal relationality through the Holy Spirit in the body of Christ. Participation in the Eucharist is the means by which faith is mediated and the pneumatic deindividualization of the person is accomplished, and the act that establishes the autonomy and the catholicity of the church in any geographical locality. Yet the monarchical structure of the Eastern understanding of the trinitarian relations—the Father as the source of the Son and the Spirit (see §5.2.1)—ultimately leads Zizioulas to an ecclesiology not too far from that of Ratzinger's. Because the one (the Father) constitutes the many (the Son and the Spirit) and the many are in turn conditioned by the one, so ecclesial relations are in symmetrical yet hierarchical fashion. Ultimately, there is a bipolarity of orders in the church, that of the laity and that of the bishops (as representatives of Christ), with the former being charismatically endowed as a whole rather than as particular individuals, with the primary purpose of acknowledging the unity of the church in their saying the "Amen" during the liturgy conducted by the latter.[11]

By contrast, Volf notes that the free-church model, descended in part from John Smyth, the sixteenth-century founder of the General Baptist movement in England, denies that the church is defined either by apostolic succession or by the communion of bishops. It highlights the unmediated presence of Christ to each believer through the Spirit instead of understanding such transmission sacramentally and values

---

11. Zizioulas's communion ecclesiology is trinitarian precisely because it is also robustly pneumatological; see John D. Zizioulas, *Being as Communion: Studies in Personhood and the Church* (Crestwood, NY: St. Vladimir's Seminary Press, 1985), esp. ch. 3; along with the claim of Michael Harper, *A Faith Fulfilled: Why Are Christians across Great Britain Embracing Orthodoxy?* (Ben Lomond, CA: Conciliar Press, 1999), ch. 15, that Eastern Orthodoxy is being charismatic rather than that Orthodoxy is having a charismatic renewal.

the subjective dimensions of ecclesial life over its objective institutions. Volf's constructive ecclesiology is thus inclusive of the best insights in both the episcopal and the free-church traditions. At its center is the confession of faith presupposing a theological anthropology that draws from the social model of the Trinity (see §5.2.3). In this model, the relations of the Trinity are understood perichoretically: each divine person indwells the other two without ceasing to be distinct. Although Volf acknowledges that this mutual coinherence is the exclusive prerogative of divinity, he extends this idea of interiority to human personhood. Human persons are constituted by God in relation to their environment, other persons, and God so as to be not only open to them but also able to internalize what is other than themselves. This process of being open to the other is central to Volf's soteriology and ecclesiology. Salvation is thereby understood pneumatologically both as the internalization of the Spirit in the individual (by faith) and as the internalization of the individual into the body of Christ (through baptism). Volf thereby attempts to negotiate the tensions faced by Ratzinger and Zizioulas between the one and the many, between unity and multiplicity, between individuality and universality, via the pneumatological, personalistic, and temporal categories of internalization/interiorization and openness.

What, then, can be said about pentecostal ecclesiology in light of this brief survey? First, pentecostalism in general does not have its own formally developed ecclesiology per se; rather, pentecostals have in general drawn uncritically from the free-church tradition. Second, pentecostal ecclesiology has been inevitably bound up with missiology; the nature of the church is essentially its missionary task. Third, pentecostal ecclesiology is inherently pneumatological; the church is founded by the Spirit, nurtured as a fellowship of and in the Spirit, and empowered by the Spirit to spread the gospel. Fourth, future pentecostal ecclesiology can no longer be attempted apart from the ecumenical conversation; the relationship between the Spirit and the sacraments, not to mention the ministry, will need to be reconsidered. Last (but certainly not least), though this is often only subconsciously assumed and hardly ever explicitly stated, pentecostal ecclesiology is intimately connected with its doctrine of salvation; the what of the church is by definition related to the question of what it means to be saved. But to say this is to confront the ecclesiological-soteriological question as understood by both the Catholic and the Orthodox theological traditions.

3.1.2 *The Contemporary Question: Whose Ecclesiology?* How, then, has the church understood this relationship between ecclesiology and soteriology? The following discussion is limited to four contemporary views. Whereas the *classical view* has connected Christian initiation and baptism as administered by the church, the *free-church* tradition has viewed salvation as dependent upon a personal confession of faith and has in the process rendered ecclesiology as a secondary reality and doctrine. Other notions include the *church as a spiritual reality* (emphasizing individual faith in terms of mystical union with Christ) and *postliberal ecclesiology* (the church as an alternative community, politics, and way of life).

The classical view: The traditional view of salvation through baptism has long been associated with the Petrine image of Noah's ark and its associated claim that a few persons "were saved through water. And baptism, which this prefigured, now saves you"; Peter goes on to say that baptism saves "not as a removal of dirt from the body, but as an appeal to God for a good conscience, through the resurrection of Jesus Christ" (1 Pet. 3:20b–21). Instead of disconnecting salvation from baptism, however, this underscores the relationship between baptism and Christian initiation (cf., e.g., John 3:5; Rom. 6:3–5; Col. 2:11–12; Titus 3:4–6) without denying the importance of either a good conscience bearing witness to the saving work of God or the future resurrection as the culmination of salvation, proleptically revealed in and experienced by Jesus. Insofar as baptism has always remained a prerogative of the church and its ministers, the traditional view has been most clearly captured by the Latin phrase *extra ecclesia nulla salus* (outside the church no salvation).[12] Just as important, the implied Lukan connection between baptism and the forgiveness of sins (Acts 2:38 and 22:16) and the postapostolic understanding of baptism as the antidote to the stain of original sin combined to give impetus to the idea of infant baptism as the means of ensuring the salvation of as many as possible (apart from other reasons for this practice).

Free churches: The Radical Reformers were the first to question seriously and extensively not only the practice of infant baptism but also the connection between salvation and baptism. If salvation is a matter of believing in one's heart and confessing with one's mouth the lordship of Jesus (cf. Rom. 10:9–13), then surely baptism follows repentance (Acts 2:38a) and signifies (not mediates) the gift of the forgiveness of sins. Further, the Protestant doctrine of the priesthood of all believers undermined the episcopal view of the church centered on her ministers and led over time to more democratic and congregationalist ecclesiologies that emphasized the importance of each individual's faith relationship with God.[13] Finally, the emergence of Pietism in the seventeenth and eighteenth centuries completed the shift within Protestantism away from

12. Francis A. Sullivan, *Salvation outside the Church? Tracing the History of the Catholic Response* (New York: Paulist, 1992).

13. See Stewart A. Newman, *A Free Church Perspective: A Study in Ecclesiology* (Wake Forest, NC: Stevens Book Press, 1986).

the sacramental definition of both church and salvation toward this more personalistic understanding. The result, however, is the interesting tension between a very propositionalistic approach to salvation, focused on the individual's verbal confession of Christ, and a very pietistic and relational view that emphasizes loving Jesus and having him in one's heart. Although evangelical and pentecostal traditions usually attempt to hold both together, there are ambiguities about what it means to confess Christ: for example, is the confession of the nontrinitarian Christ of Oneness Pentecostals, of the Arian Christ of the Jehovah's Witnesses, or of the heterodox Christ of Mormonism (albeit with its orthodox doctrine of the atonement) valid or sufficient? Further, what does it mean to be in relationship with Jesus? Is one's personal and subjective relationship with Jesus possible apart from any objective ecclesial interactions whatsoever? And finally, does not the free-church ecclesiology turn out to still hold the keys to salvation? The difference is that although salvation is mediated through baptism in the Catholic view, it is now mediated through the evangelistic activity of the priesthood of all believers.

The church as spiritual body: These ambiguities have led some theologians not only to emphasize pietistic over propositionalistic soteriologies but also to go one step further and define the human relationship with Christ in more mystical terms. Proponents of this view, usually categorized under the label of "soteriological inclusivism," assume at least (a) that Christ is not only the ontological basis for salvation but also the true light that has come into the world and has enlightened every person (cf. John 1:9); (b) that because God desires that none should perish and that all should be saved (1 Tim. 2:4; 2 Pet. 3:9), salvation by grace through faith should be understood in minimal epistemic terms, for example, that those who come to God must believe that God is and that God "rewards those who seek him" (Heb. 11:6); and (c) that God's righteous judgment will be accomplished in ways that take into account the particularities of each situation so that all will be commended or condemned according to their responses to the light that they had (cf. Rom. 2:14–16; Acts 10:35; Matt. 25:31–46).[14] Given the undeniable empirical fact that human knowledge of, and relationship with, Christ ranges widely according to these variables—for example, knowledge of Christ is spread across the spectrum of those who not only confess but also

14. Such was the response of Oneness pentecostal founding father Garfield T. Haywood when asked, "Are all those people who thought they were born of the Spirit, and were not, lost?" He replied, "No not by any means. They shall be given eternal life in the resurrection if they walked in all the light that was given them while they lived"; see Garfield T. Haywood, *The Birth of the Spirit in the Days of the Apostles* (Indianapolis: Christ Temple Book Store, n.d.), 12, repr. in *Seven "Jesus Only" Tracts*, ed. Donald W. Dayton (New York: Garland, 1985).

understand the Chalcedonian Creed, on the one end, to those who have never heard the name of Jesus, on the other, with those having varying degrees of orthodox and heterodox ideas all somewhere in between—it is suggested that the true church of Jesus Christ must exceed those who have conscious knowledge of, and relationship with, Jesus and include all those who through the grace of God are in some kind of mystical or spiritual union with him. Might these be the sheep outside the fold Jesus referred to (John 10:16)? In contemporary parlance, some theologians have followed the lead of Karl Rahner, SJ, and called them "anonymous Christians" insofar as human beings experience such mystical union with Christ by the Holy Spirit.[15] Although many evangelicals and pentecostals would take exception with Rahner's explicit characterizations, most soteriological inclusivists would agree that this view leads away from a visible, hierarchical, and institutional ecclesiology to one that sees the church first and foremost as a spiritual reality. The saved would be limited neither to the formally baptized nor even to those with formal church membership. Rather, the mystical and universal body of Christ would include the entire spectrum from all those who explicitly confess his name to all who may not be knowledgeable about Jesus but are spiritually united with him by the power of the Holy Spirit.[16]

Postliberal ecclesiology: No doubt this mystical soteriology and ecclesiology is too nebulous for many who would prefer to remain agnostic about how God deals with those either incompletely evangelized or unevangelized. Among these are postliberal theologians seeking to understand what it means to be the church neither according to the epistemic categories of modern rationalism nor according to the subjectivistic categories of Pietism or classical liberalism but according to sensibilities informed by our post-Enlightenment and even post-Christendom situation.[17] In this context, the church should resist being defined by

15. Rahner discusses this concept in many places, but he connects it specifically with the ecclesiological question in Karl Rahner, "Observations on the Problem of the 'Anonymous Christian,'" trans. David Bourke, in *Theological Investigations*, 23 vols. (New York: Seabury, 1976), 14:280–94. See also Richard Lennan, *The Ecclesiology of Karl Rahner* (Oxford: Clarendon, 1995), esp. 38–40.

16. See Avery Dulles, SJ, *Models of the Church* (Garden City, NY: Doubleday, 1974), ch. 3.

17. Representative are Rodney Clapp, *A Peculiar People: The Church as Culture in a Post-Christian Society* (Downers Grove, IL: InterVarsity, 1996); Barry Harvey, *Another City: An Ecclesiological Primer for a Post-Christian World* (Harrisburg, PA: Trinity Press International, 1999); Miroslav Volf and Dorothy C. Bass, eds., *Practicing Theology: Beliefs and Practices in Christian Life* (Grand Rapids: Eerdmans, 2002); Jeffrey Goh, *Christian Tradition Today: A Postliberal Vision of Church and World* (Louvain: Peeters, 2000); and George Lindbeck, *The Church in a Postliberal Age*, ed. James J. Buckley (Grand Rapids: Eerdmans, 2003).

outside cultural forces, whether these be the politics of Constantine or the dictates of (allegedly) universal reason. Rather, Christians should provide an alternative vision of what it means to be a community that is the people of God, a vision that at the same time overcomes the dichotomies between sacred and secular, between religion and politics, and between Christianity and culture precisely by articulating how the church provides for an entire way of life that embraces what modernity separates off as the secular, the political, and the cultural. In this way, the church develops a distinctive *habitus*, replete with its own set of ethical convictions, moral virtues, and scriptural and doctrinal narratives that regulate how Christians go about being followers of Jesus.[18] Consequently, the question of salvation is subordinated in this framework to that regarding the nature of the ecclesial, liturgical, and ethical narratives and practices that guide, inform, and structure Christian life.

None of these ecclesiologies are mutually exclusive even as each poses distinctive questions to any attempt to develop a constructive doctrine of the church. The classical ecclesiologies can no longer be simply dismissed in our ecumenical age, just as free-church ecclesiologies cannot be uncritically repeated. Further, the pentecostal disposition toward spiritualizing the nature of the church demands that the promise and challenges of soteriological inclusivism be confronted. Finally, the embodied and communal vision of postliberal ecclesiologies is attractive for various reasons today. What, then, is the way forward for any constructive ecclesiological statement in the twenty-first century?

3.1.3 *The Historical Question: Why Ecclesiology?* Given that the question about the nature of the church concerns the question about Christian identity, it is clear from the preceding that any constructive ecclesiology will need to grapple with the issues as historically understood. Even those advocating explicitly postliberal ecclesiologies retrieve and reappropriate aspects of what has been handed down. Might it therefore be that the way forward is the way back, perhaps as far back as the Nicene Creed with its confession of the church as one, holy, catholic, and apostolic?

These four notes or marks have long been at the heart of the church's self-understanding. Yet as Francis Sullivan points out, the marks have remained an undefined doctrine of faith in the sense that they have

---

18. For the notion of the church as an ethical and moral community, see the works of Stanley Hauerwas, beginning with *A Community of Character: Toward a Constructive Christian Social Ethic* (Notre Dame, IN: University of Notre Dame Press, 1981). For the idea of doctrine as ecclesiological grammar, see George Lindbeck, *The Nature of Doctrine: Religion and Theology in a Postliberal Age* (Philadelphia: Westminster, 1984); and Richard Heyduck, *The Recovery of Doctrine: An Essay in Philosophical Ecclesiology* (Waco: Baylor University Press, 2002).

been asserted but never elaborated dogmatically.[19] Newcomers to the ecclesiological block (such as pentecostals) might wonder why this is the case. The implicit response is that one asserts but does not define what seems self-evident. But further, dogmatic pronouncements without dogmatic commentary invite reflection and free the church to explore such declarations. Thus any attempt to understand the marks is an act of traditioning, a participation in the chorus of such efforts over the centuries. The church always will wrestle with the marks so long as self-understanding is sought.

But what did the early church fathers mean in declaring the *ekklēsia* to be one, holy, catholic, and apostolic? Developments during the second through fourth centuries are pivotal to any preliminary understanding of this confession. As a minority group during this period, the church was a way of life marginal to the social, political, and economic mainstream. Not infrequently the church was persecuted as a threat to the interests of society and the reigning government. Besides these pressures from outside, the church also confronted internal developments that raised questions about discerning truth from falsehood. Marcionism, Montanism, Gnosticism, and Donatism, among others, were movements that challenged the church to reflect on the apostolic tradition, on the place and role of charisma, on the meaning of morality and ethical rigor, on the nature, function, and role of the bishop, and so on. Engaging Praxeas, Celsus, Sabellius, Arius, and their followers demanded that the early Christians clarify what was believed everywhere, always, and by all. Through all of these encounters, the church was forced to ask itself repeatedly what the nature of the church of Jesus Christ is and how such is to be discerned.

The traditional marks of the church emerged amidst such developments. One might begin with the church as the one body of Christ, a body consisting of individual believers and local congregations, all of which constitute the body precisely because of the communion or fellowship they experience with each other both individually and congregationally. Insofar as the churches remain in communion with each other, the church is one; insofar as individuals or congregations remove themselves from such communion, the result is not a division of the church (for those who remain in communion continue to reflect the unity of the body) but rather heresy—withdrawal from fellowship and separation such that one no longer can be considered to be part of the body of Christ. But what is the source of this communion? Is it not the apostolic witness? Further, how is this communion mediated? Perhaps

---

19. Francis A. Sullivan, SJ, *The Church We Believe In: One, Holy, Catholic, and Apostolic* (New York: Paulist, 1988), 211–14.

through the bishops; perhaps through the sacraments; perhaps through the holiness brought about by the Holy Spirit, who is the breath of life of the body. Finally, what is the extent of this communion? Is it not to the ends of the earth (Acts 1:8), to all who actually are in communion with the body of believers and/or with its mediating structures?

The underlying concern is that of discerning true from false churches, the real body of Christ from what is not the body of Christ. Each of the marks thus presupposes and defines the others. Holiness marks the character of the church consecrated to Christ and to the work of the kingdom of God. Catholicity contrasts with sectarianism (thus opposing factionalism, heresies, and heretics) and partiality (thus opposing regionalism and elitist claims such as made by the Donatists during the early fourth century). Apostolicity points to the authority of the church, her ministry, Scriptures, sacraments, teachings, and so on, built as she is on the foundation of the apostles and prophets (Eph. 2:20). None of these marks, however, is subordinate to any other. Each is intrinsic to the church's self-understanding of its nature and definition. To dispense with or subject one to any of the others is to undermine the rest. Apostolicity is the source of ecclesiality. Catholicity is the extent of ecclesiality. Holiness is the means of ecclesiality. Unity is the fact or reality of ecclesiality.

One way forward for pentecostal ecclesiological reflection, therefore, is to engage in a self-critical dialogue with the traditional marks or notes of the church. Pentecostal self-definition, an ecclesiological matter, can be sharpened by wrestling with the church's traditional self-understanding. Further, at some point, pentecostals will need to confront the question of whether the norms for orthodox ecclesiology are established by the historical tradition. On this matter, part of the question to be negotiated is this: in what ways and why should pentecostal theology in general and ecclesiology in particular be constrained by the dogmatic traditions of the church? Finally, pentecostals surely have much to learn about ecclesiology from the Christian tradition. Yet the hypothesis I am testing is that pentecostal reflection on these traditional marks from a pneumatological perspective can not only help retrieve them for our time but also provide for an enriched understanding of the church's self-definition.

In one sense, to reread the marks of the church from a pneumatological perspective is nothing new. Yves Congar, one of the premier Roman Catholic theologians during and after Vatican II, had already attempted something similar.[20] In his own efforts to develop a pneumatological

---

20. Yves Congar, *I Believe in the Holy Spirit*, trans. David Smith, 3 vols. (New York: Seabury; London: Geoffrey Chapman, 1983).

ecclesiology, he notes, "However far we go back in the sequence of confessions of faith or creeds, we find the article on the Church linked to that on the Holy Spirit" (*BHS* 2:5). Thus the marks of the church are embedded in confession regarding the Holy Spirit. The Nicene-Constantinopolitan (381) Creed reads, "We believe in the Holy Spirit, the Lord, the giver of life, who proceeds from the Father. With the Father and the Son he is worshipped and glorified. He has spoken through the Prophets. We believe in one holy catholic and apostolic Church."[21] As ecclesiology has always been linked to the third article of the creed, Congar himself goes on to treat the traditional marks of the church in light of the Spirit, who "animates the Church" (*BHS*, vol. 2, part 1).[22]

3.2 The Marks of the Church: Pentecostal and Pneumatological Perspectives

This section compares and contrasts Congar's pneumatological approach within the Catholic framework with pentecostal perspectives, anticipating the more fully developed pneumatological ecclesiology presented in §3.3. Methodologically, it makes observations about the marks of the church in light of post–Vatican II understandings and suggests ways in which pentecostal sensibilities can contribute toward a more ecumenical and pneumatological ecclesiology.[23] This comparative exercise is especially appropriate given that the third quinquennium of the Roman Catholic–Pentecostal dialogue (1985–1989) had pneumatological ecclesiology as one of its guiding themes.[24] This window into the Roman Catholic–Pentecostal dialogue may be illuminating for both the larger ecumenical conversation in general and for pneumatological reflection on ecclesiology more specifically. My goal is to bring together the need for further pentecostal reflection on its own identity

21. Henry Bettenson, *Documents of the Christian Church*, 2nd ed. (Oxford: Oxford University Press, 1963), 26.

22. Thomas C. Oden, *Systematic Theology*, vol. 3, *Life in the Spirit* (San Francisco: HarperSanFrancisco, 1992), 297, puts it plainly: "To say the church is one, holy, catholic, and apostolic is to confess the Holy Spirit as the one who unites, cleanses, and sends the church to the whole world."

23. The need for pentecostals to wrestle with the ecclesiological tradition in general and with these traditional marks of the church in particular has been noted by others; see, e.g., Huibert Zegwaart, "The Place of the Church in the Economy of Salvation: Roman Catholic and Pentecostal Perspectives—Room for Rapprochement," *JEPTA* 21 (2001): 26–40, esp. 39.

24. See Veli-Matti Kärkkäinen, *Spiritus ubi vult spirat: Pneumatology in Roman Catholic–Pentecostal Dialogue (1972–1989)* (Helsinki: Luther-Agricola-Society, 1998), esp. 324–27.

with the task of developing a world pentecostal theology and to do so by ecumenical engagement with the historical and dogmatic traditions of the church. Along the way, some responses will also be made to the challenging questions concerning the relationship between ecclesiology and soteriology posed by contemporary ecclesiologies (§3.1.2).

3.2.1 *The Spirit and the Unity of the Church*. In Congar's discussion, the Holy Spirit is the principle of unity in the church (*BHS* 2:15–20) in three senses. First, the Spirit is not one because of the church but vice versa (1 Cor. 12:13; Eph. 4:4). The Spirit is the personal reality who makes many individuals into a community of persons. The Spirit is the source of unity amidst diversity, plurality, and difference. Yet such unity does not mean uniformity, precisely because the Spirit's unifying power enables the integrity of each one amidst the many. Second, although Christ is the author of the church and the head of the body, the Spirit is "the subject who brings about everything that depends on grace" and is therefore "the supreme and transcendent effective personality of the Church"—what the church fathers called the "soul of the Church" (*BHS* 2:19–20). Thus the church is the one body of Christ, infused with the life of Christ through the Spirit. Last, the unity of the church is understood concretely in the everyday lives of believers. Here the Spirit is poured out into hearts, resulting in solidarity and practical love. In all of this, Congar's pneumatological vision contains all the necessary elements for a sound theology of the church as the mystical body of Christ—a theology that few pentecostals will object to.

Yet in the background of Congar's exposition is the specter of Roman Catholic self-understanding. In that framework, the papacy represents the unity of the church, the episcopate, the sacraments, the liturgy, the teaching ministry, and so on. As Congar acknowledges, this unity in Roman Catholic Christianity is less uniformity than usually realized, since the accent lies more on the interiority of the Spirit's life and presence in the church and less on the exterior manifestations of the Spirit's work. At the same time, it is also undeniable that the diversity of Roman Catholic Christianity finds its cohesion and union in the bishop of Rome. Hence, any visible unity of the *ecclēsia* is located primarily in the Petrine office. The Catholic claim regarding the papacy stands in some ways as a scandal of particularity in the ecumenical church's self-understanding.

Pentecostals certainly would affirm the unity of the church.[25] They would deny, however, that any one episcopate constitutes that unity. Rather, "Pentecostals tend to view denominations as more or less legitimate

---

25. So Hollis Gause, *Living in the Spirit: The Way of Salvation* (Cleveland, TN: Pathway, 1980), 105–14.

manifestations of the one, universal Church."[26] Emphasis is thereby placed first and foremost on a spiritual and mystical reality that is never fully visible in the concrete structures of space-time.[27] But is not such emphasis on spiritual unity deceiving if the pentecostal understanding is devoid of concrete aspects? Because ecclesial unity is experienced in the fellowship of those who confess Jesus as Lord by the Holy Spirit (cf. 1 Cor. 12:3), such unity is eschatological but also supremely particularistic, perhaps even sacramental.[28]

Pentecostal sacramentality should *not* be considered in the classical sense, whereby salvation is mediated through the priesthood, through baptism, or through the (other) sacraments. Rather, insofar as pentecostals are convinced that the Spirit who resides within and presides over the church is the same Spirit who anointed Jesus of Nazareth and that the Spirit is truly encountered and manifest palpably and tangibly in the lives of individuals who constitute the church—for example, through tongues, healings, the shout, and the dance—the Spirit's reality is mediated through the particularly embodied experiences of the community of saints. There is therefore a unique sort of pentecostal sacramentality at work, an experiential and incarnational logic that acknowledges the Spirit's being made present and active through the materiality of personal embodiment and congregational life.[29]

But more important, pentecostal sacramentality means that the unity of the church comes about through the eschatological work of the Spirit. The Word made flesh and the Spirit breathing and making the Word real in and through the community of saints together constitute the one work of the triune God. Such an account of ecclesial unity as both spiritual and embodied undergirds the pentecostal notion of unity in diversity. This is not, however, for diversity's sake but for the sake of the reconciliation

26. "*Final Report* of the International Roman Catholic/Pentecostal Dialogue (1985–1989)," §34, in *PNEUMA* 12, no. 2 (1990): 124.

27. Cecil M. Robeck Jr., "Pentecostals and Visible Church Unity," *One World* (January–February 1994): 11–14; and "The Challenge Pentecostalism Poses to the Quest for Ecclesial Unity," in *Die Kirche in ökumenischer Perspektive*, ed. Peter Walter, Klaus Krämer, and George Augustin (Freiburg, Switz.: Herder, 2003), 306–20.

28. On the importance of sacramentality to ecclesiology, see Simon Chan, *Spiritual Theology: A Systematic Study of the Christian Life* (Downers Grove, IL: InterVarsity, 1998), 112–21.

29. On this idea of a pentecostal sacramentality, I follow Frank Macchia, "Tongues as a Sign: Toward a Sacramental Understanding of Pentecostal Experience," *PNEUMA* 15, no. 1 (1993): 61–76; and "Signs Too Deep for Words: Toward a Theology of Glossolalia," *JPT* 1 (1992): 47–73. See also John Gunstone, *Pentecost Comes to Church: Sacraments and Spiritual Gifts* (London: Darton, Longman & Todd, 1994), chs. 4–6; and Mark J. Cartledge, *Charismatic Glossolalia: An Empirical-Theological Study* (Burlington, VT: Ashgate, 2002), 193–99.

of a broken creation. Pentecostals also sense the pain of disunity and separation, and ecumenically conscious pentecostals would agree with Gerhard Lohfink, who calls disunity the church's "deepest wound."[30] But how is such disunity to be overcome? Recognizing the enormity of the problem, should not confession of the unity of the church also include confession of the disunity of the church in a manner similar to acknowledging God as present and yet hidden?

Here lies the significance of the pentecostal appeal to the eschatological Spirit as the one who mediates disunity into unity in a "sacramental" (pentecostal) sense. This paradigm of unity-in-diversity as reconciliation emerges from the pneumatic and charismatic intuitions derived from the pentecostal experience. The pentecostal experience at Azusa Street, which overcame gender, ethnic, racial, and socioeconomic barriers present in American life at the turn of the twentieth century, simply reembodied the eschatological outpouring of the Spirit on the day of Pentecost and in the life of the early church (§2.2.1). The pentecostal experience, then and now, brings sons and daughters together with menservants and maidservants—no small feat for a world ruled by patriarchy. It binds Samaritans, Ethiopians, and other Gentiles together with Jews—again, a major achievement in a world of ethnic and racial hostilities. It reconciles into one body the haves and have-nots through various means, whether it be the securing of justice (Zacchaeus in Luke 19:1–10), the redistribution of goods (Barnabas in Acts 4:36–37 and the widows in Acts 6:1), or the affirmation of the ministry of the well-to-do among those less well off (Dorcas in Acts 9:36–43 and Lydia in Acts 16:13–15). The case of the Ethiopian eunuch is particularly noteworthy here (Acts 8:27–39). Not only does the inclusion in the body of Christ of this high-ranking foreign official cut across ethnic, socioeconomic, and political lines; it also emphatically demarginalizes those who for physical reasons were barred from the assembly (cf. Deut. 23:1; Isa. 56:3–5).[31]

---

30. Gerhard Lohfink, *Does God Need the Church? Toward a Theology of the People of God*, trans. Linda M. Maloney (Collegeville, MN: Liturgical Press, 1999), 290–308.

31. It is bad enough to be a eunuch and excluded by the law as such; it is worse yet if one is a homosexual, as suggested by black pentecostal (and gay) theologian James S. Tinney, "'What Doth Hinder Me?' The Conversion of a Black Homosexual as Recorded by St. Luke" (sermon given at the Metropolitan Community Church of Philadelphia, November 15, 1981; typescript available from the Associated Mennonite Biblical Seminary Library, Elkhart, IN). Tinney suggests—without much documentation, given the kind of source this is—that eunuchs in the ancient Near Eastern world were at least disposed toward homosexuality, if not practicing homosexuals. Various questions, however, have to be posed to this hypothesis. First, the eunuch is a liminal category in late antiquity with a wide range of meanings—e.g., male or "temple" prostitutes, devotees of the goddess Cybele, and court officials. Further, eunuchs in the first century appear to have had the reputation of being asexual (cf. Matt. 19:12). Finally, the Ethiopian eunuch

Though beginning among the variously marginalized of American society, pentecostalism was and is driven by a convergence of a diversity of perspectives and experiences brought about by the eschatological work of the Spirit of God. Those who have continued in obedience to the Spirit's leading and have been sensitive to the church's calling toward unity have also recognized the ecumenical potential of pentecostal-charismatic spirituality and participated in the reconciling work of the Spirit through the later charismatic-renewal movements.[32] But given human fallibility and sinfulness, even the unity of pentecostal faith and experience was insufficient to keep the movement from splintering into innumerable factions. Ongoing repentance and acts of reconciliation have been and should continue to be normative (see §4.2.3).

All of this does not deny that pentecostals affirm spiritual over institutional or structured unity. Yet such spiritual unity is not devoid of concrete manifestations across the spectrum of Christian life; it is, rather, a unity that includes reconciliation and healing. And such unity is to be experienced in the Spirit, who brings those otherwise separated together in Jesus Christ in anticipation of the eschatological union before the throne of God. Perhaps this pneumato-eschatological framework provides for the possibility of convergence between the free-church confession of Jesus as Lord and the mystical-church emphasis on spiritual union insofar as both are pneumatologically constituted by the presence and activity of

---

appears to have been a Godfearer inasmuch as he is said to have "come to Jerusalem to worship" (Acts 8:28), and Jewish traditions of the first century had not abandoned the Levitical laws against homosexuality. Yet Tinney is at least correct to see that whatever the eunuch's sexual identity in this case, Philip accepted and baptized him. Much more research needs to be done to increase our understanding of biblical references to eunuchs before Tinney's thesis gains wider acceptance. But it is certainly the case that pentecostals need to begin thinking and talking about more appropriate Christian responses to homosexuals and the homosexual community than they have traditionally shown; this is how pentecostals can engage Tinney's legacy. For orienting discussions on eunuchs, see Halvor Moxnes, *Putting Jesus in His Place: A Radical Vision of Household and Kingdom* (Louisville: Westminster John Knox, 2003), ch. 4; and Theodore W. Jennings Jr., *The Man Jesus Loved: Homoerotic Narratives from the New Testament* (Cleveland: Pilgrim, 2003), ch. 9. On homosexuality and first-century Judaism, see Lewis John Eron, "Homosexuality and Judaism," in *Homosexuality and World Religions*, ed. Arlene Swidler (Valley Forge, PA: Trinity Press International, 1993), 103–34; and Martti Nissinen, *Homoeroticism in the Biblical World: A Historical Perspective*, trans. Kirsi Stjerna (Minneapolis: Fortress, 1988), ch. 5. For one model of how Christians should respond on this issue, see Willard M. Swartley, *Homosexuality: Biblical Interpretation and Moral Discernment* (Scottsdale, PA: Herald, 2003), esp. chs. 7–8. My thanks to Jan Everhart for directing me to some of the recent scholarship on biblical eunuchs.

32. See Daniel E. Albrecht, "Pentecostal Spirituality: Ecumenical Potential and Challenge," *CPCR* 2 (1997), http://www.pctii.org/cybertab.html. For more on the ecumenical potential of Pentecostalism, see the next chapter.

the present and coming Spirit. Put ecclesiologically, the church is one only even while she is being made one. In the here and now, we have a preliminary experience of the "communion of the Holy Spirit" (2 Cor. 13:13) that provides a foretaste of the final reconciliation to come.

3.2.2 *The Spirit and the Holiness of the Church.* Regarding the church as holy, for Congar, the Spirit is both the principle of the church's holiness and the sanctifying agent of individuals in the church (*BHS* 2:52–61). This is because the church is the temple or habitation of a holy God, joined as one with God through the mediatorship of the Son, who by the incarnation was betrothed to be married to his bride, the church, and now awaits consummation of this wedding at the marriage supper of the Lamb. The Spirit thus indwells the church as the firstfruits or down payment of this eschatological event. Meanwhile, however, the church struggles as a collection of sinners even while she is declared to be, and is working out her identity as, a community of saints through participation in the love of the Spirit. The holiness of the church is therefore not a human accomplishment but an eschatological gift.

Pentecostals would resonate especially with the dynamism evident in Congar's reflections on the holiness of the church. Thus much overall agreement could be reached between pentecostals and Catholics on the importance and connectedness of holiness, repentance, and ministry.[33] Holiness, in other words, is not so much a static category pertinent to Christian identity as it is an energetic, potent, and charismatic reality experienced in Christian life. This is especially the case among the pentecostals within the Wesleyan Holiness trajectory of the movement who emphasize the both-now-and-not-yet dynamic of holiness as marking authentic ecclesiality. The pentecostal perspective thus dovetails well with Thomas Oden's statement that "the chief proof of the church's holiness, ironically, is that it is found among sinners, redeeming, reaching out, healing, and sanctifying."[34]

Still, it is also the case that pentecostalism includes its fair share of legalists who understand holiness in a fairly static manner. There are also, unfortunately, too many examples of pentecostals who supposedly manifest the gifts of the Spirit but lack the fruits thereof. In these cases, pentecostals agree with Congar and the church universal that holiness is, finally, an eschatological goal. In the meanwhile, insofar as Jesus established a mercy-based rather than ritual-based approach to holiness, pentecostals also need to instantiate how a community of sinners is transformed toward saintliness through divine mercy and grace.

---

33. *"Final Report,"* §§102–8, in *PNEUMA* 12, no. 2 (1990): 138–39.
34. Oden, *Life in the Spirit,* 319.

What, then, might pentecostals possess to contribute to the broader ecclesial understanding of the church as holy? Perhaps the pentecostal gift to the church ecumenical is a pneumatologically robust notion of sanctifying transformation. Hans Küng's discussion of the church's holiness highlights the fact that holiness refers first of all to the divine nature and therefore carries the sense of being set apart or consecrated for the service of God. Rather than pointing to human activity, "what matters is the sanctifying will and word of God."[35] From the pentecostal perspective, the Spirit sets members of the body of Christ apart from the world for the work of the kingdom of God. More specifically, the Spirit clothes the believer with "power from on high" in order that he or she might bear witness to Jesus (cf. Luke 24:49; Acts 1:8).

There should be more, however, to the witness of the Spirit-filled believer than this dimension of verbal testimony. More recently pentecostals are also observing the intrinsic connection between the kerygmatic witness of the saints and the calling of the church toward participation in the prophetic activity of socioethical engagement. The church is, after all, not only a royal priesthood but also what Roger Stronstad calls a "prophethood of believers."[36] Luke-Acts shows that Jesus is the eschatological prophet who is mighty in word and deed—indeed, the paradigm for the earliest Christians, including Stephen, Philip, Barnabas, Agabus, Peter, and Paul. And among other things, prophets are called to "proclaim release to the captives and recovery of sight to the blind, to let the oppressed go free, to proclaim the year of the Lord's favor" (Luke 4:18–19). Thus Jesus' prophetic words and deeds are redemptive regarding the structures of oppression—for example, the parables of the persistent widow and the Pharisee and tax collector, Jesus' raising the only son of the widow of Nain from the dead, his acceptance of the sinful woman, his treatment of women, his attitudes toward Samaritans, and the reception and transformation of Zacchaeus. Just as redemptive are the words and actions of the early Christian community—for example, the communitarian restructuring whereby "all who believed were together and had all things in common" (Acts 2:44), caring for widows otherwise socially vulnerable, and the provision of famine relief. These prophetic actions, it could be argued, are part and parcel of the work of divinely consecrated and anointed ones, the community of prophetic saints.

35. Hans Küng, *The Church*, trans. Ray Ockenden and Rosaleen Ockenden (New York: Sheed & Ward, 1967), 324–30; quotation, 324.

36. Roger Stronstad, *The Prophethood of All Believers: A Study in Luke's Charismatic Theology*, JPTSup 16 (Sheffield, Eng.: Sheffield Academic Press, 1999).

The key to this divine restructuring lies not in the word and work of prophets in and of themselves but in the transformative power of the eschatological Spirit who comes upon them. As Matthias Wenk has pointed out, it is precisely the work of the Spirit not only to sanctify or consecrate believers apart for the prophetic word and work of the kingdom but also to accomplish such transformation in and through them.[37] Prophetically inspired speech is the medium through which the divine intent is made manifest and the believing community is transformed. In contemporary parlance, these are speech acts: words that not only tell us something but also do something and bring something about.[38] The prophetic message of John the Baptist, for example, was the means through which God warned Israel, the tax collectors, and the soldiers and that produced in them repentance (Luke 3:1–14). Yet it was also a message that left a mark on the messenger himself, since John could not be a voice proclaiming in the wilderness without having his home in the desert. Spirit-inspired speech thus has specific transformative effects on both the speaker and the audience.[39]

Elsewhere, the Spirit-inspired speeches in the infancy narratives (Luke 1–2) herald the new, restoring work of God that is about to transpire through Jesus and the believing community. Jesus' ministry of reconstituting a liberated community is itself anointed by the Spirit (Luke 4:18–19). Luke's version of what we have come to identify as the Lord's Prayer (11:2–4) is the means through which the people of God ask and receive the life-transforming and community-forming power of the Spirit of God (11:13). Pentecost (Acts 2) is a liberative and sanctifying event of the Spirit that results in the formation of the new messianic community (2:42–47). As already mentioned, throughout Acts, the Spirit's speech acts level out socioeconomic, ethnic, and gender differences even while these same speech acts identify, mark, and guide the people of God. Wenk's exposition thus highlights the restoring, reconciling, and sanctifying work of the Spirit that brings human beings

37. Matthias Wenk, *Community-Forming Power: The Socio-ethical Role of the Spirit in Luke-Acts*, JPTSup 19 (Sheffield, Eng.: Sheffield Academic Press, 2000).

38. There are three basic aspects to speech acts: locutionary, illocutionary, and perlocutionary. The first is the act of saying something; the second is doing something in the saying, e.g., when directives or requests are given; and the third is what is brought about by the saying, e.g., a marriage, when a judge says, "I pronounce you man and wife." See J. L. Austin, *How to Do Things with Words* (Cambridge, MA: Harvard University Press, 1962); and John Searle, *Speech Acts: An Essay in the Philosophy of Language* (London: Cambridge University Press, 1969); cf. Amos Yong, *Spirit–Word–Community: Theological Hermeneutics in Trinitarian Perspective* (Burlington, VT: Ashgate, 2002), 254–59.

39. Congar does mention that so long as the Spirit of God continues to speak through divinely appointed prophets today, then "the proposal of an objective revelation . . . implies a corresponding 'spirit of revelation' in the subjects who are to receive it" (*BHS* 2:30).

into relationship with God and each other. My listening to what the Spirit is saying includes my being open to being transformed by what is said—not just myself but all those who claim to be of the Spirit of God and are claimed by that same Spirit.

At the same time, the rejection of a prophecy is not only a rejection of the prophet, or of the word of the prophet, but also of the sanctifying work of the Spirit of God. Using sources from the intertestamental period, Wenk is able to show that what scholars have claimed is the cessation of prophecy during this time is perhaps better understood as reflecting the unwillingness of the people of God to hear, engage, or be transformed by the word of God.[40] In other words, it may not be—either during the intertestamental centuries, the early Christian period, or since—that the Spirit of God has ceased to speak and act; rather, a hard-hearted and hard-of-hearing people have refused to accept the message, the messenger (the inspired prophet), and the sanctifying work of God (cf. Acts 7:51; 28:25–28). Prophecy, then, never ceases; instead it is denied, ignored, neglected, or rejected by the unfaithful community resisting the purposes of God and the transformative work of the Spirit.

Clearly, Christian holiness can no longer be understood in purely individualistic terms. Rather, the *rhēma* word of the Spirit of God is formative and transformative for individuals in community. The entire church is hereby challenged by the fact that the words of the Spirit go beyond conveying information to transforming hearers open to what the Spirit is saying and doing. The holiness of the church thus marks not the accomplishments of its members but the authentic presence and activity of the Spirit of God directed toward the eschatological kingdom. In this sense, the Spirit of holiness both sets the *ekklēsia* apart, as in but not of the world, and transforms her toward the image of Jesus; the church is not only holy but also being made holy.

This identification of the church's holiness as both eschatological and communal may also mediate between the emphasis on individual holiness (especially the free-church traditions) and corporate holiness (especially sacramental and mystical ecclesiologies). The former can be upheld within a dynamic account of the Spirit's sanctifying work in the lives of believers, and the latter provides the larger historical and eschatological context in which the purified bride of Christ is set apart for the day of the Lord and the marriage supper of the Lamb (cf. Eph. 5:25–27). Additionally, in this account, the sanctification of individual believers occurs in and through each one participating in the practices of the church, as articulated by postliberal ecclesiologies.

40. Wenk, *Community-Forming Power*, 112–18, 122–33.

3.2.3 *The Spirit and the Catholicity of the Church.* The particular and yet universal mission of Jesus and his followers, both anointed by the Spirit, to many peoples, tongues, tribes, and nations informs the Roman Catholic vision of Congar. The church is thereby charismatic, reflecting the diversity of gifts from the Spirit to these peoples, tongues, tribes, and nations. Herein lies the catholicity or universality of the church (*BHS* 2:24–35). It is, after all, the Spirit who brings about the church's universality in and through the illumination of Christ in the whole counsel of the Scriptures, the teaching tradition and ministry of the church, and the liturgy. More precisely, it is the Spirit who inspires the contextualization of the gospel message in the church's missionary work throughout history precisely by enabling the discernment and interpretation of the various places, times, and events in which the gospel is planted and through which it unfolds. In all of these, it is just as well to understand the catholicity of the church eschatologically, after the eschatological Spirit who continues to form the church catholic.[41]

Various pentecostal responses follow, beginning with saying, "Amen!" to the Catholic definition of ecclesial catholicity as signifying the whole faith belonging to the whole body of Christ for the whole world. The whole faith is none other than the apostolic witness to Jesus Christ (§3.2.4). The whole body includes all who confess "Jesus is Lord" by the Holy Spirit (1 Cor. 12:3). The whole world refers not only to the eschatological gathering of peoples, tongues, tribes, and nations (Rev. 5:9b, etc.) but also to the continually expanding kingdom of God (cf. the parables of Matt. 13).

Yet along these lines, pentecostals would be hesitant to affirm catholicity in the sense of universality at the expense of particularity in the sense of locality. Here pentecostal charismology (§7.3.1) informs pentecostal ecclesiology and vice versa. The church charismatic flows from the manifestation of the gifts through each member, which serves the common good (1 Cor. 12:4–7). Each member's gifting is essential precisely because he or she constitutes the body of Christ (1 Cor. 12:12–27). Individual members constitute local congregations, which combine, finally, as the church catholic. In understanding both the charismatic giftedness and the ecclesial constitution of the church, pentecostals therefore emphasize the particularity of local congregations and individual members.

This leads to a consideration of the interdependence of the notions of catholicity (universality) and unity. If Catholicism tends to err on the side of universality, pentecostalism does on the side of locality. Therefore

---

41. In what follows, I distinguish between "Catholic" (capitalized), referring to communion with the bishop of Rome, and "catholic" (not capitalized), referring to the universality of the *ekklēsia*.

global pentecostalism has not generally been as concerned with ecumenism at either structural or institutional levels. But what about the
ecumenical movement? More specifically, what about the relationship
between the churches and the church catholic, and vice versa? Is it the
case that denominationalism and congregationalism are true expressions of New Testament Christianity, as Protestants insist? Hans Küng
has raised the issues forcefully:

> [Is it really] feasible in the light of the New Testament to regard these
> divisions as an organic development? . . . Is it not simply an easy way out
> of our obligation to work for unity here and now, to bring in eschatologi-
> cal fulfillment? . . . We should not justify these divisions, any more than
> we justify sin, but "suffer" them as a dark enigma, an absurd, ridiculous,
> tolerable yet intolerable fact of life, that is contrary both to the will of
> God and the good of mankind. . . . The Churches, apart from the so-called
> "Catholic Church," cannot achieve the necessary unity nor the necessary
> catholicity of the Church, without first sorting out their relationship to
> the "Catholic Church," from which directly or indirectly they all stem,
> and making their peace with her.[42]

As before, the initial pentecostal response would be to affirm Congar's
intuition that the church's catholicity must be understood eschatologically.[43] "The catholicity of the entire people of God is the ecclesial dimension of the eschatological fullness of salvation for the entirety of created
reality."[44] In this sense, the catholicity of the church cannot finally be
separated from the universality of the kingdom, and both will be manifest
fully on that day when the kings of the earth bring the glory and honor
of the nations into the heavenly city (Rev. 21:22–26). This means that
pentecostals would affirm catholicity both as a present reality and as an
eschatological hope: the church is catholic and being made catholic.

Although this eschatological dimension of catholicity certainly should
not be denied, the present ecumenical situation begs for a more substantive pentecostal response. Perhaps one way to approach this matter is to
inquire into the experiential reality of global pentecostalism. What is it
that binds South African, Korean, Latin American, and other pentecostals together? It could be argued that the universality of the pentecostal
community is due in part to the fact that pentecostalism is first and foremost an ecumenical experience and spirituality rather than an organized

42. Küng, The Church, 281, 283, 310.
43. For an exegetical argument that the early church understood itself to be the people
of God because of its experience of the eschatological Spirit, see Gordon D. Fee, Listening to the Spirit in the Text (Grand Rapids: Eerdmans; Vancouver: Regent College Press,
2000), 121–46.
44. Volf, After Our Likeness, 267.

network of institutions. The ties that bind pentecostals together around the world are their experiences of Jesus in the power of the Spirit. It is not that pentecostals are not concerned about Christian unity. Rather, pentecostals experience Christian unity precisely through the universality of the Spirit's presence and activity, which enable the confession of Jesus' lordship amidst the peculiarly pentecostal congregations and liturgies.

This universal catholicity is suggestive for the means of the church's missionary witness and endeavor. Here again pentecostals would affirm Congar's observation that the whole gospel belonging to the whole body for the whole world means that the world receives the gospel in its own idiom, cultural space, and historical time.[45] From its beginnings, pentecostalism has been a missionary movement assuming that the outpouring of the Spirit resulting in diverse tongues reveals the heart of God for the evangelization of the whole world. More specifically, from the perspective of pentecostal experience, the Spirit enables the confession of Jesus as Lord to come forth in many different tongues (cf. Acts 2:5–11). In the words of Vatican II, "[At Pentecost] that union [of all peoples in the catholicity of faith] was [prefigured] by the Church of the new covenant, which speaks all tongues, which lovingly understands and accepts all tongues and which overcomes the divisiveness of Babel" (*Ad gentes*, 4).

Pentecostals understand this outpouring of the Spirit to have been reenacted at the Azusa Street revival and to have continued all the way through to the present by way of the various charismatic-renewal movements (see the next chapter). Henry Pitt van Dusen long ago called pentecostalism the "third force in Christendom" beside the Catholic and Protestant churches, anticipating the explosion of pentecostal Christianity in the non-Western world.[46] Precisely because the good news belongs to all in their own language, culture, and context, pentecostal missiology has developed principles of indigenization whereby the message of the gospel and the work of the Spirit are accommodated, acculturated, and assimilated into local contexts.[47] The ruling assumption is that the

45. For a discussion of how the themes of mission, evangelization, and culture have played out in the Pentecostal–Roman Catholic dialogues, see Veli-Matti Kärkkäinen, *Ad ultimum terrae: Evangelization, Proselytism, and Common Witness in the Roman Catholic–Pentecostal Dialogue (1990–1997)*, SIHC 117 (New York: Peter Lang, 1999).

46. H. P. van Dusen, "The Third Force in Christendom," *Life*, June 9, 1958, 113–24; more accurate, perhaps, would be to identify the pentecostal stream as the fourth in Christendom, beside Orthodoxy, Catholicism, and Protestantism.

47. Besides the work of Melvin Hodges, see Paul Pomerville, *The Third Force in Missions: A Pentecostal Contribution to Contemporary Mission Theology* (Peabody, MA: Hendrickson, 1985); and John V. York, *Missions in the Age of the Spirit* (Springfield, MO: Logion, 2000).

gospel belongs to all peoples and that therefore reception of this gospel is better facilitated on their own indigenous terms.

The preceding account of the church's catholicity still necessitates the individual confession of Jesus and participation in his body (the hallmark of the free and postliberal ecclesiologies respectively) even while it does not discount the fact that this confession and participation are made possible by the Spirit of God (emphasized by mystical understandings of the church) both historically and eschatologically. Thus catholicity neither excludes nor minimizes particularity; rather, each particular is caught up into the church catholic by the Spirit poured out on all flesh. In this way, the church's catholicity is informed concretely by her historicity and locality.

But this account also raises the issue of syncretism as a possible outcome of particularization and, to use a missiological term, indigenization (also §6.1.3). How is the church catholic to recognize that elements of its confession of Jesus as Lord have been compromised in the process of translating the gospel into the language and idiom of the receiving culture? Put otherwise, how is the church to ensure that its eschatological catholicity is continuous with, rather than discontinuous from, the ecclesial catholicity by which it is marked? This concern parallels that regarding the cohabitation of tares among the wheat in the ecclesial kingdom. Confession of Jesus should not be equated with "Lord, Lord," prophetic intensity, the exorcism of demons in Jesus' name, or even the appearance of miracles (Matt. 7:22), all of which are distinguishing features of pentecostal spirituality. So pentecostals have to be wary even about the appearances of preaching the gospel "with a demonstration of the Spirit and of power" (1 Cor. 2:4), since such signs might well be misleading. But how, then, is the church catholic to be discerned? Perhaps precisely by discerning the *ekklēsia* as not only catholic but also one, holy, *and* apostolic. Is it not the case that only such a fourfold criteriology is able to identify better the true church from a false one?

3.2.4 *The Spirit and the Apostolicity of the Church*. What does a pneumatological approach to apostolicity look like in Congar's Catholic perspective? As with the marks of holiness and catholicity, the church apostolic is a gift of the Spirit and an eschatological task of coming into conformity with the apostolic message. The church apostolic is also, further, the means through which the mission of Christ is carried out by the power of the Spirit. Crucial in this regard is the category of testimony, whereby the message of the gospel is empowered by the Spirit through words and deeds, even to the point of death. These are also the means through which apostolicity of service, witness, suffering, and struggle is disclosed and confirmed. Thus "the Spirit is also given to the Church as its transcendent principle of faithfulness" (*BHS* 2:43). This apostolicity derives first from the apostles themselves but then appends itself to the people of God in general and the function of the bishops more specifically. The latter represent the ongoing communion of the people of God with the apostolic witness and thereby with the Father and the Son. Congar therefore goes so far as to say that "it is, after all, possible to speak of an apostolic succession in the case of all believers, but only in the wider context of the faithful transmission of faith" (*BHS* 2:45). In each act of transmission of the gospel (of traditioning), from that of the people of God to the magisterium, the Spirit is the one who preserves the indefectibility of the church "so that error will not ultimately prevail (see Matt. 16:18)" (*BHS* 2:46).

Regarding apostolicity, the early-twentieth-century pentecostals were driven by the conviction that theirs was the restoration of the faith and practice of the earliest disciples of Jesus.[48] More recently, the international Roman Catholic–Pentecostal dialogue agreed that genuine Christian ministry "lives in continuity with the New Testament apostles and their proclamation, and with the apostolic church. A primary manifestation of this is to be found in fidelity to the apostolic teaching."[49] The disagreement, of course, lies in the Catholic insistence on episcopal succession focused primarily on the Petrine ministry, over and against the pentecostal emphasis on the Spirit's presence and anointing power providing the endorsement of apostolic faith and ministry. Are Pentecostals and Roman Catholics, however, so far apart on this issue in light of Congar's discussion?

Veli-Matti Kärkkäinen has proposed a "conciliar understanding of apostolicity" for the consideration of his fellow pentecostal and ecumenical theologians.[50] This includes seven aspects that serve minimally as a starting point for pentecostal–Roman Catholic discussion:

- Apostolicity is first and foremost continuity with the faith of the apostles and of the New Testament church
- Charismatic life and worship are indispensable components of apostolicity
- The missionary proclamation of the gospel is at the heart of apostolicity

48. Cecil Mel Robeck Jr., "A Pentecostal Perspective on Apostolicity" (unpublished paper); a summary of this paper can be found in Jeff Gros, "Faith on the Frontier: Apostolicity and the American Born Churches," *One in Christ* 39, no. 2 (2004): 28–48. My thanks to both Mel Robeck and Jeff Gros for sharing their work with me.

49. "*Final Report*," §§88–90; quotation, §88, in *PNEUMA* 12, no. 2 (1990): 112.

50. Veli-Matti Kärkkäinen, "Pentecostalism and the Claim for Apostolicity: An Essay in Ecumenical Ecclesiology," *ERT* 25, no. 4 (2001): 323–36, esp. 333–34.

- The Scriptures are the norm of apostolicity
- Apostolicity being a dynamic concept, the issue is one of life and vitality rather than of juridical structure
- Apostolicity focuses not only on the clergy or the ecclesial authorities but also on the laity as part of the whole people of God
- Apostolicity must be regarded as a "heavily pneumatological concept"

Is Kärkkäinen separated from Congar by a chasm? Would Roman Catholics agree on the Scriptures as *the* norm of apostolicity or insist, rather, that it is the *primary* norm (*prima scriptura*)? In what ways would Catholics qualify the leveling out of the laity and the clergy in this proposal? And how conciliatory can this proposal be if it does not address the difficult question of apostolic succession?

Regarding this last issue, let us focus attention on the nature of apostolicity in its original context. The Twelve were the initially "sent ones" whose mission was to baptize and make disciples of all nations, to preach repentance and forgiveness of sins, and to witness to the suffering, death, and resurrection of Christ (cf. Matt. 28:19–20; Luke 24:45–49). Clearly, however, the first two generations of Christians did not understand the apostolic commission to be limited only to the Twelve or the apostolic message to be confined to the original disciples. Paul, Andronicus and Junia (Rom. 16:7), Silas and Timothy (cf. 1 Thess. 1:1; 2:6), and James the brother of Jesus (Gal. 1:19) were all recognized as sent ones who fulfilled the apostolic function. Paul himself notes that signs, wonders, and mighty works (miracles) were signs of true apostleship (2 Cor. 12:12).

Pentecostals have therefore generally understood the ongoing apostolic office or function (1 Cor. 12:28; Eph. 4:11) to be the Spirit-empowered ministry of missionizing, evangelizing, church planting, and discipling. From the pentecostal perspective, this fulfills all the early Christian requirements, including the charismatic components of authentic apostolicity identified by Paul.[51] And how else would pentecostals understand apostolicity except pneumatologically and charismatically?[52] If in fact apostolicity follows the original Twelve in giving testimony to

---

51. "Classical Pentecostals find an exercise of apostolic ministry wherever through the preaching of God's Word churches are founded, persons and communities are converted to Jesus Christ, and manifestations of the Holy Spirit are in evidence"; see *"Final Report,"* §79, in *PNEUMA* 12, no. 2 (1990): 111. Cf. David Cartledge, *The Apostolic Revolution: The Restoration of Apostles and Prophets in the Assemblies of God in Australia* (Chester Hill, Aus.: Paraclete Institute; Lane Cove, Aus.: McPherson's Printing Group, 2000).

52. And on this point, they would find agreement from Catholic charismatic theologian Donald Gelpi, *Charism and Sacrament: A Theology of Christian Conversion* (New York: Paulist, 1976), esp. 198–201.

the resurrection of Jesus (cf. Acts 4:33), then how is such to be accomplished in succeeding generations except by the same Spirit who raised Christ from the dead? Unlike the more than five hundred who saw the resurrected Christ (cf. 1 Cor. 15:6), later generations of believers cannot give firsthand witness to the resurrection. Yet witness is certainly given in and through the Holy Spirit, who both raised Jesus from the dead and has been given to indwell and empower believers.

For this reason Harold Hunter's distinctions between apostolic succession, apostolic teaching, and apostolic restoration are important.[53] Building on Lesslie Newbigin's paradigm of ecclesial order, ecclesial faith, and ecclesial experience, Hunter notes the emphasis on order and apostolic succession among episcopal churches, that on faith and apostolic teaching among Reformation churches, and that on experience and apostolic restoration among pentecostal churches. Each communion of churches under these categories understands the other two aspects to be most adequately understood and practiced within its own account of apostolicity. There are sociohistorical reasons each communion has emphasized one to the neglect of the others in ways that have retarded a fully healthy ecclesiality. Yet the question remains: how do all three dimensions fit together under the one category of apostolicity?

It is here that the claims of the papacy to apostolic succession may be most challenging.[54] The majority of pentecostals are not much concerned about their relationship to Roman Catholicism or the Vatican. Yet Roman Catholic charismatics are a nagging reminder that the pentecostal experience cannot avoid dealing with the ecclesial implications of unity, catholicity, and apostolicity, especially vis-à-vis the position and function of the bishop of Rome. Initially Pentecostals might be tempted to point to the plurality of authorities even within the early church itself. There are not one but four gospels alongside a multitude of apostolic traditions—for example, Paul's, James's, and Jude's. This temptation, however, exacerbates all the tensions between the one and the many, unity and multiplicity, and exclusivity and inclusivity, germane to the discussion of the criteria needed to discern the church as one, holy, and

53. Harold D. Hunter, "We Are the Church: New Congregationalism—a Pentecostal Perspective," in *Pentecostal Movements as an Ecumenical Challenge*, ed. Jürgen Moltmann and Karl-Josef Kuschel (London: SCM; Maryknoll, NY: Orbis, 1996), 17–21, esp. 18.

54. The emergence of the idea of apostolic succession is itself complex, perhaps linked to the church's battle against the excessive claims of second-century Gnosticism; see Walter Schmithals, *The Office of Apostle in the Early Church*, trans. John E. Steely (Nashville: Abingdon, 1969), esp. 286–88. In my view, the proper response to gnostic claims to accessing secret revelation is to recapture the charismatic and pneumatic dimensions of the apostolic ministry (what is attempted here) rather than to institutionalize apostolic succession.

catholic. If such a move relativizes the authority of the pope, it also relativizes the pentecostal claim to apostolic restoration.

Perhaps here the pneumatological and charismatic account of apostolicity provided by pentecostals can be of assistance in bridging the gap between their own free-church orientation and that of Catholic sacramentalism. At the first Jerusalem council, the apostolic witness emerged only after much discussion and heated debate on the question whether Gentile believers needed to be circumcised. Appeal was made to the Scriptures (James quotes various sources in the Hebrew prophets in Acts 15:16–18) and to the apostolic experience (of Peter's among Cornelius and the Gentiles). Most important for the purposes at hand is the explanation provided by the apostolic council to the non-Jewish churches: "For it has seemed good *to the Holy Spirit* and to us to impose upon you no further burden than these essentials" (Acts 15:28; emphasis added).[55] Apostolic authority to retrieve, reappropriate, and reinterpret the Scripture in accordance with ecclesial experience is sanctioned, finally, by the charismatic illumination of the Spirit.

Might this pneumatological perspective provide a way forward for pentecostals to come to grips with the claims to apostolicity as defined, symbolized, and constituted ecclesially in the Roman Catholic papacy and in other episcopal traditions (e.g., Eastern Orthodoxy)? For those who see this as a challenge that cannot be avoided—after all, their own history includes fifteen hundred years of the history of the Latin church—Congar's willingness to locate the narrower sense of apostolic succession as technically connected with the bishop of Rome within the broader reality of how apostolic faith is actually transmitted may prove to be of additional help. Insofar as the magisterium is led by the Spirit to serve the body of Christ and insofar as pentecostals (and other Christians) can discern such activity as being of the Spirit of God, is there any hindrance to pentecostals recognizing the *provisional* authority of the pope (or the episcopate) both as a symbolic re-presentation of apostolic faith and practice and as an eschatological anticipation of the full realization of the apostolic message, the *plērōma* of Christ (cf. Eph. 4:11–13)?[56] The point, after all, is not that apostolicity resides in

55. For pentecostal readings of the Jerusalem Council germane to this discussion of apostolic authority, see James B. Shelton, "Epistemology and Authority in the Acts of the Apostles: An Analysis and Test Case Study of Acts 15:1–29," *S&C* 2, no. 2 (2000): 231–47; and John Christopher Thomas, "Reading the Bible from within Our Traditions: A Pentecostal Hermeneutic as Test Case," in *Between Two Horizons: Spanning New Testament Studies and Systematic Theology*, ed. Joel B. Green and Max Turner (Grand Rapids: Eerdmans, 2000), 108–22.

56. See Clark Pinnock, "Does Christian Unity Require Some Form of Papal Primacy?" *JES* 35, nos. 3–4 (1998): 380–82. A negative response from classical Pentecostals can be

abstraction in the church but that the apostolic message and witness are preserved authentically in ecclesial life and faith as directed toward the impending kingdom of God. How else would such preservation come about except pneumatologically? And it is perhaps only from a pneumatological perspective that the dichotomies between apostolic succession and restoration, between episcopal and congregational structures, between tradition as past and as presently instantiated, between councils/creeds and kerygmatic proclamation, and so forth, might be overcome.[57] If this is the case, then the church is apostolic not only in terms of its foundation, its authority, and its message but also regarding its eschatological gathering around the throne of God (Revelation 4–5).

The preceding has discussed how pentecostal ecclesiology can be enriched by the historic self-understanding of the church and how pentecostal perspectives can contribute to contemporary ecclesiological reflection. Central to the discussion has been the dynamic element introduced by rethinking the ecclesial marks from a pneumatological perspective, so that unity, holiness, catholicity, and apostolicity are not essentially finished notes of the church but are eschatological realities produced by the Spirit's working.[58] Along the way, elements of a pneumatological ecclesiology have emerged. It is time to fill out these more abstract features of a Spirit ecclesiology within a historical, sacramental, and liturgical framework.

3.3 The Future of the Church: Elements of a Pneumatological Ecclesiology

The thesis of this chapter is that pentecostalism can contribute something substantive toward the idea of the church not only as the people of God and the body of Christ but also as the "charismatic fellowship of the Spirit."[59] When the disciples first accepted the label of "Christians" at

gauged from Ronald Kydd, "Does Christian Unity Require Some Form of Papal Primacy?" *Ecumenical Trends* 27, no. 3 (1998): 43–46.

57. As the Eastern Orthodox say, "Tradition is a *charismatic*, not a historical, principle," or, "The Councils were never regarded as a canonical institution, but rather as occasional *charismatic events*"; see Georges Florovsky, *Bible, Church, Tradition: An Eastern Orthodox View* (Belmont, MA: Norland, 1972), 47, 96; italics original.

58. This view complements Reinhard Hütter's understanding of the marks as the "core practices of the church"; see Hütter's *Suffering Divine Things: Theology as Church Practice*, trans. Doug Scott (Grand Rapids: Eerdmans, 2000), 131–32.

59. Here I am merely participating in the ongoing attempt to develop a pneumatological ecclesiology from pentecostal perspectives. See, e.g., Kilian McDonnell, introduction to *PPP*, xix–lxix, esp. xliii–xliv; Kärkkäinen, *Toward a Pneumatological Theology*, part 2; Paul D. Lee, *Pneumatological Ecclesiology in the Roman Catholic–Pentecostal Dialogue: A*

Antioch (Acts 11:26), they were acknowledging their following after the footsteps of Jesus the Christ, the one anointed by the Spirit to herald the kingdom of God. Such was also now their calling, with themselves as the new temple of the Holy Spirit (1 Cor. 3:16). The rest of this chapter discusses pentecostal Spirit ecclesiology in relationship to other pneumatological ecclesiologies that have also emerged fairly recently and sketches the basic features of a pneumatological theology of baptism and the liturgy in dialogue with recent sacramental and liturgical theology. It addresses more explicitly the issues previously raised (see §3.1.2) by sacramental views of the church as mediating the grace of God and by postliberal views of the church as an alternative grammar and way of life.

3.3.1 *The Fellowship of the Spirit: Anticipations of a Pneumatological Ecclesiology.* One of the most clearly articulated antecedents to pneumatological ecclesiology was *Unity in the Church* (1825) by the Roman Catholic theologian Johann Adam Möhler (1796–1838).[60] Responding in part to the post-Reformational fragmentation of the churches in the context of romanticist and pietist currents and in part to the Enlightenment challenges to Roman Catholic self-understanding of the church as an autonomous and self-sufficient "perfect society," Möhler's goal was to mediate between a living, affective piety and the visible, historical, and hierarchical church. Although the Catholic Church as an institutional whole provided the outward form of Christian unity, the inner spiritual unity of the church as a living organism was pneumatologically constituted: "The Church exists through a life directly and continually moved by the divine Spirit, and is maintained and continued by the loving mutual exchange of believers."[61] Further, the Spirit inspires and enables

---

Catholic Reading of the Third Quinquennium (1985–1989) (Rome: Pontifical University of St. Thomas, 1994); Ronald Douglas McConnell, *A Pentecostal in Queen Elizabeth's Church: Charismatic Experience and the Sacramental Church* (Brewster, MA: Paraclete, 2002); Gordon D. Fee, *God's Empowering Presence: The Holy Spirit in the Letters of Paul* (Peabody, MA: Hendrickson, 1994), ch. 15; Gene Mills, "The Pneumatological *ekklesia*: A Comparative and Constructive Work in Contemporary Ecclesiology," *Quodlibet Journal* 4, nos. 2–3 (2002), http://www.Quodlibet.net; Wolfgang Vondey, *Heribert Muhlen: His Theology and Praxis. A New Profile of the Church* (Lanham, MD: University Press of America, 2004); and William J. Schonebaum, "The Holy Spirit in the Life of the Believing Community: A Study in Pneumatology, Ecclesiology, and Neo-Pentecostalism" (D.Min. thesis, Luther Theological Seminary, 1979). See also Amos Yong, "The Acts of the Apostles and of the Holy Spirit: Pentecostal Reflections on the Church as Charismatic Fellowship," in *The Marks of the Church*, ed. William Madges and Michael Daley (Mystic, CT: Twenty-Third Publications, forthcoming).

60. Johann Adam Möhler, *Unity in the Church Presented in the Spirit of the Church Fathers of the First Three Centuries*, trans. Peter C. Erb (Washington, DC: Catholic University of America Press, 1996).

61. Ibid., 93.

understanding of the written word that belongs with, and emerges out of, the Spirit-inspired tradition (they are not divided): "By tradition we believe and see everything as the true expression of the Christian Spirit, which as far back as the apostles is found as apostolic doctrine."[62] Dogma becomes the "conceptual expression" of the Spirit even as tradition is conceived in terms of a vital, developmental, and communal process of reception. In this way, not only is the Spirit the theological "location" wherein Christian life begins and is sustained; the locus of the Spirit is extended toward that of the community of faith. So the Spirit comes not upon believers as individuals but upon the assembled *ekklēsia*.

In making this last claim, Möhler was responding to the threat against the inner unity of the church by the diversification of the "churches." If heretics were those who divided the church through appeal to the biblical text as their central principle, Möhler argued that they could not appeal to the Spirit's inspiration at the level of the individual to support their views. But could the individual and the ecclesial inspiration of the Spirit be separated in this way if in fact the church is pneumatologically constituted? The other question concerned the possible loss of the transcendence of the Holy Spirit when the Spirit's "location" is identified with and in the Christian community, a loss Möhler identified in the pantheism of Schleiermacher's theology (as he read it).

In his later work *Symbolism* (five editions from 1832 to 1838), Möhler sought to renegotiate the issues by resorting increasingly to an incarnational ecclesiology.[63] Clearly, his concern throughout was with Protestant sectarianism: Quakerism, Zinzendorfianism, Swedenborgianism, and Socinianism, for example, each exemplified the chaos of the Protestant situation. In *Symbolism*, then, the Spirit is always now Christ's Spirit, the Church is the "body of Christ," and the episcopate is founded by the command of Christ instead of being established by the pentecostal outpouring. The Spirit supports the community rather than founds the community. Because the Spirit is subordinate to Christ, the Spirit's presence is no longer primarily through the internal witness but through the external signs of the church. The dogmatic tradition is no longer secondary but primary. Whereas some statements in *Unity* about ecclesial office could be interpreted as saying that ordination added nothing to the charismatically endowed individual, in *Symbolism* ordination as an outward sacrament bestows inner divine realities for the task of ministry. Now even the papal office is established by Christ to provide

---

62. Ibid., 109.

63. John Adam Möhler, *Symbolism; or, Exposition of the Doctrinal Differences between Catholics and Protestants as Evidenced by Their Symbolical Writings*, trans. James Burton Robertson, 5th ed. (1843; repr., New York: Benziger Brothers; London: Gibbings, 1906).

for the centralization of the episcopacy and especially for the visible unity essential to the church's witness to revelation and to her mission to the world. Hence one can put his or her trust in the church's preaching (the testimony of a reliable witness).

Möhler justified these developments in his thinking by grounding the invisible-visible distinction of the church on the incarnation as making visible the invisible Logos. If the incarnation is taken seriously, so must the visible dimension of the church. Similarly, if Jesus worked miracles in his earthly life, so does the church: "revelation becomes null and void, fails of its purpose, and must henceforth be even called into question, and finally denied" apart from this view of the church.[64] "The abstract idea and the positive history, doctrine and fact, internal and external truth, inward and outward testimony were organically united; so must religion and Church be conjoined, and for this reason, *that God became man.*"[65] This incarnational ecclesiology is what enables Möhler to talk about the infallibility of the church, about the church and its tradition as teacher and judge on matters of faith, and about the church as the infallible interpreter of an inspired Scripture.

Möhler's concerns with the authority of the church prohibited him from explicitly developing his early pneumatological ecclesiology or from integrating his earlier and later ecclesiologies in a trinitarian direction.[66] The solution to the rampant anarchy that characterized the historical situation of the time was sought by reemphasizing the traditional Roman Catholic understanding of the papacy and ecclesial hierarchy. In this way, the truth claims of the church were grounded in the miraculous nature of the "body of Christ," itself an extension of the miracle of the incarnation. This was Möhler's direct response to the emerging liberal Protestant solution, inaugurated by Schleiermacher, that grounded theological claims on experience (in Schleiermacher's case, on the feeling of absolute dependence on the divine). These attempts to ground theology in either experience or the tradition were rejected later in the nineteenth

64. Ibid., 267.

65. Ibid., 268; italics original.

66. Since Möhler in his later work never expressly rejected wholly his earlier pneumatological ecclesiology, it could be argued that the early and later Möhler could be held together within a wider trinitarian framework. This is suggested by Bradford E. Hinze, "The Holy Spirit and the Catholic Tradition: The Legacy of Johann Adam Möhler," in *The Legacy of the Tübingen School: The Relevance of Nineteenth Century Theology for the Twenty-First Century,* ed. Donald J. Dietrich and Michael J. Himes (New York: Crossroad, 1997), 75–94; and "Releasing the Power of the Spirit in a Trinitarian Ecclesiology," in *Advents of the Spirit: An Introduction to the Current Study of Pneumatology,* ed. Bradford E. Hinze and D. Lyle Dabney (Milwaukee: Marquette University Press, 2001), 347–81. See also Michael J. Himes, *Ongoing Incarnation: Johann Adam Möhler and the Beginnings of Modern Ecclesiology* (New York: Crossroad Herder, 1997).

century by conservative Protestants in favor of the "solution" of grounding theological claims on an inerrant Scripture (see §7.3.2).

Möhler may have recoiled from his project in pneumatological ecclesiology too quickly. Kärkkäinen's survey text documents the more recent boom in pneumatological ecclesiology, observing a recurrence of pneumatic and charismatic motifs across the ecclesiological spectrum.[67] Thus Eastern Orthodoxy is not only "Spirit-sensitive" but also understands the church to be constituted by the Spirit. Post–Vatican II Catholic ecclesiology has emphasized the importance of the charisms in the life of the church (thus opening the door to the charismatic renewal in the church). Lutheran ecclesiology understands the Spirit to make alive both the word and the sacraments. Pentecostal ecclesiologies emphasize the church as a "charismatic fellowship."

Turning to contemporary ecclesiologists, Kärkkäinen notes similar connections. Zizioulas emphasizes christology and pneumatology as the dual foundation of the church. Küng writes about the church as the "creation of the Spirit." Pannenberg's is a thoroughly pneumatological ecclesiology, an understanding of the church permeated by the person and work of the Spirit. Moltmann wrote *The Church in the Power of the Spirit*, and his dedication of it to friends and colleagues in the World Council of Churches calls attention to the growing prevalence of these ideas in those circles as well. Volf focuses on the charismatic and trinitarian structure of the church (see §3.1.1). James McClendon's "Baptist vision" is very similar to those of pentecostals, emphasizing the "this is that" correlation between the present experience of the Spirit and the experiences of the earliest Christians as recorded in the book of Acts. And how can one have a missionary ecclesiology such as Newbigin's without a robust pneumatology such as that portrayed in Newbigin's notion of the church as a "community of the Holy Spirit"? Finally, pneumatic and charismatic themes are evident also in the contextual ecclesiologies, not only in the African Spirit churches but also in the Shepherding Movement's "renewal ecclesiology."[68]

But what if we take Möhler's insights toward pneumatological and incarnational ecclesiology more seriously? Might we not only derive resources toward a more robust trinitarian ecclesiology but also circumvent

---

67. See Kärkkäinen, *An Introduction to Ecclesiology*.

68. See, e.g., Zizioulas, *Being and Communion*; Küng, *The Church*; Wolfhart Pannenberg, *Systematic Theology* (Grand Rapids: Eerdmans, 1998), vol. 3; Moltmann, *Church in the Power of the Spirit*; Volf, *After Our Likeness*; Amos Yong, "The 'Baptist Vision' of James William McClendon, Jr.: A Wesleyan-Pentecostal Response," *WesTJ* 37, no. 2 (2002): 32–57; Lesslie Newbigin, *The Household of God: Lectures on the Nature of the Church* (London: SCM, 1953); and S. David Moore, "The Shepherding Movement: A Case Study in Charismatic Ecclesiology," *PNEUMA* 22, no. 2 (2000): 271–302.

altogether the modernist project of foundationalism (whether expressed in Schleiermacher's experience, Catholicism's tradition, or fundamentalism's inerrant Scripture)? My own attempt to develop a Christ-centered and Spirit-driven theology and ecclesiology is inspired in part by Möhler's uncompleted project. The result is what I have elsewhere called a shifting foundationalism that recognizes all truth claims as historically embedded without having to locate their ground on any one undeniable foundation.[69] This is because a pneumatologically driven theology acknowledges the provisionality of all theological constructions within an eschatological framework (the Spirit as the down payment of the promises to come), recognizes the unavoidable particularity of all theological understanding in history (the Spirit as the Spirit of the Son), and, following the perichoretic interpenetration of Father, Son, and Spirit, unites Christian experience of the word of God in ecclesial community (the church as the "fellowship of the Spirit").[70] Let us see how these elements of a pneumatological ecclesiology help us understand the sacraments and liturgy of the church.

3.3.2 *Born of Water and the Spirit: Toward a Pneumatological Theology of Baptism.* As is well known, the sacraments have historically been understood as mediating the grace of God. A pneumatological ecclesiology that recognizes the church as constituted by the pentecostal outpouring of the Spirit will grant that the church itself is sacramental insofar as it consists of structures, institutions, practices, congregations, and individuals, all inspired by the Spirit of God for the purposes of establishing the kingdom of God. Further, the sacraments are mediators of grace insofar as they provide ecclesial venues for the Spirit of God to accomplish the purposes of God among the people of God. As already noted (§3.2.1), pentecostal "sacramentalism" is itself empirically established, founded on the reality of the Spirit's manifestation in the material and embodied experiences—for example, glossolalia, the dance, the shout, and healings—of the gathered community of faith. How does this pneumatological theology of sacramentality apply to baptism historically understood?

The traditional claim about water baptism is that it mediates the forgiveness of sins and the Christian initiation into the body of Christ (cf. §3.1.2). The former concept has evolved into the idea known as "baptismal regeneration"—that the act of baptism itself accomplishes the forgiveness of sins—and the latter has led to the well-known "no

---

69. See Amos Yong, "On Divine Presence and Divine Agency: Toward a Foundational Pneumatology," *AJPS* 3, no. 2 (July 2000): 167–88, esp. 174; and *Beyond the Impasse: Toward a Pneumatological Theology of Religions* (Grand Rapids: Baker, 2003), 64–65.

70. This is the argument of my extended essay *Spirit–Word–Community*.

salvation outside the church" along with its view of the priesthood and sacraments as soteriological keys. Two initial responses on these matters from a pentecostal and pneumatological perspective can be noted. First, the biblical and patristic witnesses both posit an undeniable connection between water and Spirit baptism. Although Jesus' claim that those who enter the kingdom of God must be born of water and Spirit (John 3:5) has been variously interpreted in order to disconnect water from Spirit baptism, the exegesis of Acts 2:38 (and Acts 22:16) that disconnects the forgiveness of sins from water baptism is much less plausible. That the ancient church also expected catechumens to receive the Holy Spirit during the rite of initiation in general and when emerging from baptismal immersion more specifically (see §2.2.2) shows the interconnectedness of both baptisms and is suggestive for clarifying the enigmatic claim that there is, finally, only "one Lord, one faith, one baptism" (Eph. 4:5).[71] I suggest that the claim regarding baptismal regeneration should be rejected if understood to refer to the baptismal waters' magically washing away sins (1 Pet. 3:21), but can be accepted if understood pneumatically and mystically as an action of the Spirit (e.g., Titus 3:5) that includes the faith response of believers.

Second, the theology and practices of Oneness pentecostals also hold water and Spirit baptism together in ways consistent with the early church but with the explicit rejection of baptismal regeneration magically understood.[72] Oneness pentecostals not only insist on baptism "in Jesus' name," following the apostolic model in the book of Acts; they also oftentimes go further than the traditional soteriological view of baptism, to reason in this way: if full salvation includes repentance, baptism in water, and the reception of the Holy Spirit (Acts 2:38) and there is the threefold biblical witness that the baptism of the Spirit is evidenced by speaking in other tongues (Acts 2:4; 10:44–45; 19:6), then full salvation is accomplished with the manifestation of tongues signifying the infilling of the Spirit.[73] From a biblical perspective, the church has preserved a plurality of baptismal formulas. Further, the pneumatological soteriology and ecclesiology being developed in this volume

---

71. On this notion of "one baptism" of water and Spirit from a classical (Oneness) pentecostal perspective, see Andrew D. Urshan, *The Doctrine of the New Birth; or, The Perfect Way to Eternal Life* (Cochrane, WI: Witness of God, 1921), ch. 10, esp. 41–42, repr. in *Seven "Jesus Only" Tracts*, ed. Dayton. Cf. Frank D. Macchia, "Justification and the Spirit of Life: A Pentecostal Response to the *Joint Declaration*," in *Justification and the Future of the Ecumenical Movement: The Joint Declaration on the Doctrine of Justification*, ed. William G. Rusch (Collegeville, MN: Liturgical Press, 2003), 133–49, esp. 145.

72. See David Bernard, *The New Birth* (Hazelwood, MO: Word Aflame, 1984), chs. 4–6.

73. Ibid., chs. 7–9.

are capable of not only affirming but even appreciating the Oneness insistence on seeing water and Spirit baptism as connected in some way. But more problematic is the Oneness view of the soteriological signifi-cance of tongues speech. Any dogmatic stance of evidential tongues as salvific is dubious precisely because such dogmatism runs counter to the dynamic, holistic, and eschatological dimensions of Christian life and experience (see §2.3.3).

This said, further connections between Oneness and patristic bap-tismal understandings can be established in dialogue with the Syriac fathers, given the pneumatological orientation of both traditions.[74] The Syriac writers agree that water baptism gives the Holy Spirit (Acts 10:45–47) even if they disagree on when this occurs (e.g., in one of the anointings, in immersion, or in the imposition of hands). Yet reception of the Spirit is crucial to a proper understanding of water baptism, since the gifts of the Spirit—sonship, membership in the body of Christ, priest-hood and kingship, and purification and sanctification—come with the Spirit's person. Thus the Syriac Fathers believed that "baptism is also a Pentecost, a charismatic event," even as they recognized that "the pentecostal effects of baptism do not necessarily manifest themselves at baptism itself, but may be delayed until later: the 'pledge of the Spirit,' the potential, however, is already present as a result of baptism."[75] These manifestations and signs of the effective working of the Spirit are love of God, true humility, kindness toward others, true love for others, and the illuminated vision of the mind.

Against this background, the key elements of a pentecostal and pneu-matological theology of water baptism can be articulated with the help of the recent ecumenical document *Baptism, Eucharist, and Ministry* (*BEM*).[76] First and fundamentally, the celebration of baptism as a Chris-tian rite should include, centrally, the invocation of the Holy Spirit (*BEM* §20). This invitation identifies the ritual as explicitly Christian and locates its sacramentality not in the materiality of consecrated water but in the presence and activity of the Spirit of the living God.[77]

74. Sebastian Brock, *The Holy Spirit in the Syrian Baptismal Tradition*, The Syrian Church Series 9 (Poona, India: Anita, 1979). The Syriac tradition includes the Syrian Orthodox, Maronite, Melkite, and Church of the East churches.

75. Ibid., 134, 137.

76. *Baptism, Eucharist, and Ministry*, Faith and Order Paper 111 (Geneva: World Coun-cil of Churches, 1982). For pentecostal responses, see Cecil M. Robeck Jr. and Jerry L. Sandidge, "The Ecclesiology of *koinonia* and Baptism: A Pentecostal Perspective," *JES* 27, no. 3 (1990): 504–34; and Harold D. Hunter, "Reflections by a Pentecostalist on Aspects of *BEM*," *JES* 29, nos. 3–4 (1992): 317–45.

77. According to the description given by G. C. Oosthuizen, this interconnectedness between the Spirit and the baptism rite is explicitly evident in the Zionist Spirit churches

Second, baptism in water not only enacts our participation in the death and resurrection of Christ and our conversion/cleansing but also represents our reception of the gift of the Holy Spirit (*BEM* §5).[78] Baptism is, in this sense, a concrete experiencing of the death and life of Jesus (the body of Christ) (cf. Rom. 6:4; Gal. 3:27; Col. 2:12). It is both an invitation to identify with the death and life of Jesus and an actualization of this reenactment. Baptism becomes the concrete act in a historical point in time—the "crisis experience," to use Wesleyan and pentecostal language—that is the means by which we experience the life of Jesus by the Holy Spirit. Thereby empowered, believers are enabled to follow in the footsteps of the Christ, to do the things that he did. So long as we recall the image of salvation as fluid, with past, present, and future tenses always operative and shifting, baptism can serve as the identifiable experience that initiates, confirms, and anticipates this dynamic movement. In saying this, we come close to the understanding of the early church fathers, who saw water baptism as signifying and encapsulating an entire process of initiation, confirmation, discipleship, and ongoing, deepening, and even intensifying conversion.[79]

Third, in an intriguing study on foot washing in the Johannine community (John 13), John Christopher Thomas suggests a sacramental interpretation of foot washing as linked to the ongoing cleansing from sin that supplements the initial cleansing received at water baptism.[80] Given the prevalence of the rite in many apostolic pentecostal churches and denominations, has foot washing been adopted as an explicitly pentecostal expression of sacramentality—classically understood, that is, as a sign or mediator of grace—to fill in the lacuna felt with the rejection of the Catholic view of the sacraments?[81] And if so, might the foot-washing ritual not also inform the continued elaboration of a distinctive pentecostal theology of the sacraments in general and of

---

of South Africa; see G. C. Oosthuizen, *Baptism in the Context of the African Indigenous/Independent Churches (A.I.C.)* (KwaDlangezwa, South Africa: University of Zululand Press, 1985), esp. 26–37.

78. By "enacts" and "represents," I wish to find a way beyond the impasse of saying either "baptism saves/gives the Spirit" or "baptism merely symbolizes." Here I find myself solidly within the classical Pentecostal tradition; see J. Narver Gortner, "The Importance of Water Baptism," ch. 3 in J. Narver Gortner, Donald Gee, and Hy Pickering, *Water Baptism and the Trinity* (Springfield, MO: Gospel Publishing House, n.d.), esp. 39–46; and James Lee Beall, *Rise to Newness of Life: A Look at Water Baptism* (Detroit: Evangel, 1974), ch. 7.

79. As argued by Gelpi, *Charism and Sacrament*, ch. 5.

80. John Christopher Thomas, *Footwashing in John 13 and the Johannine Community* (Sheffield, Eng.: JSOT, 1991), ch. 5.

81. Some of these questions are asked by Frank D. Macchia, "Is Footwashing the Neglected Sacrament? A Theological Response to John Christopher Thomas," *PNEUMA* 19, no. 2 (1997): 239–49.

baptism in particular by providing a liturgical forum for experiencing the ongoing sanctifying work of the Spirit (cf. §3.2.2)?

Fourth, contemporary pentecostal understandings of the gifts of the Spirit can be enriched in ecumenical dialogue on water baptism. As the Syriac fathers identified the gifts of the Spirit in not only charismatic but soteriological terms, so also is the distinction between the two rightly blurred for contemporary theological purposes. All too often the charismatic gifts and the fruits of the Spirit are separated, or the charisms are sensationalized signifiers adrift from any soteriological meaning. The truth is that the charisms are soteriological insofar as they are given for the edification of a needy people of God whose full salvation is yet to be eschatologically experienced. Similarly, the saving work of the Spirit is also charismatic insofar as justification and sanctification, for example, give the charisms their distinctively Christian character.

Finally, if the above sketch has any validity, pentecostals can cease to be suspicious of sacramental language regarding water baptism. Minimally, if baptism is understood as our obedient participation in the death of Christ and our realization of new life in the power of the Spirit, then there is at least a protosacramental character to baptism as Christian initiation.[82] Maximally, if baptism is understood not as a "dead ritual" but as a living and transformative act of the Spirit of God on the community of faith, then baptism is not only protosacramental but fully sacramental in the sense of enacting the life and grace of God to those who need and receive it by faith. Although I am challenging my pentecostal colleagues and churches to go beyond affirming "a purely symbolic view of the ordinances,"[83] I believe that this and the proposal below regarding the Lord's Supper are fully consistent with pentecostal intuitions regarding the Spirit's presence and activity in the worshiping community.

3.3.3 *Meeting Daily in the Spirit: Toward a Pneumatological Theology of the Liturgy*. From this initiatory rite (we *were* saved) emerges a distinctive pentecostal and pneumatological theology of the liturgy whereby the entire liturgy (or worship service) becomes a "sacrament of the Spirit" (whereby we *are being* saved).[84] To put it in thesis form, I suggest that the

82. See Stanley E. Porter, "Baptism in Acts: The Sacramental Dimension," in *Dimensions of Baptism: Biblical and Theological Studies*, ed. Stanley E. Porter and Anthony R. Cross (New York: Sheffield Academic Press, 2002), 117–28.

83. Richard Bicknell, "The Ordinances: The Marginalised Aspects of Pentecostalism," in *Pentecostal Distinctives*, ed. Keith Warrington (Carlisle, Eng.: Paternoster, 1998), 204–22; quotation, 205.

84. Theological-Historical Commission for the Great Jubilee of the Year 2000, *The Holy Spirit, Lord and Giver of Life*, trans. Agostino Bono (New York: Crossroad, 1998), 92. See also Walter Hollenweger, *Pentecostalism: Origins and Developments Worldwide* (Peabody, MA: Hendrickson, 1997), ch. 21.

Holy Spirit breathes life and grace into the believing community by making present and available the resurrection power of Jesus Christ, which inaugurates the eschatological kingdom of God. More concretely, the Holy Spirit transforms the community of faith from moment to moment so that it can more fully realize and embody here and now the image and likeness of the eschatological Christ. This happens liturgically (among other means) in the word of worship that is directed to God and enlivened by the Spirit of God, in the word of proclamation of Jesus as the Messiah, and in the word of consumption that is the eucharistic fellowship of the body and blood of Christ.[85] Let me briefly elaborate on each.

A pneumatological theology of the liturgy emphasizes the centrality of the Spirit's presence and activity to enable the true praise and worship of God (John 4:23–24), precisely because no true encounter with God is possible apart from such divine initiative. When the Spirit is present and active, the vertical dimension of relationship between God and the people of God opens up (as experienced by John, who visited the throne of God only in the Spirit; Rev. 4:2). Human beings realize their fallenness, finitude, and unworthiness in the presence of God and their need for the confession of their sins (cf. Isa. 6:5) and are enabled to experience, if only in part, the glory of God because of the mediating and sanctifying work and word of Christ by the Spirit. At this juncture, the life-giving word of Christ is transformed into living words of praise and worship by the people of God, given to God for no other reason than that God is worthy to be magnified. This becomes in turn a transformative experience for the people of God, leading to an ever intensifying realization of the eschatological glory of God amidst the worshiping community.

Yet this relationship opened by the mediating word and work of Christ is not limited to its vertical or eschatological dimension but carries over into the believing community's engagement with reality here and now. Thus a pneumatological theology of the liturgy recognizes the necessity of the Spirit quickening the word of Christ in order to give life to the people of God. When this happens, the letter of the law becomes living and active (John 6:63; 2 Cor. 3:6; Heb. 4:12). This is what pentecostals often call the "*rhēma* word," which speaks God's word anew and afresh to the here-and-now situation of the believer and the believing community. This certainly occurs in the contemporary sermon, the central form of kerygmatic proclamation of the living word of Christ by the power of the

---

85. All I mean by "liturgy" here is its plain etymological sense of the people of God doing the work of God in the worship of God. In this sense, pentecostals are liturgical like anyone else, except that their liturgical movements include patterns of spontaneity amidst the ordered elements. So Daniel E. Albrecht, *Rites in the Spirit: A Ritual Approach to Pentecostal/Charismatic Spirituality*, JPTSup 17 (Sheffield, Eng.: Sheffield Academic Press, 1999).

Spirit. But because the Spirit of God is no respecter of persons and has been poured out upon all flesh, the *rhēma* word can be spoken at any moment and by any one.[86] Thus the importance of the testimony and confessional praise in pentecostal liturgy[87] as well as ordered moments for the manifestation of the charisms, including the word of wisdom, the word of knowledge, and tongues and their interpretations. The living word of the Spirit is best understood doing things with words and bringing things about with words (illocutionary and perlocutionary speech acts, respectively; see §3.2.2). So the word of Christ spoken by the power of the Spirit accomplishes the transformation of the soul and of the believing community—for example, in the bringing about of a new situation ("Brother Saul, . . . regain your sight and be filled with the Holy Spirit"; Acts 9:17); in the granting of forgiveness ("Your sins are forgiven"; cf. Luke 7:48; John 20:22–23); in the releasing of those captive and oppressed ("There is therefore now no condemnation for those who are in Christ Jesus . . ."; Rom. 8:1); in the reconciling with those estranged ("Go and show yourselves to the priests . . ."; Luke 17:14); and in exorcising the demonic ("Come out of him!" Luke 4:35)—so that the world of the Scriptures becomes alive in the here and now of the liturgical community.[88] In one sense, the Spirit enables us to step into and inhabit the world of the scriptural narrative; in another sense, the Spirit of God calls and empowers the believer and believing community to actualize the word of God in the image and likeness of Jesus.

But the word of God not only returns to God in worship and accomplishes the purposes of God in the world (cf. Isa. 55:11); it is also internalized and, through the Supper, literally embodied by the people of God. So a pneumatological theology of the liturgy highlights the centrality of the working of the Spirit in the fellowship of the meal. In this case, the invocation (*epiklēsis*) of the Spirit becomes essential to the church's memory (*anamnēsis*) of Christ, both in the sense of enabling

86. Note the prevalence of kerygmatic activity, emboldened speech, and the widespread impact of the word of God following movements of the Spirit in Acts—e.g., 1:5–8; 2:4; 4:8, 31; 6:3–8; 7:55–56; 9:17–20; 10:44–46; 11:15–17; 11:24; 13:9–10, 49–52; 19:1–7. I am indebted for this insight to James B. Shelton, *Mighty in Word and Deed: The Role of the Holy Spirit in Luke-Acts* (Peabody, MA: Hendrickson, 1991), ch. 11, esp. 136–48.

87. For discussions of pentecostal testimony, see Scott A. Ellington, "History, Story, and Testimony: Locating Truth in a Pentecostal Hermeneutic," *PNEUMA* 23, no. 2 (2001): 245–63; "The Costly Loss of Testimony," *JPT* 16 (2000): 48–59; and Mark J. Cartledge, *Practical Theology: Charismatic and Empirical Perspectives* (Carlisle, Eng.: Paternoster, 2003), ch. 3. For the role of confession, see James K. A. Smith, *Speech and Theology: Language and the Logic of Incarnation* (New York: Routledge, 2002), esp. 134–50.

88. An excellent contemporary perspective on Christian ritual is George D. McClain, *Claiming All Things for God: Prayer, Discernment, and Ritual for Social Change* (Nashville: Abingdon, 1998).

the recollection of the historical Jesus in the present remembering of the body of Christ and in the sense of making present the living Christ in the "membered" elements of the bread and cup and in the "members" of the congregation as the living body of Christ.[89] As such, the Lord's Supper becomes a sacramental rite (in the senses defined above) that transforms the worshiping community through word and Spirit. We can see this in at least five dimensions.

First, the Supper is a physical act wherein the word of God is consumed by the body of Christ through the working of the Spirit. The physicality of this experience can be understood in the literal sense of eating and drinking. Indeed, the eating and drinking of the elements used to be literally nourishing (cf. Acts 2:46). Because of abuses, however, Paul instructed the Corinthians to eat and drink to their fill at home before coming to participate around the Lord's Table (1 Cor. 11:17–22). Since Paul's concern was that factions not develop in the body between the haves and the have-nots, there is no reason the Lord's Supper cannot once again become a communal celebration that nourishes physical bodies so long as the congregation is alert to the have-nots in their midst.

But even more than a source of nourishment, the Supper as a physical act, taken with self-discernment, also is an occasion for God's healing grace to be manifest.[90] This is so not only in the sense in which the church fathers understood the Eucharist as a *pharmakon* (or pharmaceutical medicine) but also in the sense in which many pentecostals believe healing to be in the atonement—"by his wounds you have been healed" (1 Pet. 2:24b)—so that to internalize the body and blood of Christ is to release its healing virtues for broken bodies.[91] And why not, if in fact the material elements of bread and wine or juice somehow mediate the presence of Christ by the power of the Spirit? If pentecostals believe that the healing powers of God and the gift of the Holy Spirit can be and are communicated through material means—for example, handkerchiefs, aprons (Acts 19:12), and the laying on of hands (Acts 8:14–17; 9:17; 13:3; 19:6)[92]—then why not through the eucharistic elements (cf.

---

89. See Neville S. Clark, "Spirit Christology in the Light of Eucharistic Theology," *HeyJ* 23, no. 3 (1982): 270–84; and, from a Catholic charismatic perspective, Peter Hocken, *Blazing the Trail: Where Is the Holy Spirit Leading the Church?* (London: Bible Alive, 2001), chs. 4–5. On Hebraic memory as not just recollection but also the power of what is recollected to impact the present, see Brevard Childs, *Memory and Tradition in Israel* (Naperville, IL: A. R. Allenson, 1962).

90. See Kärkkäinen, *Toward a Pneumatological Theology*, ch. 10, esp. 142–44.

91. Bicknell, "The Ordinances," 216; cf. his study of the Lord's Supper in the Elim Pentecostal churches in Britain: Richard Bicknell, "In Memory of Christ's Sacrifice: Roots and Shoots of Elim's Eucharistic Expression," *JEPTA* 17 (1997): 59–89.

92. Ronald A. N. Kydd, "Jesus, Saints, and Relics: Approaching the Early Church through Healing," *JPT* 2 (1993): 91–104.

John 6:51–58)? Believers encounter the living Christ who is present, understood not in the physicalist or consubstantive terms of Aristotelian and neoscholastic substance philosophy but in the interpersonal and intersubjective terms of contemporary pneumatological theology.[93]

This means, second, not only that Christ is present to us but that we are present to Christ. This mutual presence is made possible by the Spirit, invited to reign over the Supper. The Spirit enables us to "respond to Christ's 'bodily presence' and [to] share in the formation of a mutual, personal presence."[94] In this pneumatological framework, what is important is not the alleged "transubstantiation" of the elements into the actual body and blood of Christ, nor the moment of full or mutual presence between Christ and the believing community, but the intersubjective mutuality that is always a matter of degree: the Supper now becomes a mysterious interpersonal encounter wherein Christ and his body are brought into real relationship by the Spirit.[95]

Third, the Supper is thus an ecclesial and social act of solidarity whereby Jesus the resurrected Word is united with the body of Christ through the fellowship of the Spirit.[96] It goes beyond the interpersonal union brought about by consuming the elements, toward the fellowship brought about by the Spirit among those nourished by the body and blood of Jesus. This effects a transformation of human relationships within and without the congregation. Not only are those who gather around the Lord's Table required to be sensitive to each other and to be discerning about the body of Christ (cf. 1 Cor. 11:22, 27–34); insofar as the Supper is the consummation of the liturgical activity of the church, the members of the body are not to approach this moment without being reconciled to any and all from whom they are estranged (cf. Matt. 5:23–24). In this way, the Supper becomes a moment of intimate and yet catholic (§3.2.3) fellowship brought about by the Holy Spirit around the body (and blood) of Christ even as it hastens the process of reconciliation between believers and other believers and those not yet followers of the way of Jesus.[97] The eucharistic fellowship can never be only inward-looking but is always

93. I am helped here by John H. McKenna, *Eucharist and Holy Spirit: The Eucharistic Epiclesis in 20th Century Theology* (Great Wakering, Eng.: Mayhew-McCrimmon, 1975), part 3.

94. Ibid., 184.

95. Ibid., 203. Gelpi, *Charism and Sacrament*, 249, also talks about the experiential dimension of the Eucharist.

96. Paul McPartlan, *Sacrament of Salvation: An Introduction to Eucharistic Ecclesiology* (Edinburgh: T & T Clark, 1995), ch. 6.

97. The power of the Eucharist to bring the divided together is powerfully illustrated by Harold E. Dollar in his discussion of how Jewish eating habits informed their sociocultural relationships and vice versa: *A Biblical-Missiological Exploration of the Cross-Cultural Dimensions in Luke-Acts* (San Francisco: Edwin Mellen, 1993), ch. 12.

already opened to the world, at least in attitude and eschatological anticipation if not in participatory actuality.

Fourth, connected to this is that the Supper is a political and prophetic act whereby the enacted and enacting body of Christ provides and mediates an alternative way of life through the gracious activity of the Spirit. By "political," I am drawing both on themes of exodus and liberation connecting the Supper with the Passover meal and on postliberal perspectives that consider how the Supper in particular and the liturgy in general provide imaginative possibilities for and actually instantiate alternative modes of space-time existence in this world.[98] The church gathered around the Table of the Lord is a spatiotemporal and public body that celebrates its constitution through the transgression of all legal, class, gender, sexual, ethnic, racial, and national boundaries (§3.2.3). Hence, against modernity's privatization of the religious dimension of human experience, the fellowship of the Supper opens up a truly free space for human habitation and provides for a counterdiscourse to the prevailing ideologies of any time, thereby making concrete God's redemptive activity in all spheres and aspects of life. In this way, the Eucharist is also a prophetic act, sanctifying, renewing, and empowering the church for its mission of reconciliation to the world (see *BEM* §§14, 17; §3.2.4 above). It makes real, through the working of the Spirit, a "participatory politics" that catches up the members of the body into a transformative narrative, thereby freeing individuals-as-communities to enact the kingdom of the future in the present.

This leads, finally, to an understanding of the Supper as an eschatological act whereby the people of God anticipate embodiment of the word of God according to the full image and likeness of Jesus Christ through the resurrection power of the Spirit. After all, the Supper is not only an act of remembering but also an act of anticipation until Jesus returns (1 Cor. 11:26). And this eschatological dimension is the realm of the Spirit, who graces—sometimes violently breaking through—history's times and places with foreshadowings of the coming kingdom. As the Oriental Orthodox put it, it is the Holy Spirit who "'recaptures' the salvific events of the past into the *Now* and anticipates the 'not yet' into the present."[99] Doing so renders the Supper in particular and the church in general as signs of the eschatological kingdom, which banishes the fallen powers of this world (Luke 11:20) and ushers in justice, righteousness, peace, and

---

98. See also William T. Cavanaugh, *Theopolitical Imagination: Discovering the Liturgy as a Political Act in an Age of Global Consumerism* (New York: T & T Clark, 2002).

99. Jacob Vellian, "Role of the Holy Spirit in the Sanctifying Effect of the Sacraments according to the Oriental Perspective," in *Oriental Churches—Theological Dimensions: International Theological Conference of the Catholic Oriental Churches*, ed. Xavier Koodapuzha (Kerala, India: Oriental Institute of Religious Studies, 1988), 101–11; quotation, 101.

the fruits of the Spirit (cf. Isa. 11:1–2; 32:15–17). It also requires that, eschatologically speaking, "we must regard all human beings, Christians and non-Christians alike, as at least potential members of the body of Christ."[100]

The Spirit ecclesiology developed here has enabled envisioning a pneumatological theology of the sacraments and of the liturgy. Herein lies the pentecostal response to the postliberal vision of the church as an alternative praxis. Though agreeing with the postliberal ecclesiology in its basic senses, pentecostals would want to emphasize the pragmatic, transformative, and eschatological dimensions of being and becoming the people of God. Put this way, the sacramental liturgy, a gift of God and the Holy Spirit, is now a performance that redeems and transforms all persons, along with their times and places, for the kingdom and glory of God. Here, we are in and not of the world, but also open to the world as the world is opened to the coming kingdom by the presence and activity of the Spirit.

This chapter has extended the reflections on pneumatological soteriology in chapter 2 within an ecclesiological framework. It proceeded in three directions: laying out the present ecclesiological *status quaestionis*, engaging the ecclesial tradition's self-understanding, and dialoguing with recent sacramental and liturgical theology. The basic idea is that a pneumatological approach to the church emphasizes the holistic (multidimensional), transformative, dynamic, and eschatological dimensions of what it means to be the people being saved by God. The marks of the church, reread in pneumatological key, contribute to this ecclesiological vision as seen in the concrete depiction of the liturgy and the sacraments. This exercise has provided further opportunity to render a social and communal account of the pentecostal experience of the Spirit. Jesus the Savior, healer, sanctifier, baptizer, and coming King becomes the body of Christ as the saving, healing, sanctifying, baptizing, and—if I may be granted a neologism—"eschatologicalizing" (making the future kingdom present here and now) presence and activity of God by the Spirit. The next chapter explores further the broader ecclesial and ecumenical implications of the Spirit poured out on all flesh. Come Holy Spirit, breathe upon the church . . .

100. Cavanaugh, *Theopolitical Imagination*, 5.

4

"From Every Nation under Heaven"

The Ecumenical Potential of Pentecostalism for World Theology

If the argument in the preceding chapter that world pentecostalism contributes distinctive elements to the traditionally understood marks of the church has merit, then world pentecostalism participates in the catholicity of the church of Jesus Christ. As we have already seen (§3.2.3), the catholicity of the church both assumes an eschatological dimension—the church also being made catholic—and reflects a missionary vision of the church being represented, manifest, and contextually enacted in the diversity of its local congregations. This raises the ecumenical question of the brokenness of the church in its most challenging pentecostal form: how can the divided and dividing pentecostal churches adequately represent the catholicity of the church, much less present to the world a united witness to Jesus and the kingdom? Put in Johannine terms, has the prayer of Jesus that the church may be one failed, and if so, how can the world know that the Father has sent Jesus and that he loves the world as he loves the Son (cf. John 17:22–24)? Although many pentecostals have dismissed the ecumenical question for various reasons,[1] the church's ecumenical failure needs to be confronted insofar as pentecostalism is a missionary movement that emphasizes evangelism and the lack of demonstrated love between believers undermines the church's witness (see John 13:35).

For this reason, an entire chapter is devoted to a discussion of this matter in this pentecostal contribution to world Christian theology in the late modern world. The thesis (§2.2.1; §3.2.3) that the pentecostal experience of the Spirit provides a reconciling dynamic able to heal the fragmentation of the church will be developed here.[2] The ecumenical potential of pentecostalism resides precisely in its conviction that the gathering of those "from every nation under heaven" (Acts 2:5) on the day of Pentecost continues to the present day because the Spirit continues to be poured out upon all flesh. The emphasis lies on *potential*: in reality, pentecostalism is fragmented perhaps even more than other Christian traditions. There is something about the charismatic movement of the Spirit that resists institutionalization insofar as hierarchies, structures, and denominationalism sometimes inhibit the freedom of the Spirit's activity. Thus the ecumenical potential of pentecostalism is a task to be realized, even as the pentecostal experience of the Spirit is a gift to be eschatologically fulfilled.

This chapter develops the biblical and thematic bases for our pneumatological and pentecostal ecumenism (§4.1), surveys the promise of this vision in what I call the ecumenical tradition of pentecostalism (§4.2), and elaborates on the remaining challenges prohibiting the full realization of the ecumenical potential of pentecostalism (§4.3). The aim is to thereby deepen insights into the soteriological and ecclesial nature of the pentecostal outpouring of the Spirit upon all flesh. Put this way, the focus will subordinate the practical questions regarding how to go about doing ecumenism to the theoretical and theological issues that inform our ecumenical vision and identity. Yet as the discussion will show, pentecostal praxis informs pentecostal theory even on this matter, as there is always the hermeneutical spiral between praxis and theory. For the purposes at hand, however, the ecumenical promise and challenge will be presented not only as an organizational and structural

---

1. Some of these—the pentecostal valuing of spiritual over visible unity; pentecostal fears that ecumenical relationships erode the doctrinal foundations of the gospel; and the influence of dispensational eschatology, which identifies the ecumenical movement with the apostasy of the end times—are discussed in Amos Yong, "Pentecostalism and Ecumenism: Past, Present, and Future," part 2, *PR* 4, no. 2 (2001): 36–48.

2. Terrence Robert Crowe, *Pentecostal Unity: Recurring Frustration and Enduring Hopes* (Chicago: Loyola University Press, 1993), has already proposed this, but his discussion was focused on the Assemblies of God.

matter for world Christianity but as representing the very heart of the soteriological and ecclesial gift of God.

4.1 Pentecost and Ecumenism: Biblical and Thematic Considerations

We begin our discussion by articulating the bases for a biblical and pentecostal ecumenism and developing themes for a pneumatological and charismatic ecumenical perspective. The argument here is that the ecumenical event of the day of Pentecost points to an eschatological horizon even as it holds promise for the ongoing work of healing the divisions of the churches.

4.1.1 *Biblical Perspectives on Ecumenism.* The word "ecumenism" is derived from the Greek word *oikoumenē*. The substantive of a participle of *oikeō*, "dwell," which is related to *oikos*, "house," *oikoumenē* (from *oikoumenē gē*, literally, "inhabited earth") is sometimes translated "world" or "whole world." In these cases, *oikoumenē* signifies the world's inhabitants and functions as a figure of speech describing a pervasive reality. It is not used in the modern sense of the term as related to the unity of the church except in a very indirect way, when referring to the widespread influence of Christian actions such as preaching the gospel (e.g., Matt. 24:14; Acts 17:6; 24:5; Rom. 10:18). Instances of the term in the New Testament do not therefore advance our understanding of contemporary ecumenism. Its current meaning derives more from the etymology of the term—the whole world or the entire household or inhabitants of the world—rather than from specific New Testament usage.

Contemporary ecumenism, however, is intimately connected with ecclesiology in general and with the first mark of the church in particular. In fact, the metaphor of household is applied to the church (*tous oikeious*; Gal. 6:10). In the Letter to the Ephesians, the household of God (2:19) is composed of both Jews and Gentiles, is governed by the gospel (*tēn oikonomian*; 3:2), and is united together "in the promise in Christ Jesus" (3:6). Later on this same letter says, "[Make] every effort to maintain the unity of the Spirit in the bond of peace. There is one body and one Spirit, just as you were called to the one hope of your calling, one Lord, one faith, one baptism, one God and Father of all, who is above all and through all and in all" (4:3–6). Clearly, the oneness of God extends to the effects of the work of God (cf. §3.3.2).

Paul confirms this in no uncertain terms in his First Letter to the Corinthians. Factions had developed among those baptized by Paul, Apollos, Peter, and others (1 Cor. 1:10–16; 3:4, 21–23). In response, Paul emphasizes the unity of the body of Christ (e.g., 12:12–13). The intention of God is that "there may be no dissension within the body, but the members may have the same care for one another. If one member suffers, all suffer together with it; if one member is honored, all rejoice together with it. Now you are the body of Christ and individually members of it" (12:25–27). Some might respond that Paul is speaking here to the various individual persons who make up the one body of Christ at Corinth, and say that these words provide no justification for thinking about the unity of various churches as understood by the contemporary ecumenical movement. This ignores, however, the plain meaning of Paul's usage of the metaphor "body of Christ" to describe the church, and the fact that in his salutation he addresses not only the Corinthians but also "all those who in every place call on the name of our Lord Jesus Christ, both their Lord and ours" (1:2). It is therefore reasonable to conclude that the metaphor of various parts of the one body is meaningful at a number of levels: various individual persons in one local congregation, various congregations in a city or geographic region, various groups of churches in the world, and so on.

To stop with Paul, however, would be to leave the discussion at a fairly abstract level. A much more concrete picture emerges when we consider the Gospel accounts. Ecumenists have frequently pointed to Jesus' "high priestly prayer" for the disciples and all believers in John 17. Note first that Jesus' prayer extends far beyond the circle of the twelve disciples and embraces all of those who believe in him (v. 20). The unity that is prayed for is universally inclusive of believers in Jesus. Further, this expected unity derives from the unity between the Father and the Son (v. 21). This is important because the Father-Son unity appears to be all-encompassing: ontologically in terms of shared presence (1:1–2; 10:38; 14:10–11; 16:32) and the divine name (8:58; cf. Exod. 3:14); imagistically in terms of the Son revealing (1:18; 14:7–9) and representing (13:20) the Father; actually in terms of the Son doing (only) what the Father does (5:19; 8:29; 14:31); gloriously in terms of equal honor being due to Father and Son (5:23) and bestowed by each on the other (8:49–50, 54; 13:31–32); judicially, as rendered by the Son on behalf of the Father (5:22, 26–27, 30; 8:16); mutually in terms of witness and testimony (8:18) and will and intention (6:38; 12:27–28); evangelistically in terms of Jesus' proclaiming and teaching (only) the Father's message (7:16–17; 8:28; 12:49; 14:24; 15:15); salvifically in terms of Jesus being the way to the Father (14:6); communally in terms of fellowship (11:41–42) and love (14:21); and so on. This is a deep unity that cannot be simply explained in only one way. As prayed for by Jesus, then, the unity of believers should be understood not simplistically at any one level, but holistically, embracing every aspect or dimension of reality.

This unity thus transcends all artificial lines of demarcation that human beings, even those in churches, so often erect to distinguish themselves from others.

Finally, for our purposes, it would be remiss not to mention the centrality of love to the Father-Son unity and the unity for which Jesus prayed for those who believe in his name (17:26). Love is what characterizes the trinitarian relationship between the Father and the Son, between the Son and the world, and between the Father and the world. Earlier in the gospel, Jesus had said, "By this everyone will know that you are my disciples, if you have love for one another" (13:35). Failure to demonstrate such love to the world betrays our witness to nonbelievers. On the other hand, the loving unity that should bind believers together in Jesus is precisely the testimony by which others realize God's love for them.

The unity between Father and Son is also connected to the sending of the Spirit. Jesus promised the arrival of the Counselor, the Spirit of truth, from the Father and foretold, "On that day you will know that I am in my Father, and you in me, and I in you" (14:20). Later in the same upper-room speech, Jesus indicates that the common message of Father and Son will be made known to the disciples by the Spirit of truth (16:12–15). Yet the Spirit is only implied, not mentioned, in Jesus' ecumenical prayer.

4.1.2 *The Day of Pentecost as an Ecumenical Prototype.* The Pentecost narrative of Acts 2 illuminates the Spirit's ecumenical role:

> When the day of Pentecost had come, they were all together in one place. And suddenly from heaven there came a sound like the rush of a violent wind, and it filled the entire house where they were sitting. Divided tongues, as of fire, appeared among them, and a tongue rested on each of them. All of them were filled with the Holy Spirit and began to speak in other languages, as the Spirit gave them ability.
>
> Now there were devout Jews from every nation under heaven living in Jerusalem. And at this sound the crowd gathered and was bewildered, because each one heard them speaking in the native language of each. Amazed and astonished, they asked, "Are not all these who are speaking Galileans? And how is it that we hear, each of us, in our own native language? Parthians, Medes, Elamites, and residents of Mesopotamia, Judea and Cappadocia, Pontus and Asia, Phrygia and Pamphylia, Egypt and the parts of Libya belonging to Cyrene, and visitors from Rome, both Jews and proselytes, Cretans and Arabs—in our own languages we hear them speaking about God's deeds of power." All were amazed and perplexed, saying to one another, "What does this mean?" (vv. 1–12)

I propose that a pneumatological grounding of ecclesial identity in diversity, and of unity in plurality, is implicit in this passage. This thesis has been argued by a Reformed theologian who has served as a provocative dialogue partner for Pentecostals: Michael Welker.[3]

Welker's pneumatology is self-characterized as a "realistic biblical theology" that pays as much attention to the diversity as to the unity of the biblical narratives and traditions. In his chapter concerning the Spirit on the day of Pentecost and in the book of Acts, Welker suggests that the miracle of Pentecost

> lies not in what is difficult to understand or incomprehensible, but in a totally unexpected comprehensibility and in an unbelievable, universal capacity to understand. . . . This difference between the experience of plural inaccessibility to each other and of enduring foreignness, and unfamiliarity, on the one hand, and of utter commonality of the capacity to understand, on the other hand—this is what is truly and shocking about the Pentecostal event. . . . An astounding, indeed frightening clarity in the midst of the received complexity and variety, a dismaying familiarity in the midst of the received inaccessibility and unfamiliarity—this is what is miraculous and wonderful about the revelation at Pentecost. The Pentecost event connects intense experiences of individuality with a new experience of community.[4]

Welker's account calls attention to the radical pluralism implicit in the Pentecost account. Yet this pluralism, instead of being erased or sublated by the universal outpouring of the Spirit on all flesh, is what constitutes the powerful universality of the pentecostal gift. The result is what Welker calls an "overcomprehensibility" that both amazes and perplexes the spectators.[5] The response "What does this mean?" (v. 12) was not a request for an explanation of what was spoken; it was an expression of the bewilderment that the crowd felt in being able to understand the testimony of the 120 about "God's deeds of power" (v. 11). Read in this light, the Pentecostal event signifies nothing less than that "God affects a world-encompassing, multilingual, polyindividual testimony to Godself."[6]

This unity-in-diversity theme of the day of Pentecost should not be underestimated. As already suggested (§2.2.1), the first *ekklēsia* (2:37–47)

3. Michael Welker, *God the Spirit*, trans. John F. Hoffmeyer (Minneapolis: Fortress, 1994), esp. ch. 5. Cf. Frank Macchia, "Discerning the Spirit in Life: A Review of *God the Spirit* by Michael Welker," *JPT* 10 (1997): 3–28; and Michael Welker, "Spirit Topics: Trinity, Personhood, Mystery, and Tongues," *JPT* 10 (1997): 29–34.

4. Welker, *God the Spirit*, 230–31, 233.

5. Ibid., 232.

6. Ibid., 235.

emerged precisely out of those who congregated that day on the streets of Jerusalem. Notice again some of the regions represented from around the Mediterranean. There were devout Jews, and possibly Gentile proselytes, from Egypt, perhaps denoting what is now called the African continent and thereby including the black race. There were the despised Cretans, long stereotyped as untrustworthy (Titus 1:12–13). There were the Arab descendants of Ishmael. The early church was truly constituted by a diversity of voices, perspectives, and particularities.

The cumulative fruit of the Spirit's outpouring on the day of Pentecost finds its fulfillment in the eschatological consummation of God's saving work. We are told in the revelation to the seer on the isle of Patmos that those gathered before the throne of God and the Lamb are "from every tribe and language and people and nation" (Rev. 5:9; cf. 7:9). This is in part because the gospel is being sent "to every nation and tribe and language and people" (14:6). On that final day, the great multitude representing such a staggering diversity of persons will lift up a resounding chorus of voices to the Lord God almighty as they celebrate the great wedding feast joining together once for all the Lamb and his bride (19:6–9). The one body of those who are saved, as this picture and that depicted at Pentecost show, knows no boundaries, whether such is conceived politically, socially, linguistically, racially or ethnically, or otherwise.

To recapitulate, a biblically conceived ecumenism begins with the one work of God represented during the New Testament era as and through the church of Jesus Christ. The unity of this body is—or should be—a reflection of the unity between the Father and the Son. Put another way, this unity is demonstrated in the love that members of this body have for each other, in the same way that the Father loves the Son and vice versa. It is therefore appropriate to consider this love as "the unity of the Spirit in the bond of peace" (Eph. 4:3), eschatologically inaugurated at Pentecost.

4.1.3 *Pneumatological Themes from the Pentecostal Experience*. From the preceding, two themes emerge that are central to any ecumenism founded on the Pentecost narrative: the reality of what I call the diversities of the Spirit and the missionary thrust of the church.

The diversity of tongues on the day of Pentecost gave witness to the works of God. This appears to be one of the marks of the Spirit, who is most fully present and active in the "varieties of gifts, . . . varieties of services, . . . varieties of activities" (cf. 1 Cor. 12:4–6). Paul envisioned such diversification of giftings through the metaphor of the body of Christ having many parts, many members, many functions, and many components (1 Cor. 12:12–31). This diversity and pluralism therefore are intrinsic to the church itself. The sending of the Spirit on the day of Pentecost resulted in one living organism, the body of Christ, with many members. The many find their wholeness in the one, and the one's effectiveness and beauty are to be found in the diversities of its members, including the sons and daughters, men and women, young and old (Acts 2:17–18) from around the world.

This emphasis on the diversities of the Spirit is a central value of the contemporary ecumenical movement, manifested and expressed variously but also in the microcosm of the World Council of Churches. Although all institutions need to be discerned—even Paul strongly cautions the Corinthian believers that charismatic phenomena inevitably come mixed with human and, at times, demonic influences and require discernment and judgment—the present orientation of the ecumenical movement in general and the WCC in particular is not about imposing a like-mindedness or uniformity of belief or practices on its constituency. Rather, its goal is to lift up the name of Jesus Christ through common witness and common mission, and its conviction is that such common witness and common mission sustain, not destroy, national, regional, local, and indigenous expressions of the gospel. In other words, the present ecclesiology of the ecumenical movement is profoundly pluralistic rather than totalistic or hegemonistic, representing the biblical emphasis on the diversities of the Spirit.[7]

On the practical level, then, the ecumenical movement is more about affirming differences than it is about making churches the world over fit into one mold. In fact, as the *Baptism, Eucharist, Ministry* document illustrates, the plurality of churches, liturgies, and traditions is affirmed. Each church is understood to play a vital role in the overall mission of the church; each contributes to the symphony that declares God's saving presence and activity in the world by the power of the Spirit; each provides distinct witness to the world and brings its own gifts to the head of the church. Indeed, as the contingent of churches from the non-Western world has consistently grown in the WCC, it is increasingly clear that the traditional (i.e., Western) norms for discernment—whether at the level of the manifestation of the *charismata* or even at the more fundamental level of ecclesiologies as a whole—will continue to be challenged, resulting in a reemphasis on scriptural criteria.[8]

Embracing the diversities of the Spirit, however, includes with it potential problems as well. There is, for example, the important matter

7. See, e.g., Yacob Tesfai, *Liberation and Orthodoxy: The Promise and Failures of Interconfessional Dialogue* (Maryknoll, NY: Orbis, 1996).

8. It is ironic that some in the ecumenical movement are threatened by the possibility that the presence of hundreds, if not thousands, of independent pentecostal churches, the majority of them deriving from the two-thirds world, will some day dominate the WCC. See Donald W. Dayton, "Yet Another Layer of the Onion; or, Opening the Ecumenical Door to Let the Rifraff In," *ER* 40 (1988): 87–110.

of an extreme tolerance that might set in, such that truth is compromised. Ecumenists have been charged with being pluralistic relativists, refusing to offend others who might believe or practice differently than they do. On this score, the ecumenical movement needs the pentecostal movement, but only insofar as the latter does not mute the prophetic voice of the Spirit of God. An ecumenism without truth is simply a vacuous, outward unity. Pentecostals who are fearful on this point should be critically engaged on this front. Our obligation should be a discerning participation and engagement, not sectarian withdrawal and condemnation.

I suggest further that the diversities of the Spirit manifest in the present ecumenical movement are a further sign of the missionary impulse that originated modern ecumenism. Few Pentecostals today realize that the ecumenical movement was initially launched as a missionary movement and retains that focus today. As missiologists and historians have noted, although the twentieth was the century of pentecostal missions, the nineteenth was that of the Protestant missionary enterprise. It was during the nineteenth century that the mainline churches established themselves on every continent. It was also during this same time that problems were identified, many of which were too large for the mission agencies of these individual churches and denominations to resolve on their own. The heart of the modern ecumenical movement was birthed at a global mission conference that convened at Edinburgh, Scotland, in 1910, and from which the International Missionary Council (IMC) was established in 1921. At the same time, it was realized that missionary work could not proceed apart from confronting both the social and political injustices prevalent during the interwar years and the doctrinal differences that separated the churches. Thus emerged the Life and Work world conference (1925) and the Faith and Order world conference (1927). These combined to form the WCC in 1948.[9] In 1961, the IMC officially joined forces with the WCC, thus reaffirming the WCC's commitment to the missionary witness of the churches.

The early twentieth century was thus a time during which churches in the West awoke to the power of ecumenical unity for carrying out the task of the Great Commission. As the various churches began to assess the daunting project of world evangelization, they realized that such could be accomplished much more efficiently if they worked together instead of separately. In short, it was the missionary endeavor that brought hitherto self-sufficient groups, movements, and denominations together. Likewise, the central impetus toward classical pentecostal organization

---

9. Marlin Van Elderen, *Introducing the World Council of Churches*, rev. ed., Risk Book Series (Geneva: WCC Publications, 1992), ch. 2.

was the collaborative power of common mission. Fulfilling the missionary mandate has done more to bring the church together since the Reformation than anything else.

This task has not been lost on the ecumenical movement today. Certainly, the world at the beginning of the twenty-first century is quite different from when the IMC was founded. Yet missions remains the raison d'être of the WCC, as clearly reasserted in the WCC's *Ecumenical Affirmation on Missions and Evangelism*, published in 1982. The *Affirmation* emphasizes the importance of conversion, the application of the gospel to every realm of life, the centrality of the churches to God's mission, mission as the way of Christ, the mandate of taking the good news to the poor, the mandate regarding global witness, and the challenge to witness among people of other faiths. In short, ecumenism is missions and vice versa.

It goes without saying, however, that the missionary focus of the ecumenical movement has shifted. Clearly, the evangelistic edge has been blurred and, in some cases, been replaced among some denominations almost completely by socioeconomic and political projects. Yet it is also the case that many of these projects will never be accomplished by individual churches or single denominations working alone. Instead the resources and cumulative power of the entire range of the church of Jesus Christ in all its diversity will need to be mobilized toward action if such changes are to be realized. Should this not lead us to pray for another pentecostal outpouring of the Spirit?

4.2 The Ecumenical Tradition of Pentecostalism

This is exactly how some pentecostals understand the emergence of modern pentecostalism, as an answer to prayer for the unity and mission of the churches. My claim here is to give further impetus to the thesis that modern pentecostalism was not only an ecumenical movement from the beginning but was and has been ecumenical precisely in the pneumatological and charismatic sense of valuing the diversities of the Spirit's gifts and activities and of enacting the power of the Spirit's witness. This will be clear in our discussion of modern pentecostal origins at the beginning of the twentieth century, of the neopentecostal or charismatic renewal movement at midcentury, and of the "color line" in pentecostalism. This discussion will emphasize the distinctive pneumatological and charismatic features of what I call the ecumenical tradition of pentecostalism.

4.2.1 *Modern Pentecostal Origins: Local and Global.* Most histories of modern pentecostalism posit at its origins both the initial manifestation of tongues at Charles Parham's Bethel Bible College in Topeka, Kansas, in January 1901 and the highly publicized revival facilitated by William Seymour at Azusa Street from 1906 to 1908. Focusing on Azusa Street, we observe both that racial and ethnic distinctions were rendered secondary to the fellowship of the Spirit (see §4.2.3) and that there were women—both black and white—in public leadership roles (see §4.3.2). But note the interdenominational character of the revival. Even when we focus only on the black and evangelical roots of pentecostalism identified by Hollenweger,[10] we find a diversity of Christian traditions represented: Keswick Reformed, Wesleyan Holiness, revivalist, Baptistic, African American, and the like. There was a type of separatism quite prevalent among these early pentecostals, many of whom were unsatisfied with the lifeless spiritual state of their existing churches and looking for alternatives. The pentecostal revival seemed to them to be dynamic encounters with God conducive to the Spirit's invigorating movement when compared with the "dead" ecclesial organizations in their backgrounds.

Thus did the founding of classical Pentecostal denominations such as the Assemblies of God in the second decade of the revival unite this disparate group of men and women under a common experience. But not only that: their motivation was also common mission in the power of the Spirit, whether such be regarding the taking of the gospel to foreign lands, social, publication, or educational projects, or the cultivation of pentecostal faith.[11] Since most of them recognized the denominationally schismatic nature of the body of Christ, this also explains why the Assemblies of God as well as other early pentecostal groups saw themselves initially as movements rather than denominations (which most became).

But not only did the early pentecostal revivals attract and unite individuals from a wide variety of Protestant denominations; they also effectively transformed denominations. More specifically, leaders of existing churches and denominations returned to their congregations and organizations taking the pentecostal experience of the Spirit with them. Because of this, "existing denominations were split, while others were totally transformed into pentecostal vehicles."[12] The former included the establishment of the Pentecostal Free Will Baptists (separating from the Free Will Baptists). The latter included the Church of God in Christ

10. See Walter J. Hollenweger, *Pentecostalism: Origins and Developments Worldwide* (Peabody, MA: Hendrickson, 1997); also §I.2.

11. See a reliable history of classical pentecostalism, e.g., Gary B. McGee, *This Gospel Shall Be Preached: A History and Theology of Assemblies of God Foreign Missions to 1959*, 2 vols. (Springfield, MO: Gospel Publishing House, 1986), vol. 1, ch. 4.

12. C. M. Robeck Jr., "Azusa Street Revival," *NIDPCM* 344–50; quotation, 348.

(black Holiness); the Church of God, Cleveland, Tennessee (founded by a Missionary Baptist preacher, R. G. Spurling); and the Pentecostal Holiness Church (Wesleyan Holiness). Thus, pentecostalism was ecumenical not only in bringing individuals from different Christian backgrounds together but also in uniting whole denominations under the one experience of the Spirit.

It was precisely this ecumenical vision that animated many of these early pentecostal pioneers. In almost every instance, their encounter with the Spirit led them to envision that the pentecostal outpouring would be central to experiencing Christian unity. Such unity, they thought, could not emerge from structural or organizational efforts but only through the reconciling presence of the Spirit. Even so, this unity would be accomplished within the framework of the existing denominations as individuals were swept up into the movements of the Spirit. This tradition has spawned a long line of ecumenical pentecostals who, even in the early days, understood their own vocation as pentecostals and charismatics to be bridge builders between the existing churches as empowered by the Spirit.[13] Thus a German Lutheran pastor, Jonathan Paul (1853–1931), began a loose association of churches (the Mülheim Association of Christian Fellowship) that nevertheless remained partly within the established Reformed and Lutheran churches of Germany. From his background in the French Reformed Church, Louis Dallière (1887–1976) worked diligently to ensure the continuation of the charismatic tradition in that denomination. Alexander Boddy (1854–1930) remained a lifelong rector in the Anglican Church, even after coming into the charismatic gift. The founder of Dutch pentecostalism, Gerrit Roelof Polman (1868–1932), was the go-between not only for the churches in the Netherlands but also for those in Germany and Britain during the Second World War.[14] Last but certainly not least is David Du Plessis (1905–1987), one of the few pentecostal bridge builders to those in the mainline churches during the first three decades of the charismatic-renewal movement.[15] For each of these individuals in the ecumenical tradition of pentecostalism, leaving one's denomination was neither a prerequisite for, nor a requirement following, the reception of the pentecostal experience. Rather, it was precisely the experience of the Spirit

13. On the ecumenical ministries of the following individuals, see Hollenweger, *Pentecostalism*, chs. 25–26.

14. See Cornelis van der Lan, *Sectarian against His Will: Gerrit Roelof Polman and the Birth of Pentecostalism in the Netherlands* (Metuchen, NJ: Scarecrow, 1991).

15. Remarkably, we are still awaiting the definitive book length publication on Du Plessis. Meanwhile see Martin Robinson, "David Du Plessis—a Promise Fulfilled," in *Pentecost, Mission, and Ecumenism: Essays on Intercultural Theology*, ed. Jan A. B. Jongeneel et al., SIHC 75 (Frankfurt, Ger.: Peter Lang, 1992), 143–56.

that knit together the followers of Jesus Christ, even those who had not yet manifested all the signs of the Spirit's presence and activity.

This ecumenical tradition of pentecostalism can be more easily understood within an alternative account of pentecostal origins that identifies the movement in global context from the very beginning. In contrast to the standard history, which defines pentecostalism in terms of Parham's Bethel Bible College or Seymour's Azusa Street revival, alternative historiographies are emerging that locate these events in world context.[16] In this broader framework, what was happening at Azusa Street was neither paradigmatic nor prototypical but, rather, illustrative of a much wider move of the Spirit of God. Thus Andrew Harvey Argue, pioneering evangelist and leader of the Pentecostal Assemblies of Canada, reflecting on the revival in November 1908, wrote,

> Our hearts rejoice to hear of many faithful witnesses, many precious souls from nearly every part of the globe, receiving the Holy Ghost according to Acts 2.4, in Jerusalem, Syria, Arabia, Persia and Armenia, and a number of places in China. . . . In India it has broken out in many quarters and . . . in forty places in Scotland. . . . Also many have been baptized in England, Ireland, Wales, Sweden, Norway, Switzerland, Holland, Germany, Australia, Russia and Tibet. In Africa, West and South; San Marcial, New Mexico; Jeruca, Cuba; Egypt, Toronto, Italy; and in Japan.[17]

This worldwide outpouring of the Spirit was not merely a series of disconnected revivals but a complex and differentiated unity as well. Clearly, as Michael Bergunder has noted, original pentecostalism was not only worldwide with the emphasis on geographical diversity but also global by virtue of the complex networks of publications, correspondences, personal contacts/travels, and missionary connections.[18] In a very real sense, many different sites of the revival were epicenters of pentecostal activity, even if none were completely removed from the

16. See, e.g., David Bundy, "Bibliography and Historiography of Pentecostalism outside North America," *NIDPCM* 405–17; Cecil M. Robeck Jr., "Pentecostal Origins in Global Perspective," in *All Together in One Place: Theological Papers from the Brighton Conference on World Evangelization*, ed. Harold D. Hunter and Peter D. Hocken, JPTSup 4 (Sheffield, Eng.: Sheffield Academic Press, 1993), 166–80; and Allan Anderson, *An Introduction to Pentecostalism: Global Charismatic Christianity* (Cambridge: Cambridge University Press, 2004), ch. 9.

17. A. H. Argue in *The Apostolic Messenger*, quoted in D. William Faupel, *The Everlasting Gospel: The Significance of Eschatology in the Development of Pentecostal Thought*, JPTSup 10 (Sheffield, Eng.: Sheffield Academic Press, 1996), 226.

18. Michael Bergunder, "Constructing Indian Pentecostalism: On Issues of Methodology and Representation," in *Asian and Pentecostal: The Charismatic Face of Christianity in Asia*, ed. Allan Anderson and Edmond Tang (Oxford: Regnum; Baguio City, Phil.: Asia Pacific Theological Seminary Press, 2005), 177–213, esp. 179–86.

others. In this case, can we say that original pentecostal ecumenism was, in some sense, orchestrated by the Holy Spirit as a nexus of events wherein each particular occurrence contributed and gave local expression to the wonderful works of God in its own way and language?

4.2.2 *Neopentecostal Ecumenism.* Pentecostal "denominationalism" set in rather quickly toward the end of the first generation, effectively squelching the ecumenical impulse of the movement. I suggest viewing the neopentecostal revival as an antidote to this development. Also known as the charismatic-renewal movement of the mainline churches, neopentecostalism has, like early modern pentecostalism, touched denominations and individual lives. It has revitalized the churches through the emergence of charismatic streams in all the major denominations, including the Roman Catholic Church and the Eastern Orthodox churches.[19]

Not surprisingly, those who participated in or observed the renewal movements in the mainline churches also began to see the ecumenical potential of the experience of the Spirit.[20] These neopentecostals or charismatics recognized that the vitality imparted to Christian faith by the pentecostal outpouring was a common experience that cut across creedal, denominational, liturgical, traditional, and theological/doctrinal lines. Ecumenical activities were sustained and furthered precisely because of the acknowledged commonality of experiencing the Spirit's presence and activity. For them, the pentecostal experience of the Spirit meant a revitalized spiritual life, increased Bible reading, intensified devotional piety, the manifestation of the *charismata*, including speaking in other tongues, renewed appreciation for liturgical and sacramental worship, and deeper motivation toward social action. Aside from personal revival, there has also been the emergence of formal pentecostal dialogues with the established churches—for example, with the Roman Catholic Church and with the World Alliance of Reformed Churches—along with the emergence of new denominations. The Charismatic Episcopal Church (1992) and the Communion of Evangelical Episcopal Churches (1995)

19. See Charles Edwin Jones, *The Charismatic Movement: A Guide to the Study of Neo-Pentecostalism with Emphasis on Anglo-American Sources* (Metuchen, NJ: American Theological Library Association and Scarecrow, 1995). Given that the charismatic-renewal movement is a phenomenon mainly of the Western denominations and churches, the focus in this subsection is on Euroamerican pentecostalism.

20. E.g., "Malines Document II," *PPP* 3:82–174; Philip J. Rosato, "Called by God, in the Holy Spirit: Pneumatological Insights into Ecumenism," *ER* 30 (1978): 110–26; Albert C. Outler, "Pneumatology as an Ecumenical Frontier," *ER* 41 (1989): 363–41; Konrad Raiser, "The Holy Spirit in Modern Ecumenical Thought," *ER* 41 (1989): 375–87; and Henry I. Lederle, "The Spirit of Unity—a Discomforting Comforter: Some Reflections on the Holy Spirit, Ecumenism, and the Pentecostal-Charismatic Movement," *ER* 42 (1990): 279–87.

are examples of organized expressions of the Convergence Movement (from the 1970s), which has sought to blend charismatic, evangelical, liturgical, and sacramental dimensions of church life and spirituality.

More recently the globalization of the charismatic renewal has given further impetus to the idea of pentecostalism as an ecumenical movement. The remarkable power of the pentecostal experience to bridge not only denominational differences but also to speak to the hearts of people who come from divergent institutional, geographic, cultural, and political backgrounds has been recently made even more evident in revivals such as those at Toronto, Brownsville, and Pensacola. These have reached staggering numbers, bringing people together whose paths would never have crossed apart from their life-transforming encounter with the Spirit of God. The masses have come from every continent to experience the power of God and have returned to their places of origin full of the Holy Spirit.[21] This is not to affirm all that goes on at these prolonged evangelistic campaigns. It is, however, to testify to the uniting power of the ecumenical tradition of pentecostalism.

In light of these developments, classical Pentecostal fears regarding the charismatic renewal in the established churches have been somewhat calmed. This has been enabled in part by the development of pentecostal relationships with more evangelical-type denominations and groups. Models of Christian unity centered on common mission such as Billy Graham crusades, World Vision famine relief endeavors, and parachurch ministries such as InterVarsity, Women Aglow, and the Full Gospel Businessmen's Fellowship International have mollified pentecostal apprehensions and actually encouraged pentecostal participation and koinonia with nonpentecostals.

Further, the charismatic explosion in the mainline churches also opened the door for further pentecostal participation in formal ecumenical activities. As previously noted (§1.1.3), the Iglesia Pentecostal de Chile and the Misión Iglesia Pentecostal both joined as member churches of the WCC in 1961. Since then, there has been a slow but steady escalation of pentecostal involvement in things ecumenical. Today pentecostal churches from Brazil, Argentina, and Chile and various sub-Saharan churches have taken out WCC memberships. In addition to WCC involvement, various pentecostal churches have established long-term relationships with mainline denominations, and individual pentecostals are found at national, regional, and other levels of ecumenical activity. Some have even served on the committees of the WCC, the National Council of Churches (in the U.S.A.), and other regional ecumenical

---

21. See Margaret M. Poloma, *Main Street Mystics: The Toronto Blessing and Reviving Pentecostalism* (Lanham, MD: Altamira, 2003).

organizations, such as the Latin American Council of Churches, actively contributing to the development of the theological literature of the ecumenical movement.

As pentecostals have gotten to know nonpentecostals in a deeper way in these joint efforts, they have come to appreciate the diversity present in the body of Christ. Indeed, some have even begun to realize the common convictions that they share with their Roman Catholic brothers and sisters on some issues. And they have also begun to open themselves up to the power that a biblical ecumenism affords the church's witness. Most important has been the realization of the potential of pneumatology for the present and the future of Christian ecumenism. This was nowhere more evident than in the seventh WCC convocation, held in Canberra, Australia, in February 1991.[22] The theme of this gathering was "Come Holy Spirit, Renew the Whole Creation" (cf. Ps. 104:30). Work sections were formed under the headings "Giver of Life—Sustain Your Creation!" "Spirit of Truth—Set Us Free!" "Spirit of Unity—Reconcile Your People!" and "Holy Spirit—Transform and Sanctify Us!" Reports from those who attended testified to the powerful spirit of unity present as Christians from all over the world gathered to worship, pray, sing, dance, and rejoice together in Jesus' name. Such an event probably would not have been possible apart from the charismatic renewal and the pentecostal presence in the WCC. Events exactly like these—recall Toronto, Brownsville, Pensacola, and so forth—are what transform the lives of delegates and, by extension, the congregations to which they belong.

But there have also been challenges. Certainly, not all that has flown under the banner of charismatic renewal in the ecumenical movement can or should be endorsed. Even as pentecostals have dropped the ball regarding specific issues in their own history, so have ecumenists as well. Thus, when one of the plenary speakers of the Canberra conference invoked the spirits of war-torn and destitute Korean people and prayed for healing, this went too far for most participants and delegates.[23] Again, however, discerning participation rather than sectarian withdrawal is in order. Pentecostal revivals have by no means been free of controversy themselves. The proper response is not to ban revivals but to sift the wheat from the chaff. In the same way, one can and should expect that

22. See Michael Kinnamon, ed., *Signs of the Spirit: Official Report of the 7th Assembly of the World Council of Churches, Canberra, Australia, 7–20 February 1991* (Geneva: WCC Publications; Grand Rapids: Eerdmans, 1991); and Krister Stendahl, *Energy for Life: Reflections on the Theme "Come, Holy Spirit—Renew the Whole Creation"* (Geneva: WCC Publications, 1990).

23. For a pentecostal report, see Cecil M. Robeck Jr., "A Pentecostal Reflects on Canberra," in *Beyond Canberra: Evangelical Responses to Contemporary Ecumenical Issues*, ed. Bruce J. Nicholls and Bong Rin Ro (Oxford: Regnum, 1993), 108–20, esp. 111–12.

all genuine movements of the Spirit in the ecumenical world will be accompanied by manifestations that require discernment. This makes pentecostal participation all the more important, given that we, of all persons, are (or should be) the ones most sensitive to the need for discernment of spirits and for openness to that particular gift of the Spirit.

Against this backdrop, the question is no longer whether pentecostals are ecumenical but what kind of ecumenists they should be. In one sense, the ecumenical movement cannot be avoided, since pentecostals have always been ecumenical even though most of us have not realized this before.[24] And those who wish to withdraw will be challenged from the pentecostal fold (within) rather than from the neopentecostal or other quarters (without). This challenge, with all the promise and problems attached thereto, can be most clearly seen in the relationship between black and white pentecostals.

4.2.3 *Pentecostalism and the Color Line: An Ecumenical Case Study.* Having previously provided an overview of black pentecostalism in the U.S.A. (§1.3.4), I now focus on the question of pentecostal ecumenism through the lens of black pentecostalism and black-white pentecostal relationships in North America. One of the least-known facts about the Azusa Street revival is its multiracial environment. This is especially remarkable given the segregationism prevalent in North America during the first half of the twentieth century. From 1906 to 1908, the Azusa Street mission drew together persons from several races, ethnic groups, cultures, and nationalities. This integration of blacks and whites (not to mention Hispanics and Asians) was practically unheard of given the American context more than fifty years before the civil rights movement. Blacks and whites were found worshiping and singing together, tarrying before the Lord and praying for one another, "mingling and even touching in the mission."[25] One participant recollected that at Azusa Street "the 'color line' was washed away in the blood."[26] These events were unprecedented. The result was not only a transformation of hearts but also a tearing down of barriers inhibiting the experience of genuine Christian unity such that "there is no longer Greek and Jew, circumcised and uncircumcised, barbarian, Scythian, slave and free; but Christ is all and in all!" (Col. 3:11; cf. 1 Cor. 12:13; Gal. 3:28, which adds "male and female").

24. See Cecil Mel Robeck Jr., "Taking Stock of Pentecostalism: Reflections of a Retiring Editor," *PNEUMA* 15, no. 1 (1993): 35–60, esp. 39.

25. Dale T. Irvin, "'Drawing All Together into One Bond of Love': The Ecumenical Vision of William J. Seymour and the Azusa Street Revival," *JPT* 6 (1995): 25–53; quotation, 46.

26. Frank Bartleman, *Azusa Street: The Roots of Modern-Day Pentecost* (1925; repr., Plainfield, NJ: Logos International, 1980), 54.

That the ecumenical miracle at Azusa Street did not last is also a well-known historical fact. Whites and blacks formed their own denominations because of the socioeconomic and political pressures in force at that time. White pentecostals drifted toward their Yankee (i.e., fundamentalist and, later, evangelical) relatives, forging alliances that have, in more recent times, left many pentecostals wondering what has happened to the pentecostal fervor. Black pentecostals, however, have continued to emphasize the shout, the dance, the sway, the clap, and the many other electrifying features of the original Azusa Street revival. This parting of ways has signified, in some respect, the socioeconomic distinctions between whites and blacks in North America. Upwardly mobile whites moved further and further away from lower-class blacks, leaving in places a chasm unbridgeable (sad to say) even for a Spirit-led people. In hindsight, it is seen that pentecostals squandered a golden opportunity to continue as a prophetic voice not only on racial and ethnic issues but also on socioeconomic ones as well. Racial discrimination and socioeconomic segregation would persist for another sixty and more years before being legally confronted. What might have happened if the original ecumenical character of pentecostalism had persisted and developed instead?

Even in light of the civil rights movements of the 1960s and 1970s, however, pentecostals have been slow to respond to the need for racial reconciliation. It was not until October 1994 that the all-white Pentecostal Fellowship of North America (PFNA) voted to dissolve and reconstitute as a racially inclusive group.[27] The result was the emergence of the Pentecostal/Charismatic Churches of North America (PCCNA). Whites and blacks were led first to remember and acknowledge the racism of the past; then to seek forgiveness from, and dispense forgiveness to, each other; celebrate the Lord's Supper together; and, at one point, participate jointly in a spontaneous foot-washing ceremony. The result included a "Pentecostal Partners Racial Reconciliation Manifesto," written jointly by black and white pentecostal leaders, which proposed a "reconciliation strategy for 21st century ministry."[28] Its eleven articles included a repudiation of racism in all its forms along with a commitment to retrieve and reenact the reconciliatory message of Azusa Street.

One should not disparage the import of this "Memphis Miracle," as it has been acclaimed. Better late than never, as the old saying goes. Still, one cannot help but lament the fact that instead of being the pacesetters, pentecostals have been sluggish in acting out the impulses toward racial

27. For details, see Frank Macchia, "From Azusa to Memphis: Evaluating the Racial Reconciliation Dialogue among Pentecostals," *PNEUMA* 17, no. 2 (1995): 203–18.

28. Ibid., 217–18; see also the PCCNA website, http://www.pctii.org/pccna/manifesto .html.

reconciliation inherent within its original ecumenical experience. Though symbolically significant, the "Racial Reconciliation Manifesto" needs to be followed by sustained and concrete action to address the actual racism and the social, political, and economic divides between black and white pentecostalism, especially in North America. On the theological front, what about the fact that many black pentecostals—perhaps up to 30 percent of all black churches and denominations—are Apostolics who affirm a Oneness understanding of God?[29] In this case, is not the trinitarian statement of faith adopted by the PCCNA (mainly from the white National Association of Evangelicals) a step backwards for pentecostal ecumenism in general and for black-white relations in particular? Further, in light of the original multiculturalism of the Azusa Street revival, what about reconciliation beyond black and white to include Hispanic, Asian, and other ethnic pentecostals? Why are we not surprised to hear that black and Hispanic trinitarians and black and Hispanic Oneness congregations fellowship together much more than white trinitarians and Oneness?[30] Finally, does not any reconciliation remain incomplete if it fails to address the subordination of women?[31]

Three observations can be made about the ecumenical tradition of pentecostalism when viewed through the lens of black-white pentecostal relations. First, the slow healing of the breach between black and white pentecostals can only revive pentecostalism, for various reasons. At the very least, the emergence of multicultural congregations featuring blacks and whites worshiping together will restore to pentecostalism a richer sense of the charisms of the Spirit. Whereas not uncommonly among white pentecostals "the charismata were soon restricted to the nine referred to in 1 Corinthians 12," among black pentecostals the Spirit continues to be perceived as working in and through the people of God "in the gifts of story and song, testimony and prayer, vision and dream, dance and motor behaviour, shouting and the drama of the sermon—all manifestations of the power and love of God."[32] Similarly to the pentecostal dialogue

29. Of the 124 black denominations or bodies of churches listed under "Pentecostal/Apostolic, Holiness and Deliverance" churches in Wardell J. Payne, ed., *Directory of African American Religious Bodies: A Compendium by the Howard University School of Divinity* (Washington, DC: Howard University Press, 1991), 82–116, there are 37 identified as Oneness.

30. David D. Daniels, "Dialogue among Black and Hispanic Pentecostal Scholars: A Report and Some Personal Observations," *PNEUMA* 17, no. 2 (1995): 219–28, esp. 226–27.

31. These and many other pointed questions are posed in the "Roundtable: Racial Reconciliation" articles by Frank Macchia, Ithiel Clemmons, Leonard Lovett, Manuel Gaxiola-Gaxiola, Samuel Solivan, Barbara M. Amos, and Cecil M. Robeck Jr. in the spring 1996 issue of *PNEUMA*.

32. Iain MacRobert, *The Black Roots and White Racism of Early Pentecostalism in the USA* (New York: St. Martin's, 1988), esp. 90–93; quotation, 92.

with the Syriac Orthodox tradition submitted earlier (§3.3.2), in this case the mundane workings of the Spirit are retrieved alongside the ecstatic manifestations of the Spirit.

Second, insofar as black pentecostalism emphasizes the experiential dimension of ecumenism much more than it does the doctrinal, black-white ecumenism will restore to center stage pentecostal witness as a way of life. White pentecostals will be required once again to own up to the experiential matrix of their theologies even while black pentecostals will be confronted with the richness of the Christian theological tradition. Sure, blacks and whites can stay within their own comfort zones, but doing so prompts this question: "How does one interpret the predominately African American membership within Wesleyan Pentecostalism, the predominately white and Hispanic membership within Reformed Pentecostalism, and the predominately African American membership of Oneness Pentecostalism?"[33] Might not a renewed black-white pentecostal ecumenism contribute to the overcoming of various dogmatisms, whether it is between Reformed and Wesleyan pentecostalisms or even trinitarian and Oneness pentecostalisms?

Finally, black-white pentecostal ecumenism will energize the movement for the social, economic, and political tasks that confront the churches in general and world pentecostalism in particular. As Russell Spittler, Assemblies of God educator and exegete, notes: "White Pentecostals are by their doctrines very otherworldly. . . . [They] are far more influenced by fundamentalism than blacks are. And blacks are far more influenced by factors and forces in social change."[34] Black pentecostals have been immune neither to the fundamentalist-dispensationalist eschatological leaven—with many black churches having succumbed to processes of "spiritualization" (instead of taking sociopolitical action) and "pacification" (internalizing oppression in order to respond pacifistically)[35]—nor to accommodation to the dominant capitalist ideology of upward social movement, as exemplified by the emergence of a productionism/consumerism of spirituals and gospel music, black amusement,

33. David D. Daniels, "'Everybody Bids You Welcome': A Multicultural Approach to North American Pentecostalism," in *The Globalization of Pentecostalism: A Religion Made to Travel*, ed. Murray W. Dempster, Byron D. Klaus, and Douglas Petersen (Irvine, CA: Regnum International; Carlisle, Eng.: Paternoster, 1999), 222–52; quotation, 247.

34. Quoted in Marlon Millner, "We've Come This Far by Faith: Pentecostalism and Political and Social Upward Mobility among African-Americans," *CPCR* 9 (2001), http://www.pctii.org/cyberj/cyber9.html.

35. See Robert Beckford, "Black Pentecostals and Black Politics," in *Pentecostals after a Century: Global Perspectives on a Movement in Transition*, ed. Allan H. Anderson and Walter J. Hollenweger, JPTSup 15 (Sheffield, Eng.: Sheffield Academic Press, 1999), 48–59; also idem, *Dread and Pentecostal: A Political Theology for the Black Church in Britain* (London: SPCK, 2000).

clubs, shows, and so on.[36] Yet by and large, black pentecostalism remains much more aware of the social dimension of religious faith than white. So whereas white pentecostals in North America are concerned first and foremost about doctrinal orthodoxy and evangelism directed toward conversion, black pentecostals are more concerned with social issues.[37] Thus the well-known and influential black pentecostal churches are in many cases—for example, the West Angeles Church of God in Christ (Bishop Charles E. Blake), the Church of God in Christ in Brooklyn (Reverend William Dougherty), and the Mason Temple Church of God in Christ, Memphis[38]—active both in providing communal networks of support for the marginalized and in being actively engaged in sociopolitical processes of transformation. In all of these ways, the contribution of the black churches to the ecumenical tradition of pentecostalism is to restore to a central position the concerns for uplifting the black race, empowering sociopolitical and economic transformation of the church, acting as the prophetic conscience of the nation in general and of the believing community in particular, encouraging socially informed theological reflection, and reintegrating (black) evangelicalism into the black community and melding the former's agenda of spiritual concerns with the latter's agenda of social concerns.[39]

4.3 PENTECOSTALISM AND ECUMENISM: PRESENT AND FUTURE CHALLENGES

The preceding overviews demand further reflection on the present and future challenges confronting the ecumenical tradition of Pentecostalism. Here we focus on matters related to social witness, gender issues, and multifaith ecumenism.

4.3.1 *Ecumenism and Social Justice.* The discussion of black-white pentecostal relations sets the social-justice question firmly on the church's ecumenical agenda. The questions here are pointed: How can the church provide a unified witness to the gospel when it is itself fragmented be-

36. Clarence Taylor, *The Black Churches of Brooklyn* (New York: Columbia University Press, 1994), ch. 3.

37. With some exceptions among whites; see Sharon Linzey Georgianna, "The American Assemblies of God: Spiritual Emphasis and Social Activism," in *Faces of Renewal: Studies in Honor of Stanley M. Horton Presented on His 70th Birthday,* ed. Paul Elbert (Peabody, MA: Hendrickson, 1988), 263–77.

38. All are noted by Andrew Billingsley, *Mighty like a River: The Black Church and Social Reform* (New York: Oxford University Press, 1999), 137.

39. Mary R. Sawyer, *Black Ecumenism: Implementing the Demands of Justice* (Valley Forge, PA: Trinity Press International, 1994).

tween the haves and the have-nots? How can the message of the church be good news to the poor when they are being exploited by the rich? How can the call for church unity be authentic given the socioeconomic disparities currently in place?

Black pentecostals have already been of tremendous assistance in formulating a pentecostal social ethic (see §§1.3.2–1.3.4). Most striking among their contributions is the raising of historical consciousness regarding the religious and theological ideologies that legitimate racism and racial prejudice. Black pentecostals have also consistently retrieved and reappropriated the Azusa Street experience as a model for present and future interracial and interethnic relationships: the Spirit poured out upon all flesh is no respecter of persons and values the various shades of color that define human beings. Finally, in uniting spirituality and social awareness and in attending to the economic and political dimensions of religious practice, black pentecostals provide important perspectives on the nature of Christian worship and piety even as they show that all Christian practice and theory occur within, and need to engage, their social and historical contexts.

These insights provide a solid foundation for the kind of pentecostal social ethic that needs to inform and enrich the ecumenical tradition of pentecostalism. Such insights are immensely valuable when brought into dialogue with the work in ethics conducted from Roman Catholic charismatic perspectives. Post–Vatican II Catholicism has repeatedly emphasized social witness alongside dialogue and proclamation. Convinced not only that the Spirit comes upon individuals but also that the Spirit renews the face of the earth, Catholic charismatics have sketched out a pneumatological theology of social action emphasizing the charisms of the Spirit, the fruits of the Spirit, the Spirit's work to evangelize and humanize and to redeem sin and relieve suffering, and the apostolic empowerment of the Spirit.[40] Catholic charismatic social ethics has focused on concrete social issues—the aged; correctional reform; drugs and addictions; the environment; hunger; the media and their usage; mental illness; poverty; race relations; consumerism, education, government/politics, and housing; and the sick[41]—with emphasis upon the

40. Cardinal Léon-Joseph Suenens and Dom Helder Camara, "Malines Document III," in *Charismatic Renewal and Social Action: A Dialogue* (Ann Arbor, MI: Servant, 1979), repr. in *PPP* 3:291–357.

41. All are discussed in Sheila Macmanus Fahey, *Charismatic Social Action: Reflection/Resource Manual* (New York: Paulist, 1977).

But what about war and peacemaking? They are strikingly absent in Fahey's discussion. There is a movement to retrieve and reappropriate the pacifist stance of many pentecostals during the early days of the movement. The argument is that pacifism is a moral sign of the restoration of the apostolic church, is a critique of the existing moral order,

charismatic giftings of the Spirit as essential to adequate engagement (see §7.3.2). Black pentecostalism explicitly identifies the racial and ethnic dimensions of social problems even as the Catholic charismatic renewal provides the kinds of institutional commitment required for concrete and effective social transformation.

Further, black pentecostal and Catholic charismatic concerns come together in the ethical vision of Latino/a pentecostals. Defining Christian salvation in terms of liberation, shalom, and reconciliation, pentecostal theologian Eldin Villafañe asks how this can be realized in Hispanic communities.[42] To answer this question, he recognizes the need to identify the cultural, sociodemographic, and anthropological analyses of the Latino situation and the religious, cultural, and spiritual resources available to Hispanics for addressing their concerns. The central characteristics of Hispanic pentecostal spirituality—their passion, personalism, communal emphases, festiveness, and so forth—are then correlated with the signs of the Spirit's presence and activity, whether this be the Spirit's brooding over the waters of history, the Spirit's grieving over personal and social sin, or the Spirit's empowering baptism for witness. Villafañe draws on this correlation to talk about "ethics as pneumatology" and "pneumatic political discipleship": the Spirit challenges the church to participate in the reign of God, to confront and dismantle structural sin and evil, and to fulfill its prophetic and vocational missions of establishing koinonia through liturgy, kerygmatic proclamation, and discipleship and service.[43]

Assemblies of God social ethicist Murray W. Dempster also utilizes this emphasis on koinonia, kerygma, and *diakonia* (discipleship). Dempster is after a holistic model of evangelism that not only proclaims the kingdom of God but also manifests its eschatological presence through social action.[44] The church's social witness—both social welfare for

and puts into practice the universal valuation of human life. See Murray W. Dempster, "Pacifism in Pentecostalism: The Case of the Assemblies of God," in *The Fragmentation of the Church and Its Unity in Peacemaking*, ed. Jeff Gros and John D. Rempel (Grand Rapids: Eerdmans, 2001), 137–65; Joel Shuman, "Pentecost and the End of Patriotism: A Call for the Restoration of Pacifism among Pentecostal Christians," *JPT* 9 (1996): 70–96; and Paul N. Alexander, "Spirit Empowered Peacemaking: Toward a Pentecostal Peace Fellowship," *JEPTA* 22 (2002): 78–102.

42. See Eldin Villafañe, *The Liberating Spirit: Toward an Hispanic American Pentecostal Social Ethic* (Lanham, MD: University Press of America, 1992).

43. Ibid., ch. 5; also Eldin Villafañe, "The Politics of the Spirit: Reflections on a Theology of Social Transformation for the Twenty-First Century," *PNEUMA* 18, no. 2 (1996): 161–70.

44. Murray W. Dempster, "Evangelism, Social Concern, and the Kingdom of God," in *Called and Empowered: Global Mission in Pentecostal Perspective*, ed. Murray W. Dempster, Byron D. Klaus, and Douglas Petersen (Peabody, MA: Hendrickson, 1991), 22–43.

individuals and social action that transforms social systems—makes tangible the church's kerygmatic proclamation, confirms the truth of and validates the gospel's claims, and serves to exemplify the church as a countercommunity even as it transmits/bears the church's moral tradition. To do all this, Dempster urges, is to follow in the footsteps of Jesus and do what he did under the power of the Spirit: proclaim and inaugurate the kingdom of God among the poor, the oppressed, the sick, the demon-possessed, and others. In this way, we have "a Kingdom ethic made operational within the charismatic community by the empowerment of the Spirit."[45] Taking Dempster's suggestions seriously would not only continue the reconciliation of blacks and whites but also propel the black pentecostal vision for social justice to the front of contemporary pentecostal thought and practice. After all, this perspective legitimates the prophetic tradition of black pentecostalism, which seeks, following the footsteps of the Hebrew prophets, to address social injustices in the name of God. And in the end, following the life and ministry of Jesus leads to a healthy reformulation of pentecostal eschatology.[46] Instead of being derived from dispensationalist time charts that undermine social action through emphasis on otherworldly salvation, pentecostalism will be able to develop themes from within the pentecostal experience itself that allow the impending kingdom of God to break through into the historical present. The result will be the kind of holistic eschatology that values the embodiment of the present even while awaiting the resurrection of the body; that actualizes the "fellowship of the Spirit" even while awaiting the eschatological banquet given through the Spirit's invitation; and that participates in the incarnational and pentecostal movements of history even while awaiting the taking up of this history into the eternal kingdom of God (see §1.2.3; §2.2.1).

In all of this, the church's social witness remains its most powerful means of proclaiming the full gospel, since the gospel is not just talk but action. Empowered by the Spirit, such witness overcomes the structures and carriers of evil, heals the divisions between human beings, and actualizes the unity and catholicity of the church as far as possible in awaiting the eschatological kingdom. These are the normative marks of the Spirit's presence and activity in the ecumenical tradition of pentecostalism.

4.3.2 *Ecumenism and Gender: Women and Pentecostalism.* But what if you're black, poor, *and* a woman? The ecumenical tradition of pentecostalism may be bringing black and white *men* together, some might respond,

45. Murray W. Dempster, "Pentecostal Social Concern and the Biblical Mandate for Social Justice," *PNEUMA* 9, no. 2 (1987): 129–53; quotation, 147.

46. Murray W. Dempster, "Christian Social Concern in Pentecostal Perspective: Reformulating Pentecostal Eschatology," *JPT* 2 (1993): 51–64.

but still be leaving out women in general, not to mention black women in particular.[47] Although many important issues need to be addressed regarding the category of gender, the focus here is on the ecumenical question of how the unity of the church can be fully realized if more than half of its constituency is subordinated to the rest and/or marginalized from the centers of power and authority. On the basis of previous discussions (§1.1.2; §2.2.1), pentecostal ecumenism cannot and should not avoid this issue and, further, has resources within the tradition to redress it.

Historically, when discussing gender, most pentecostals see men and women as equals before God. Various ecclesial and cultural factors, however, have left women subordinated under the "headship" of their husbands in the home and under the leadership and authority of males in the churches. Being the biblical literalists they are, pentecostals have justified this simply by quoting the relevant scriptural texts (for example, 1 Cor. 11:3; Eph. 5:22–24; 1 Tim. 2:12–15; and 1 Pet. 3:1–6).

Yet the matter is not so easily decided. The Scriptures provide their own internal qualifications to the preceding texts. The Corinthians text should be read in light of 11:11–13, which presumes that women continue to pray and prophesy so long as they observe the proper etiquette,[48] and the Ephesians passage follows 5:21, which calls for the mutual submission of everyone to others. Timothy and Peter include injunctions regarding the dress of women that are undeniably culture-relative rather than universal prescriptions. Why insist on a literal reading of the portions dealing with women in ministry and not on the dress codes in the broader context? Further, in the case of Timothy's congregation, there were undoubtedly troublesome matters involving some of the women (e.g., 1 Tim. 5:11–16; 2 Tim. 3:6), and there is the apparent fact that the Paul who denied women the opportunity to teach and minister is also the one who had coworkers in the gospel, such as Euodia, Syntyche, and Priscilla (Phil. 4:2–3; Rom. 16:3), and recognized the ministry of deaconesses such as Phoebe (Rom. 16:1). Finally, what about women judges (Deborah) and prophetesses (Miriam, Huldah)?

Partly because of the scriptural ambiguity, there has always been an ambivalence among pentecostals regarding the ordination of women. But more important in the pentecostal case has been the prominence of

47. Black pentecostals are beginning to contribute explicitly to womanist conversations; see, e.g., Lorine L. Cummings, "A Womanist Response to the Afrocentric Idea: Jarena Lee, Womanist Preacher," in *Living the Intersection: Womanism and Afrocentrism in Theology*, ed. Cheryl J. Sanders (Minneapolis: Fortress, 1995), 57–66.

48. In addition to this point, Jenny Everts Powers, "Recovering a Woman's Head with Prophetic Authority: A Pentecostal Interpretation of 1 Corinthians 11.3–16," *JPT* 10, no. 1 (2002): 11–37, argues that the same hermeneutic that uses this passage to restrict women from ministry is employed against the pentecostal doctrine of Spirit baptism.

women called and empowered by the Spirit for ministry in the churches from the earliest days of the revival. At Azusa Street, the prominence of pentecostal women may have anticipated the accomplishments of the women's suffrage movement, culminating in the passage of the Nineteenth Amendment, allowing women the right to vote, in 1920. Since that time, women have served in almost every type of ministry position available. Names such as Minnie Abrams (missionary to India), Florence Crawford (founder of the Apostolic Faith Church in Portland, Oregon), Lucy Farrow (missionary and evangelist), Alice Luce (church pioneer and educator), Aimee Semple McPherson (founder of the International Church of the Foursquare Gospel), Carrie Judd Montgomery (transdenominational minister, teacher, writer, and social worker), Agnes Ozman (evangelist), Lillian Trasher (missionary to Egypt), Maria Woodworth-Etter (healing evangelist), Ida B. Robinson (founder of the Mount Sinai Holy Church of America), and, more recently, Kathryn Kuhlman (healing evangelist) are representative of the legacy of pentecostal women.[49] Yet in the main, most of the scores of other pentecostal women in ministry struggled to reconcile their call to ministry with the prevailing expectations of their times, their churches, and even their spouses.[50]

Unsurprisingly, we have seen a decline in the number of women in ministry since the first generation of modern pentecostal pioneers. The ever-increasing institutionalization of pentecostalism led to the further marginalization of women from positions of authority in the churches.[51] They could be active in the ministry in various ways so long as they did not have authority over men, according to the Pauline injunction (1 Tim. 2:12). Further, the increasing alliances forged between pentecostalism and evangelicalism from the 1940s onward meant that evangelical battles between complementarians and egalitarians (as these positions have come to be called)[52] now also belonged to pentecostals. Finally, the rise of feminism with its liberal hermeneutic of suspicion scared

49. Each of the women named has her own entry in *NIDPCM*; cf. also James R. Goff Jr. and Grant Wacker, eds., *Portraits of a Generation: Early Pentecostal Leaders* (Fayetteville: University of Arkansas Press, 2002).

50. This ambiguity continued almost to the present time, as documented by Elaine J. Lawless, *Handmaidens of the Lord: Pentecostal Women Preachers and Traditional Religion* (Philadelphia: University of Pennsylvania Press, 1988), esp. ch. 5.

51. So Margaret M. Poloma, "Charisma, Institutionalization, and Social Change," *PNEUMA* 17, no. 2 (1998): 245–52; Jacqueline Grey, "Torn Stockings and Enculturation: Women Pastors and the Australian Assemblies of God," *AusPS* 5–6 (2001): 95–106; and Mickey Crews, *The Church of God: A Social History* (Knoxville: University of Tennessee Press, 1990), ch. 5.

52. See James R. Beck and Craig L. Blomberg, eds., *Two Views on Women in Ministry* (Grand Rapids: Zondervan, 2001).

off pentecostals, who were and remain, generally speaking, theological conservatives.

As we have seen, the tension felt by modern pentecostal women exists in the biblical texts, even perhaps in the communities to whom Luke wrote.[53] Yet although we need to be careful of reading contemporary understandings of androcentrism, patriarchalism, and egalitarianism into first-century horizons and self-understandings, it is also clear that, on the whole, Luke's presentation of women is quite positive compared with the prevailing views of his time. Following Ben Witherington, I propose to recognize Jesus as working to dismantle class distinctions and to reform Jewish attitudes toward women *within* a patriarchal culture.[54] Jesus not only receives women as disciples (Luke 8:1–3) and teaches them (10:38–42) but also breaks social (7:36–50), political (18:1–8), ritual (8:42b–48), religious (13:10–17), and other taboos against women prevalent in his day. Furthermore, from the perspective of the day of Pentecost, the role of women in Luke-Acts is a fulfillment of Joel's prophecy regarding the Spirit being given fully also to women (cf. Joel 2:28–29; Acts 2:17). "It is clear that the realization of Joel's prediction that 'your daughters shall prophesy' is one of the signs that the last days have arrived."[55] Women were among those who waited for the promise of the Spirit in the upper room (Acts 1:14), and there is no reason to doubt that they received the pentecostal baptism and spoke about God's deeds of power (2:11b). Further, there is the explicit teaching ministry of Priscilla (18:1–3, 26; in the latter verse teaching Apollos, a man), the four prophesying daughters of Philip (21:9), and the host of women, such as Dorcas and Lydia, who ministered variously to the needs of those around

53. This is the thesis of Barbara Reid, *Choosing the Better Part? Women in the Gospel of Luke* (Collegeville, MN: Liturgical Press, 1996): that Luke's portrayal of women in silent, passive, and supporting roles and as being in need of wholeness (which Jesus restores) reveals both his patriarchal mindset and his theological understanding of women as subordinate to men, at least in terms of public ministry—even Philip's four prophesying daughters are silent. Reid suggests that a feminist liberation interpretation of Luke today will still need to read against the grain of Luke's (textual) intention and "choose the better part" (full egalitarianism) in order for the gospel to be good news to women. See also Robert J. Karris, "Women and Discipleship in Luke," in *A Feminist Companion to Luke*, ed. Amy-Jill Levine and Marianne Blickenstaff (New York: Sheffield Academic Press, 2002), 23–43.

54. Ben Witherington III, *Women in the Ministry of Jesus*, Society for New Testament Studies Monograph Series 51 (Cambridge: Cambridge University Press, 1984), 128; "On the Road with Mary Magdalene, Joanna, Susanna, and Other Disciples—Luke 8:1–3," in Levine and Blickenstaff, eds., *A Feminist Companion to Luke*, 133–39; and Allen Black, "Women in the Gospel of Luke," in *Essays on Women in Earliest Christianity*, ed. Carroll D. Osburn (Joplin, MO: College Press, 1995), 445–68, esp. 465–68.

55. Jenny Everts Powers, "'Your Daughters Shall Prophesy': Pentecostal Hermeneutics and the Empowerment of Women," in Dempster, Klaus, and Petersen, eds., *The Globalization of Pentecostalism*, 313–37; quotation, 330.

them. Finally, in retrospect, the women were the first evangelists to announce the good news of the resurrection, even before the outpouring of the Spirit on the day of Pentecost (cf. Luke 23:55–24:10).

When these data are set alongside the other New Testament references, it is no wonder that pentecostals have argued both that the life and work of Christ have broken the curse on women from the fall and that the last days' outpouring of the Spirit on women has anointed them for ministry.[56] Thus the need for an authentic "Pentecostal-charismatic feminism" is acknowledged as essential to the future of the ecumenical tradition of pentecostalism.[57] This is a kind of pneumatic feminism, conferred not by any rite of ministerial ordination but by the authority of the Spirit manifest in the operation of the charisms in the lives and ministries of women.[58] And is it not possible that, given the widespread patriarchalism and sexism that (pentecostal) women have had to endure, they have been the most broken and therefore the most open to the infilling and empowerment of the Spirit?[59] Surely at the level of the basic and ongoing ministries of the church of Jesus Christ, women have carried the load. Is it not time for the ecumenical tradition of pentecostalism to affirm unequivocally that God's being no respecter of persons requires the acknowledgment of the full equality of women not only in terms of human standing before God but also in terms of male-female relationships in the home, the churches, and society?[60]

56. See Jenny Everts Powers, "Reversing the Curse: Menstruation, Childbirth, and the Status of Women in the New Testament" (paper presented at the annual meeting of the Society for Pentecostal Studies, Marquette University, Milwaukee, WI, March 13, 2004; to be published in *JPT*).

57. Cheryl Bridges Johns, "Pentecostal Spirituality and the Conscientization of Women," in Hunter and Hocken, eds., *All Together in One Place*, 153–65; also Pamela S. Holmes, "An Educational Encounter: A Pentecostal Considers the Work of Elisabeth S. Fiorenza," *Refleks—med karismatisk kristendom i fokus* 2, no. 1 (2003): 52–67.

58. See David Roebuck, "Perfect Liberty to Preach the Gospel: Women Ministers in the Church of God," *PNEUMA* 17, no. 1 (1995): 25–32.

59. This is the thesis of Jenny Meyers Everts [Everts Powers], "Brokenness as the Center of a Woman's Ministry," *PNEUMA* 17, no. 2 (1995): 237–43.

60. Here classical Pentecostals can perhaps learn from the Marian piety of their Catholic charismatic brothers and sisters, which honors Mary as the "perfect model" of the "apostolic spiritual life," so long as this does not result in objectifying motherhood as the dominant or exhaustive model of a liberative "pentecostal feminism." The challenges are the established Marian doctrines, such as the perpetual virginity of Mary, the Immaculate Conception, and the Assumption. For Catholic-Pentecostal interactions regarding Mary, see the ninth Roman Catholic–Pentecostal dialogue session held at Vienna, Austria, in 1981, documented by Jerry L. Sandidge, *Roman Catholic/Pentecostal Dialogue (1977–1982): A Study in Developing Ecumenism*, 2 vols., SIHC 44 (Frankfurt, Ger.: Peter Lang, 1987), 1:234–53, 335–41. The papers presented at this meeting and published include Laurence R. Bronkiewicz, "The Catholic Veneration of the Virgin Mary, Mother of God and of our Lord and Savior, Jesus Christ," 2:274–88; and Jerry L. Sandidge, "A Pentecostal Perspective

4.3.3 *The Church in Conversation with the World's Religions*. For pentecostals who are suspicious about expanding the ecumenical task to include the church's social witness and to address gender discrimination, the question about the relationship between Christians and those in other faiths will be off limits. Although this is an issue I have addressed elsewhere at much greater length,[61] I would like to present some new insights that suggest why the interfaith challenge is related to the intra-Christian ecumenical challenge. In particular, I wish to provide further exegetical grounding for the claim that the Christian encounter with religious others arises out of the presence and activity of the same Spirit of God who also enables the intra-Christian ecumenical relationship.

Pentecostal theologian Jean-Jacques Suurmond has called attention to seeing the outpouring of the Holy Spirit upon all flesh as signaling "a decisive new change in the relationship between God and the world and thus also in relationship between human beings."[62] More specifically,

on Mary," 2:289–351. Cf. Louis P. Rogge, OCarm, "The Woman Named Mary," *PNEUMA* 4, no. 2 (1982): 19–32; and, in response to Rogge, Jerry L. Sandidge, "A Pentecostal Response to Roman Catholic Teaching on Mary," *PNEUMA* 4, no. 2 (1982): 32–42. In addition, "Mother" Ida Robinson (Mount Sinai Holy Church of America) is cited as saying, "If Mary can carry the Word of God in her womb, why can't I carry the Word of God on my lips?" (Harold Dean Trulear, "Ida B. Robinson: The Mother as Symbolic Presence," in Goff and Wacker, eds., *Portraits of a Generation*, 308–24; quotation, 322).

For Catholic charismatic perspectives on Mary, see "Malines Documents II," *PPP* 3:150–51; Leon Joseph Cardinal Suenens, *A New Pentecost?* trans. Francis Martin (New York: Seabury, 1975), ch. 11; René Laurentin, *Catholic Pentecostalism*, trans. Matthew J. O'Connell (Garden City, NY: Doubleday, 1977), ch. 10; James F. Breckenridge, *The Theological Self-Understanding of the Catholic Charismatic Movement* (Washington, DC: University Press of America, 1980), ch. 6; Marilyn C. McCarthy, "A Comparative Study of Popular Marian Piety and the Charismatic Renewal Movement in the Roman Catholic Church of the United States" (M.A. thesis, Andover Newton Theological School, 1985); and Paul Josef Cordes, *Call to Holiness: Reflections on the Catholic Charismatic Renewal* (Collegeville, MN: Liturgical Press, 1997), 27–28, 37. Other Catholic perspectives include pneumatological theologies of Mary developed by Pope Paul VI and Brazilian theologian Leonardo Boff; see Edward D. O'Connor, *Pope Paul and the Spirit: Charisms and Church Renewal in the Teaching of Paul VI* (Notre Dame, IN: Ave Maria, 1978), 101–8; and Leonardo Boff, *The Maternal Face of God: The Feminine and Its Religious Expressions*, trans. Robert R. Barr and John W. Diercksmeier (London: Collins, 1979).

61. See Amos Yong, *Discerning the Spirit(s): A Pentecostal-Charismatic Contribution to Christian Theology of Religions*, JPTSup 20 (Sheffield, Eng.: Sheffield Academic Press, 2000); and *Beyond the Impasse: Toward a Pneumatological Theology of Religions* (Grand Rapids: Baker, 2003). Other pentecostals sensitive to the challenges of living in a religiously plural world are beginning to wrestle with this issue; see M. Stephen, *Towards a Pentecostal Theology and Ethics* (Ktm., India: Christhava Bodhi, 1999), ch. 7; and Veli-Matti Kärkkäinen, *An Introduction to the Theology of Religions: Biblical, Historical, and Contemporary Perspectives* (Downers Grove, IL: InterVarsity, 2003).

62. Jean-Jacques Suurmond, *Word and Spirit at Play: Towards a Charismatic Theology*, trans. John Bowden (Grand Rapids: Eerdmans, 1995), 198–203; quotation, 201.

Suurmond suggests that the coming of the Spirit into the world on the day of Pentecost released charismatic gifts that enable human beings to encounter each other as authentically other rather than as projections of and for the self. And of decisive importance, this possibility of new modes of relationship extends beyond what Christians experience with other Christians to what Christians experience with those outside the church.

Suurmond's proposal is developed here by digging deeper into the Pentecost narrative. Among the many miracles of Pentecost, the most important for our purposes is that it made possible the encounter of human beings who, left to themselves, would not have entered into relationship. Whether such was a miracle of speech or of hearing is not of concern here (see also §4.1.2). The crucial issue is that understanding occurred across linguistic lines: "in our own languages we hear them speaking about God's deeds of power" (Acts 2:11). Galileans who spoke Aramaic were able to communicate with those from around the Mediterranean world (Luke's identification of native languages is a nonexhaustive listing of the visitors present in Jerusalem). Therefore, one of the miracles of Pentecost was to reconcile a human race divided by language since the tower of Babel, and the uniting tongue was not merely human but spoken as the Spirit gave utterance.[63]

---

63. Also, although the traditional understanding of the day of Pentecost is that it reversed the curse of Babel—see Raniero Cantalamessa, OFMCap, *The Mystery of Pentecost*, trans. Glen S. Davies (Collegeville, MN: Liturgical Press, 2001), ch. 1, esp. 8–18—a postcolonial reading suggests that, set in the context of the Babylonian exile, the Babel episode concerns not so much divine punishment in the form of language diversification as a judgment of collective human (i.e., Babylonian) hubris attempting to unify the human experience through linguistic and social modes of domination (i.e., the Babylonian Empire). Three conclusions are drawn from this perspective. First, the diversification of tongues is a blessing (to the Jews) because it disables the systems of domination that inhibit their freedoms. Consequently, the Acts narrative is not about unintelligibility but about intelligibility and, perhaps more important, about sanctioning the plurality of languages concerning the divine before an audience who would have expected nothing less than Hebrew (or Aramaic) as God's preferred means of communication. Second, Babel is God's means of securing the scattering over all the earth that was commanded to Noah and his family (Gen. 9:1), even as Pentecost becomes the divine means for the promulgation of the gospel to the ends of the earth. Finally, only God is one, creation being division and even *ha adam* being plural, and the tongues of Pentecost are a polyvalent testimony to the beautiful artistry of the Creator God. See J. Severino Croatto, "A Reading of the Story of the Tower of Babel from the Perspective of Non-identity: Genesis 11:1–9 in the Context of Its Production," in *Teaching the Bible: The Discourse and Politics of Biblical Pedagogy*, ed. Fernando F. Segovia and Mary Ann Tolbert (Maryknoll, NY: Orbis, 1998), 203–23; and Hinne Wagenaar, "Babel, Jerusalem, and Kumba: Missiological Reflections on Genesis 11:1–19 and Acts 2:1–13," *IRM* 92, no. 366 (2003): 406–21, esp. 411–13.

Yet the encounter made possible here goes beyond linguistic lines toward what we might call intercultural or cross-cultural communication. Certainly, those present at Jerusalem were identified as "devout Jews" (v. 5) and, to that extent, were not culturally other than the 120 who descended from the upper room. But to identify Jews only as a cultural category during the first century is problematic, since there is an anachronistic distinction between "cultural Jews" and "religious Jews" that derives more from the modern period than from the Second Temple period. Diaspora Jews during the Second Temple period were certainly ethnically distinct but less certainly culturally demarcated. More important, that Jewishness also functioned during the first century as an ethical and political marker complexifies the cultural and linguistic distinction.

In addition, to assume that no Gentiles were present in Jerusalem because Luke explicitly identifies devout Jews at the scene is to overlook other exegetical clues. First, Luke qualifies his description of these Jews by noting their derivation "from every nation under heaven" (v. 5). Second, they also heard the 120 speaking "in the native language of each" (v. 6). Finally, most revealing is the presence of proselytes—Gentile converts to Judaism—on the scene (v. 10). Although most commentators read Luke straightforwardly and see these proselytes as hailing only from Rome, it is also grammatically possible that "Jews and proselytes" does "not refer to any specific national group with its own language . . . , but covers *all* the preceding groups with respect to religious affiliation."[64]

In any case, we have here the presence of both the Jewish Diaspora and Gentile converts to Judaism. The Jews present had remained devout worshipers of God in spite of their dispersion abroad and had visibly set themselves apart through various practices—for example, their observances at mealtime, male circumcision, and the Sabbath. Still, removed from their homeland for generations if not centuries, they had certainly grown up in other places, learned other languages that were now native to them, and been shaped by the languages and cultures within which these languages flourished. In the case of the Gentile converts to Judaism, the situation is even more complex. Some proselytes stopped short of circumcision, even while adhering to Jewish law. Is it also possible that others were not pure monotheists or perhaps had not severed ties with the pagan communities from which they came?[65] The fact that

64. Ernst Haenchen, *The Acts of the Apostles: A Commentary*, trans. Bernard Noble and Gerald Shinn (Philadelphia: Westminster, 1971), 171; italics original.

65. This question is posed because such was clearly the case with the Godfearers who become prominent later in the book of Acts (e.g., 10:1–2); see John J. Collins, *Between Athens and Jerusalem: Jewish Identity in the Hellenistic Diaspora* (New York: Crossroad, 1983), 270.

there were degrees of conversion to Judaism should caution us against homogenizing the "proselytes" Luke identifies as eyewitnesses on the day of Pentecost. This group of persons undoubtedly had fused (or were in the process of fusing) a variety of practices, values, customs, and traditions into their Jewish identity.

In either case (devout Jew or Gentile proselyte), whereas generations previous to ours may have overlooked the interconnectedness between language and culture, no longer can we responsibly do so. To speak a language fluently because one has grown up with it is significantly different from taking on a second language. The former includes the socialization that language provides. That those present in Jerusalem were natives of places as disparate as Asia (Minor), Mesopotamia, and North Africa, among others, means that their experience of the one God had been similarly shaped by the particularities of their linguistic, socio-historical, and cultural experiences. The Pentecost narrative therefore portrays an intercultural encounter of wide magnitude.

To make the association between language and culture, however, raises a further connection: that between language, culture, and religion. Current scholarship in religious studies continues to debate the links between religion and language and between religion and culture. Can religion be clearly demarcated from language and culture? Is it possible to understand religion in its purity, apart from cultural considerations? What would religion abstracted from language and culture sound or look like? On the other side, are there purely linguistic, cultural, or cultural-linguistic phenomena apart from religion? In these various disciplines arguments are made about the interdependence of language and religion and of culture and religion. Although language, culture, and religion are certainly distinguishable for purposes of communication and reflection, in reality they overlap and are deeply interconnected. The boundaries between these domains of human experience, if existing at all, are seriously contested.[66]

Although the question whether Luke understood Pentecost as an intercultural or interreligious event cannot be decided exegetically, the reading provided here is by no means implausible when set against the Jewish background of Luke-Acts. Following the work of James Scott, I see the Pentecost narrative to be universal in scope for various reasons. First, it is undeniable that Luke's list of nations in the Pentecost narra-tive has its own genealogy, beginning with Genesis 10 and continuing with the Chronicler (1 Chron. 1) and the intertestamental tradition of

---

66. The beginnings of the deconstruction of the concept of religion go back one genera-tion to Wilfred Cantwell Smith, *The Meaning and End of Religion* (New York: Macmillan, 1962).

the table of seventy/seventy-two nations.[67] Given the first-century Jewish understanding of the comprehensiveness of the seventy/seventy-two nations as representing all the peoples of the earth—note the translation of the seventy that resulted in the Septuagint, and the seventy languages needed among the Sanhedrin so that proper and full testimony to the truth could be given to enable the rendering of accurate judgments[68]—Luke's shorter sample signifies the universality of the gospel rather than limits its scope. Second, the structure of Acts, beginning in Judea and proceeding through Samaria to the ends of the earth (1:8), parallels the church's universal mission to include all the children of Shem (Israel, or the Jews), Ham (the African race), and Japheth (the remaining Gentiles).[69] For these reasons, the ministry of Philip to Samaria and that of Peter to Cornelius are especially highlighted. Third, the sons of Shem, Ham, and Japheth are the seventy/seventy-two nations of Genesis 10, and it is only Luke who preserves both Jesus' genealogy of seventy-two generations (Luke 3:23–38) and the story of Jesus' sending the seventy/seventy-two (Luke 10:1) alongside the sending out of the Twelve (Luke 9:1–6).[70] All of this implies that Luke understood the universality of the gospel according to the reigning categories of his day: that whereas Yahweh had previously apportioned spaces for all humankind according to their "gods" (Deut. 32:8) and then foretold through the Isaianic prophecy that Yahweh is "coming to gather all nations and tongues; and they shall come and shall see my glory" (Isa. 66:18–20; quotation, v. 18), now the gift of the Holy Spirit was to empower the witness of the gospel to "the ends of the earth" and to "all nations" (Acts 1:8; 17:26).

This analysis establishes the interconnections between language, the nations, and their religious traditions. The point is the arbitrariness of separating language from culture, nation, and religion. The universality

67. There has been a long-standing debate about whether there are seventy or seventy-two nations; various manuscripts attest to each figure. For discussion of some of the issues and of the Lukan point made here, see James M. Scott, "Luke's Geographical Horizon," in *The Book of Acts in Its First Century Setting*, vol. 2, *The Book of Acts in Its Graeco-Roman Setting*, ed. David W. J. Gill and Conrad Gempf (Grand Rapids: Eerdmans; Carlisle, Eng.: Paternoster, 1994), 483–544, esp. 527–30; *Paul and the Nations: The Old Testament and Jewish Background of Paul's Mission to the Nations with Special Reference to the Destination of Galatians* (Tübingen: J. C. B. Mohr, 1995), 5–54; and *Geography in Early Judaism and Christianity* (Cambridge: Cambridge University Press, 2002), 68–84.

68. See Babylonian Talmud, *Sanhedrin* 88a; Laurie Zoloth, "Seeing the Doubting Judge: Jewish Ethics and the Postmodern Project," in *Textual Reasonings: Jewish Philosophy and Text Study at the End of the Twentieth Century*, ed. Peter Ochs and Nancy Levene (Grand Rapids: Eerdmans, 2003), 214–28, esp. 224–25.

69. Scott, "Luke's Geographical Horizon," 530–41; and *Paul and the Nations*, 167–76.

70. Scott, *Geography in Early Judaism and Christianity*, 51–55. The majority of manuscripts indicate that seventy were sent by Jesus.

of the Spirit's outpouring in the Pentecost narrative has implications
not only for those committed to the translation of the Bible into all
the known languages or for the present multicultural agenda but also
for the multifaith encounter. It suggests that testimony to the truth
is provided not just in one language but through many.[71] Hence the
contribution of a diversity of cultures and religious traditions should
not be underestimated. At the same time, the unity of the truth did not
and should not undermine the particularity of each voice. Although the
Pentecost narrative may undermine the thesis that languages, cultures,
and religions are radically incommensurable, it is also the case that the
outpouring of the Spirit preserves rather than erases the differences.
The integrity of each way needs to be protected and not subsumed into
an all-inclusive system that either ignores or transmutes illegitimately
its distinctiveness.[72]

When will we begin mining the resources for the intercultural and
interreligious engagement implicit in the Pentecost narrative? Might
not our theological enterprise be transformed altogether if we take the
interreligious dialogue seriously in our time? While put rhetorically, this
hypothesis is easily confirmed in the broader context of the church's
expansion to include Gentiles in the first century. Missiologist Andrew
Walls suggests that the present Gentile-dominated church has for too
long taken for granted the Gentile identity of the people of God and
neglected the revealed mystery that astounded even the angels: that in
Christ, God has accomplished a new, reconciled humanity from that
which was formerly antagonistically set off as Jew and Gentile and that
it was precisely the goal of the unity of the Spirit to produce an eschatological unity of faith according to the full measure of Christ.[73] Walls
further suggests that, reread in this way, the Letter to the Ephesians
reveals how the early church struggled with deep theological issues
as the presence of Gentiles in the community of faith grew. Instead of
retrenching into the secure confines of its Jewish identity, however, the
church creatively incorporated Gentile (i.e., pagan) elements into its
language and liturgy. The adoption of the Greek *Kyrios*, used by Gentiles

71. Samuel Solivan, *The Spirit, Pathos, and Liberation: Toward an Hispanic Pentecostal Theology*, JPTSup 14 (Sheffield, Eng.: Sheffield Academic Press, 1998), 112–18; and
Frank D. Macchia, "The Tongues of Pentecost: A Pentecostal Perspective on the Promise
and Challenge of Pentecostal/Roman Catholic Dialogue," *JES* 35, no. 1 (1998): 1–18.

72. For further exposition, see Amos Yong, "The Spirit Bears Witness: Pneumatology,
Truth, and the Religions," *SJT* 57, no. 1 (2004): 1–25. See also a similar argument by Ulrich
Dehn, "Life and Spirit: A New Approach to a Theology of Religions," in *Theology and the
Religions: A Dialogue*, ed. Viggo Mortensen (Grand Rapids: Eerdmans, 2003), 457–62.

73. See Andrew F. Walls, "The Ephesian Moment," in *The Cross-Cultural Process in
Christian History* (Maryknoll, NY: Orbis; Edinburgh: T & T Clark, 2002), 72–81.

for their cult divinities, as a christological title and the interpretation of Jesus as having cosmic significance were their boldest accomplishments. Read in this way, the universality of Christian faith was established not so much through the negation of other religious traditions as through a process of reinterpretation and reappropriation.

The Christian theological enterprise is yet to be surprised by what will happen if its primary dialogue partners are not Western philosophers, such as Plato and Aristotle, but Eastern "philosophers," such as Laozi, Mengzi, Nagarjuna, and Shankara. Might not their voices also witness to the truth, beauty, and holiness of God?[74] For this reason, the ecumenical tradition of pentecostalism stands to deepen its missionary calling and to be enriched by engaging those in other faiths. Does not the reading of the Pentecost narrative proposed here lead us to celebrate the plurality of languages, cultures, and people groups through which the Spirit's presence and activity are manifest? As sociologist of pentecostalism David Martin notes, "Once the Bible is your text there are as many interpretations as there are readers, and the Spirit is unbound."[75] Of course, we need to be alert that this open space for a plurality of perspectives does not lead to uncritical relativism. But critical interactions with perspectives one does not agree with do not need to be polemical. Rather, guided by what Mark Roberts calls a "hermeneutic of charity," we should discern the occasion of the "other" reading, rejoice in its good fruit, and preserve such even amidst attempts to reread all texts—"ours" and "theirs"—more accurately.[76] In this way, a critical, charismatically inspired response does not tear others down but builds them up. This approach to religious others results in our own conversion and transformation, by the power of the Spirit, into the image of Jesus (see ch. 6 below).

This chapter has drawn from the pneumatological soteriology and ecclesiology of chapters 2 and 3 a pneumatological vision for Christian ecumenism in the late modern world. Plumbing the depths of the mystery of Pentecost through a robustly Lukan hermeneutic, we have uncovered an ecumenical tradition of pentecostalism that cuts across all traditional divisions—ethnic, racial, linguistic, social, class, gender, and religious—even as it finds pneumatic empowerment to work for and hasten the eschatological day of the Lord. Within the holistic and

74. Such voices are rightly acknowledged to be present in the world religions by the Second Vatican Council; see *Nostra aetete*, §2.

75. David Martin, *Pentecostalism: The World Their Parish* (Oxford: Blackwell, 2002), 170.

76. Mark E. Roberts, "A Hermeneutic of Charity: Response to Heather Landrus," *JPT* 11, no. 1 (2002): 89–97.

eschatological framework of our soteriology and ecclesiology, pentecostal ecumenism necessarily combines social ethics, spirituality, dialogue, and evangelism focused on empowering congregations "as viable centers of Christian formation and totalistic transformation that engage in meaningful ministry and worship, inclusive of all who desire to respond to the call to holiness, irrespective of sex, race, or economic status"[77]—and perhaps also irrespective of religious affiliation. Directed toward the day of the Lord, pentecostal ecumenism yearns for the Spirit to establish peace, justice, and righteousness and break down the barriers between people even as it anticipates the coming kingdom, when all the people of the world "will bring into it the glory and the honor of the nations" (Rev. 21:26). Yet our concluding reflections, which attempted to ground the interreligious encounter upon a pneumatological imagination and pentecostal foundation, raise an important question: What is the identity of the Spirit who allegedly brings together those who call upon even the names of other gods? Is not the Holy Spirit the Spirit of the Father and of the Son Jesus Christ? Is this not the Spirit of the triune God? Come Holy Spirit, continue to enlighten our minds . . .

77. Cheryl J. Sanders, *Saints in Exile: The Holiness-Pentecostal Experience in African American Religion and Culture* (New York: Oxford University Press, 1996), 125–42; quotation, 132.

5

Oneness and Trinity

Identity, Plurality, and World Theology

Unlike standard texts in systematic theology since the dawn of the Protestant era, this work has not followed the established loci of Father-Son-Spirit. Rather, it has attempted a pneumatologically driven and Christ-centered theology from the start, and for that reason, it began with our experience of the Spirit. Nevertheless, the time has come to wrestle with the identity of the Spirit in whom we live, move, and have our being, and as intimated in the preceding pages, to ask about the Spirit is to ask about Jesus and about God. Partly for this reason, the theological tradition was led to a triune understanding of God. From a modern pentecostal perspective, however, the doctrine of God has been a watershed, dividing the trinitarian pentecostals from the Oneness pentecostals since the second decade of the twentieth century.

Perhaps some might say that the Spirit christology developed in chapter 2 may be of assistance in getting us beyond this impasse. After all, historically, trinitarian theology emerged mainly from the early church's wrestling with the identity of Jesus, and it was the affirmation that Jesus was of the same substance (*homoousios*) with the Father that secured the fundamental structure of the trinitarian understanding of God. If we revert to a Spirit christology that affirms Jesus as the man who did what he did as empowered by the Spirit of God, then the driving force behind trinitarian theology will lose much of its momentum. This move will not work, however, since Spirit christology is meant to complement Logos christology, not replace it (see §2.3.1). Additionally, the import of Logos christology for the Oneness doctrines of God and incarnation means that we will need to respect this aspect of its contribution toward a world pentecostal theology for our time.

The objective of this chapter is twofold. First, it aims to go beyond just making space for Oneness pentecostal theology (as did Kenneth Gill; see §I.2) and provide justification for engaging Oneness pentecostal perspectives as equal dialogue partners in the task of Christian theological reconstruction in the late modern world (as intimated in §3.3.2 and §4.3.3). Second, this chapter aims to work toward an ecumenical doctrine of God that both Oneness and trinitarian pentecostals can affirm, and to do so along two lines. Initially, the chapter emphasizes the unity of God. As Jesus himself said, "No one is good but God alone" (Luke 18:19). It also calls attention to the modes of Oneness and trinitarian worship and practice and builds at this level toward a narrative understanding of the trinitarian orientation of Christian faith, an understanding that both pentecostal traditions can affirm. This chapter proceeds to lay out the Oneness-trinitarian problematic (§5.1), then explores contemporary constructive trinitarian theological proposals with the challenges of Oneness theology firmly in hand (§5.2), and concludes with a proposal for Oneness-trinitarian rapprochement (§5.3).

The method here assumes the validity of the previous argumentation: from pentecostal experience and practice toward theological reflection. Those who demand an alternative methodology will probably resist both the approach and the conclusions here, however provisionally stated. But for the rest (most of my readers, I hope) who are willing to continue the journey with me, I trust that the reflections that follow will serve not only the ecumenical purpose of bridging the theological gap between Oneness and trinitarian pentecostals but also the broader Christian theological task of "faith seeking understanding" in the late modern world.

5.1 The Oneness-Trinitarian Debate

This section formally introduces the Oneness pentecostal doctrine of God, surveys the Oneness-trinitarian pentecostal polemic, and presents some observations about the relationship between pentecostalism and the theological tradition in general and about the Oneness revisioning of the tradition more particularly. Because the Oneness-trinitarian debate has been especially heated in North America—Oneness churches and movements in the two-thirds world either have been much less engaged in the theological debates or have been dismissed as sectarian or cultic—our focus in this chapter will be on the Missouri-based United Pentecostal Church International (UPCI).[1]

5.1.1 *The Oneness Doctrine of God.* The origins of the Oneness emphasis on the unity of God have been traced to the revelation, to John Schaeppe and Frank Ewart in 1913, of Jesus as "the Name" (singular) of God understood as Father, Son, and Holy Spirit.[2] Pentecostal practice was immediately characterized by mass rebaptisms "in Jesus' name" following the apostolic precedent as recorded throughout the book of Acts.[3] This revelation of "the Name" soon overran the nascent (trinitarian) Assemblies of God, officially formed in 1914, resulting in the expulsion of believers in the "new doctrine" from the parent organization in 1916. In that year, the Assemblies of God General Council formulated its "Statement of Fundamental Truths" mainly to counter the threat posed by the "New Issue." The extensively developed statement 13, "The Essentials as to the Godhead" (in ten subsections), insisted that although the terms "Trinity" and "Persons" are "not found in the Scriptures, yet [they] are words in harmony with Scripture. . . . We, therefore, may speak with propriety of the Lord our God, who is One Lord, as a Trinity or as one Being of three Persons, and still be absolutely Scriptural."[4]

In contrast, the Oneness doctrine of God can be summarized by the two central doctrinal affirmations of the United Pentecostal Church: "(1) There is one God with no distinction of persons; (2) Jesus Christ is the fullness of the Godhead incarnate."[5] Although the second affirmation distinguishes Oneness theology from the Socinian and modern unitarian

---

1. Publications of UPCI theologians are also the most easily accessible among the many Oneness denominations. Most important, the UPCI is discussed here simply because I am most familiar with it among Oneness organizations.

2. For a trinitarian view of this history and the ensuing division, see William W. Menzies, *Anointed to Serve: The Story of the Assemblies of God* (Springfield, MO: Gospel Publishing House, 1971), 106–21; a more neutral presentation is Edith L. Blumhofer, *The Assemblies of God: A Chapter in the Story of American Pentecostalism*, vol. 1, *To 1941* (Springfield, MO: Gospel Publishing House, 1989), ch. 10. For a Oneness view, consult Arthur L. Clanton, *United We Stand: A History of Oneness Organizations* (Hazelwood, MO: Pentecostal Publishing House, 1970), 13–26.

3. For a concise look at North American Oneness theology and practice, see David A. Reed, "Oneness Pentecostalism," *NIDPCM* 936–44.

4. "Statement of Fundamental Truths Approved by the General Council of the Assemblies of God," 13(a), in Minutes of the General Council of the Assemblies of God, St. Louis, October 1–7, 1916.

5. David Bernard et al., *Meet the United Pentecostal Church International* (Hazelwood, MO: Word Aflame, 1989), 56.

denials of the Trinity,[6] it is more important to point out that, historically, these distinctive Oneness emphases served to reject what was perceived at the turn of this century as tritheistic interpretations of the Trinity, on the one hand, and both Arian and modern theological liberal rejections of the deity of Christ, on the other. They are also corollary doctrines, neither being explicable in the Oneness scheme without the other. In what is better understood as a contemporary revival of the Jewish-Christian theology of the name, Oneness Pentecostals understand Jesus to be the name of God's redemptive means in the New Testament. Jesus therefore refers both to the Nazarene having divine and human natures and to the soteriologically efficacious name of the Godhead.

In the new covenant, then, Jesus is the "exact imprint of God's very being" (Heb. 1:3). As the human figure in whom "the whole fullness of deity dwells bodily" (Col. 2:9), Jesus is able to say, "I am in the Father and the Father is in me" (John 14:10). The Oneness explication of the relation between the Son and the Father thus takes its orientation from the Jewish Shema, "The LORD our God, the LORD is one!" (Deut. 6:4 NKJV), and its Pauline echoes: "but God is one" (Gal. 3:20), "there is no God but one" (1 Cor. 8:4b), and "one God and Father of all" (Eph. 4:6). Father, Son, and Holy Spirit are accepted as the revelation of the modalities of the one God with no implicit reference to divine personalities or distinct centers of consciousness.

In this sense, the term "Son of God" is understood as biblically revealed regarding the humanity of God in Jesus whereas "God the Son" is rejected as an unwarranted philosophical reification. This is an important point. Oneness theology distinguishes between the Word (Logos) and the Son of God. "In the beginning was the Word, and the Word was with God, and the Word was God" (John 1:1). Whereas the Word preexisted as a "thought or a plan in the mind of God," it is not considered an eternal or hypostatic distinction in the Godhead. At the incarnation, however, this Word was spoken, and "the Word became flesh" (John 1:14).[7] "Only begotten Son" of God (John 3:16 KJV) is therefore taken as a reference to the incarnation and not to the preexistent Son. Because Oneness thinkers reject the absurdities deployed in explicating how it is that the Father begets the Son (such as that proposed by Origen in his doctrine

---

6. Bernard reminds us that Socinus's (1539–1604) denial of the Trinity was predicated on his rationalistic rejection of the deity of Jesus; see Bernard's discussion and rejection of Socinus and the unitarianism movement he spawned in David Bernard, *A History of Christian Doctrine*, vol. 2, *The Reformation to the Holiness Movement, A.D. 1500–1900* (Hazelwood, MO: Word Aflame, 1996), 108–10.

7. David Bernard, *The Oneness of God* (Hazelwood, MO: Word Aflame, 1983), 60. See also Marvin D. Treece, "The Oneness Exposition of John 1:1–14," in *Symposium on Oneness Pentecostalism, 1986* (Hazelwood, MO: Word Aflame, 1986), 223–58.

of the eternal generation of the Son), they deny the ontological preexistence of the Son as a separate person from the Father.[8] The full deity and humanity of the incarnate God are then explicated, not, however, by resorting to trinitarian categories.

Oneness thinkers have allied themselves with aspects of Nestorian christology, by which they distinguish between Jesus' acts as a man and as divine. Thus Jesus slept, thirsted, and died as a man but produced miracles, forgave sins, and was resurrected as God.[9] The Gospel records are interpreted so as to stress pure Judaic monotheism rendered compatible with the absolute deity of Christ.

> The Bible speaks of Father, Son, and Holy Ghost as different manifestations, roles, modes, titles, attributes, relationships to man, or functions of the one God, but it does not refer to Father, Son, and Holy Ghost as three persons, personalities, wills, minds, or Gods. God is the Father of us all and in a unique way the Father of the man Jesus Christ. God manifested Himself in flesh in the person of Jesus Christ, called the Son of God. God is also called the Holy Spirit, which emphasizes His activity in the lives and affairs of mankind.[10]

5.1.2 *Oneness-Trinitarian Polemics*. Classical Pentecostalism has generally adhered to the traditional doctrine of the Trinity as bequeathed by historic Christianity. Simply stated, orthodox trinitarianism holds that "within the one essence of the Godhead we have to distinguish three 'persons' who are neither three gods on the one side, nor three parts or modes of God on the other, but coequally and coeternally God."[11] The doctrine can be elaborated in three distinct propositions: "1) There is one God and one only. 2) This God exists eternally in three distinct persons: the Father, the Son and the Holy Spirit. 3) These three are fully equal in every divine perfection. They possess alike the fullness of the divine essence."[12]

8. Bernard, *The Oneness of God*, 103–8. The reference is to Origen, *First Principles* 1.2.4.

9. See, e.g., Bernard, *The Oneness of God*, ch. 8. Bernard's insistence that "one cannot merge Christ's humanity and deity totally and still maintain the Oneness doctrine" inevitably leads him to affirm the broad contours of Nestorius's christology even if he does not follow that patriarch of Constantinople on every point; see David Bernard, "Oneness Christology," in *Symposium on Oneness Pentecostalism, 1986*, 127, 143.

10. Bernard, *The Oneness of God*, 144.

11. G. W. Bromiley, "Trinity," in *Evangelical Dictionary of Theology*, ed. Walter A. Elwell (Grand Rapids: Baker, 1984), 1112.

12. Roger Nicole, "The Meaning of the Trinity," in *One God in Trinity: An Analysis of the Primary Dogma of Christianity*, ed. Peter Toon and James D. Spiceland (Westchester, IL: Cornerstone, 1980), 1–2. Few trinitarian pentecostals would disagree with this evangelical articulation, even as most Oneness pentecostals would see this as representative of the trinitarian understanding.

In similar fashion, trinitarian pentecostal theologians have approached the doctrine of God in typical Western fashion by discussing the unity of the Godhead and then emphasizing the three eternal and personal distinctions within the divine essence.[13] Especially in its older versions, however, pentecostal theological manuals have neglected dogmatic arguments in favor of biblical proof-texting. This reflects the classical Pentecostal—trinitarian and Oneness—distrust in philosophical and historical argumentation and human reason. It is, after all, "beyond the power of the finite mind to explain the Infinite; but it is not beyond the power of man to declare what is revealed."[14]

The "New Issue" raised by Oneness pentecostals in the modern pentecostal revival questioned the traditional trinitarian view of the Godhead and resulted in both groups being diametrically opposed to, and historically suspicious of, each other. The disagreement centered on two related matters: the oneness of the Godhead and baptism in Jesus' name. Oneness pentecostals strenuously objected to the perceived tritheism of three-person language whereas trinitarian pentecostals feared the Socinian and Nestorian implications of the Oneness message. Over the decades, both sides have ignored each other at best and occasionally fired polemical salvos. Trinitarians accuse Oneness pentecostals of theological and doctrinal heresy, but Oneness pentecostals accuse trinitarians of deviating from the biblical witness or subjecting Scripture to foreign philosophic categories. Partly because the Oneness pentecostals found themselves on the defensive against not just trinitarian pentecostals but almost the entire Christian world, they developed a more sectarian identity.[15]

At the lay and ecclesial levels, trinitarians and Oneness laypersons and leaders still do not speak to one another, as each group is suspicious that the other has strayed from the truth. The emergence of the scholarly Society for Pentecostal Studies (SPS) in the early 1970s, however, has jump-started the Oneness-trinitarian conversation. Oneness pentecostals are still a very small minority, but the SPS was established without a doctrinal statement precisely because its founders saw the need to provide a forum for constructive theological dialogue between the two estranged traditions. Yet after almost thirty years of discussion, we may be no closer to agreement now than when we first

13. See, e.g., Ernest Swing Williams, *Systematic Theology*, 3 vols. (Springfield, MO: Gospel Publishing House, 1953), 1:199–202; Stanley M. Horton, ed., *Systematic Theology*, rev. ed. (Springfield, MO: Logion, 1995), chs. 4–5; and Raymond M. Pruitt, *Fundamentals of the Faith* (Cleveland, TN: White Wing Publishing House, 1981), 97–100.

14. Williams, *Systematic Theology*, 1:199.

15. See Joseph H. Howell, "The People of the Name: Oneness Pentecostalism in the United States" (Ph.D. diss., Florida State University, 1985), esp. part 1.

began. This is clear in the recent exchange between Ralph Del Colle, a Catholic charismatic theologian, and David Bernard, senior theologian of the UPCI. Del Colle offered a set of irenic theological theses aimed at securing agreement between Oneness and trinitarian pentecostals on the issue of the Godhead.[16] Bernard's formal response revealed a sympathy toward these proposals but unearthed that the stumbling block to a united pentecostalism remains centered on divergent views on the Godhead *ad intra* (internal to itself). Bernard pointed out that insofar as trinitarian pentecostals focus on "the necessity of the work of the Father, Son, and Holy Spirit in the economy of salvation . . . , this is precisely what Oneness theology affirms and even emphasizes." On the economic side, God is triune as revealed by the Scriptures. Trinitarians are concerned, however, that "this economic 'Trinity' does not translate into an ontological Trinity" for their Oneness siblings. Bernard responded that "this is a philosophical argument, not a scriptural one," and insisted on the oneness of God.[17]

Two related observations emerge at this juncture. First, what is strongly implied in historically orthodox trinitarianism is that God can be defined in terms of an eternal essence. This presumption has been assumed by both trinitarian and Oneness pentecostals and lies behind their own contrary theological formulations. Thus the trinitarian pentecostal theologian Myer Pearlman introduces his discussion of the doctrine of the Trinity by asking the rhetorical question "How could God have any fellowship before finite creatures came into existence?" He answers that "the Divine Unity is a compound unity, and that in this unity there are really Three distinct Persons, every One of whom is the Godhead, and yet is supremely conscious of the other Two. So we see that there was an Eternal Fellowship before any finite creatures were created; therefore God was never alone."[18]

The entire Oneness polemic against the doctrine of the preexistent Son also reflects this basic assumption. Oneness theology therefore necessarily wrestles with the New Testament passages that speak of creation by or through the Son and is centrally concerned with the question "What does creation 'by the Son' mean, since the Son did not have a substantial preexistence before the Incarnation?"[19] They proceed

16. The published version is Ralph Del Colle, "Oneness and Trinity: A Preliminary Proposal for Dialogue with Oneness Pentecostalism," *JPT* 10 (1997): 85–110.

17. David Bernard, "A Response to Ralph Del Colle's 'Oneness and Trinity: A Preliminary Proposal for Dialogue with Oneness Pentecostalism'" (presented at the twenty-fifth-anniversary meeting of the Society for Pentecostal Studies, Toronto, March 7–9, 1996), 7.

18. Myer Pearlman, *Knowing the Doctrines of the Bible* (Springfield, MO: Gospel Publishing House, 1937), 68–69.

19. Bernard, *The Oneness of God*, 115.

to distinguish between the human, incarnate spirit of Jesus as the Son and the divine, eternal Spirit of Jesus (identical with the Holy Spirit, modalistically conceived) as the Creator. Since God "does not live in time and He is not limited by time as we are," it is by divine foreknowledge that the Son is used to create the world, that is, "with the knowledge of His [God's] plan for the Incarnation and the redemption of the cross in mind."[20]

This leads to our second observation: a presumed dualism of time and eternity underlies both the Oneness and the trinitarian pentecostal understandings of creation. God's eternality is defined in terms of immortality and everlastingness, suggestive of infinite temporal extension to the past and future, in contrast with the finite and bounded created order.[21] It is ironic that pentecostals have given scant attention to both the metaphysical assumptions and the doctrine of creation that undergird this view. To do so may lead pentecostals either down the road traveled by the church fathers, perhaps even to the Platonic worldview through which trinitarian orthodoxy was established, or, in our present post-Enlightenment context, to a revised cosmological or metaphysical vision. But trinitarian pentecostals have not taken the time to engage these matters at the philosophic level (simply assuming uncritically what has been handed down in the tradition), and Oneness pentecostals are reluctant to do so (given their conviction that the later tradition was led astray by foreign philosophic ideas).

5.1.3 *Oneness and the Trinity: Fundamental Issues.* The preceding overview illuminates the central issues dividing Oneness and trinitarian pentecostals. They include disagreements in three interrelated areas: biblical interpretation, the authority of the dogmatic tradition of the church, and the philosophical underpinnings of theological reflection.

Most obviously, the Oneness-trinitarian debate turns on the question of which understanding of God the Bible most clearly supports. Insofar as the classical Oneness-trinitarian debates proceeded through the biblicistic method of proof-texting and insofar as the word "Trinity" does not appear in the pages of the Bible, Oneness pentecostals are confident of their conclusions. But on the other side, since the personality and personhood of Father, Son, and Spirit could be established from Scripture by pointing to texts that showed each one exhibiting personlike traits, the trinitarians are also confident of their view as a biblical doctrine.

Oneness pentecostals grant the biblical revelation of the triune manifestation of God relative to salvation history—for example, God is manifest first as Father-Creator, then as Son-Redeemer, and now as

---

20. Ibid., 116.
21. Ibid., 30; and Williams, *Systematic Theology*, 1:182.

Spirit-Baptizer. Much like the third-century modalists, however, they claim that this does not translate into eternal persons in Godself. Rather, they say, the trinitarian doctrine arose as the early church was seduced by the worldly spirit of *philosophia*. Thus Bernard laments that "the root problem of the trinitarian error, both historically and theologically, is a failure to heed and comprehend Colossians 2:8–10."[22] This response, however, fails to take into account that trinitarian pentecostals do not resort to philosophic categories in their own theological formulations. Further, the most sustained trinitarian pentecostal defense to date against Oneness theology not only refrained from philosophic argumentation but also avoided historical and dogmatic ones in favor of the argument from Scripture.[23]

But to return to the point granted by Oneness pentecostals, does not the triune revelation of God in salvation history tell us something about God as trinitarian in Godself? The Oneness negative response to this question is countered by trinitarian arguments that if God in Godself does not correspond to God as revealed, then revelation is deceptive and untruthful. What is at stake and needs to be exposed in the Oneness interpretive scheme, according to former Oneness pentecostal Gregory Boyd, is the "authenticity of God's self-revelation."[24] For trinitarian pentecostals, the doctrine of the Trinity is at least latent in the Scriptures, and the Nicene and Chalcedonian developments do not violate but, rather, clarify the scriptural witness.

This leads to the question of the role of the dogmatic tradition for the ongoing task of Christian theological reflection. Generally speaking, trinitarian and Oneness pentecostals are in agreement with *sola scriptura*, basic to the Reformation. At least for early modern pentecostals, the revival was a divinely ordained restoration of biblical Christianity, obscured since the passing of the apostles at the end of the first century. On this point, many pentecostals would share the radical Reformers' (the Anabaptists') general suspicion regarding the dogmatic tradition in general and the ecumenical creeds in particular.

Clearly, trinitarian pentecostals have followed the dogmatic tradition selectively, affirming the doctrine of the Trinity of the Nicene and Chalcedonian creeds but often rejecting or at least neglecting the christological doctrine of the *theotokos*—regarding Mary as the "mother of God"—and other elements in these same confessions. The rationale given is that

---

22. David Bernard, *Oneness and Trinity, A.D. 100–300: The Doctrine of God in Ancient Christian Writings* (Hazelwood, MO: Word Aflame, 1991), 179.

23. See Carl Brumback, *God in Three Persons* (Cleveland, TN: Pathway, 1959).

24. Gregory A. Boyd, *Oneness Pentecostals and The Trinity* (Grand Rapids: Baker, 1992), 114, 178–80.

only the doctrines that are biblical are retained. But this is precisely the point of contention between Oneness and trinitarian pentecostals. There is the further point that the goal of a purely biblical theology is not attainable. All theological reflection depends upon, and emerges from, the experiential, existential, and sociocultural matrix wherein it finds itself. Even the various scriptural texts have their complex contexts that need to be heeded in order to be interpreted more accurately. Thus the dogmatic tradition cannot be rejected merely on the grounds that it appeared after the apostolic age. But then neither trinitarian nor Oneness theologies are either purely biblical or historically contaminated. Both are, to some degree or other, biblical and historically situated.

To their credit, Oneness thinkers have at least begun to grapple with the historical issues. They have devoted much more attention to the historical Christian tradition than their trinitarian siblings, even if they are motivated to rescue their own doctrinal emphases by revisiting the history of doctrinal development.[25] Yet Oneness historiography has produced some interesting results. Certainly, their modalistic theology and uniquely Jesus-centered christology have motivated their argument that Christian "orthodoxy," the trinitarianism of the Nicene-Constantinopolitan Creed and the later Athanasian Creed, was the result of a perverted synthesis of biblical teaching and Hellenistic philosophic speculation.[26] Yet Bernard also notes that although Nicaea was

a victory for the deity of Christ[,] it was not a clear rejection of Oneness. Some participants could have been essentially Oneness in their thinking, and most were not trinitarian in the modern orthodox sense. Some supporters of the winning side were modalistic or were accused of being modalistic. Many opponents of Nicea as well as some supporters interpreted the original Nicene formula in a modalistic fashion. . . . When the theological heirs of Nicea finally distanced themselves from modalism, they did so at the expense of tainting their doctrine with subordinationism and tritheism, despite their denials. And those problems still beset trinitarianism today.[27]

25. See, e.g., William B. Chalfant, *Ancient Champions of Oneness: A History of the True Church of Jesus Christ* (Hazelwood, MO: Word Aflame, 1979). Also, in addition to his *Oneness and Trinity*, see David Bernard, *The Trinitarian Controversy in the Fourth Century* (Hazelwood, MO: Word Aflame, 1993); and *A History of Christian Doctrine*, 3 vols. (Hazelwood, MO: Word Aflame, 1995–1999).

26. Thomas Weisser, "Was the Early Church Oneness or Trinitarian?" in *Symposium on Oneness Pentecostalism, 1986*, 53–68; see also William B. Chalfant, "The Fall of the Ancient Apostolic Church," in *Symposium on Oneness Pentecostalism, 1988 and 1990* (Hazelwood, MO: Word Aflame, 1990), 351–85.

27. Bernard, *The Trinitarian Controversy in the Fourth Century*, 59.

In arguing toward this conclusion, Oneness theologians have developed their own "orthodox" tradition. Noteworthy in the Oneness pedigree are the defenders of Monarchianism, who emphasized the unity of God. Figures hereticized by Nicene orthodoxy, such as Noetus, Praxeas, Theodotus, and Sabellius, have been revived as "ancient champions of Oneness" whereas the champions of trinitarianism, such as Justin Martyr, Tertullian, Origen, Novatian, and especially the post-Nicene Athanasius and the Cappadocians, are regarded as corrupters of the biblical faith in their move away from the essential oneness of God first to a binitarian and later to a trinitarian plurality. Tertullian, the first theologian to draw attention to the conceptual difference between the divine economy and the personal relations in the Godhead, is specifically ostracized as the architect of trinitarian theology; in contrast, Irenaeus, a much earlier church father, "could be called at most an economic trinitarian" and is accepted as a mediating thinker and patristic ally to Oneness theology.[28]

Can Oneness pentecostals have it both ways? Can they reject the dominant Christian tradition as aberrant while identifying their own Oneness genealogy? On the other side, can trinitarians embrace the classical theological tradition without also adopting the tradition's philosophic or metaphysical presuppositions? Both groups agree that it is appropriate, at least in some senses, to speak of the trinitarian revelation relative to salvation history. Their dispute arises regarding what to extrapolate from the biblical evidence about the divine reality apart from the created order. The difficulty is exacerbated, since the implicit language of the Trinity in the Bible cannot adequately clarify the internal relations of the three apart from philosophic assistance. Both are therefore caught on the horns of a dilemma. Oneness Pentecostals cannot deny the revelation of God in triune terms, but to grant this would force the question of the divine truthfulness on them, assuming, as they do, the philosophic coherence of talking about God existing "before" the created order. Trinitarian Pentecostals, on the other hand, though affirming the economic Trinity on the basis of revelation, are forced to rely on the tradition's extrabiblical philosophic categories, foreign to their sensibilities, in order to explicate the eternal essence of the divine life "before" the world.

5.2 Contemporary Trinitarian Theology

We will now explore the issues by enlarging the ecumenical conversation to include various tributaries to the contemporary discussion on

---

28. Bernard, *Oneness and Trinity*, 170.

the doctrine of God. Given the renaissance in trinitarian theological reflection during the last generation (is it surprising that it coincides with the explosion of pneumatological reflection during almost the same period of time?), our dialogue partners will be trinitarian thinkers: the Orthodox theologian Vladimir Lossky; Karl Barth; and a trio of two-thirds-world theologians. Given the specific problematic at hand and space constraints, the exposition of each theologian's thinking will be necessarily brief and focused. The goal is threefold: to get a broad sense of the contemporary thinking on the doctrine of God in general and on trinitarian theology in particular; to assess the role of pneumatology in reflection on God and Trinity; and to glean resources from the contemporary scene that might help in overcoming the Oneness-trinitarian impasse.

5.2.1 *Retrieving the Tradition: Lossky*. Perhaps the most outstanding of Eastern theologians in the first half of the twentieth century, Vladimir Lossky (1904–1958) and his contributions to displaying the ecumenical significance of Orthodox theology are inestimable. True to his tradition, Lossky's theological vision was characterized by the centrality of the church fathers and Orthodox themes such as deification, the essence-energy distinction, and mystical spirituality. Yet also in tune with Orthodoxy was his trinitarian vision, featuring central patristic emphases.

First, without apology, Lossky retrieved especially the Greek patristic trinitarian terminology, seeking only to make it intelligible to the contemporary world.[29] God was thus one *ousia* ("essence") in three *hypostases* ("subsistences"). The latter term was preferred to *prosōpon* (colloquially, "person"; literally, "face" or "mask"), equivalent to the Latin *persona* ("person"), since *prosōpon* points only to the apparent, and thereby not essential, character of the individual face. This leads Lossky to argue that the church fathers did not uncritically articulate their theological ideas in Greek linguistic categories, as the older Harnackian thesis or the Anabaptist and Oneness critiques would have it. Rather, the fathers accomplished a fundamental transformation of the available vocabulary so as to allow a truly new synthesis of ideas to emerge.[30] Thus Lossky notes the repeated denials of especially the Cappadocian fathers that the triune Father, Son, and Holy Spirit are simply the mathematical addition of individual persons. Further, the Plotinian

29. Vladimir Lossky, *Orthodox Theology: An Introduction*, trans. Ian Kesarcodi-Watson and Ihita Kesarcodi-Watson (Crestwood, NY: St. Vladimir's Seminary Press, 1978), 40–45.

30. Vladimir Lossky, *The Mystical Theology of the Eastern Church* (Cambridge, Eng.: James Clarke, 1957; repr., Crestwood, NY: St. Vladimir's Seminary Press, 1976), esp. 47–52.

trinity of the One, the Intelligence, and the World Soul was not adopted by the early church because of its emanationism and descending hierarchy. Against this backdrop, given the virtual synonymy of *ousia* and *hypostasis* in fourth-century usage, the trinitarian idea that emerged was truly novel. The triune "persons" are not "individuals" that are part of and divide their species (as denoted by *prosōpon*); in fact, following Saint Basil, Lossky saw that an uncritical adoption of *prosōpon* would lead to the Sabellian error of seeing Father, Son, and Spirit as merely successively appearing modalities (masks) of the hidden divine substance. Against these conclusions, each *hypostasis* "assumes in its fullness divine nature. . . . [They] are infinitely united and infinitely different: they *are* the divine nature, but none possesses it, none breaks it to own it exclusively. It is precisely because each one opens itself to the others, that they share nature [divine *ousia*] without restriction, that the latter is not divided."[31] Herein lies the emergence of the trinitarian concept of personhood as interpenetrating—see the Greek *perichōrēsis* and the Latin *circumincessio*—and dynamic subsistences (*hypostases*). Neither masked appearances (modalism) nor separate individuals (tritheism), the divine persons are unique and yet unfathomable in their infinite openness to, and interrelationship with, each other. This is the unique Christian theological understanding of human personhood: men and women are finite beings created in the image, and being re-created in the likeness, of the triunely personal God.

Second, Lossky defended the Orthodox rejection of the *Filioque* ("and the Son")—the Spirit proceeding not just from the Father but from the Father *and the Son*—added to the Latin version of the Nicene-Constantinopolitan confession (57–62).[32] The issues go beyond biblical proof-texting (cf. John 14:26; 15:26) and concern neither merely ecclesial authority nor the changing of the creed of the church. Rather, the issues are theological, beginning with the Greek emphasis on the real distinction between the persons (as defined above) over and against the Latin emphasis on the unity of the divine nature. In the *Filioque*, the Greek fathers saw the stress on Father-Son unity as undermining the personal differentiation of not only Father and Son but also Spirit (hence Lossky's rejection of the Augustinian metaphor of the Spirit as the "bond of love"). From this follows the impairment of the monarchy of the Father, in and through whom the Greek fathers saw the originating source of the Godhead. The *Filioque* either would posit two originating principles or would demand definition of the divine unity "behind" the divine persons,

31. Lossky, *Orthodox Theology*, 42.
32. Unless otherwise noted, all numbers in parentheses in the text of this discussion of Lossky refer to pages in Lossky, *The Mystical Theology of the Eastern Church*.

tending in an impersonalistic direction (this flowered later in Eckhart's "God beyond God"). Finally, the *Filioque* would effectively subordinate the mission and economy of the Spirit to that of the Son's, resulting, in practice Lossky argued, not only in the Roman hierarchical (rather than charismatic) ecclesiology but also in the constriction of the Spirit's presence and activity within the church.

Third, the removal of the *Filioque* thus allows the Orthodox retrieval of Irenaeus's image of the Son and Spirit as the "two hands of the Father." The separate—that is, related but distinct—economies of the Son and the Spirit then lead to the soteriological and ecclesiological thesis that "Pentecost is not a 'continuation' of the Incarnation. It is its sequel, its result. The creature has become fit to receive the Holy Spirit" (159). That is, "the work of Christ concerns human nature which He recapitulates in His hypostasis. The work of the Holy Spirit, on the other hand, concerns persons, being applied to each one singly. Within the church the Holy Spirit imparts to human hypostases the fullness of deity after a manner which is unique, 'personal'" (166). So Jesus confers the Spirit on human nature (*ousia*) collectively (John 20:22), followed later (at Pentecost) by the Spirit's infilling or "pneumaticizing" of individuals personally (*hypostasis*), enabling each one to fully realize his or her personhood as created in the image and likeness of God (167–68). In this way, the selflessness or *kenōsis* of the Spirit's personhood (as seen in traditional theology's silence about pneumatology) is explained, since the Spirit gives its divinity to human beings, identifying with them, fully preserving their freedom and personhood, and valuing their particularity and diversity even while bringing them into communion with God and with each other. But lest the church be left without concrete witness of the Spirit's mission, the Spirit descended not only initially upon Mary to purify her as *theotokos* ("mother of God") but also pentecostally upon her to enable her deification as the down payment for the eschatological deification of the body of Christ (193–95).

Herein lie not only the pneumatological underpinnings for the Eastern doctrine of deification but also the rationale for the linking of confirmation (the receiving of the Holy Spirit) and baptism in the Orthodox rite. As important is Orthodoxy's rejection of papal primacy in favor of a fully charismatic ecclesiology wherein each individual person, full of the Holy Spirit, plays his or her distinct role in the work (*leitourgia*) of the church. Reminiscent of (without referring to) Möhler's early ecclesiology emphasizing the inner dimension of the church and anticipating Zizioulas's famous articulation of the church as constituted both christologically and pneumatologically, Lossky writes, "The Church is not only one nature in the hypostasis of Christ: it consists also of multiple hypostases in the grace of the Holy Spirit" (182).

5.2.2 *Reconstructing the Tradition: Barth's Trinitarian Theology.* The theology of Karl Barth (1886–1968) is certainly much too rich for any survey to do justice to it. The goal here is to summarize his trinitarian theology while paying special attention to his proposal for replacing the traditional "person" language with "modes of being." Secondarily, we will explore the role of the Spirit in his thought, including his defense, contra Lossky, of the *Filioque*.

To begin, the Trinity is not just one doctrine alongside others in Barth's theology.[33] Rather, Barth's entire *Dogmatics* is structured according to the trinitarian self-revelation of God.[34] Thus God is Revealer, Revealed, and Revealedness. The One who reveals himself (the Father) as himself (the Son) is identical with the effects, purpose, and meaning of this self-revelation to others (the Spirit). The revelation of God is thereby a single act of God repeated thrice: God as subject (Father) reveals himself objectively (Son) as God (Spirit). For Barth, this revealing God is God as he is in himself: God who speaks himself as himself and who shows himself as himself.

The resulting revelation brings us to the triune economy manifest as revelation (primordially, of the Father), reconciliation (historically, of the Son), and redemption (eschatologically, of the Spirit). Yet the economy of revelation is identical to the inner trinitarian being of God, since both the economic and the immanent trinities are derived from the Word of God manifest in Jesus Christ and preserved in the scriptural narrative.[35] It is Jesus who reveals the one who speaks, even as it is Jesus' sending of the Spirit (hence Barth's defense of the *Filioque* clause) that accomplishes this revelation in the hearts and lives of human beings. And because Barth's doctrine of revelation is his doctrine of salvation, his trinitarian theology is in that sense unfinished, anticipating the full redemption of creation, of which Christ is the firstfruits and the Spirit is the down payment.

In light of the Oneness-trinitarian problematic we are discussing, our analysis is limited to Barth's early trinitarian theology, up through

33. There are many good introductions to Barth's trinitarian theology. The best are Eberhard Jungel, *The Doctrine of the Trinity: God's Being Is in Becoming*, trans. Horton Harris (Grand Rapids: Eerdmans, 1976); Robert W. Jenson, *The Triune Identity: God according to the Gospel* (Philadelphia: Fortress, 1982); and Alan J. Torrance, *Persons in Communion: An Essay in Trinitarian Description and Human Participation* (Edinburgh: T & T Clark, 1994).

34. William Stacy Johnson, *The Mystery of God: Karl Barth and the Postmodern Foundations of Theology* (Louisville: Westminster John Knox, 1997), brings this out clearly.

35. See David Ford, *Barth and God's Story: Biblical Narrative and Theological Method of Karl Barth in the Church Dogmatics* (Frankfurt, Ger.: Peter Lang, 1985).

volume 1 of his *Church Dogmatics*.[36] We begin with the opening thesis of §9, "God's Three-in-Oneness":

> The God who reveals Himself according to Scripture is One in three of His own modes of existence, which consist in their mutual relationships, Father, Son, and Holy Spirit. In this way He is the Lord, i.e. the Thou who meets man's I and unites it to Himself as the indissoluble Subject, and who actually thus and thereby becomes manifest to him as his God. (400)

The most obvious point is that Barth's doctrine of the Trinity is rooted in the saving revelation of God to human beings. The divine intention is to reconcile estranged humanity to Godself.

More important is Barth's substitution of "modes of being" or "modes of existence" (German: *Seinsweise*) for the traditional language of trinitarian "persons." Given the misleading connotations of the early church's *persona* and *prosōpon* and the modern individualistic conception of "person" as self-existing and self-conscious rationality, Barth sees this as the more suitable rendition for the patristic *hypostasis/subsistentia*—that is, "mode of existence of one who exists" (413). This is his reading of the Son as "the exact imprint of God's very being" (Heb. 1:3): the Son's mode of existence is "an 'impress,' a countertype of God the 'Father's' mode of existence" (413). Barth is careful to qualify his usage so that "modes of being" is to be regarded neither as referring to divine attributes (415) nor as affirming third-century subordinationism or modalism (437–39). This is because the three modes of existence are neither accidental to nor economic manifestations of God, but "it is precisely only in this three-time otherness that He is God" (414). Positively, "modes of being" provides a safeguard against polytheism (503) or tritheism insofar as we are not talking about three subjects but about one subject thrice. This preserves the unity of God's action according to the traditional formula *opera trinitatis ad extra sunt indivisa* ("The external works of the Trinity are undivided").

Given the Oneness rejection of the tripersonal confession of God because of its tritheistic connotations, it is not surprising that Oneness scholars have been drawn to Barth's proposal.[37] Superficially, Barth's "modes of existence" parallels the Oneness scholars' retrieval and revision of modalism for their own doctrine of God. More substantively, they would agree with Barth that "the meaning of the doctrine of the Trinity is not that there are three personalities in God. That would

---

36. Karl Barth, *Church Dogmatics*, vol. 1, part 1, *The Doctrine of the Word of God*, trans. G. T. Thomson (Edinburgh: T & T Clark, 1936; repr., 1960). Unless otherwise noted, all references to this volume will be by page number in parentheses in the text.

37. E.g., Bernard, *A History of Christian Doctrine*, 3:171–78.

be the worst . . . expression of tritheism, against which we must here guard" (403). Further convergence between Barth and the Oneness doctrine of God is found in his claim that "the trinitarian baptismal formula could not be more wrongly interpreted, than by regarding it as the formula of a baptism into three divine names"; following Tertullian, "the *honoma* [name] of Father, Son, and Holy Spirit, Matt. 28:19, is one and the same. . . . Baptism is in *nomina* [in the *name*], not *in nominibus Patris, Filii et Spiritus sancti* [in the *names* of Father, Son, and Holy Spirit] . . ." (401).

Yet this is where the convergence between Barth and Oneness pentecostalism ends. Barth affirms unequivocally what Oneness theology denies: the eternal nature of the Son's mode of existence. Indeed, Barth insists that to deny Christ's eternal preexistence as the Son of God would be to render the incarnation necessary and eliminate the divine freedom (481). Further, it would be unwarranted theological speculation to think of the Son of God only in economic terms instead of "antecedently in himself" (482). Defending the Nicene formulation, he states that "begotten by the Father before all time" means "did not come into being in time as such" (488), since "before all time" is not a temporal designation (489). Barth's polemic is directed not at Oneness pentecostalism (of which he knew nothing) but against the ancient Arian heresy. Yet Barth acknowledges that to defend the Son's eternal begottenness and generation by the Father is not fully possible for human rationality; it is an act of faithful piety (492–96).

The same mystery applies to the procession of the Spirit (543–45). Yet Barth defends the *Filioque* on the grounds that the revealed Spirit must be the Spirit antecedently in eternity as well and that the Spirit, as the communion of love between God and human beings, must also be the communion of love between the Father and the Son (548–50). More pointedly, the *Filioque* signifies for Barth not a double procession (of the Father and the Son) but a common origin of the Spirit that preserves the oneness of Father and Son not in two persons but in two modes of existence (556–57).

Alar Laats's comparison of Barth and Lossky on the *Filioque* makes explicit that Barth could not abolish the *Filioque* without abolishing at the same time the christocentrism and rejection of natural theology that were dominant at least in the first half of *Church Dogmatics*.[38] To say, as Barth did, that the objective reality of revelation is the incarnation of the Son (which was independent of anything) and the subjective reality of revelation is the Spirit (who applies the reconciliation achieved

38. Alar Laats, *Doctrines of the Trinity in Eastern and Western Theologies*, SIHC 114 (Frankfurt, Ger.: Peter Lang, 1999).

by the Son) is to make the Spirit's mission dependent upon the Son's and to preserve the *Filioque*. But the counterquestion that arises at this point is how the robustness of the Spirit's distinct mode of existence is preserved, at least in Barth's early theology. This is an alternative formulation of Volf's criticism that Barth's theology of the Trinity—God is an indissoluble subject in threefold repetition—is based on a "logic of the same" that reinforces the traditional Western emphasis on the unity of the divine essence.[39]

I do not wish here to defend Volf's social trinitarianism, but only to observe that although the early Barth made a good pneumatological start, he did not see it through and acknowledged this later in life.[40] That good start was his 1929 lecture "The Holy Spirit and the Christian Life," which shows the Holy Spirit as being integral to Barth's theology of creation, reconciliation, and redemption.[41] *Church Dogmatics*, however, subordinates pneumatology to christology, congruent with Barth's defense of the *Filioque*. Much later, in a 1957 address, Barth reflected, "There is certainly a place for legitimate Christian thinking starting from below and moving up, from man who is taken hold of by God to God who takes hold of man. . . . One might well understand it as a theology of the third article. . . . Starting from below, as it were, with Christian man, it could and should have struggled its way upward to an authentic explication of the Christian faith."[42] Does Barth's coming full circle to pneumatology hold promise for a pneumatological healing of the Oneness-trinitarian pentecostal rift?

5.2.3 *Reappropriating the Tradition: Latino, Asian, and African Trinitarian Theologies*. Although much more can and should be said about the resurgence of trinitarian theology, any attempt to resolve the Oneness-trinitarian pentecostal dispute must take place in the world context. For this reason, our attention turns to the constructive work in trinitarian theology performed by those in Southern and Eastern

---

39. See Miroslav Volf, *After Our Likeness: The Church as the Image of the Trinity* (Grand Rapids: Eerdmans, 1998), 176–81.

40. Even though acknowledging that Barth "becomes more and more a pneumatocentric theologian" (which is still too much, I think), Philip Rosato presents Barth as "perhaps first and foremost, a pneumatologist." Rosato ends up with a skewed reading of Barth that is corrected by John Thompson. See Philip Rosato, *The Spirit as Lord: The Pneumatology of Karl Barth* (Edinburgh: T & T Clark, 1981), quotations, 43 and viii, respectively; and John Thompson, *The Holy Spirit in the Theology of Karl Barth* (Allison Park, PA: Pickwick, 1991).

41. Karl Barth, *The Holy Spirit and the Christian Life: The Theological Basis of Ethics*, ed. Robin W. Lovin, trans. R. Birth Holye, rev. ed. (Louisville: Westminster John Knox, 1993).

42. Karl Barth, "Evangelical Theology in the 19th Century," in *The Humanity of God* (Richmond: John Knox, 1972), 24–25.

churches. Representative thinkers—Brazilian liberation theologian Leonardo Boff, Korean Jung Young Lee, and Nigerian Okechukwu Ogbonnaya—will illuminate trends that may be helpful for considering further the question of the contemporary philosophical underpinnings of trinitarian theology.

Boff has written two books on the Trinity, the earlier more technically argued and the latter more accessible.[43] Though doing theology in the Latin Catholic tradition, Boff's trinitarian theology features three specific ecumenical and constructive moves. First, he retrieves the Orthodox (Cappadocian, more specifically) starting point of the three persons rather than the traditional Western focus on the divine nature. This leads Boff to a social trinitarian model that emphasizes the perichoretic interrelationships of the triune community. Starting with the divine communion accords better with the biblical revelation of Father, Son, and Spirit, even if it runs the risk of tritheism. As a liberation theologian, however, Boff also believes that God as triune community provides a better theological basis for social and environmental liberation than the traditional Western model.[44] Second, in order to avoid the traditional subordination of the Spirit to the Son (as in the Barth of *Dogmatics*) and to preserve the full mutuality and reciprocity of the Spirit and the Son, Boff draws further from the Orthodox tradition in arguing for an *ex Patre Spirituque* (from the Father and/through the Spirit) alongside the *ex Patre Filioque*. This preserves the biblical truth that "the Son through his begetting receives the Holy Spirit from the Father and is then, in his being, eternally inseparable from the Holy Spirit."[45] Boff proceeds to argue for the mission of the Spirit as "pneumatizing" creation (language reminiscent of Lossky's), redeeming it from death and uniting it once again with the life of the Trinity. Third, in this sense, Boff suggests that we understand the Spirit's serving as the womb of creation's rebirth to represent the feminine dimension of the divine mystery.[46]

43. Leonardo Boff, *Trinity and Society*, trans. Paul Burns (Maryknoll, NY: Orbis, 1988); and *Holy Trinity, Perfect Community*, trans. Phillip Berryman (Maryknoll, NY: Orbis, 2000).

44. Boff further develops especially the latter claim in Leonardo Boff, *Cry of the Poor, Cry of the Earth*, trans. Phillip Berryman (Maryknoll, NY: Orbis, 1997).

45. Boff, *Trinity and Society*, 205; Boff cites Paul Evdokimov (1901–1970), esp. his *L'Esprit saint dans la tradition orthodoxe* (1969).

46. Boff, *Trinity and Society*, ch. 11. Boff had earlier developed, much further than did Lossky, the connection between pneumatology, the divine feminine, and Mariology; see Leonardo Boff, *The Maternal Face of God: The Feminine and Its Religious Expressions*, trans. Robert R. Barr and John W. Diercksmeier (London: Collins, 1989). For an alternative Catholic reading of pneumatology and the divine feminine with a lesser emphasis on Mary, see Donald L. Gelpi, *The Divine Mother: A Trinitarian Theology of the Holy Spirit* (Lanham, MD: University Press of America, 1984).

The feminine dimension of God is also articulated in Jung Young Lee's (1930–1996) Asian (Methodist-Presbyterian) perspective on the Trinity.[47] Meaning not to replace but to complement traditional (Western) articulations of the doctrine, Lee intentionally rethinks the Trinity in light of Asian categories and concepts. The Father thus represents the heavenly principle (*li*) that is the unifying source of creativity and of moral and spiritual order, and the Son represents the acme of filial piety in responding to the Father's preeminence. Yet the Father-Son relationship is possible only within a triadic structure that includes the Spirit as the maternal principle of the Godhead. In addition, the Spirit is also the material principle (*ch'i*, or vital energy) of the universe. The *Dao* (the Way) points to the mysterious comings and goings of the Spirit (cf. John 3:8) that cannot be named, even as the miraculous and ecstatic experiences of human beings call attention to the enabling and transcending power of the Spirit.[48]

In the background is Lee's "yin-yang symbolic thinking." Based on the *I Ching* (Book of Changes), yin-yang symbolic thinking emphasizes holism (harmonizing opposites rather than conflict), inclusivism (both-and rather than either-or), relationality (interaction rather than substance), organicism (interconnectedness between heaven, earth, and embodied humanity rather than dualisms of whatever kind), and dynamism and alteration (movement rather than stasis).[49] Further, yin-yang symbolic thinking illuminates Christian theology by providing a metaphysics and logic more in tune with trinitarian thinking than the dyadic and dualistic assumptions of the Western philosophical tradition. Lee is thus able to explicate the central features of the Christian claim in terms of unity and distinctiveness—for example, the divine and human natures of Christ; the spiritual and material dimensions of creation; God's transcendence and immanence; the community and the individual; male and female; death and resurrection; creation and redemption—for theology in world context.

Most intriguingly, Lee's yin-yang approach demands that the *Filioque* be recognized only as one of the six possible orders of the trinitarian symbols. Together these orders reflect a thoroughly mutualistic and yet radically differentiating inner-trinitarian life: (1) Father-Spirit-Son (the Asian Trinity of heaven, earth, and humanity, correlated in part with Spirit christology); (2) Father-Son-Spirit (the Confucian or patriarchal model,

---

47. Jung Young Lee, *The Trinity in Asian Perspective* (Nashville: Abingdon, 1996).
48. Ibid., ch. 5, "God the Spirit."
49. See Jung Young Lee, *Theology of Change: A Christian Concept of God in an Eastern Perspective* (Maryknoll, NY: Orbis, 1979). Cf. Nozomu Miyahira, *Towards a Theology of the Concord of God: A Japanese Perspective on the Trinity* (Carlisle, Eng.: Paternoster, 2000).

correlated with the traditional *Filioque*); (3) Spirit-Father-Son (the Daoist or matriarchal model, correlated with the epistemic order of general revelation); (4) Spirit-Son-Father (the shamanic model, correlated with the return trajectory of the traditional Irenaean recapitulation soteriology); (5) Son-Father-Spirit (the mutuality of Son and Father, complementing model 2, correlated with the christocentric model); (6) Son-Spirit-Father (the existential model of encountering transcendence, correlated with the apostolic experience).[50] Although Lee realizes that these analogies drawn from the Asian experience can only partially illumine the trinitarian mystery, he does provide insights from the biblical narrative read through the East Asian context and perspective.

Social trinitarianism is given distinctive articulation from the African context by Okechukwu Ogbonnaya (Methodist).[51] Retrieving the peculiarly Hebraic concept of the "council of the gods"[52] and rereading this in light of the complex and high-god-yet-differentiated cosmologies of African traditional religions and the communal orientation of African societies, Ogbonnaya proposes a "divine communalism" as a mediating trinitarian model that emphasizes both the unity and the plurality of deity. This background illuminates not only trinitarian metaphors but also the early trinitarian conceptualization of Tertullian, operating as he did in the North African context.[53] Bringing these various threads together, Ogbonnaya's trinitarian vision highlights the images of relational interplay within the divine community—for example, God is one in substance, status, and power and three in persons and manifestations/uses of power. Following the functional subordination of cosmic powers under the high god within the ontological matrix of the unity of divine beings, Ogbonnaya also affirms a functional christological and pneumatological subordination within the ontological equality of the triune God. Finally, however, Ogbonnaya says relatively little about the Holy Spirit except that, at the level of the divine economy, the divine community as spirit is compatible with the African concept of pervasive forces while, at the level of theology, "Spirit is that substance which is

50. See Lee, *The Trinity in Asian Perspective*, ch. 7. The correlations made are in part my own.

51. A. Okechukwu Ogbonnaya, *On Communitarian Divinity: An African Interpretation of the Trinity* (St. Paul: Paragon House, 1994).

52. E. Theodore Mullen Jr., *The Divine Council in Canaanite and Early Hebrew Literature* (Chico, CA: Scholar's Press, 1987).

53. Ogbonnaya, *On Communitarian Divinity*, ch. 4. This is Ogbonnaya's boldest hypothesis, as Tertullian's trinitarian theology has been perennially heralded as coming from Roman, particularly Stoic, sources. Understandably, Ogbonnaya's argument relies on conceptual correlations rather than historical genealogy. In any case, as one of the first to study implications of the African context on Tertullian's theology, perhaps Ogbonnaya's efforts will open up new vistas for research in due time.

common to all the members of the Divine community."[54] Unfortunately, the tendency toward the impersonalism of the Spirit in Ogbonnaya's articulation results in a less than robust trinitarian theology.

5.3 Oneness and Trinity: Back to the Future

What stands out from this survey of trinitarian theology pertinent to the Oneness-trinitarian pentecostal debate? A balance sheet, first on the trinitarian side and then on the Oneness side, is appropriate before concluding with a provisional Oneness-trinitarian rapprochement.

5.3.1 *Trinitarian Theology: Alterity and Mutuality.* Although the preceding survey has been exactly that—a very brief overview of five trinitarian theologies—three conclusions clearly stand out pertinent to the Oneness-trinitarian dispute. First, trinitarian theology has perennially been on guard against tritheism. From the Cappadocians to Lossky in the East and from Augustine to Barth in the West, Christian trinitarianism has worked consciously to articulate the triune rather than tritheistic character of its understanding of God. Indeed, as Lossky's retrieval shows, the church fathers created a new category from their reflections on the doctrine of God—the *person*—which post-Enlightenment sensibilities have corrupted. To understand God as tripersonal is not to declare God as having three distinctly individual personalities (tritheism) but to affirm the fully interpenetrating and dynamic modes of relations that constitute the divine mystery.

Second and building on the first, the result in contemporary theology is not only the kind of social trinitarianism seen in Boff but also the relational trinitarianism of Lee and the communalism (albeit weakened by a deficient pneumatology) of Ogbonnaya. Even more important are the themes that these trinitarian articulations have contributed toward the world theological enterprise. Clearly in Boff's theology, trinitarian perichoresis not only includes the created order within the divine life but also provides a model for human mutuality and liberated communities. In Boff and Lee, trinitarian relationality provides for an ecological and theoanthropocosmic theology desperately needed in our time. In Lee and Ogbonnaya, trinitarian communality serves as a bridge toward dialogue with other religious traditions, thus enabling a deeper and more authentic

---

54. Ibid., 71. Ogbonnaya is severely handicapped in his pneumatology because of his attempt to follow and develop Tertullian on most points. He could have said much more about pneumatology if he had relied on the rich pneumatological capital found in African traditional religions. See Allan Anderson, *Moya: The Holy Spirit in the South African Context* (Pretoria: University of South Africa Press, 1991).

contextualization of the gospel message and theological reflection in the Eastern and Southern hemispheres. In short, trinitarian theology is not merely a speculative enterprise concerning the inner life of God apart from creation; it is also a concretely applicable doctrine pertinent to the various orders of human and created existence. The value of these recent developments is that difference, otherness, and plurality are preserved not just because they are politically correct ideologies of our time but because they are theologically grounded in the very identity of God. But they are also important given the multidimensional soteriological vision associated with the pneumatological and pentecostal theology being developed in this volume. From this perspective, trinitarianism is not only first-order descriptions of the way God "is" but also more about the ways in which Christians talk about God and God's relationship with the world in light of their experiences of the Son and the Spirit.

Finally, theology is only fully trinitarian when due attention is given to pneumatology. Most clearly demonstrated in Ogbonnaya's case, this matter is also illuminated through the debate concerning the *Filioque*. Although Barth's acceptance of the *Filioque* does not result in a weakened trinitarianism, I agree with Laats that the *Filioque* buttressed Barth's christocentrism in ways that prevented him from developing a richer pneumatological and trinitarian theology. In the case of Lossky, rejection of the *Filioque* enabled maintenance of the triune persons, each with "his" own integrity, as starting point. For Boff and Lee, the *Filioque* needed to be complemented by other theological models of the triune relationships in order to capture more fully the perichoretic mutuality and reciprocity of the trinitarian mystery.

For this reason, one way forward for pentecostal theology in the twenty-first century is to confront the dividing theological issue between East and West: the question of the *Filioque*. This does not mean that pentecostals should side with one or the other side; clearly, there are more alternatives available, and these are not limited to either Boff's or Lee's proposals. But pentecostals have not really even begun to think through this matter for themselves.[55] A number of interrelated issues present themselves: is the economy of the Spirit to be subordinated to that of the Son's, and depending on the answer to this question, what are the implications for Oneness-trinitarian pentecostal theology and for pneumatological theology? At stake is something like this: if pentecostals affirm the *Filioque*, then they will be adopting a christological framework that, though conducive to the Jesus-centeredness of Oneness

---

55. Not much has changed since this same observation was made almost two decades ago by Gerald T. Sheppard, "The Nicene Creed, Filioque, and Pentecostal Movements in the United States," *Greek Orthodox Theological Review* 31, nos. 3–4 (1986): 401–16.

pentecostalism, may also short-circuit the quest for a pneumatological theology. Of course, my sympathies lie with pneumatological theology even as I hope to remain Christ-centered. Can I have my cake and eat it too? Put alternatively, can one pull off a pneumatological theology within a christological framework?

This project is an attempt to show one way to do so. Let me state, at least provisionally, where I am now. Although I had previously tended toward the Orthodox answer, I have since come to see the value of the *Filioque* insofar as it provides for one clear model of trinitarian salvation history in which redemption is accomplished in, and dynamically experienced by, those who are being saved.[56] Building on this, let me propose one way forward for an ecumenical pentecostal and pneumatological theology, in dialogue with Boff and Lee.

With Boff, I wish to affirm not so much that we add *Spirituque* to the Creed—multiplying potentially controversial terms does nothing for the solidarity of the church's confession—but that we acknowledge the Spirit both sends Jesus and is sent by Jesus (compare §2.1.2 with Luke 3:16b and John 20:22). What must be avoided is subordinating either Spirit to Son or vice versa.[57] Against any and all forms of subordinationism, we must affirm the mutuality of the economies of Word and Spirit in order to guard against either the fanaticism, enthusiasm, and individualism of a Spirit-dominated theology or the dogmatism, hierarchicalism, and institutionalism of a Word-dominated theology. Discerning Christ and the Spirit is neither relativistic (without criteria) nor absolutistic (without ambiguity). Because of the perichoretic mutuality and reciprocity of Christ and Spirit, I believe it possible to develop a pneumatologically driven and christologically centered theology.

But with Lee, I agree also that there is now a broader theological context within which Christian theology must proceed: that which includes the religious quest of all humankind. Lee's multiple-patterned divine orders are helpful for relocating the *Filioque* within this world theological context. Orthodox-Catholic polemics has resulted in a stalemate, and

---

56. For my initial thoughts, see Amos Yong, *Discerning the Spirit(s): A Pentecostal-Charismatic Contribution to Christian Theology of Religions*, JPTSup 20 (Sheffield, Eng.: Sheffield Academic Press, 2000), 64–70. My more recent reflections are in *Spirit–Word–Community: Theological Hermeneutics in Trinitarian Perspective* (Burlington, VT: Ashgate, 2002), 59–72. The following presents an update on my thinking on this important issue.

57. Kilian McDonnell thus talks about the "simultaneity of the . . . missions of Son and Spirit" and of the "reciprocity of 'in Christ' and 'in the Spirit'": "At this moment in history I choose a christology dependent on pneumatology as an antidote to the imbalance arising from the dominance in the West of pneumatology dependent on christology." See Kilian McDonnell, *The Other Hand of God: The Holy Spirit as the Universal Touch and Goal* (Collegeville, MN: Liturgical Press, 2003), 194; cf. 88–90, 203–4.

trinitarian theology transposed into the world context may invigorate the discussion or render the traditional disagreements moot.

5.3.2 *Oneness Theology in the World Religious Context.* But do these moves require leaving the Oneness pentecostal witness behind? In view of the preceding discussion, let me present three reasons why I believe not. First, Oneness pentecostalism reminds trinitarians that Christianity is a monotheistic faith. The doctrine of the Trinity is not about three gods but, rather, about the God who transcends merely numerical one-ness or threeness. Precisely because trinitarianism bears witness to the subtlety and complexity of the Christian theistic conception, the Oneness voice prevents trinitarianism from falling into tritheism. This threat is especially real for social trinitarian constructs; the Oneness confession of the unity of the Godhead checks the tendency toward a literalistic individualizing of the three persons.

Second, the Oneness means of articulating the divine unity nevertheless includes a robust incarnational christology that defends the divinity of the historical Jesus Christ. Here is where Oneness pentecostal theology differs from any kind of Arianism, with its subordinationist christology, and from any kind of unitarianism that denies the divinity of the Son, even as Oneness formulations preserve the irreducible complexity of the one God. Here we come to the second important rationale for keeping the Oneness voice in play in the contemporary theological climate: its unique articulation of both the divinity of Christ and the strict unity of the Godhead. I see this Oneness contribution in terms of what David Reed calls the early Jewish Christian theology of the name.[58] Seeing the fundamental role of Jesus'-name baptism in Oneness belief and practice, Reed suggests that Oneness theology provides an alternative kerygmatic understanding of revelation focused on the name of God. This theology of the name is consistent with the diversity of first-century Jewish un-derstandings regarding the various personified manifestations of the presence and nature of Yahweh, such as Shechinah, Angel of the Lord, Word, Wisdom, and Spirit. In this context, the early Jewish Christian claim regarding Jesus as revealing God reflects a kind of personification of the divine revelation in history that does not compromise the unity of the Godhead. More precisely, the unutterable name of Yahweh now becomes fully known in the name Jesus. Given the ancient Near Eastern convic-tion about the revelatory character of names, the name of Jesus reveals Yahweh not only as Savior present with his people (Matt. 1:21–23) but also as the most high covenant-keeping Father of Jacob, David, and their descendants (Luke 1:32–33). For this reason, not only does gathering in

58. David A. Reed, "Oneness Pentecostalism: Problems and Possibilities for Pentecostal Theology," *JPT* 11 (1997): 73–93, esp. 81–91.

the name of Jesus mark the early Jewish followers of the Galilean (Matt. 18:20) but healing and, more important, salvation are received in the name of Jesus (Acts 3:6; 4:12). Baptism into the name of Jesus thereby solidifies in practice this revelatory and saving work of God.

Third, this leads to the unexpected but important contribution of Oneness pentecostalism for Christian theology in the world context: the bridges it affords to the Christian-Jewish and Christian-Muslim encounters. Given the previous call for expanding intra-Christian ecumenism to include dialogue with other faiths (§4.3.3), the potential Oneness pentecostal contribution toward the interreligious conversation should not be underestimated. Jewish-Christian relationships have seen an especially dramatic change since the Holocaust. Although anti-Semitic and supersessionist attitudes have certainly drawn a fair share of their argument from the New Testament, more recent post-Shoah readings have highlighted instead the Pauline insistence on the steadfastness and eternal character of God's covenant with the Jews (see esp. Rom. 9–11).[59] Might not a "Jewish-Christian theology of the name" provide additional resources to advance the Jewish-Christian dialogue?

Granted, it is still premature to expect Oneness pentecostals in particular, not to mention pentecostals in general, to flock to the interreligious dialogue table. Yet insofar as even conservative evangelicals are opening up lines of dialogue with Jews,[60] how far behind are the pentecostals? Further, even if pentecostals are still a generation away from multifaith ecumenism, the resources of the Oneness theology of the name are available now to the Christian-Jewish encounter. And if the following observations are any indication, I am optimistic that unexpected convergences can be found when Oneness convictions and insights are brought to the dialogue table.

To begin, how might the Oneness theology of the name engage Orthodox Jewish monotheism today? The results of the dialogue held in 1978 between Pinchas Lapide, an Orthodox Israeli Jew, and Jürgen Moltmann, a German Lutheran theologian and social trinitarian, are suggestive along at least three lines.[61] First, Lapide's admission that Jewish monotheism is not mathematical oneness but an ethical piety and orientation toward the ground of the universe can be brought into dialogue not only with the early church's denial that "one" and "three"

---

59. For an overview of developments through the last half of the twentieth century, see Tikva Frymer-Kensky et al., eds., *Christianity in Jewish Terms* (Boulder, CO: Westview, 2000).

60. E.g., Marc H. Tanenbaum, Marvin R. Wilson, and A. James Rudin, eds., *Evangelicals and Jews in an Age of Pluralism* (Lanham, MD: University Press of America, 1984).

61. See Pinchas Lapide and Jürgen Moltmann, *Jewish Monotheism and Christian Trinitarian Doctrine: A Dialogue*, trans. Leonard Swidler (Philadelphia: Fortress, 1981).

are mathematical quantities but also with the Oneness "praxis of the name"—for example, baptism, healing, and praying. In each case, "our God is one God" is not an abstract confession of God "in self"—this is, as Lapide points out, the "god of the philosophers"[62]—but a way or path of salvation. Second, Lapide's granting the resurrection as a historical fact—this explains for him the profound change in the demeanor of the disciples[63]—and the messianic ministry of Jesus without accepting the ontological claim regarding Jesus as divine begs to be juxtaposed with the Oneness confession of Jesus' divinity but denial of historical trinitarianism. In both cases, uncompromising commitment to the oneness of God will allow for a Jewish-Christian dialogue on christology that may further Jewish-Christian relations and yield new theological and christological insights.[64] Finally, Lapide's observation of the many triadic traces in Jewish faith—for example, the God of Abraham, Isaac, and Jacob; God's self, spirit, and word; the Trisagion, or "Holy, Holy, Holy," of the prophet Isaiah (6:3)[65]—can be brought alongside the Oneness acknowledgment of God as Father, Son, and Spirit, within the mutual context of the theology of the name. The many names of God in the Hebrew Bible do not undermine the oneness of Yahweh, just as Father, Son, and Spirit do not threaten the one God whose name is Jesus.

In this context, the recent call by Rabbi Jonathan Sacks for a monotheistic theology of difference that goes beyond toleration and pluralism is suggestive of further opportunities for the Oneness theology of the name to make a contribution. Sacks rightly sees that in our globalizing context, we need "a way of locating the celebration of diversity at the very heart of the monotheistic imagination."[66] Yet for Sacks as a rabbi, the way forward can never compromise the oneness of God at the center of Jewish faith. Sacks's strategy, then, is to articulate an understanding of God as creator of diversity. How might the fact that the one name of God is revealable in the diversity of human tongues and languages represent a Oneness contribution to Sacks's proposal?

62. Ibid., 65.

63. Ibid., 59–60.

64. Lapide believes in Jesus' resurrection as compatible with Jewish faith but does not accept the Christian claim of Jesus' messiahship because Jesus' life and even resurrection did not establish the messianic kingdom expected by Jews. Still, Lapide holds that the rejection of Jesus by the Jews opened up the door for Christianity to fulfill the promise of God to bless the world through the Jews. Pentecostals will be seriously challenged to rethink their theology of Judaism in light of Lapide's argument. See also Pinchas Lapide, *The Resurrection of Jesus: A Jewish Perspective*, trans. Wilhelm C. Linss (Minneapolis: Augsburg, 1983).

65. Pinchas Lapide, in Lapide and Moltmann, *Jewish Monotheism and Christian Trinitarian Doctrine*, 34–38.

66. Jonathan Sacks, *The Dignity of Difference: How to Avoid the Clash of Civilizations* (New York: Continuum, 2002), xi.

Along this same vein, the late John Howard Yoder's (1927–1997) unfinished project of arguing for the one covenant of God with humankind not only denies the traditional reading of the Babel event as divine judgment but sees it as expressing God's affirmation of diversity and pluralism as good.[67] Yoder sees both Judaism and Christianity as diaspora movements charged with bearing witness to the one self-revealing God to the ends of the earth. Thus the prophetic word to the Jews in Babylon—"But seek the welfare of the city where I have sent you into exile, and pray to the LORD on its behalf, for in its welfare you will find your welfare" (Jer. 29:7)—requires a stronger translation: "Seek the salvation of the culture to which God has sent you."[68] Does not the outpouring of the Spirit both preserve the blessing of Babel and confirm Yoder's insights given the inextricable connections between language and culture? And in this case, does not Pentecost also point to the possibility of the full and final redemption of Judaism specifically as one of the divine means of grace (without implying that historical Judaism is fully a means of divine grace in all its specificities)? In this reading, Christianity becomes another vehicle through which the Jewish witness to the divine name is transformed and carried to the Gentiles (again, without implying that historical Christianity is fully a means of divine grace in all its specificities), even while Christians will need to grapple with the implications of God's eternal covenant with the Jews for the Christian mission. Might the Oneness pentecostal paradigm that retrieves to center stage the early Jewish Christian theology of the name be serviceable for such a time and task as this?

Providing additional bridges to the Jewish-Christian dialogue is no minor achievement given the interconnections between this conversation and the emergence of the Jewish-Christian-Muslim trialogue.[69] Here we are talking not only about the trialogue between these three Abrahamic traditions[70] but also about the more specific Christian-Muslim dialogue.

67. John Howard Yoder, *The Jewish-Christian Schism Revisited*, ed. Michael G. Cartwright and Peter Ochs (Grand Rapids: Eerdmans, 2003), ch. 10, esp. 188–90, 194.

68. Ibid., 202 n. 60.

69. Initial forays include Ignaz Maybaum, *Trialogue between Jew, Christian, and Muslim* (London: Routledge & Kegan Paul, 1973); and Joseph Gremillion and William Ryan, eds., *World Faiths and the New World Order: A Muslim-Jewish-Christian Search Begins* (Washington, DC: Interreligious Peace Colloquium, 1978). The most recent developments include the emergence of the National Society for Scriptural Reasoning (see http://www .depts.drew.edu/ssr/nationalssr/), whose goal is to facilitate theological reflection in a postcritical key emergent from the dialogical retrieval of the founding texts of the three Abrahamic traditions by their adepts.

70. F. E. Peters has done more than most to make this explicit; see Peters, *Children of Abraham: Judaism, Christianity, Islam* (Princeton, NJ: Princeton University Press, 1982).

There is increasing realization after the September 11, 2001, attack on the World Trade Center in New York City that the Christian encounter with Islam needs to be rebuilt from the ground up. In addition, the pervasiveness and the global reach of pentecostal mission require it. What about the Oneness pentecostal contribution to this task? Anticipating further discussion (§6.3), let me identify two particular trajectories. First, I have elsewhere called attention to the fact that the Oneness pentecostal encounter with other monotheistic faiths in general and with Islam in particular is not burdened by the doctrine of the Trinity.[71] The Oneness confession of the deity of Jesus and the Muslim connection of the doctrines of *tawhid* (the unity of God) and *shirk* (the blasphemy of attributing deity to any creature) means that much more theological discussion is necessary.[72] But the discussion can proceed apart from the difficult matters surrounding the complex trinitarian claims. Further, the Oneness Jewish Christian theology of the name can surely be brought into conversation with the Muslim *Shadadah*—"There is no God but Allah . . ."—and the various personifications of the name in the Jewish Christian tradition can be fruitfully compared and contrasted with the ninety-nine names of Allah.[73] The goals of these encounters are manifold. But they include neither the syncretistic amalgamation of two or three faiths toward a supposed "new world religion" nor the politically correct politeness of postmodern relativism and tolerance. Rather, these encounters could constitute a distinctive (Oneness) pentecostal contribution both to the deeper understanding of self and otherness in our time and to the development of a uniquely pentecostal and pneumatological "hermeneutic of peace."[74]

5.3.3 *Toward Oneness-Trinitarian Rapprochement on the Doctrine of God*. What, then, about the future of the Oneness-trinitarian pentecostal dispute? Let us be honest about the challenges confronting any project in pentecostal theology. On the one side, pentecostal theology can no longer proceed as if Oneness pentecostalism did not exist; on the other, pentecostal theology is also informed by the dogmatic tradition of the church, especially important to the Catholic charismatic theologians in its midst. So let me attempt a via media by recalling Kenneth Gill's

71. See Yong, *Discerning the Spirit(s)*, 191.

72. See Muzammil H. Siddiqi, "God: A Muslim View," in *Three Faiths—One God: A Jewish, Christian, Muslim Encounter*, ed. John Hick and Edmund S. Meltzer (Albany: State University of New York Press, 1989), 63–76, esp. 69–71.

73. This was initially noted by Edwin Arnold, *Pearls of the Faith; or, Islam's Rosary: Being the Ninety-Nine Beautiful Names of Allah* (New York: J. W. Lovell, 1882).

74. See the call of Mennonite theologian Michael G. Cartwright for a "hermeneutic of peace" in his afterword to Yoder, *The Jewish-Christian Schism Revisited*, 205–40, esp. 232.

proposal (§I.2) about viewing Oneness theology as being underdeveloped from the trinitarian perspective. Still, the Oneness position brings back to center stage certain important features of the biblical witness. The concluding remarks to this chapter will highlight the platform for further Oneness-trinitarian discussion within the overall proposal for reconstructing Christian theology in the late modern world.

To begin, Oneness theology is not devoid of trinitarian features, just as trinitarian Pentecostals have never ceased to emphasize the unity of God. In their official theological statements, both groups take account of the biblical revelation of the divine unity and the divine plurality in turn. Thus the official United Pentecostal Church introductory handbook does not fail to discuss the Father, Son, and Holy Ghost, even as Assemblies of God theological textbooks begin their discussion of the Trinity by stating explicitly that "the Scriptures teach that God is One, and that beside Him there is no God."[75] Further, both groups agree that the biblical testimony sanctions a trinitarian revelation of God relative to the economy of salvation. David Reed's observation, as far back as 1975, that Oneness theologians and apologists spoke of God "solely in terms of His redemptive activity" is also true for trinitarian pentecostals.[76]

Oneness-trinitarian agreement grounded in the pentecostal experience of the Spirit highlights and emphasizes "God for us" rather than God in Godself. This is itself an important admission because it provides the basis for the kind of pentecostal ecumenical theology difficult to come by at the doctrinal and propositional level. Put succinctly, Oneness and trinitarian pentecostals are bound together by a "oneness of experience."[77] Bernard states that the work of salvation—understood as justification, regeneration, adoption, and sanctification—"originates in God's grace, are purchased by Christ's blood, and comes to us through faith in Christ. Furthermore, all four occur when we repent, are baptized in the name of Jesus, and are filled with the Holy Spirit."[78] The trinitarian character of salvation is here evident. Further, both theologies are confessionally Jesus-centered and experientially Spirit-oriented. While this has led to a sort of eclipse of the Father,[79] pentecostal spirituality is nevertheless

75. Pearlman, *Knowing the Doctrines of the Bible*, 68. On the Oneness side, see Bernard et al., *Meet the United Pentecostal Church International*, 60–62; and David Bernard, "God," in Hall and Bernard, eds., *Doctrines of the Bible*, 15–22; in the latter manual, Bernard has successive sections entitled "The Oneness of God" and "Father, Son, and Holy Spirit."

76. David Reed, "Aspects of the Origins of Oneness Pentecostalism," in *Aspects of Pentecostal-Charismatic Origins*, ed. Vinson Synan (Plainfield, NJ: Logos International, 1975), 143–68; quotation, 152.

77. Bernard, "Response to Ralph Del Colle," 4.

78. David Bernard, *The New Birth* (Hazelwood, MO: Word Aflame, 1984), 334–35.

79. Thus Thomas A. Smail, *The Forgotten Father* (Grand Rapids: Eerdmans, 1980), calls for a retrieval of the Father.

undeniably concerned with the historical dealings of God in the world, the church, and especially the individual, understood as redeemed by the Son and mediated through the Spirit. Thus Jesus is confessed as "*my* Savior and baptizer*," and the Holy Spirit is welcomed as "*my* empowerer." "The tripartite experience of early Christians patterned in Acts 2:38 may suggest that, while [Oneness Pentecostals] have a Oneness view of God, they have a trinitarian experience of God."[80] The same holds true for trinitarian pentecostals by virtue of their "oneness of experience" with their separated siblings. Both Oneness followers and trinitarians experience God as Creator, Redeemer, and Sanctifier.[81] Reed's earlier conclusion remains accurate: "There is little in the Oneness teaching on functions of the Father, Son and Holy Spirit that would distinguish it from trinitarian doctrine except in its insistence upon the belief that the three are really only one."[82]

This means that the Oneness-trinitarian debates may be adjudicated at the level of the underlying narrative base more appropriate to the Jewish theology of the name and the kerygma of Jesus' life, death, and resurrection at the heart of the trinitarian construct. Herein may lie a strategy that is not only more conducive to Oneness sensibilities than its current attempts to rehabilitate the Logos category for theological and christological purposes, but also more helpful in articulating the gospel in a post-Enlightenment and postmetaphysical world. Further, resorting to the narrative base of the gospel to ground an ecumenical theology for the late modern world would enable retrieval of the pentecostal and pneumatological dimension of the gospel. This emphasis prevents superficial trinitarianism from lapsing back toward a binitarian theology. Finally, retrieval of the gospel narrative not only provides the opportunity for but also necessitates (how else can a narrative be retrieved?) its retelling, repetition, and reenactment, all of which are crucial to the realization of the truth of the gospel for our time. Here again, to start with the Spirit as we have attempted to do is to realize that theology follows after the self-revealing and saving work of God, which catches human beings up in the gospel story. This would be trinitarian theology about the one God at the height of its effectiveness because the testimony of encountering God in Jesus Christ by the Spirit moves us further toward the divine mystery than does reliance solely on creedal

80. Reed, "Oneness Pentecostalism: Problems and Possibilities for Pentecostal Theology," 91.

81. Thus Yves Congar observes that "the texts that speak of the Spirit of the Son or of Christ are all concerned with the economy, God's plan in the world"; see Yves Congar, *The Word and the Spirit*, trans. David Smith (San Francisco: Harper & Row, 1986), 103.

82. David A. Reed, "The Origins of the Theology of Oneness Pentecostalism in the United States" (Ph.D. diss., Boston University, 1978), 249.

propositionalism (see further §7.3.2). This does not mean, however, that the philosophic and metaphysical dimensions of theological reflection are no longer necessary. All theology has assumptions at this level that need to be acknowledged and admitted. It only means that articulation of the philosophic underpinnings of a pentecostal and pneumatological theology will emerge from the basic encounter with God through the Spirit (see §7.2.3).

But as important is the fact that to tell and live the Pentecost story is to realize proleptically the eschatological achievements of the triune God (see §2.2.1). This is because God will be all in all only after the Spirit lifts up the Son and the Son returns or subjects all things to the Father. Hence pentecostal experience is oriented toward both a realized and a future eschatology. The kingdom of God is at hand, yet it is also coming. Dreams and visions anticipate the kingdom; glossolalia heralds the kingdom; healings and exorcisms are signs that its invasion is partly realized. The kingdom is the Father's, inaugurated by the Son, and ushered in by the Spirit.[83] In this eschatological consummation, the groaning of creation will cease as it "will be set free from its bondage to decay and will obtain the freedom of the glory of the children of God" (Rom. 8:21), and as the Oneness vision of the Godhead insists, the unity of the economic Trinity will be realized and secured in the divine union of the all in all (1 Cor. 15:28).

The preceding has shown that trinitarian pentecostals affirm the oneness of God and deny tritheism whereas Oneness pentecostals affirm the one God revealed in Jesus as Father, Son, and Holy Spirit. An ecumenical pentecostal theology will go a long way toward repairing the breach between these sibling movements. More important, since the doctrine of God poses difficulties for ecumenical relationships between pentecostalism and the other churches, the benefits to be gleaned for the church catholic are at present incalculable. But I believe that the foregoing discussion has cleared the way not only for further intra-Christian ecumenical theology but also, unexpectedly, for the Christian encounter with other faiths. Our journey so far has led us inexorably to raise this question here again, even as we did at the end of the previous chapter: what is or can be the response of a pentecostal and pneumatological theology to the religiously plural world context of our time? Does the Spirit blow in or through the world's religions, and if so, can we trace her tracks? Come Holy Spirit, breathe upon the world . . . of the religions . . .

---

83. See the trinitarian revision of Steven J. Land, *Pentecostal Spirituality: A Passion for the Kingdom*, JPTSup 1 (Sheffield, Eng.: Sheffield Academic Press, 1993), esp. 197.

6

The Holy Spirit and the Spirits

Public Theology, the Religions, and the Identity of the Spirit

I have argued so far that we cannot separate the interreligious ecumenical question from the intra-Christian ecumenical one (§4.3.3; §5.3.2). It is time to confront this matter head-on. Along with the questions deriving from the interaction between science and religion, the challenges emerging from the encounter between the world religions have intensified since the middle to late nineteenth century. Precipitated by the emergence of Darwinism in the 1860s and the turn East by the American transcendentalist movement in the 1870s, the questions have come fast and furious as the horizons have broadened. The next chapter will take up the science-and-religion question; here our attention is on the knotty problem of doing theology in a world religious context.

Three interrelated questions demand special attention for a Christian theology of religions in our time. First, what is the role of the religions in the providence of God? Second, does God save through the religions, and if so, how? Third, what should be the Christian response to other faiths? The hypothesis proposed here is that a pneumatologically driven theology is more conducive to engaging these matters in our time than

235

previous approaches. I have suggested elsewhere that the religions are neither accidents of history nor encroachments on divine providence but are, in various ways, instruments of the Holy Spirit working out the divine purposes in the world and that the unevangelized, if saved at all, are saved through the work of Christ by the Spirit (even if mediated through the religious beliefs and practices available to them).[1] Until both the questions and the answers are broadened so as to take into account the religions themselves, however, those tentative proposals will be necessarily incomplete at best and immaterial at worst, since apart from these developments, Christians pronounce judgment on the religions without knowing what it is they are actually making pronouncement about. In other words, as any theology needs to follow after the experiences and empirical actualities that it strives to understand, the theology of religions is not exempt. Only a pneumatological approach to the religions enables us to hold in tension the distinctive confessional claims of Christian faith alongside the actual claims of the religions themselves, because the Spirit's being poured out upon all flesh does not cancel out but instead preserves the diversity of human voices.

This pneumatological hypothesis, which has guided this volume from the beginning, will continue to inform our reflections. Some repetition is unavoidable, but distinctively new arguments will also be brought to bear on the pneumatological thesis. In particular, this chapter will provide further exegetical warrants for my pneumatological theology of religions (§6.1), buttress the argument historically through the retrieval of an ally in the Wesleyan theological tradition (§6.2), and illustrate the potential of the pneumatological approach through a concrete case study in the Christian-Muslim dialogue (§6.3). This will supplement previous arguments and demonstrate the potential of pneumatological theology for the global religious context of late modernity.

6.1 THE SPIRIT, THE PUBLICS OF THEOLOGICAL REFLECTION, AND RELIGIOUS PLURALISM

If the Spirit has been poured out upon all flesh, then the public of theological reflection is as wide as humankind. This section explores further this new world context for Christian theological reflection, develops a fresh line of response to the multireligious character of this

---

1. See Amos Yong, *Discerning the Spirit(s): A Pentecostal-Charismatic Contribution to Christian Theology of Religions*, JPTSup 20 (Sheffield, Eng.: Sheffield Academic Press, 2000); and *Beyond the Impasse: Toward a Pneumatological Theology of Religions* (Grand Rapids: Baker, 2003).

context from Jesus' parable of the Good Samaritan, and suggests the role of pentecostalism at this crossroads of doing theology in a religiously plural world.

6.1.1 *The New World Context: Cultures and Religions.* In our time of increasing awareness of the challenges raised by the various reactions to modernity, modern science, and the diversity of religions, Christian theology faces at least three tasks. First, it must learn to speak the various languages—of the sciences, of the religions, and of the various postmodernisms—that pose these challenges, so that it can understand the issues at stake. Second, the understanding of these various other languages should reach a level of sufficient depth and sophistication to allow rearticulation of these languages in ways that are recognized by their advocates and that in turn enable critical interaction with them. Finally, these other languages need to be appropriately translated into the terms and categories of Christian faith and vice versa if there is to be any means for their challenges to be posed to Christian theology or for the latter to respond. Indeed, once translation successfully occurs, transformation has already taken place. We will return to this important matter. But for the moment, it is especially important that Christian theology not erect "straw" positions and then presume to declare Christian superiority after demolishing these nonexisting (except in the minds of zealous Christian apologists) fictions.

In one sense, the preceding five chapters have attempted to follow these insights by rethinking the doctrines of salvation, the church, and God within the global context of the pentecostal experience. This chapter more specifically addresses the cultural and religious dimensions of this new world context. After all, Christian theology is the thinking by the church not only for the church but also for the world. In its broadest sense, theology—the *logos*, or the word, about God—is done by any and all interested in the subject matter of divine things and is not limited to Christians or even to monotheists. For these reasons, Christian theology needs to engage the multicultural and the multireligious realities of our times.

In many ways, pentecostals are still at the very beginning of this process. We have contented ourselves so far with dialoguing only with the languages closest to ours—evangelical and fundamentalistic forms of Christianity—and have either ignored the rest or warned our pentecostal faithful against consorting with these "enemies" of the faith. Yet vital pentecostal faith in the late modern world requires that we open things up. If a sectarian attitude that withdraws from the world is motivated by fear, a dialogical attitude that engages the world is motivated by the truth that sets people free. Yet the dynamics of such broad-ranging engagements are indeed challenging.

The complexity of the issues can be seen in the call by Latino theologian Benjamin Valentin for a fully public theology.[2] Valentin's proposal concerns the current state of Latino/a theology in the United States. He challenges his North American Latino/a colleagues to move from identity and cultural issues to the public spaces of social, economic, and political analysis/criticism. The former, characteristic of much of Latino/a theology over the past generation, is a defensive posture focused on solidifying the diasporic identity of Latino/a cultures in North America. The latter, however, presumes that Latino/a theology has something to say not only to Latinos/as but to the broader public. Given Valentin's definition of public theology—"a form of discourse that couples either the language, symbols, or background concepts of a religious tradition with an overarching, integrative, emancipatory sociopolitical vision in such a way that it movingly captures the attention and moral conscience of a broad audience and promotes the cultivation of those modes of love, concern, and courage required both for individual fulfillment and broad-based social activism"[3]—his attempt to engage Latino/a theology with public issues such as diversity, equality, plurality, and multicultural and multiethnic relations can be better understood. The result is the connection of the theological with the cultural and the social, the fusing of identity politics and emancipatory projects, and the expansion of the theoretical and practical relevance of theology. In the end, Latino/a theology bears witness to "God's crossing over between and among us."[4]

There is much to commend Valentin's theological project. For one thing, his starting point is not an abstract theological position but that of the Hispanic community. Yet he still recognizes the necessity for theology to speak to the contemporary issues of our time and is confident that Latino/a theology has something to offer to the (North American) public on issues of vital importance. Of course, there are also dangers in any enterprise in public theology. Will such projects be coopted by the agendas of others in ways that are theologically compromising? In particular, is not a public theology driven by an "emancipatory sociopolitical vision" liable to turn theology into anthropology? Finally, even if it is insisted that there be built-in checks to protect our public theology from these seductions, does not all engagement with other

2. Benjamin Valentin, *Mapping Public Theology: Beyond Culture, Identity, and Difference* (Harrisburg, PA: Trinity Press International, 2002). Although Valentin theologizes more explicitly as a Latino than as a pentecostal, his ideas are engaged here because of his pentecostal background and church affiliation.

3. Ibid., xx.

4. Ibid., xxii; also 136–40.

thought forms on their terms shift, even if ever so subtly, the terms and convictions of the originating language?

Valentin's response would be that all theologies assume some kind of cultural self-understanding. Whereas fundamentalisms of all stripes see themselves as culture-negating, Valentin suggests that Latino/a theologies acknowledge their cultural rootedness and therefore affirm the centrality of the category of culture for theological reflection. This includes cultural appropriation, in light of culture not as a bounded set of beliefs and practices but as a dynamic environment of practices and agency. In this sense, Latino/a theologies are inherently collaborative and dialogical—*teología en conjunto*, theologies in conjunction—crisscrossing various lines of differentiation. It is better, then, to acknowledge up front that all theologies have their cultural dimension (as do Valentin and other Latino/a theologians) than to deny the cultural matrices of one's theologizing. The attempt to do the latter results either in an anticultural stance or in theology informed negatively and unconsciously by the cultural conditions.

Here Miroslav Volf's reflections on the cultural contexts of theology are worth pondering.[5] Volf suggests that none of the following strategies for negotiating the intersection of gospel and culture work: liberal accommodationism, postliberal traditionalism, and sectarian retreat. His response is to go beyond the dualism or dichotomy of gospel and culture and argue both that Christian difference is internal to any given cultural world and that it should be from this site of marginality that the gospel makes its contribution. How does this come about? In some instances cultural features are adopted, in others not; in some instances the gospel leads to a change of cultural direction, in others not; in some instances cultural features are discarded and replaced, in others not. This leads to Volf's thesis: "Christian difference is always a complex and flexible network of small and large refusals, divergences, subversions, and more or less radical alternative proposals, surrounded by the acceptance of many cultural givens. There is no single correct way to relate to a given culture as a whole, or even to its dominant thrust; there are only numerous ways of accepting, transforming, or replacing various aspects of a given culture from within."[6]

Let me put it this way: if in the twenty-first century we are looking for a rigidly defined theological methodology that will enable us to engage

---

5. Miroslav Volf, "When Gospel and Culture Intersect: Notes on the Nature of Christian Difference," in *Pentecostalism in Context: Essays in Honor of William W. Menzies*, ed. Wonsuk Ma and Robert P. Menzies, JPTSup 11 (Sheffield, Eng.: Sheffield Academic Press, 1997), 223–36.

6. Ibid., 233.

culture without getting our gospel hands dirty, then we may as well quit now. No such approach is available because gospel and culture are not two separate things. Rather, the gospel always comes in cultural dress. Even Jesus came as a first-century male Jewish carpenter. This leads to the incarnational principle whereby God redeems, at least potentially, all that is taken up historically in the life of Christ. Therefore we proceed best in our time if our theologies are multiperspectival, multidisciplinary, and multicultural. Multiperspectivalism requires taking seriously the insights of all voices, especially those previously marginalized from the theological conversation—for instance, women, the poor, the differently abled or disabled, perhaps even the heretics![7] Multidisciplinarity requires taking seriously the insights of the wide range of human learning, especially those in the hard and soft sciences. And multiculturalism requires that we take seriously the insights of the various ethnic and cultural groups and their experiences.

But to open the multicultural door is to open the multireligious door (§4.3.3). Is there anything Christians can learn from those in other faiths that we need but do not already have? If we answer yes, then are we not saying the gospel is insufficient? And if we say no, then why not jettison the interreligious dialogue in favor of the traditional missionary and evangelization approaches?

My initial response would be that Christians should be open to learning from other religious traditions similarly to the ways in which Christians have learned from the findings of the sciences over the centuries. Christian theologies have adjusted to scientific advances, sometimes easily, other times with considerable difficulty and struggle. Why not with the religions, which themselves are not static entities but are dynamically reconstituting themselves even as Christian traditions are (as in §2.3.3)? Christians can refuse to engage the religions as they can reject science, but this would not be a Christian theology *for the twenty-first century*.

My long-run response is that Christians should be open to learning from other religious traditions because of the unfinished character of Christian identity. While we are being formed into the eschatological image of Jesus, we continue to look through the glass dimly. If others have something to say about God, should we not at least listen both sympathetically and critically? Further, not only are we being formed; also our knowledge of God remains finite on this side of the eschaton. Finally, given the infinitude of God, how can this be *exhaustively* conveyed in finite time and words?

---

7. I am working on a project tentatively titled, "Down Syndrome and the Human Condition: Theological Reflections on Intellectual Disability."

6.1.2 *The Spirit's Teaching through the Religions: Lessons from the Good Samaritan.* When read in the present multicultural and multireligious context, the story of the good Samaritan (Luke 10:25–37) shows how we can learn from those in other faiths.[8] Jesus told the parable in response to a lawyer who had initially asked him about how one inherits eternal life. When Jesus answered that eternal life came with fulfilling the two greatest commandments—loving God and neighbor—the lawyer sought to justify himself with the counterquestion "Who is my neighbor?" The story of the good Samaritan can be read in two complementary senses: either as a straightforward answer to this question—my neighbor is anyone in need—or as Jesus' means of humbling the pride and arrogance of the lawyer (who sought self-justification) by showing that one as despicable as a Samaritan could indeed be a neighbor and fulfill the requirements of the law.[9]

But who was this Samaritan? In what ways would this story have humbled this self-justifying Jewish interlocutor? For a better sense of this parable's evocative power, some background about Jewish-Samaritan history and relations is needed. The emergence of the Samaritans goes back perhaps to the eighth century BCE with the fall of Samaria to the Assyrians (cf. 2 Kings 17:24–41).[10] The cities of Samaria were settled by peoples from various parts of the Assyrian Empire who brought with them their own cultural and religious practices. The ensuing process of integration resulted, at least early on, in a kind of religious syncretism, so that the newly formed Samaritan people worshiped the Lord but also continued their worship of the deities they brought with them. Not surprisingly, this marked the beginnings of suspicion and hostility between Israelites and Samaritans. Conflict flared especially after the Babylonian exile, when those allowed to return by the decree of Cyrus the Persian were resettling the land (Ezra 1:1–4) and attempts were made to rebuild the temple at Jerusalem (the story of Nehemiah).

During the fourth century BCE, the Samaritans obtained authorization from their Persian regents to build their own temple on Mount Gerizim. Although this exacerbated relationships with the Jews over the next few generations, the Samaritans had clearly discarded their

8. Hints of the following reading of this pericope appear in Robert Cummings Neville, *Symbols of Jesus: A Christology of Symbolic Engagement* (Cambridge: Cambridge University Press, 2001), 179.

9. The latter emphasis is from Bastiaan van Elderen, "Another Look at the Parable of the Good Samaritan," in *Saved by Hope: Essays in Honor of Richard C. Oudersluys*, ed. James I. Cook (Grand Rapids: Eerdmans, 1978), 109–19.

10. For an overview, see H. H. Rowley, "The Samaritan Schism in Legend and History," in *Israel's Prophetic Heritage: Essays in Honor of James Muilenburg*, ed. Bernhard W. Anderson and Walter Harrelson (New York: Harper & Brothers, 1962), 208–22.

syncretistic practices and solidified their monotheistic commitment. Indeed, Samaritan literature confirms their own sense of being the true Israelites, given the various exilic experiences of the children of Jacob. They were devoted to the singular prophethood of Moses, to the Torah (his composition), and to Mount Gerizim as the center of their religious lives.

By the second century BCE, Jewish-Samaritan lines were drawn. From the Samaritan perspective, insofar as the Jews did not worship on Mount Gerizim, they were apostates from the true faith and to be resisted.[11] On the other side, toward the end of the Maccabean revolt in 107 BCE, John Hyrcanus destroyed the temple of Mount Gerizim, partly in response to the Samaritans' denial of their relationship to the Jews amidst Antiochus IV's persecution of the Jews and partly in response to the Samaritans' permitting "their temple to be known as the temple of Zeus Hellenios."[12] This marked, it seems, the final schism between these two people groups.

Although the data even in the Hebrew Scriptures conflict about Israelite views regarding the Samaritans, the New Testament presents a more unambiguous picture, perhaps indicating that attitudes had hardened during the intertestamental period. The Gospel of John gives important insights into Jewish-Samaritan relations. The editorial gloss added after Jesus requests a drink from the Samaritan woman at the well—"Jews do not share things in common with Samaritans" (John 4:9)—may provide insight into Matthew's account (written to Jews) of Jesus' explicit prohibition of the Twelve from taking the good news to the Samaritans (cf. Matt. 10:5). Further, Jewish and Samaritan identities were clearly contrasted in their respective commitments to worship at the temple in Jerusalem and on Mount Gerizim (John 4:20–22). This is confirmed in Luke's Gospel, which not only says that the Samaritans have rejected Jesus "because his face was set toward Jerusalem" but relates the response of Jesus' disciples, "Do you want us to command fire to come down from heaven and consume them?" (Luke 9:53–54). Finally and more tellingly, the Jewish accusation against Jesus also communicates a sense of how Jews viewed Samaritans: "Are we not right in saying that

11. Hasanein Wasef Kahen, *Samaritan History, Identity, Religion and Subdivisions, Literature, and Social Status* (Jerusalem: Greek Convent, 1966), 28–29. The Samaritan perspective on the apostasy of the Jews as this perspective evolved during the intertestamental period and came to inform Samaritan identity is preserved in some of the documents collected in John Bowman, trans. and ed., *Samaritan Documents Relating to Their History, Religion, and Life* (Pittsburgh: Pickwick, 1977), ch. 2.

12. Bruce W. Hall, *Samaritan Religion from John Hyrcanus to Baba Rabba* (Sydney: Mandelbaum Trust and University of Sydney, 1987), 163–67, summarizing Josephus's *Antiquities*; quotation, 167.

you are a Samaritan and have a demon?" (John 8:48). It appears the feelings were mutual: Samaritans considered Jews apostates, and Jews considered the religion of the Samaritans to be demonic.

Reading this parable from the perspective of the encounter of religions is of value. Clearly, there are parallels between contemporary Christian views of other religions and first-century Jewish views of the Samaritans: as apostates; as a marginal sect at best and a dangerous cult at worst; as proponents of a completely foreign (i.e., untruthful and incorrect) set of religious beliefs and practices; as holders of a religious perspective inspired by the devil himself; and so on. How does Jesus' telling of this story address these perspectives and attitudes?

This story has at least four implications for shaping Christian approaches to other faiths. First, if Jews could learn something from Samaritans, so can Christians learn from those in other faiths, even those we have previously defined as cultic, irreligious, or even demonic.[13] Second, if the Samaritan could love selflessly and demonstrate this in his actions, so are those of other faiths capable of demonstrating selfless love. Third, insofar as the Samaritan's actions show him to be not only the "comrade of God" but also the embodiment of God's comradeship to human beings,[14] does he also not show us the possibility of Jesus meeting us in religious others? Why not, if Jesus is to be found in the faces of little ones (Matt. 18:5) and in the hungry, the thirsty, the stranger, the naked, the sick, and those in prison (Matt. 25:40, 45)?

Finally, perhaps what is most important but also most controversial, Jesus told the story of the good Samaritan in the context of the lawyer's question about how to inherit eternal life. From the preceding discussion, it is possible that the Samaritan fulfilled both conditions in Jesus' initial response. Clearly, first-century Samaritans were monotheistic lovers of God. Equally clearly from the parable, this Samaritan loved his (Jewish) neighbor as himself. Insofar as the text then implies that the Samaritan satisfies the conditions for inheriting eternal life, is it not also possible in today's religiously plural world that there are some in other faiths who might love God and their neighbor as did the Samaritan? In contrast, insofar as the lawyer is indicted for loving God but not his non-Jewish neighbor (remember, he tried to justify himself), is not the Christian

13. Thus COGIC theologian Alonzo Johnson: "I have learned much in recent years from my explorations into the mythical and theological systems of people of faith from various religious communities around the world" (*Good News for the Disinherited: Howard Thurman on Jesus of Nazareth and Human Liberation* [Lanham, MD: University Press of America, 1997], 149).

14. Llewellyn Welile Mazamisa, *Beatific Comradeship: An Exegetical-Hermeneutical Study on Lk 10:25–37* (Kampen, Neth.: J. H. Kok, 1987), esp. 164–72.

also indicted for his or her love for God but not for the (non-Christian) neighbor (cf. James 2:1–17; 1 John 4:20–21)?

I am only raising this question. Clearly, our salvation is by grace through faith as a gift from God, "not the result of works, so that no one may boast" (Eph. 2:9). But does not the Jewish legalism in the background of the Pauline Letters suggest that this addresses first and foremost the ritual works directed to salvation? Further, what if the religious other neither has the intention to work for his or her salvation nor boasts of having attained such through good deeds (contrast the Pharisee and the tax collector in Luke 18:9–14)? If neither of these pertain to the Samaritan (or any religious other), then is it not still the loving prerogative of God to save this Samaritan (or any religious other)? Finally, there is also the New Testament witness of divine blessing and judgment meted out for what people do (cf. 1 Cor. 3:10–15; Rev. 20:12–13; Matt. 25:31–46).[15] But as important for Christians is Jesus' warning, "Not everyone who says . . . , 'Lord, Lord,' will enter the kingdom of heaven, but only the one who does the will of my Father in heaven" (Matt. 7:21).

The preceding should be read less as a dogmatic claim about the salvation of those in other faiths than about reorienting Christian perceptions and attitudes toward religious others, whom we often define in terms Jews applied to Samaritans. I submit this reading of the parable to be faithful both to the particular interest Luke has in Samaria (cf. the healing of the Samaritan leper in Luke 17:11–19) and to the explicit focus on the gospel's engagement with Samaria on its way to the ends of the earth (cf. Acts 1:8; 8:1–25). Further, God "has not left himself without a witness" (Acts 14:17), and this applies not only to the God-fearing Gentiles but also to the supposedly despicable Samaritans. Indeed, God "shows no partiality, but in every nation anyone who fears him and does what is right is acceptable to him" (Acts 10:34b–35; cf. 17:26–28). Why, then, have Christians in general and pentecostals in particular tended historically to subordinate these images of God's presence and activity in and through all human beings to other selected (especially Pauline) passages regarding human depravity and thoroughgoing unrighteousness?

6.1.3 *Pentecostalism and the Interreligious Encounter.* Here are two brief responses and one lengthier response to the above question. First,

15. Matthew's discussion of the judgment between sheep and goats on the basis of what people do should be read against the background of his apparent openness to the Gentile world—as seen in the pericope regarding the Magi (ch. 2), the faith of the officer with the sick daughter (ch. 8), and the Syro-Phoenician woman (ch. 15)—a remarkable openness for a document addressed to first-century Jews. See Jacques Matthey, "Pilgrims, Seekers, and Disciples: Mission and Dialogue in Matthew," *IRM* 91, no. 360 (2002): 120–34.

internal to the question of theological method, the Protestant disposition to subordinate (Lukan) narrative genres of Scripture to (Pauline)
didactic genres for purposes of doctrinal articulation is related to privileging Romans over Luke and Acts for understanding our religiously
plural world. It is part of the purpose of this volume to articulate a
coherent and systematic theology through the Lukan lens to complement, not replace, those developed through the perspective of Paul.
Second, in light of the pentecostal (and evangelical) commitments to
the Great Commission, the emergence of pentecostalism at the turn of
the twentieth century meant that it would adopt the nineteenth-century
mottoes and rationales for world evangelization that were dependent
upon images such as those portrayed in Jonathan Edwards's famous
sermon "Sinners in the Hands of an Angry God." Motivation for mission and evangelism, in other words, was found in the many souls who
would be lost eternally apart from hearing the gospel. From the Lukan
perspective, however, mission is never connected to the fear of hellfire
and brimstone, but to the empowering work of the Spirit.

More important and problematic for this question of why the Lukan
witness to the universal presence and activity of God is subordinated
to the Pauline insistence on the total depravity of human beings is the
practical issue of how to communicate properly the gospel in and among
the various cultures of the world. As already mentioned, pentecostal missionary strategies early on emphasized the importance of establishing
the indigenous church (see §3.1.1). Yet this indigenization brings with
it the risk of syncretism, a concern that repeatedly arises for pentecostal
theology (see I.2; §1.2.1; §3.2.3). Is there a way to follow Luke's lead in
the book of Acts, which reveals a consistent wariness of, and vigilance
against, syncretism in its pejorative form, even as it contains neither
an overly excessive or heavily aggressive form of polemics nor a wholly
negative view of the human race?[16] Can we discern an uncompromising
witness to the one God of Jesus Christ through the beliefs and practices
of those in other faiths (cf. Paul at the Aeropagus in Acts 17) and at the
same time avoid syncretism?

It is fruitful here to bring Valentin's and Volf's comments discussed
earlier (§6.1.1) into conversation with those of Chilean pentecostal theologian Juan Sepúlveda (also §1.1.3).[17] In the Chilean context, Sepúlveda
notes the instability of the idea of syncretism. What he considers to be

16. This is the thesis argued throughout Hans-Josef Klauck, *Magic and Paganism in
Early Christianity: The World of the Acts of the Apostles*, trans. Brian McNeil (Minneapolis:
Fortress, 2003), esp. 119–21.

17. Juan Sepúlveda, "To Overcome the Fear of Syncretism: A Latin American Perspective," in *Mission Matters*, ed. Lynne Price, Juan Sepúlveda, and Graeme Smith, SIHC 103
(Frankfurt, Ger.: Peter Lang, 1997), 157–68.

the expression of popular culture in Christian form—Chilean pentecostalism—indigenous Chileans consider to be a sign of the "economic, political, cultural and religious domination of the West."[18] Chilean pentecostals such as Sepúlveda are caught between having a sense of cultural and ethnic pride about their Chilean identities and wishing to be in solidarity with their (usually North American) pentecostal missionaries and their constituencies. But apart from these issues, other factors need to be considered, such as what has happened and continues to happen through the process of *mestizaje* ("miscegenation," or racial mixing); how to understand the nature of conversions that occur through missionary and evangelistic efforts, versus discoveries of newfound spiritualities by those disoriented for various reasons, versus the transformation of religious communities renegotiating their identities in the face of modernity (which arrived at about the same time in Chile as did the pentecostal missionaries). Further, as Valentin has informed us, Hispanics are rather culturally attuned; this, along with the open-endedness of Andean (and Latin American) indigenous religious traditions, combines to make the synthesis of Christian beliefs and practices a rather natural process. So, congruent with Volf, Sepúlveda understands syncretism as a natural process, so that "we cannot grasp any meaning without the help of our precarious cultural categories." In that case, can we be wary about syncretism in its pejorative form even while proceeding with a more intentional "incarnational dynamic" that inspires the Christian mission to be more fully and genuinely dialogical rather than monological?[19]

Sepúlveda's approach not only points the way forward for pentecostals concerned with syncretism but also provides a further theological rationale for the pentecostal encounter with other faiths. Let us face it: like it or not, the world religions, at least, are here to stay. Syncretism is and should be a concern not only for pentecostals in the two-thirds world but also for pentecostals in the Euroamerican West, where Southerners and Easterners are steadily emigrating and Asian, African, and Latin American religions are increasingly sending their own missionaries. More than ever, other religionists are our neighbors, coworkers, schoolmates, and business contacts. We need a theological rationale for engaging dialogically with them, not just a pragmatic (missionary) one. Pentecostalism's global presence and the realization of Buddhism, Hinduism, Islam, and Judaism as *world* religions require a more informed and sophisticated Christian approach.

18. Ibid., 159.
19. Ibid., 167; also Juan Sepúlveda, "Gospel and Culture in Latin American Protestantism: Toward a New Theological Appreciation of Syncretism" (Ph.D. diss., University of Birmingham, 1996).

Again, a pneumatological approach to the interreligious encounter provides the kind of theological justification for multifaith relations that world Christianity badly needs. Acknowledgment that the Spirit is poured out on all flesh requires a respectful Christian orientation to those in other faiths. Recognizing the possibility that the Spirit can speak through even religious others demands a listening ear, a willingness to be self-critical, and an openness to learning from, and even being corrected by, them. And perhaps most important, the potentiality of the Spirit's presence and activity in the religions and their adherents means both that the religious traditions of humankind are redeemable for the glory of God and that the gospel can be communicated (i.e., contextualized, accommodated), even found manifest in new ways, in other faiths. The Spirit poured out on all flesh enables the miracle of human communication—hearing and speaking, tongues and their interpretations—so that what was once far off is brought near (cf. Eph. 2:13) and what was strange is now intelligible (cf. 1 Cor. 14:21). All of these combine to confirm the missiological principle of indigeneity, long ago embraced by pentecostals (see §3.1.1), except that it demands extension of this principle in the twenty-first century from the realm of culture to the realm of the religions.

6.2 TOWARD A PNEUMATOLOGICAL THEOLOGY OF RELIGIONS

This section develops the preceding exegetical and pentecostal perspectives toward a theological framework for our encounter with other faiths. With help from the early Wesleyan theological tradition, it elaborates the basic framework of a pneumatological theology of religions and sets out guidelines for discerning the Spirit's presence and activity in other faiths. A concrete case study focused on the question of how and to what extent it is possible to learn from other faiths appears in the next section.

6.2.1 *An Assist from the Wesleyan Theological Tradition.* John Fletcher's contributions to the Holiness movement's emphasis on the baptism of the Spirit as a second work of grace (§2.3.3) have already been mentioned. Less well known, however, are Fletcher's "doctrine of dispensations" and its implications for Christian attitudes toward, and interactions with, those in other faiths. Laurence Wood has brought Fletcher's ideas to the attention of contemporary theologians and made available some of Fletcher's key writings on this topic.[20] It is apropos here to summarize

---

20. See Laurence W. Wood, *The Meaning of Pentecost in Early Methodism: Rediscovering John Fletcher as John Wesley's Vindicator and Designated Successor* (Lanham, MD: Scarecrow, 2002), ch. 7; and John Fletcher, "The Language of the Father's Dispensation"

and then highlight the central features of what I call Fletcher's proto-pneumatological theology of religions.

In a nutshell, Fletcher understood the various covenants between God and humankind as differing dispensations through which God dealt with five different classes of human beings: (1) nonbelievers; (2) those under the Noahite covenant, including the Gentile (non-Jewish) believers in the one God, which Fletcher called the dispensation of the Father; (3) those under the Mosaic covenant, that is the Jews, in a mediating dispensation between that of the Father and that of the Son; (4) those under the ministration of John the Baptist and initiated into Christ, best represented by Anna, Simeon, and the believing disciples during the ministry of Jesus, all "carnal believers" and "imperfect" followers of the Lord; (5) those who have come into Pentecost, that is, who have experienced the fullness of perfection and the abiding grace/witness of the baptism of the Holy Spirit.

Within this framework, Fletcher developed a set of categories within which to locate much of what was known to him as an eighteenth-century Anglican clergyman. One could be trinitarian in confession but not in experience. Further, Roman Catholics may not be entirely perfected by the baptism in the Holy Spirit, but they are nevertheless like the Moravians and as such are members of the kingdom under the dispensation of the Son, following in the footsteps of the disciples of Jesus and John the Baptist. More important were all those whom Fletcher saw as within the divine grace under the dispensation of the Father: Deists, Socinians, unitarians, Moralists, and even Arians.

> As we see daily good mistaken men, yea gospel-ministers, who in the sincerity of their hearts, turn antinomians in theory, and decry the doctrines of justice and holiness, out of a *partial* regard for the doctrines of grace; may not good mistaken men, in the sincerity of their hearts, turn Arians, or Socinians, and oppose the doctrine of the *Trinity*, out of a partial regard for the doctrine of God's *Unity*. Are not both those mistakes equally unscriptural? Have we any more right to doom *such* Arians to destruction than to threaten *such* Antinomians with the damnation of hell? . . . Nay, if we believe the Scriptures, we must candidly allow, that it is possible to be under the dispensation of *the Son*, without having clearer views of his divinity than John the Baptist *seems* to have had. (FD 73)[21]

---

and "A Charimeter; *or*, A Scriptural Method of Trying the Spirits and Knowing the Proportion of Our Faith," both edited by Laurence W. Wood, *Asbury Theological Journal* 53, no. 1 (1998): 65–78 and 83–90 respectively. The italics in the quotations from the former article is Fletcher's underlining, as preserved by Wood.

21. It is against antinomianism that Fletcher's major theological concerns are directed; see John Fletcher, *Five Checks to Antinomianism*, 2 vols. in 1 (London: Wesleyan-Methodist Book Room, 1885). This leads him to "show the cruelty of those opinions which

For our purposes, the result for Fletcher is that all Christian bigotry toward non-Christians and those in other faiths is undermined, since, "as God had formerly children among the gentiles, as well as among the Jews; so he has now sons and daughters among the heathen, as well as among the Christians" (FD 66). It is not that Fletcher wishes to condone Arianism, Socinianism, or other religions, but neither does he want "to send to hell all the righteous men, who are *strong* in the dispensation of the *Father*, and all the believers who are *weak* in the dispensation of the *Son*, merely because the former have not been blessed with a revelation of the Trinity, and because the latter cannot admit human and philosophical explanations of that deep mystery" (FD 75–76). Rather, the various dispensations of God enable each class or category of persons to "speak the truth in love *according to the proportion of* their *faith*, and according to *the measure of the rule, which God hath distributed*, and they have attained" (FD 76).

In short, Christians who come into an understanding of the doctrine of dispensations as articulated by Fletcher "would not be so ready to enter the lists of dispute to prove, that there cannot be salvation for sincere *heathens* under the dispensation of the *Father*, as well as for sincere *Christians* under the dispensation of the *Son*" (FD 70). Fletcher thereby affirmed not universalism[22] but only the possibility of the salvation of the unevangelized *if* they responded to the light that they had. Further, Fletcher was aware that his doctrine could certainly be taken in directions fostering elitism, and so he insisted that "those in the highest dispensation of grace would reflect the humility of Christ."[23] Finally, Fletcher's doctrine of dispensations has a trinitarian progression, somewhat akin to Joachim of Fiore's triune dispensationalism. Yet Fletcher was clear that "at whatever stage one may experience faith in God, it is always faith in the one God of Jesus Christ. It also means that the Father, Son, and Holy Spirit are at work at each stage of salvation."[24] Within this scheme, Fletcher felt able to harmonize the universal salvific will of God (e.g., 1 Tim. 4:10; Titus 2:11; Heb. 11:6; Rom. 2:6, 15) with the empirical fact of the masses of unevangelized "heathen."

---

directly or indirectly doom to eternal perdition all the heathens, who never read the law of Moses, or heard the Gospel of Christ" (cited in Wood, *The Meaning of Pentecost in Early Methodism*, 134).

22. Thus Fletcher insisted that although all true worshipers at each dispensation are accepted by God and therefore saved, "on the other hand, if a man be *not* a *true* worshipper according to any one of the three above-described dispensations, he is still a worldling, a child of wrath, and an inheritor of the kingdom of darkness" ("A Charimeter," 87).

23. Wood, *The Meaning of Pentecost in Early Methodism*, 127.

24. Cited ibid.

Why do I call Fletcher's doctrine of dispensations a protopneumato-logical theology of religions? Partly because of the place allowed within the Fletcherian scheme at least for the monotheistic traditions and their orientation toward the baptism of the Holy Spirit as the culmination of the full revelation of the triune God and partly because of his claim that the works of each triune member are present during each dispensation. Still, Fletcher conceived his model fundamentally in linear terms, and only with great difficulty are we able to locate in it those in Eastern religious traditions (of which Fletcher shows little awareness).

I suggest reframing Fletcher's doctrine of dispensations within the pneumatological soteriology developed in this book (§2.2). Two shifts in particular are important. One is that the doctrine of dispensations can also be understood more concretely, in terms of the dynamic processes of conversion that stretch across human lives. This more accurately describes the human experience of the multidimensional saving work of God even as it enables clearer recognition of the work of the Spirit throughout the entire process. The other is that the doctrine of dispensations can be understood as directed toward the eschatological appearance of the kingdom. This eliminates the static connotations of the concept of dispensation in favor of the more pneumatological concept of the reign of God, thus allowing clearer articulation of the dynamism of Fletcher's doctrine. These moves, incorporating the dynamic, holistic, and relational theology of conversion previously developed, can carry Fletcher's dispensational and inchoate theology of religions toward a pneumatologically informed understanding more consistent with the overall emphases of his theological system.

6.2.2 *The Holy Spirit as God Present, Active, and Absent in the Religions.* Traveling in this direction, we arrive at three hypotheses that provide a rudimentary framework for a pneumatological theology of religions:[25] (1) Granted that God is universally present by the Spirit, God in this sense sustains even the religions for divine purposes. (2) Granted that the Spirit's work is to usher in the kingdom of God, the Spirit is active in and through various aspects of the religions insofar as the signs of the kingdom are manifest. (3) Granted that the Spirit's universal presence and activity presume a resistant and retarding presence and activity that work against the kingdom of God, the Spirit is also absent from the religions to the extent either that the signs of the kingdom are absent or that they are being prohibited from being manifest.

---

25. What follows brings together the three foundational pneumatological categories developed in Yong, *Discerning the Spirit(s)*, esp. 122–32, with the three axioms presented in Yong, *Beyond the Impasse*, 44–46.

First, to affirm the Spirit's presence in the religions is to make nothing more than a basic theological statement about the omnipresence of God. Where, after all, can we go away from the Spirit of the Lord? the Psalmist asks (Ps. 139:7–12). Put alternatively, using Pauline language, what in all creation can separate us from the love of God in Christ (Rom. 8:39), which is no less than the Holy Spirit given to our hearts (Rom. 5:5)? Following out the scriptural witness, why would the realm of the religions be exempt from the Spirit's presence? This is not to say that all religions are good, holy, and truthful, nor is it to say that the entirety of any particular religion (including Christianity as a historical religion)[26] is good, holy, and truthful. Further, this claims neither that any religion is fully salvific in the Christian sense nor that any religion is fully revelatory of God's mystery. To say that all governing authority is from God (Rom. 13:1) requires saying neither that all governments are from God nor that the entirety of any particular government is from God. Whether any or all are from God is something that we will have to discern, and this goes also for the religions. Therefore, to affirm that the religions are not accidents of history that catch God by surprise is, at one level, a theological truism.

Second, to affirm the Spirit's activity in the religions is to confess much more, though all the qualifications of the first hypothesis apply here as well. One classic example is Cyrus the Medo-Persian king and patronizer of the Babylonian god Marduk, who was yet anointed with the Spirit of God to act on behalf of the people of God (Isa. 45:1; cf. Ezra 1).[27] In this case, we have a pagan who was also a Christ figure (an anointed one) accomplishing the purposes of God. But it is not simply that God can use pagans (e.g., Balaam and his divination). Consider the nature of human religiosity (dependent, of course, on the world religious traditions) and its mediation through the material, social, cultural, political, economic, and other spheres of human existence. Human religiousness is not an accidental feature of human life that can be put on and taken off at will. Rather, it informs these spheres even as it is formed in and through them. Thus religion is resolutely intertwined with the human condition and with human hopes and aspirations and is only arbitrarily divorced from individual and communal identities. So the Christian claim that the kingdom of God is now coming (even if also not yet) cannot be limited only to any one sphere (e.g., the social, political, or

26. This follows Karl Barth, "The Revelation of God as the Abolition of Religion," in *Church Dogmatics*, vol. 1, pt. 2, *The Doctrine of God*, trans. G. T. Thomson and Harold Knight (Edinburgh: T & T Clark, 1956), §17.

27. On Cyrus the pagan, see Christian E. Hauer and William A. Young, *An Introduction to the Bible: A Journey into Three Worlds*, 5th ed. (Upper Saddle River, NJ: Prentice-Hall, 2001), 132, 136, 198, 200.

economic) and detached from any other (e.g., the religious). This is no more than the claims previously made about the multidimensionality of salvation (§2.2.2), which locates God's saving deeds not only in the private space of the human heart but in the material, social, political, and other domains of life. For similar reasons, religious conversion, as previously discussed (§2.2.3), is precipitated by conversion in other realms even as it transvalues conversion in these other realms. In short, given this interconnectedness, to say that the Spirit is active in the world at all is to say that the Spirit is active in the world of the religions in some way.

Third, although the Spirit is God present and active in the world, this presence and activity are still eschatological—not yet fully experienced but punctuated here and now by the Spirit. This points to our human experience of God's hiddenness or God's absence. Using religious parlance, I identify this with the demonic in order to preserve some means to retrieve and reappropriate the traditional claim that the religions are bearers not only of the divine but also of the demonic.[28] But the demonic signifies not only the apparent absence of the divine but also the forces that actively resist the arrival of the divine kingdom. Because of this, the specifics of any demonology make sense only with an understanding of the perceived threats precipitating demonological reflection. Thus, insofar as the medievals were concerned with monastic purity, on the one side, and with the Turks, on the other, the demonic was identified with the seductions of the flesh and with the Islamic religion. Insofar as the fundamentalists were concerned with theological liberalism, on the one side, and with Darwinism, on the other, the demonic was identified with higher criticism and with the carriers of evolutionary theory—teachers, textbooks, school systems. Today, insofar as (evangelical) Christianity is concerned with terrorism and the Arab nations are concerned with secularization, the demonic is identified with Al-Qaeda, on the one hand, and with Western capitalism, on the other; and so on. Yet although religious persons and communities usually demonize religious traditions other than their own, the demonic is pervasive, from a

---

28. Since Tillich reintroduced the category of the demonic into Christian theological discourse, a number of proposals have been put forward to reconstruct a theology of the demonic for our time by, e.g., Walter Wink, Nigel Wright, Rene Girard, and Jeffrey Burton Russell. See my previous discussions in Yong, *Discerning the Spirit(s)*, 127–32, 235–45; *Beyond the Impasse*, 137–39, 154–56, 164–66; "The Demonic in Pentecostal-Charismatic Christianity and in the Religious Consciousness of Asia," in *Asian and Pentecostal: The Charismatic Face of Christianity in Asia*, ed. Allan Anderson and Edmond Tang (Oxford: Regnum; Baguio City, Phil.: Asia Pacific Theological Seminary Press, 2005), 93–128; and "Spirit-Possession, the Living and the Dead: A Review Essay and Response from a Pentecostal Perspective," *DD* 8, no. 2 (2004): 77–88.

Christian theological perspective, with traits of its presence and activity throughout the domains of human experience and even in Christian lives and institutions—anti-Semitism, the Crusades, the witch hunts, sexism, racism, and classism, to name a few of the demonic's most obvious manifestations in Christian history.

What about the demonic and the pentecostal imagination? Pentecostal demonologies respond to at least three kinds of threats. First is the threat of the former life from which we have been saved and that still may retain a certain degree of attractiveness to us (thus acting as a competitor for our Christian commitment); at this level, the demonic is identified with everything that stands for that life—for example, sex, drugs, and rock 'n' roll. A second response is the personalizing and the psychologizing of the demonic; André Corten is right to say that "the Devil is a symbolic device used to designate social ills which oppress the poor: unemployment, hunger, prostitution, street children, drugs, and so on."[29] A third response is the socializing and the politicizing of the demonic, that the demonic is all that opposes the values of the kingdom and inhibits the fulfillment of the Great Commission, from the "spirit of blindness" to other kinds of territorial spirits. Insofar as the forces resisting the kingdom operate at every level and in every domain of human life, pentecostals are right to say, "The Devil is a ubiquitous presence."[30]

6.2.3 *The Spirit and the Spirits: Discerning the Spirit(s) in the Religions*. The challenge is to discern which spirit is which in the world of the religions. Where is the Holy Spirit? What is the Holy Spirit doing? What other spirits are present in the religions, and what are they doing? This task of discerning the religions can be an exceedingly complex affair.[31] I suggest three interrelated sets of questions that pertain to this challenge.

First, we need to discern the various background factors in our encounter with other faiths. There are not only a pluralism of religions but a plurality of contexts in and through which the religions subsist: geographical, historical, economic, political, and social. As important, there is also a pluralism of encounters between persons of faith: daily coexistence, domestic settings (interfaith marriages), social interactions,

29. André Corten, *Pentecostalism in Brazil: Emotion of the Poor and Theological Romanticism*, trans. Arianne Dorval (London: Macmillan; New York: St. Martin's, 1999), 61–62.

30. David Lehmann, *Struggle for the Spirit: Religious Transformation and Popular Culture in Brazil and Latin America* (Cambridge, MA: Polity, 1996), 139.

31. See Yong, *Beyond the Impasse*, ch. 6; and Amos Yong, "Spiritual Discernment: A Biblical-Theological Reconsideration," in *The Spirit and Spirituality: Essays in Honor of Russell P. Spittler*, ed. Wonsuk Ma and Robert P. Menzies, JPTSup 24 (New York: T & T Clark, 2004), 83–104.

spiritual practices (meditation, worship, multifaith prayer), doctrinal understanding, the comparative science of religions (which brackets truth claims), formal intrareligious discourse (as in the Christian attempt at self-understanding in a religiously plural world), and formal inter-religious dialogue. To discern the religions requires that we accurately discern the contexts within which our discernment proceeds.

Second, we need to pay close attention to what demands understanding—in this case, the multifarious phenomena of the religions. Insofar as discernment is always about concrete realities, discerning the religions will need to focus on the particularities of other faiths. How can we say anything about the Spirit's presence, activity, or absence in the world of the religions without empirical investigation of this complex reality? We need to learn how to observe other faiths from an insider's perspective (so far as that is possible) so as to avoid our own biases, which pick out only what we have been trained to pick out. Still, discernment is about measuring a reality with previously established criteria (e.g., the marks of the kingdom) to determine congruence or divergence. So does not each side of the process undermine the other? Is it possible to fully adopt an insider's perspective so as to understand the religions and at the same time retain our Christian criteria in assessing them?[32]

I suggest that the pneumatological imagination derived from the outpouring of the Spirit enables this kind of impartial (so far as that is possible), sympathetic, and yet critical inquiry to proceed. This is because we realize that the pentecostal mission of the Spirit is never abstract but concretely and historically realized and manifest in actual persons, bodies, communities, experiences, languages, and so forth. The miracle of Pentecost is that the Spirit enables the difficult and even impossible task of understanding the other in all his or her otherness, strangeness, and difference (see §4.3.3). Only in the Spirit are we able to follow in the footsteps of Jesus, who fulfilled his mission by empty-ing himself and taking the form of another (Phil. 2:5–8). Granted, the process of discernment is never easy. Discerning the Spirit in the world of the religions can never be the merely intellectual exercise of reading the doctrinal texts of other faiths (although this is a necessary task). Discernment further requires an incarnational mindset, made possible by the Spirit of Pentecost, that is willing to get one's hands dirty with and in the particularity of religious lives and practices of those in other faiths. And given that the religions are never static entities, discernment

32. This is a complex matter, as brought out in Amos Yong, Frank D. Macchia, Ralph Del Colle, and Dale T. Irvin, "Christ and Spirit: Dogma, Discernment, and Dialogical Theology in a Religiously Plural World," *JPT* 12, no. 1 (2003): 15–83. The following at-tempts to advance this conversation.

is always provisional—sufficient for the moment but requiring us to check again and again to see if our previous conclusions hold up. It is important to discern the various goals, purposes, and functions of the diversity of religions. But most important, with the Christian conviction that the Spirit is ever active in the world, even that of the religions, who knows whether a determination of the Spirit's absence today in a given religious phenomenon may not produce a determination of the Spirit's presence tomorrow in a phenomenon that is now both the same and yet different?

Finally, to discern the Spirit in the world of the religions is to pursue a multileveled inquiry that is best measured by its fruits. At one level, discerning the religions transforms (as does increased knowledge most of the time) our understanding, attitudes, and approaches to those in other faiths. Here our neighborly, social, and missionary relationships are affected. We interact with those in other faiths who have a different demeanor and strategies because we see religious others first as complex human beings and only then as Buddhists, Hindus, Muslims, and so forth. To discern the Spirit in the world of the religions correlates with living in the Spirit with the world of the religions.

At another level, the interreligious encounter transforms us as Christians not only in relationship to religious others but also regarding our own self-understanding. To enter into relationships is to be transformed by them, as all genuine relationships are dialogical. This transformation affects our Christian identity.[33] To discern that other spirits are present and active there and then is to discern both the otherness of the religions and the presence and activity of the Spirit of Jesus and of his body here and now. In this sense, discernment is always twofold: of self and other simultaneously. On the one hand, to be a Christian is not to be a Buddhist, Hindu, or Muslim insofar as there are mutually contradictory elements of these identities. At the same time, there may be essential elements of Buddhism, Hinduism, or Islam that are not contradictory to the fruits of the Spirit and the marks of the kingdom. In these cases, that in itself enriches the Christian self-identity even while the challenging process of engaging religious others on their terms also deepens the Christian self-understanding.

33. Harold Dollar points to the conversion of Peter and the Twelve in their encounters with Cornelius and the pagan converts to Christ (Acts 9–10; 15). Cornelius and the Gentile converts were not religious others in the contemporary sense of the term, but they were surely religious others, measured by the crisis of self-understanding these experiences precipitated in these early Jewish followers of Jesus. See Harold E. Dollar, *A Biblical-Missiological Exploration of the Cross-Cultural Dimensions in Luke-Acts* (San Francisco: Edwin Mellen, 1993), chs. 6, 8.

Is it possible that our Christian identity might be transformed altogether? Theoretically, yes; since authentic relationships never decide in advance about how things will end up, we must be open to the idea that those who are doing the discernment may undergo various levels of conversion depending on what they find and on whether they are open to being transformed by their findings. This is how I understand the journey of faith, which requires that my confidence lie not in myself but in the Spirit of God, who is able to bring this work to completion.

At the third level of discerning the Spirit in the world of the religions is the question of criteria for discernment. According to the pneumatological soteriology and pneumatological ecclesiology developed in this volume, what are minimal clues to the Spirit's presence and activity? First, are the fruits of the Spirit being manifest in the religious phenomenon in question? Second, are the works of the kingdom manifest in the life and ministry of Jesus—after all, the Spirit witnesses to Jesus—seen in the religious phenomenon (§2.1.2)? Third, is salvation, understood in its various dimensions (§2.1.3; §2.2.1), discernible in the religious phenomenon? Fourth, is conversion in the various human domains (§2.2.3) occurring in the lives of those in other faiths? Fifth, is the ecclesial mark of holiness (§3.2.2), understood in its realized and eschatological senses, discernible, however dimly, in the religious phenomenon? Put alternatively, can the processes of purification according to a trajectory anticipating the coming kingdom be discerned in the religious tradition in question? These criteria are abstract in the extreme. Knowing how to apply them to the various contexts and religious phenomena will itself affect our understanding not only of the criteria—since the religions will have their own criteria—but also of how criteria function epistemologically and theologically. They are nevertheless heuristic devices representing our best, even if feeble, attempts to discern the Spirit in the world of the religions in our time.

For these reasons, then, at the level of theology proper, discernment will always leave as many questions as answers. And why should this not be the case in the theology of religions when it is the case in theology's relationships with the sciences and even in understanding the world of the Bible on its own terms? The point here is to forestall those who want to insist that unless discerning the religions can provide some hard and fast answers on whether the Spirit is present, revealing and saving through them, the interreligious encounter (and interreligious dialogue in particular) is a waste of time. Three brief responses are in order. First, not all are called to formal interreligious dialogue, even though all Christians are called to bear the witness of Jesus to their neighbors, including those in other faiths (§6.1.2). Second, if bearing Christian witness takes the form of establishing dialogical relationships with others, including those in other faiths, then the question to ask is whether having relationships is ever a waste of time. For those who measure valuable activities only by conversion to Christian faith, most things done in life are a waste of time. Finally, the Christian life is a journey toward the truth that is to be revealed fully in the day of the Lord. Life in the Spirit, directed toward that eschatological goal (cf. John 16:13; 1 John 2:27), will be impoverished and debilitated if the hard questions concerning the religions are subordinated to the pragmatic tasks of world mission and evangelization, traditionally understood.

6.3 The Spirit and the Christian-Muslim Encounter: A Case Study

Now that the biblical, pneumatological, and theological grounds for the interreligious encounter have been developed, this section returns to the theological question, opened up at the end of chapter 4 and discussed in the context of the Christian doctrine of the Trinity in chapter 5, concerning the identity of the Spirit. Here, however, this question is pursued in the world religious context, in dialogue with Islam. We will survey the Christian-Muslim encounter, focus in on the pneumatological question through an exegesis of relevant Qur'anic passages, and step back from the exercise to assess our progress (or digress, as the case may be). This section is also concerned throughout with two other related matters: to test the above theory of discernment in a concrete multifaith engagement and to suggest a way forward for interreligious dialogue and comparative theology in the late modern world.

6.3.1 *The Christian-Muslim Encounter: An Overview*. In many ways, the history of Christian-Muslim relations is better characterized as confrontation rather than encounter.[34] Although the spread of Islam by the sword during the first few Islamic centuries was welcomed by some Christians who saw Islamic rule as relief from oppression at the hands of other Christian rulers, Christian-Muslim interactions were characterized, for the most part, from the beginning by mutual criticism and hostilities rather than by dialogue. Polemical and oftentimes acrimonious debates; forced conversions (on both sides); extended wars, the Crusades being the most bloody; and, most recently, the Arab-Israeli conflicts—these have combined to inform the powerful and negative images both sides use to characterize the other. In the process, the cordiality that has

---

34. Thus Rollin Armour Sr., *Islam, Christianity, and the West: A Troubled History* (Maryknoll, NY: Orbis, 2002).

existed at times has been all but forgotten, whether it be the scholarly interchange of ideas in the East during the eighth and ninth centuries and in the West during the medieval period or the peaceful coexistence of Christians and Jews in Muslim-occupied territories throughout the centuries.

Intrafamily feuds are often more heated and prolonged than those between strangers, and this has certainly been the case between the grandchildren of Isaac (Christians) and those of Ishmael (Muslims). From the Muslim perspective, the revelation of Allah to Muhammad supersedes the corrupted revelations to the Jews and the Christians.[35] The latter especially have twisted the truth by compromising the oneness of God with the doctrine of the Trinity, and the transcendence of God with the doctrine of the incarnation. From the Christian perspective, the Muslim rejection of Jesus as the one mediator of salvation between God and humankind occurs not in ignorance of the gospel message but with an intentionality that adds to and deforms the gospel narrative (both prohibited according to one reading of Rev. 22:18–19). As a result, the history of Christian-Muslim relations at the level of theological and doctrinal interaction has been dominated by apologetics, negatively erected to ward off potential victors over one's own position and positively directed toward the undermining of the other position.

The emergence of the academic study of religion in the West has produced more recently a generation of scholars less interested in adjudicating the doctrinal and theological disagreements between these two traditions and more interested in fostering mutual understanding and toleration. The former approach is claimed to have been a dead end, answerable (if at all) only in the eschaton but meanwhile only producing misunderstanding, motivating strife, and even resulting in bloodshed. Sympathetic and open-minded investigation of each other, it is claimed, will reveal that there are as many continuities as discontinuities between the two traditions[36] and that neither tradition is the devil's tool to undermine the other, as has so often been thought. The result

---

35. It is debated among Muslims whether Jewish and Christian misunderstandings "are the result of errors in their scriptural matter or errors in interpretation of the text by the Jewish and Christian communities"; see Kathryn Johnson, "The Lessons from the Garden: An Examination of the Scriptural Legacy of Islam," in *Living Traditions of the Bible: Scripture in Jewish, Christian, and Muslim Practice*, ed. James E. Bowley (St. Louis: Chalice, 1999), 103–31; quotation, 123.

36. This is best displayed in F. E. Peters, *Judaism, Christianity, and Islam: The Classical Texts and Their Interpretation*, 3 vols. (Princeton: Princeton University Press, 1990), which collects material from all three traditions according to common themes and motifs and shows that the disagreements between the traditions are so strong because they derive from fundamental commonalities.

of the second approach, however, has been an emphasis on descriptive methods and studies to the neglect of engaging the normative questions of truth—witness the separation of departments of religion from divinity schools and seminaries. The scholarly study of both traditions has facilitated open and civil conversation, but at the expense of the things that really matter to most Christians and Muslims.

Still, many have come to see that acknowledgment of the interconnectedness between religion and culture (e.g., §4.3.3) has implications for the relationship between religion and theology and therefore that this division of labor between the science of religion and the theological sciences is also rather arbitrary. No doubt, they can be demarcated; but equally without doubt, they are inseparable. Witness how scholars of religion operate with theological assumptions in their work—for instance, defining religion in social (Durkheim), economic (Marx), or psychological (Freud) terms is already reductionistic, revealing a theological bias—and how theologians who ignore the findings of religious studies do so to their own detriment and produce an ivory-tower theology of abstraction. Another way forward is needed, one that builds on the gains made in the scholarly study of religion but that also wrestles with the normative theological and doctrinal matters at the heart of all religious traditions, including Christianity and Islam.

What has emerged is a new kind of comparative theology. Its features include (a) an approach to other faith traditions on their own terms as much as possible, which includes the recognition of the need to develop adequate and yet revisable categories for comparison that are able to register the important values and aspects of other traditions from their perspectives; (b) the commitment to engage other faiths, including their theological and doctrinal claims, first and foremost from standpoints internal to the traditions themselves; and (c) the willingness to allow the deliverances of these comparative theological projects to challenge and perhaps inform one's own theological thinking alongside the need for critical analysis of the other tradition from the perspective of one's own position. In short, comparativists must recognize that they do not stand on neutral ground but must allow their biases to be checked by insider perspectives from the other tradition. Further, comparativists must cultivate an awareness of the complex dynamics that drive a religious tradition to be critical of itself, resulting in a pluralism of discourses within it. Finally, only then can outside criticism of a tradition proceed, and even so, not apart from a willingness to be critiqued by the other faith as well. The model proposed here is therefore a relational and dialogical one that includes critical engagement moving in both directions at various moments in the interreligious encounter.

Making Christian-Muslim interaction operate at this level is no simple task, but sympathetic Christian interpreters of Islam such as Wilfred Cantwell Smith, Kenneth Cragg, and F. E. Peters and sophisticated Muslim interpreters of Jesus such as Seyyed Hossein Nasr and S. Nomanul Haq have taken the first steps. Even evangelicals are attempting to reengage Islam by listening and learning instead of only asking polemical questions.[37] The kind of energy and effort applied to understanding Christian texts from historical-critical and literary perspectives is now being applied also to Islamic texts[38]—a development especially pertinent to the future of Christian-Muslim interaction. John Kaltner, for example, has proposed an "intracanonical reading" of the Bible and the Qur'an, seeking illumination of the biblical text from the Qur'anic perspective (as a Christian, Kaltner is less focused on how the Bible can illuminate the Qur'an) and hoping to further the dialogical relationship between these two traditions instead of exacerbating their historical polemics.[39]

Our immediate question, however, concerns the identity of the Spirit in the world religious context. Following the lead of Kaltner and others, I propose to explore this question in dialogue with the Qur'an. I claim no particular expertise on either Islam or the Qur'an. My motivation is simply to follow out the interreligious path of inquiry charted by the pneumatological imagination and to learn from Islam.

6.3.2 Ruh *in Qur'anic Perspective.* The word translated "spirit" in the Qur'an, *ruh,* has etymological roots similar to those of the Hebrew *ruah,* "wind."[40] *Ruh* and its derivatives occur only twenty-one times in the Qur'an: 2:87, 253; 4:171; 5:110; 12:87; 15:29; 16:2, 102; 17:85; 19:17; 21:91; 26:192–95; 32:9; 38:71–72; 40:15; 42:52; 58:22; 66:12; 70:3–4; 78:38; and 97:4.[41]

---

37. Exemplary in this regard is Gerald R. McDermott, *Can Evangelicals Learn from World Religions? Jesus, Revelation, and Religious Traditions* (Downers Grove, IL: InterVarsity, 2000), ch. 9.

38. Thus D. W. Pack's historical-critical interpretation of Muhammad as an orphan looking for peace and security and finding such in the dreams and visions that are now recorded in the Qur'an is a marked advance from previous evangelical apologetic literature; D. W. Pack, "An Evangelical Assessment of Muhammad," *JAM* 3, no. 2 (2001): 243–65; 4, no. 1 (2002): 63–77.

39. John Kaltner, *Ishmael Instructs Isaac: An Introduction to the Qur'an for Bible Readers* (Collegeville, MN: Liturgical Press, 1999); and *Inquiring of Joseph: Getting to Know a Biblical Character through the Qur'an* (Collegeville, MN: Liturgical Press, 2003).

40. I have been helped greatly throughout my reading of *ruh* in the Qur'an by Colin Chapman, "Discerning the Spirit in Engagement with Islam"; and esp. Mohammad Kazem Shaker, "The Spirit of God in the Qur'an and the Bible" (papers presented at the "Ysbryd—the Spirit in a World of Many Faiths" Conference, University of Wales College, Newport, Wales, July 14–17, 2003).

41. All references to the Qur'an are drawn from the widely reprinted Mohammed Pickthall translation; see http://www.sacred-texts.com/isl/pick/index.htm.

First, a rough categorization of *ruh* as it appears in the Qur'an yields at least six associations, some interrelated. (1) *Ruh* is associated with the revelation of the Qur'an in various ways. On the one hand, *ruh* is the deliverer of the Qur'an (16:102; 26:192–95); on the other, *ruh* is allied with, and derivative from, the word of command of Allah (16:2; 17:85; 40:15). Further, *ruh* is explicitly identified as the source of Muhammad's inspiration (42:5).[42] (2) *Ruh* is associated with the angels of Allah (16:2; 70:3–4; 78:38; 97:4). The angels are also deliverers of Allah's word and warning to the world. (3) *Ruh* is said to be the source of human breath (15:29; 32:9; 38:71–72). This is a marvelous creation of Allah, one before which even the angels are admonished to prostrate themselves. (4) *Ruh* is also given to Mary, the mother of Jesus (4:171; 19:17; 21:19; 66:12). She who was chaste was nevertheless enabled to believe the word of Allah through the *ruh* of Allah in order to bear the prophet of Allah. (5) *Ruh* is also said to assume the form of Jesus, the son of Mary (2:87, 253; 4:171; 5:110). Jesus is the Messiah, a messenger of Allah who accomplished signs and wonders of the Spirit. He is also declared to be the "perfect man" (19:17) and a token for all people (21:91) by the powers of *ruh*. (6) None who have *ruh* despair; rather, they are comforted and strengthened as believers in Allah (12:87; 58:22). Even this simplistic classification shows that, like *ruah* in Jewish thought and *pneuma* in Christian theology, no one reading of *ruh* has been received in the Islamic tradition.

Second, a Christian reading of *ruh* in the Qur'an cannot but ask to what extent Muhammad depended, in his understanding of this concept, on prevailing ideas circulating about the Arabian peninsula in the early seventh century. None of these associations seem particularly novel, and many have a biblical warrant at some level. Yet Christian apologists should curb their zeal on this point, since originality is not a necessary authentification of divine revelation. The Bible itself draws from a wide range of sources in the surrounding ancient Near Eastern culture, and yet Christians affirm the entirety of the Bible as the word of God and inspired by the Spirit.

Third, with the realization that the order of suras in the Qur'an is not chronological but by length, from longest to shortest, how can historical criticism illuminate the progression of the usage of *ruh*, if at all? Here Thomas O'Shaughnessy's work is very helpful.[43] One of the few to explore

42. Partly from this, Ibn Sina (980–1037) concludes that the human beings who are the inspired of Allah, including the prophets of Allah, are breathed upon by the Spirit; see Peters, *Judaism, Christianity, and Islam*, 2:66.

43. Thomas O'Shaughnessy, SJ, *The Development of the Meaning of Spirit in the Koran* (Rome: Pontificium Institutum Orientalium Studiorum, 1953). Unlike C. G. Mylrea and Shaikh Iskandur 'Abdul-Masíh, *The Holy Spirit in Qur'an and Bible* (London: Christian

this topic, O'Shaughnessy concludes that references to *ruh* emerge from four distinct stages or layers of Qur'anic composition: the first Meccan period, which connects *ruh* with angels; the second Meccan period, which associates *ruh* with human beings, especially Adam and Mary; the third Meccan period, which identifies *ruh* with the Lord's *amr* (command or word); and the final Medina period, in which *ruh* is the spirit of holiness imparted to Jesus. O'Shaughnessy finds confirmation of this thesis in the classical commentarial tradition of Tabairi (d. 923), Zamakhshari (d. 1143), al-Razi (d. 1209), and Baidawi (d. 1286). He concludes that the resulting Qur'anic concept of *ruh* is a creative contextualization and appropriation of previous sources rather than just a bland plagiarism.

Finally, before attempting a theological synthesis, however provisional, we should note the limitations of the preceding map of *ruh* in the Qur'an. First, we are obviously hampered by reliance upon *one* English translation. This itself will undermine, in the eyes of devout Muslims, for whom the divine word should not be translated from the Arabic, the authority of any conclusions we might draw. Second, the Qur'anic texts identified above beg for further historical-critical, rhetorical, and literary analysis, and each verse needs explication within the broader Qur'anic narrative. Third, usage of the texts in question—whether in the mosque, in devotional life, or elsewhere—should be taken into account to determine how each text functions in Muslim life and piety. Fourth, the Islamic commentarial tradition needs to be consulted at far greater depth, especially the classical Muslim commentators, just as Christians value the postapostolic and patristic interpretations of the apostolic tradition because of their proximity to the New Testament writings. Fifth, the symbol of *ruh* needs to be analyzed in terms of its role within the broader scope of Islamic life and thought. I have neither the space nor the expertise for these further tasks and therefore defer to others more capable than I. Our more limited goals in this exercise, however, have been twofold: the pedagogical goal of providing a model for what the interreligious dialogue can look like from a pentecostal perspective, and the theological goal of reflecting on this encounter in the global religious context. What can we say about these objectives, given these limitations?

6.3.3 *Discerning the Spirit/*Ruh: *Toward a Comparative Christian-Muslim Pneumatology.* The most obvious observation about the Qur'anic concept of *ruh* is its convergence with Christian pneumatology, including many ideas already discussed in these pages. *Ruh's* relationship to Jesus, so pronounced in the Qur'an, justifies consideration of at least a kind

---

Literature Society for India, n.d.), O'Shaughnessy's work is not explicitly apologetically motivated by Christians polemics. In this sense, his is the more reliable approach even if both works arrive at similar historical-critical conclusions.

of Spirit christology, especially since Jesus is also recognized to be the Messiah (4:171). Further, the connection between *ruh* and the revelatory word (*amr*) of Allah is consistent with the Christian understanding of the Spirit as inspiring the word of God. In addition, *ruh* as the breath of human beings points, along with *nafs* ("soul") and *qalb* ("heart"), to the "trinitarian" anthropology of the Qur'an.[44] Last for our purposes, *ruh* is also the "comforter," Allah's means of strengthening and encouraging believers especially. This is connected to the controversy in the Muslim interpretation of 61:6: "And when Jesus son of Mary said: O Children of Israel! Lo! I am the messenger of Allah unto you, confirming that which was (revealed) before me in the Torah, and bringing good tidings of a messenger who cometh after me, whose name is the Praised One." Is this "Praised One" to be understood as *Ahmad* (some texts), that is, Muhammad, or as *períklytos* (other texts), that is, the Paraclete ("advocate" or "comforter") also promised by Jesus (John 14:16)?[45]

In spite of these similarities, Christians and Muslims entertain clearly documented theological disagreements on Spirit/*ruh*. Most obvious is the Christian understanding of the Spirit as fully divine. In contrast, "the general conception among Muslims is that the Spirit is a created, empowered entity who is not coeternal with God, and who does not share in the divine nature."[46] This theological and dogmatic issue threatens to terminate the conversation, even if not as dramatically as does the christological question. What, if anything, can be done to keep the discussion afloat? How might our pneumatological imagination see the way forward?

At the level of comparative exegesis, John Kaltner appropriately reminds us that the New Testament authors did not have the post-Nicene trinitarian pneumatological understanding. Rather, their view (Kaltner calls attention to Luke's in particular) "of the nature of the Holy Spirit is probably closer to that found in the Isaiah and Psalm texts of the Hebrew Bible where it refers to God's bestowal of a spirit of holiness on an individual."[47] This reminder enables us to contrast the historical factors

44. Annemarie Schimmel, *Mystical Dimensions of Islam* (Chapel Hill: University of North Carolina Press, 1975), 191.

45. The former readings are summarized in JoEllen C. Delamatta, "The Affinities in Muslim Theology in Relation to the Christian Doctrine of the Holy Spirit" (M.A. thesis, Trinity Evangelical Divinity School, 1989), 10–12. But cf. Islamic scholar Josef van Ess: "One thing for certain is that Muhammad did not see himself as the Holy Spirit"; see van Ess, "Islam and the Other Religions: Jesus in the Qur'an—Islamic Perspectives," in Hans Küng et al., *Christianity and the World Religions: Paths to Dialogue with Islam, Hinduism, and Buddhism*, trans. Peter Heinigg (New York: Doubleday, 1986), 97–132, esp. 99–100; quotation, 100.

46. A. Christian van Gorder, *No God but God: A Path to Muslim-Christian Dialogue on God's Nature* (Maryknoll, NY: Orbis, 2003), 120.

47. Kaltner, *Ishmael Instructs Isaac*, 263.

leading to the Christian trinitarian understanding with the historical factors sustaining Islamic monotheism and antitrinitarianism. In what ways does the Qur'anic understanding of *ruh* reflect a pre-Nicene viewpoint perhaps prevalent in the Arabian peninsula of the sixth century? Further, in what ways can we discern in the Islamic tradition of monotheism the Spirit who calls attention not to himself but to the Son *and* the Father?

At the dogmatic level, I propose a way forward that I am somewhat ambivalent about: to apply the Oneness pentecostal witness (see §5.3.2). According to the Oneness conviction, "the Spirit of the Father, the Spirit, and the Holy Spirit, and the Spirit of His Son, were different expressions of the one and self-same Spirit."[48] Can this mediating point invigorate the Christian-Muslim dialogue? The high Oneness christology still needs to be confronted, even as the Oneness articulation of the gospel narrative remains at best a marginal Christian perspective. Nevertheless, is it not possible for the Spirit, who empowers the diversity of voices to bear witness to the wonders of God, to bring forth unexpected gains from this specific Christian-Muslim dialogue?

At the theological level, we have yet to ask in a more nuanced way if we can learn anything about the Holy Spirit from the Qur'an.[49] The connection between *ruh* and the angels certainly comes to mind as calling for deeper investigation. More intriguing for our purposes, however, are the connections between *ruh* and the command or word of Allah. Kenneth Cragg notes that the command of God (*Amr*) represents the creative power of God (6:73; 16:40; 36:81; 40:68) and "is also closely linked in the Qur'an with the Spirit (e.g. *al-Ruh min Amrihi*, 40:15) whence flows the revelation."[50] The implications of this Qur'anic motif for Islamic and Christian wisdom theology, for a Jewish theology of the word (*dabar*), and for a more pneumatologically robust Christian theology of revelation can propel the interreligious trialogue between Christians, Jews, and Muslims into the next generation. Is it too much to expect from the Spirit, who blows from where no one knows, to energize even Christian theological reflection from Islamic sources?

At the grassroots level, can we observe through a pneumatological lens what is happening in the Christian-Muslim encounter on the ground? This means not so much the use of "power-encounter" concepts in evan-

48. G. T. Haywood, "Divine Names and Titles of Jehovah" (Indianapolis: Christian Temple Bookstore, n.d.), 12, repr. in *The Life and Writings of Elder G. T. Haywood*, ed. Paul Dugas (Stockton, CA: Western Apostolic Bible College, 1968).

49. See James Kritzeck, "Holy Spirit in Islam," in *Perspectives on Charismatic Renewal*, ed. Edward D. O'Connor, CSC (Notre Dame, IN: University of Notre Dame Press, 1975), 101–12.

50. Kenneth Cragg, *Muhammad and the Christian: A Question of Response* (Maryknoll, NY: Orbis; London: Darton, Longman & Todd, 1984), 126.

gelizing Muslims, advocated by those who recognize the prevalence of Islamic concepts of power especially in the popular understanding.[51] Rather, I'm referring to situations where the Christian presence stimulated Islamic growth, even as Muslim influences have informed Christian development. Thus James Haire calls attention to the rural Indonesian context, where Islamic Wahhabism has flourished partly through Christian activity and where Christian doctrines and practices have emerged with a distinctively Muslim shape—for example, the reinforced doctrine/idea of predestination; the adoption, in the Christian rite of the remission of sins during the Lord's Supper, celebrated twice a year (Easter and October), of the popular Muslim practice of warding off evil during Ramadan; and the emergence of a congregational government influenced by Muslim concepts and language and functioning in ways similar to Muslim courts.[52] In the West African context, the need for improved ecumenical and interreligious relations has led to new "revelations" from charismatic Aladuran (West Africa) church leaders such as Elijah Oshitelu, who proclaimed in 1952, "Let one Friday be separated for the Moslem community to worship for thanksgiving in their mosques right round the country; while a Sunday should be separated for all the Christians . . . for the same purpose. . . . Christianity and Mohammedanism alone should be recognized in the nation throughout, and paganism and the worshipping of idols should be totally discountenanced."[53] Much more controversial are African prophets of independent charismatic churches who assume that the two genuine religions recognized by God/Allah are Christianity and Islam; that the true prophethood of Muhammad is inspired by the Holy Spirit; and that acquiring the Holy Spirit as a Muslim amounts to experiencing the salvation of Allah and deliverance from the grip of Satan.[54] My point is not to embrace all of these developments but to be spurred on to discernment and theological reflection by what is happening in the Christian-Muslim encounter.

The long-term result, I believe, will be at least threefold. First, there will be a deepened contextualization of the gospel, a more coherent articulation of the message of Jesus in Islamic and even Qur'anic terms. From a

---

51. See, e.g., Sobhi Malek, "Islam Encountering Gospel Power," in *Called and Empowered: Global Mission in Pentecostal Perspective*, ed. Murray W. Dempster, Byron D. Klaus, and Douglas Petersen (Peabody, MA: Hendrickson, 1991), 180–97, esp. 185–86.

52. James Haire, *The Character and Theological Struggle of the Church in Halmahera, Indonesia, 1941–1979*, SIHC 26 (Frankfurt, Ger.: Peter Lang, 1981), esp. 242–48.

53. Harold W. Turner, *History of an African Independent Church*, 2 vols. (Oxford: Clarendon, 1967), 2:92; also 1:56, 96, 128, 193.

54. Prophet Dr. M. A. Olujide and Prophetess D. A. Olujide, *Quran Testifies to the Existence of the Holy Spirit* (Lagos, Ghana: Loyal Printers Industries, n.d.), esp. 44–52.

missiological and theological perspective, this represents the Christian message of redemption, in this case, the redemption of the languages, cultures, and even religious traditions of the world for the sake of the gospel. Second, the church will thereby be a servant to the religions, seeking after and contributing toward their welfare in ways similar to those envisioned by John Howard Yoder (§5.3.2)—for example, by challenging other faiths to be true to their original commitments, enabling their reform or purification from corrupting elements, or empowering their contribution to human well-being and flourishing.[55] Finally, the Christian faith will also be transformed in anticipation of the impending kingdom of God. Pentecostals have always been told that at the great banquet feast of God, they will be surprised both by who they thought would be there and are not, and who they did not think would be there and are. Might this not also apply to those in other faiths?

This chapter presents concrete suggestions for pentecostals and, more generally, Christians to come to grips with our religiously plural world. These include initially orienting ourselves properly to the religions through a conscious attempt to wrestle with our most authoritative sources (especially the Bible); developing a plausible hypothesis or theory (theology) for this situation that informs our interreligious relationships; and testing and refining (as necessary) our theory through concrete engagement with the religions. Perhaps over time our theory (theology) will show itself to be seriously deficient and will have to be discarded, or perhaps living religious traditions, like human persons, will forever resist objectification and our attempts to neatly theorize (theologize) about them. But this itself would be acceptable, as the heart of a pneumatological theology is precisely its dynamism, which demands an open-endedness commensurate with its eschatological orientation toward the future. Following after the Spirit, who leads us into all truth, is an acknowledgment that the truth is in some ways yet ahead of us. That this fundamental disposition and trust in the process of inquiry informs and shapes our attitudes and actions toward religious others is itself a testimony to the truth. And this is no less so than when we deal with the other major theological question confronting Christian theology in late modernity, the encounter between religion (and theology) and science. Come Holy Spirit, breathe upon the natural world . . .

---

55. See also George Lindbeck, "The Gospel's Uniqueness: Election and Untranslatability," in Lindbeck, *The Church in a Postliberal Age*, ed. James J. Buckley (Grand Rapids: Eerdmans, 2002), 223–52, esp. 251–52.

7

The Heavens Above
and the Earth Below

Toward a Pneumatological Theology of Creation

For the most part, pentecostals have avoided talking about science and the natural world, as they have about the world of the religions, except in polemical and defensive ways. Times are changing, however, as the boldness and confidence that come with the Spirit's outpouring are understood to include but not be limited to the straightforward proclamation of the gospel. Rather, the "power to witness" occurs not only in the interreligious dialogue but also in academic inquiry in the natural and social sciences. This is an important development, since pentecostals are citizens of the modern world (see §I.2).

The thesis argued here is that the pneumatological imagination undergirding the pentecostal orientation to the world illuminates not only the scientific enterprise but also the human engagement with the natural world in all its complexity. This might seem an odd hypothesis, given the perennial disjunction understood between spirit and nature. At one level, this disjunction is true: the concept of nature as bequeathed by the Enlightenment often presumes a materialistic metaphysics that has explained away the spiritual realm as a figment of the mythological imagination. This is part of the reason our goal in this chapter is a pneumatological theology of creation rather than of nature.[1] My point is that the spirit-nature opposition is a false one to begin with and that resources from the pneumatological imagination help us understand why science is not antithetical to a theistic worldview and enable a more sophisticated and informed engagement with the various orders of creation.

The cues derive from the phenomenology of the day of Pentecost. Not only was there the "sound like the rush of a violent wind"; there were also "divided tongues, as of fire" (Acts 2:2–3). Further, the outpouring of the Spirit resulted in

> . . . portents in the heaven above
> and signs on the earth below,
>   blood, and fire, and smoky mist.
> The sun shall be turned to darkness
> and the moon to blood. (Acts 2:19–20)

At one level, this is metaphorical language functioning, in both Acts and its original context (the prophecy of Joel), as apocalyptic discourse that calls attention to the cataclysmic events attending the arrival of the Day of the Lord and the salvation and vindication of the people of God. But if we remained at this level and then concluded that this language has nothing really to tell us about the created world, then the fact that the Bible is replete with metaphorical language may lead to the correlative conclusion that the Bible also has nothing to say about reality or the human condition. I prefer instead to ask about the theological implications of such phenomenological metaphors. Two converging responses

---

1. There are two distinctions that are important. The first is the notions of "creation," "created world," and "orders of creation" used in the following as inclusive of, and sometimes synonymous with, "nature." My thanks to Greg Zuschlag for calling this distinction to my attention. His unpublished paper, "The Ecological Promise of Peirce and the Problem of Human Exceptionalism in the West," was a gift of the Spirit to me as I rethought the structure of this chapter as the last chapter of the book late in the writing process rather than as the seventh of nine originally planned. The second is the distinction between natural theology (which begins from nature and proceeds to theology) and theology of nature/creation (which begins from theological, in my case pneumatological, premises and proceeds to reflect on the created order). For more on this latter distinction, see Ian G. Barbour, *Nature, Human Nature, and God* (Minneapolis: Fortress, 2002), 2.

For introductory discussions to theology of creation, see John Carmody, *Ecology and Religion: Toward a New Christian Theology of Nature* (New York: Paulist, 1983); Claude Y. Stewart Jr., *Nature in Grace: A Study in the Theology of Nature* (Macon, GA: Mercer University Press, 1983); David A. S. Fergusson, *The Cosmos and the Creator: An Introduction to the Theology of Creation* (London: SPCK, 1998); and Zachary Hayes, *The Gift of Being: A Theology of Creation* (Collegeville, MN: Liturgical Press, 2001).

to this question motivate what follows. On the one hand, the presence and activity of the Spirit are amenable to phenomenological portrayal drawn from our experience of the natural world. On the other hand, the phenomenon of nature in particular and the orders of creation in general are intrinsically able to carry and convey theological and pneumatological expression.

From this starting point, we inquire into the relationship between religion and science (§7.1), sketch a pneumatological, semiotic, and philosophical theology of creation (§7.2), and conclude with some theological and ethical implications for spiritual life in the late modern world (§7.3). Our goal throughout is at least threefold: first, to encourage further pentecostal reflection on the theology and philosophy of science and the theology and philosophy of nature, topics still in their embryonic stage in pentecostal scholarship; second, to articulate in the discourses of the sciences the pentecostal and Christian claim about divine presence and activity in the world, both because the pentecostal charism of the interpretation of tongues enables such translation and because the commitment to doing theology in a fully public context requires that we engage any and all conversations, including the sciences, that directly or indirectly implicate theological claims; and finally, to contribute to the religion/theology-and-science conversation from an explicitly pneumatological perspective. These are bold and far-reaching endeavors, and in the scope of one chapter, the discussion can only be programmatic. Yet the preliminary and provisional success (or not) of this venture even at this basic level will be another indicator of whether pentecostal theology is ready and able to participate in the articulation and reformulation of Christian theology in the world context of the twenty-first century.

7.1 Approaching Creation: Science in Search of the Spirit

To begin this particular assignment toward a theology of creation in dialogue with the sciences, we need to get our bearings on the state of the question regarding the complex relationship between religion and science.[2] This section sets out the broad landscape, obtains another assist from the Wesleyan tradition toward a theology of science, and surveys the emerging engagement of pentecostals with the sciences.

2. Throughout this chapter, the "religion and science" and "theology and science" relationships are considered synonymous. Thus *religion-science* is used here as shorthand except when I am making an explicit theological point, which will then be clear from the context of the usage.

7.1.1 *The Challenge of Modern Science.* The emergence of modern science over the last few hundred years has posed one of the most sustained challenges to Christian theology. Christian thinkers have responded either by subordinating one to the other, separating the two completely, or attempting some kind of synthesis. Let me speak briefly to each in turn.[3]

The subordinationist response works both ways. On the one side are those who say science should always be subordinate to religious revelation. A range of positions prevails even in this camp. On the far right are those who reject science completely, partly because of a misreading of the entire scientific enterprise as requiring atheistic, naturalistic, and materialistic presuppositions. For those on this end, science is the most pervasive example of unbelief and is oftentimes caricatured as such. Toward the left are those who are cautiously accepting of the scientific endeavor but vigilant about not compromising theological convictions in order to learn from science. For these, contradictions between theology and science are the result of scientific inaccuracies. Science will need to reassess its presuppositions, refine its experiments, and revise its conclusions in order to be theologically acceptable. Among conservative Christians, especially in popular pentecostalism, it is still commonplace to find widespread adherence to this subordinationism of science to divine revelation.

On the other side of the subordinationist response are those who insist on the reverse: that religion and theology should always be subject to the advances of the sciences. Here again is a spectrum of positions. At the far left are those who reject religion completely, partly because of a misreading of religious commitment as signaling intellectual weakness at best or superstitiousness at worst. For those on this end, religion is a hindrance not only to science but to the progress of humankind. Toward the right are those who are cautiously accepting of the tenets of religion—some may even be religious practitioners—so long as religious authoritarianism does not hinder the advance of science. For these, contradictions between science and theology are the result of theological ineptness, religious misinterpretations, scientific misunderstandings, or just plain ignorance. They hold that theology needs to be shorn of religious mythology before it is able to engage adequately the world (of

---

3. Here are summarized the discussions from a wide range of religion-science literature, from Ian G. Barbour, *Issues in Science and Religion* (1966; New York: Harper Torchbooks, 1971); through John F. Haught, *Science and Religion: From Conflict to Conversation* (New York: Paulist, 1995); to Niels Henrik Gregersen and J. Wentzel van Huyssteen, eds., *Rethinking Theology and Science: Six Models for the Current Dialogue* (Grand Rapids: Eerdmans, 1998).

science) as we know it. Not surprisingly, this position remains popular primarily among practicing scientists.

These two subordinationist positions divide on various issues, but most emphatically on that concerning methodology. The question is, What is the most reliable approach to discovering truth? Those who subordinate revelation to science insist on an empirical approach that pays close attention to what there is. Those who subordinate in the other direction are not necessarily rationalists but nevertheless are convinced that some kind of a priori starting point inevitably informs our engagement with the natural world, and they ask why it should not be God-given Scripture. What, in other words, should be the authority that guides our scientific inquiries?

Another response completely separates the realms of religion and science. For some who practice this separation, there is an incommensurability between the domains and methods of religion and science; for others, religion and science might be two parallel discourses, each providing alternative perspectives on human life in the world. But both would agree that the domain of religion includes the spiritual, moral, and aesthetic dimensions of life whereas the domain of science includes the natural, physical, and material dimensions of the world. Because of this fundamental conviction, the separatist position denies that religion and science can ever truly conflict with each other. All contradictions are only apparent, the result of either science overreaching its domain of expertise (the natural world) or religion overreaching its domain (the spiritual, moral, and aesthetic worlds). According to this position, theology can never contribute anything of substance to a scientific understanding of the natural world, even as the sciences cannot illuminate the authentically religious life. Although this division of labor seems awkward and forced, it is quite widespread especially among those who do not wish to (or cannot) give up their religiosity as practicing scientists and cannot find any other way forward except through such compartmentalization.

There is, however, an alternative to both subordinationism (in its two forms) and separatism—the way of synthesis. Again, there is a spectrum of positions within this camp, ranging from those who see both religion and science as mystical practices, on the left, to seeing both religion and science as empirical modes of knowledge, on the right. In between these extremes are those who believe there are convergences between religion and science: at times they overlap, providing confirmation one to the other, and at other times they remain in a dialogical relationship, each seeking to provide a more comprehensive account of reality and acknowledging the need for help from the other in order to do so. Contradictions between religion and science could be the fault of either or both. In any case, because both are concerned with ultimate truth and reality, they cannot finally disagree.

My own view of this matter includes three components. First, I want to emphasize the fluidity and dynamic nature of both the religious and the scientific pursuit. Neither is a static or infallible enterprise. This leads, second, to the recognition that on any particular issue, either kind of subordinationism, separatism, or synthesis may be most appropriate. This is not only a descriptive claim about what happens in the science-religion interface but also a normative claim about the unpredictability of the relationship. On any issue, the "correct" response may be to subordinate either to the other, or to acknowledge that they concern divergent realities or domains, or to see that a genuine synthesis is uncovered. Finally, then, as in the interreligious dialogue, the integrity of both theology and science must be preserved. Each must be allowed to speak in its own voice, to define its own categories of importance, to identify its own values and perspectives. The other side must be ever ready to learn but should also be given opportunity to speak a critical or cautionary voice in turn. Instead of attempting to justify theology through science or vice versa, we should proceed, on the one hand, with the conviction that religious beliefs and theological claims should not be counterindicated by scientific or empirical evidence,[4] even as we recognize, on the other, the provisionality of the deliverances of science and the fact that all inquiry, scientific and otherwise, is based on assumptions that can never be questioned wholesale and are yet constantly being revised. In short, the quest for a theology of creation should include nothing less than an ongoing dialogical relationship between theology and science, each clarifying, complementing, and perhaps even correcting the other's self-understanding at appropriate junctures in the human quest for truth.

But to ask that we take the voice and perspective of science seriously is to raise the question of the exact nature of scientific discourse. Here the debate proceeds in two related trajectories. On the one hand, philosophers of science argue over the epistemological and linguistic underpinnings of the scientific enterprise. Some hold to a traditional view of science as providing a language that describes an objectively existing world as it actually is. Others hold an assortment of positions advocating a view of the language of science as instrumental for human purposes, internal to the discourse of science, or simply metaphoric and

---

4. This is the position enunciated most clearly by Philip Clayton, *Explanation from Physics to Theology: An Essay in Rationality and Religion* (New Haven: Yale University Press, 1989), 161–67; and *God and Contemporary Science* (Edinburgh: Edinburgh University Press; Grand Rapids: Eerdmans, 1998), esp. 5–9.

self-referencing.[5] On the other hand, this raises the question whether the world exists independent of knowers (realism) or whether the real is a creation or projection of (at least) human minds (idealism).

At one level, the argument could be made that insofar as science serves the human purpose of getting around in the world, at least a critical-realist position begs to be assumed. At another level, however, that science rests on unprovable assumptions—for example, about the correspondence between scientific concepts and models with the external world, especially at the quantum level—raises some concerns about the scientific enterprise that move us into the realm traditionally known as metaphysics. My view is that pneumatology is what opens us up to the possibility of a participatory epistemology that overcomes the dualistic and dichotomous thinking of subject and object without collapsing the distinction between self and otherness and that mediates between the opposing metaphysics of idealism and realism without lapsing into either positivism or skepticism. This chapter explores this pneumatological approach to science and the natural world.

7.1.2 *Toward a Theology of Creation: Another Assist from the Wesleyan Tradition*. As pentecostalism is located at least partly in the Wesleyan-Arminian tradition, we have periodically referred to this tradition for theological insights (esp. §2.2.3; §6.2.1). Here we look to Wesley himself—not Wesley the evangelist, homiletician, or theologian but in his lesser-known role as observer of the natural world—to see if and how he can help us articulate a theology of creation.[6]

Granted, Wesley was not a scientist *simpliciter*. As Robert Schofield informs us, Wesley deemphasized experimentation altogether and had no use for theory development.[7] This was because of his conviction that science is a matter of observing what God has made rather than an authorization for us to tamper with nature and because of the speculative, continually changing, and hence unreliable nature of scientific theorizing and hypothetical abductive reasoning. So the mysterious nature of

5. This was given initial expression by Thomas Kuhn, *The Structure of Scientific Revolutions*, 2nd enl. ed. (Chicago: University of Chicago Press, 1970); and argued more radically later by philosophers of science such as Paul Feyerabend, *Against Method: Outline of an Anarchistic Theory of Knowledge* (London: NLB, 1975; repr., London: Verso, 1978); cf. John Preston, Gonzalo Munéver, and David Lamb, eds., *The Worst Enemy of Science? Essays in Memory of Paul Feyerabend* (New York: Oxford University Press, 2000).

6. For a basic overview of the state of science and its relation to Christian theology in Wesley's day, see David W. Bebbington, "Science and Evangelical Theology in Britain from Wesley to Orr," in *Evangelicals and Science in Historical Perspective*, ed. David N. Livingstone, D. G. Hart, and Mark A. Noll (New York: Oxford University Press, 1999), 120–41.

7. Robert E. Schofield, "John Wesley and Science in 18th Century England," *Isis* 44 (1953): 331–40.

causation debated in mid-eighteenth-century philosophy and science led Wesley to see causal connections as belonging to the realm of God and not worthy of experimentation.

But Wesley, well versed in the tradition of Baconian empiricism,[8] cultivated and exercised remarkable powers of observation despite being but an amateur scientist. He did not ignore the findings of science, incorporated science into his writings and teaching, and considered science to have great utilitarian value, especially in terms of its medicinal effects. This is seen in Wesley's three "scientific" compilations: *Primitive Physic; or, An Easy and Natural Method of Curing Most Diseases* (1747; 13th ed., 1768), *The Desideratum; or, Electricity Made Plain and Simple* (1759), and *A Survey of the Wisdom of God in the Creation; or, A Compendium of Natural Philosophy* (2 vols., 1763; 5 vols., 1777).

Primitive Physic and *The Desideratum* were in effect medical manuals. The former begins with a preface discussing the maintenance of good health and presents an alphabetized list of 274 sicknesses and recipes for their cure. The latter is basically an introduction to electricity, advocating a variety of therapeutic uses for physical, physiological, and psychological ailments. By modern standards, Wesley's proposals are more commonsense practices than solid medical treatises or scientifically rigorous arguments. In the eighteenth-century context, however, these are far from the quackery found in the popular literature and, in the case of *The Desideratum*, perhaps even on the cutting edge of electrotherapeutic studies.[9]

Clearly, these manuals emerged out of Wesley's ministry to the sick, especially in the free medical clinics he established for the poor. This is important because it points to the pragmatic and soteriological context of Wesley's "scientific" inquiries. Further, both manuals exhibit Wesley's empirical orientation. He made sure to commend only remedies with empirical confirmation. Taken together, Wesley's work in this area convinced him of the interconnectedness of natural, human, and divine processes. Medical cures were but attempts to capture the movement of nature's rhythms and harness its powers toward healing the sick.

Against the backdrop of this work done in the 1740s and 1750s, Wesley was led to a more intense study of nature itself. Called natural philosophy in his time, the subject matter included the entire scope of the created order. Wesley's *Survey of the Wisdom of God in the Creation* therefore includes selections from the broad spectrum of scientific literature,

8. See John C. English, "John Wesley's Scientific Education," *Methodist History* 30, no. 1 (1991): 42–51.

9. See H. Newton Malony, "John Wesley and the Eighteenth Century Therapeutic Uses of Electricity," *Perspectives on Science and Christian Faith* 47 (1995): 244–54.

covering, in order, the realms of human beings, animals, organic life, the earthly elements, and the cosmos.[10] This eighteenth-century version of the Great Chain of Being reflects Wesley's wide-ranging scientific interests.

Although a quick perusal of Wesley's *Survey* reveals that he was not trained in any of these fields of inquiry, the compilations do show that Wesley was a voracious reader who was well aware of the major developments in the sciences of his time and quite discerning about the most promising trajectories of scientific inquiry.[11] They also illuminate Wesley's theological conviction that all creation revealed the glory of God. Wesley's articulation, throughout the *Survey*, of a pre-Darwinian doctrine of evolution in terms of the "gradual progression" of the accepted "Scale of Being" did not question God as ultimate Creator, apart from whom creation would not be self-sustaining. Yet Wesley also spoke very pointedly of evolutionary transitions within the animal kingdom: from worms to insects, to reptiles, to fish, to birds, to quadrupeds.[12] Although he seemed to suggest that human beings were but the last step in the evolutionary process, he never explicitly said so.[13]

My purpose is not to defend Wesley's scientific conclusions but to retrieve his scientific orientation as a model for those in the Wesleyan-Arminian scholarly tradition, particularly in pentecostalism. Wesley's scientific legacy is significant for various reasons. First, although Wesley's

10. See John Wesley, *A Survey of the Wisdom of God in the Creation; or, A Compendium of Natural Philosophy*, ed. B. Mayo, 3rd American ed., rev. and enl., 2 vols. (New York: Bangs & Mason, for the Methodist Episcopal Church, 1823).

11. Among the more than forty scientists whom Wesley read in some depth were Tycho Brahe and Edmund Halley (astronomers), Albrecht von Haller (the father of modern "nervous physiology"), John Kepler (who found the laws of planetary motion), Christan Huygens (who invented the pendulum clock), Charles Bonnet (a biologist who originated the term "evolution" in parthenogenetic experimentation), Joseph Priestly (who discovered oxygen and experimented with electricity), and John Ray (the first to classify plant and animal "species"). See Frank W. Collier, *John Wesley among the Scientists* (New York: Abingdon, 1928), 23–28.

12. E.g., Wesley wrote, "Hairy birds having projected ears, a mouth furnished with teeth, and whose body is carried on four paws armed with claws—are they birds in reality? Are quadrupeds, that fly by the assistance of great membranous wings, really such? The bat and flying squirrel—are these strange animals, which are so proper for establishing the graduation that subsists between all the productions of nature? The ostrich with the feet of a goat, which runs rather than flies, seems to be another link which unites birds to quadrupeds" (*Survey*, 2:209).

13. Collier, *John Wesley among the Scientists*, 148–49, notes that Wesley differed from the Darwinian evolutionists in positing a supernatural origin of creation and the indestructibility of species, thus negating the time element. He reminds us that although Wesley was an ardent evolutionist, his avowed goal was "not to account for things; but only to describe them."

science was not systematically integrated into his theological system, he was not a systematic theologian, nor was he interested in writing systematic theological treatises. Rather, Wesley was a practical theologian who nevertheless recognized the importance of engaging the science of his day. As such, he provides a model for pentecostal practitioners to emulate even as his commitment to scientific inquiry challenges those who think that Christian life and thought in the twenty-first century can proceed in ignorance of the sciences. That Wesley's scientific pursuits originated in the context of his healing ministry testifies to the interconnectedness of science and faith, theory and practice.[14]

Second, if we step back to locate Wesley's scientific interests against the broader intellectual currents of his time, we see better the theological stakes involved. The reigning theological model of the mid–eighteenth century was Deism, the idea that God had created the world and left it to run according to its built-in laws and mechanisms. On the left of the Deistic position was the atheistic materialism of the *philosophes*, and on the right were the reactionary subjectivism and enthusiasm of Pietism and popular religion. In this context, Wesley was looking for ways to understand God's activity in the world and the human experience of freedom.[15] My point here is not to determine whether Wesley was successful but to highlight the unavoidable challenge to any theology: that it has to engage in the questions of its time if it is to speak forcefully beyond a small parochial circle. In our late modern world, any theology that neglects the sciences and the natural world will be severely handicapped in addressing many of the pressing issues calling for reflection. But in what would be even more detrimental for a pneumatological theology, how can we avoid engaging these matters, given that the root metaphor driving our theological vision is that of God's presence and activity in the world by the Holy Spirit?

Last but certainly not least, however, it is precisely a pneumatological theology that can provide the means for integrating Wesley's scientific orientation within a systematic theological and philosophical framework.

---

14. If for no other reason than credibility, pentecostals are beginning to recognize the unavoidability of this interconnectedness in our time. The healing evangelist Benny Hinn, e.g., has begun to deploy trained medical doctors in his crusades in order to validate miraculous healings before a skeptical public. For more on the need for a "public hermeneutic" related to Pentecostal healing, see Jean-Daniel Plüss, "The Commercialization of Drugs; or, Can Pentecostals Maintain Their Therapeutic Ministry?" in *Experiences of the Spirit: Conference on Pentecostal and Charismatic Research in Europe at Utrecht University, 1989*, ed. Jan A. B. Jongeneel, SIHC 68 (Frankfurt, Ger.: Peter Lang, 1991), 103–14, esp. 108.

15. See John W. Haas Jr., "Eighteenth Century Evangelical Responses to Science: John Wesley's Enduring Legacy," *Science and Christian Belief* 6 (1994): 83–102.

Wesley's methodical instincts are sound. I propose to build on Wesley's legacy with a complementary assist: that of the pneumatological imagination derived from the outpouring of the Spirit.

7.1.3 *Pentecostalism and Science: A New Conversation?* Although anti-intellectualism and, with it, suspicions regarding the scientific enterprise continue in many quarters of the pentecostal world, advances have been made in the pentecostal encounter with modern science.[16] Especially in the second half of the twentieth century, pentecostals are increasingly pursuing graduate education not only in the humanities but in the natural, social, and even technological sciences.[17] Not surprisingly, the increasing number of such students has correlated with the transformation of pentecostal Bible schools and institutes into centers of higher education granting degrees across the disciplines. The quest for accreditation has required that these institutions find ways to mentor and nurture gifted pentecostal students through the maze of higher education in order to return with terminal degrees to teach in their faculties. Although many of these students struggle to integrate their pentecostal faith and their scientific learning and vocation (somewhat in the separatist model discussed in §7.1.1), the more reflective are confronting the issues more straightforwardly.

Though remaining theologically conservative on most issues, pentecostal reflections on science cannot be simplistically pigeonholed into fundamentalistic or even conservative evangelical categories. To take the theory of evolution as an example (still controversial among the theologically conservative), already in the early 1970s, the Society for Pentecostal Studies was alerted to the wrongheadedness of the vicious polemics against science in popular pentecostal circles and was called to carefully "distinguish between fact and theory, original works (experimental evidence) and philosopher's thinking."[18] Pentecostals have therefore sought to carve out their own space to reflect on the scientific data. Although their theological dialogue partners on this topic remain primarily other evangelical thinkers, the results so far, even if minimal, have not been constrained by the conservative evangelical subculture. Literal, twenty-four-hour-day scientific creationism is by no means the

16. For an overview, see Amos Yong and Paul Elbert, "Christianity, Pentecostalism: Issues in Science and Religion," in *Encyclopedia of Science and Religion*, ed. J. Wentzel van Huyssteen, 2 vols. (New York: Macmillan Reference Library, 2003), 1:132–35.

17. E.g., as in Assemblies of God minister and educator Dennis Cheek, *Thinking Constructively about Science, Technology, and Society Education* (Albany: State University of New York Press, 1992).

18. The speaker was Myrtle Fleming, the head of the science department at Lee University, Church of God (Cleveland, Tennessee); see Ronald Numbers, *The Creationists: The Evolution of Scientific Creationism* (Berkeley: University of California Press, 1993), 307.

norm for pentecostals who have taken science seriously—witness Paul Elbert's defense of an evolutionary position that sees the biblical days as cosmological and geological phases.[19] Charles Hummel suggests what he calls a "partial-view" understanding whereby science and the Bible offer complementary but nonexhaustive perspectives on reality (a version of the synthesis position above).[20] And even back in the 1970s, Duane Thurman adopted a liberal-arts approach and insisted on laying out the creation-evolution issues in a very open-ended and inconclusive way instead of indoctrinating conservative pentecostal students in either direction.[21]

The gains made in such efforts have spurred some pentecostals to reflect on the scientific enterprise within the broader framework of a world theory or worldview. Edited by Michael Palmer, *Elements of a Christian Worldview* contains chapters in philosophy, Scripture, history, natural science, human nature, work, leisure, ethics, music, literature, media, and politics.[22] Especially pertinent to our topic are Lawrence McHargue's chapter on natural science, Billie Davis's on human nature, and Dennis McNutt's on politics.[23] McHargue is concerned with the history and philosophy (basic assumptions) of science, especially with the fact that the assumptions of modern science have come to permeate contemporary Western culture. Though not looking to curb the direction of research suggested by such scholars as Elbert and the others noted above (none of whom McHargue mentions), he focuses on highlighting the limits of the scientific method along three lines. First, the haphazard nature of scientific progress should caution us against an overenthusiastic embrace of science's capabilities. Second, following Thomas Kuhn, he points out that the shifting nature of scientific paradigms not only underscores the

19. Paul Elbert, "Biblical Creation and Science: A Review Article," *JETS* 39 (1996): 285–89. Elbert is a trained physicist and longtime faculty member at Lee University of the Church of God (Cleveland, TN).

20. Charles E. Hummel, *The Galileo Connection: Resolving Conflicts between Science and the Bible* (Downers Grove, IL: InterVarsity, 1986). Hummel, a neopentecostal, has training in chemical engineering and biblical literature. See also Charles E. Hummel, *Fire in the Fireplace: Charismatic Renewal in the 90s*, 2nd ed. (Downers Grove, IL: InterVarsity, 1993).

21. Duane L. Thurman, *How to Think about Evolution and Other Bible-Science Controversies* (Downers Grove, IL: InterVarsity, 1978). Thurman taught for years in the biology department at Oral Roberts University.

22. Michael Palmer, ed., *Elements of a Christian Worldview* (Springfield, MO: Logion, 1998).

23. McHargue is a biologist with a Ph.D. from the University of California, Irvine, teaching at Vanguard University; Davis is trained, in part, in sociology at the University of Miami, Florida, and is former chair of the Department of Behavioral Sciences at Evangel University; and McNutt is a Ph.D. in government from Claremont Graduate School and now teaches history and political science at Vanguard University.

subjectivity of the scientific enterprise but also reveals the uncertainty underneath all scientific endeavors. Finally, science answers only questions that can be empirically investigated; it cannot tell us anything about "what is worthy of attention, cannot tell us what we should aspire to or what we should hope for, and cannot tell us what finally matters in life."[24] These limitations enable reflective criticism on both our scientific assumptions and activity and our efforts to (re)construct a Christian worldview. Even with these limitations, however, McHargue emphasizes the importance and legitimacy of Christian participation in the scientific enterprise.

Davis's "A Perspective on Human Nature" is a multidisciplinary discussion of the theological, anthropological, psychological, and sociological dimensions of what it means to be human. Her purpose is to provide a Christian framework for personal knowledge and sociorelational understanding in order to evaluate other scholarly and popular ideas about human nature. The discussion weaves through the maze of contemporary psychological and sociological models of the human being. These, like the assumptions of modern science, have become central to the worldview of the West, especially among secularists. Davis's conclusion that human behavior is shaped and perhaps determined biologically, psychologically, and socially would indeed be pessimistic apart from Christian understanding. What is basically true about secular explanations of human behavior needs to be supplemented by biblical revelation. The latter is a source both of increased pessimism in pointing to the impact of sin, on the one hand, and of optimism in revealing the activity of the Holy Spirit, on the other. Working diligently to integrate faith with social-scientific learning, Davis finds that her Christian commitments enable her to affirm the insights and wisdom gained from all sources of study and research.

McNutt's "Politics for Christians (and Other Sinners)" deserves mention because he includes discussions about politics, human nature and politics, the nature and problem of power, and ecclesiastical, governmental, national, and international politics. Especially helpful is McNutt's analysis of power. This brief discussion shows awareness of the pervasiveness of power in the sociopolitical realms and of its tendencies toward being used exploitatively and manipulatively. McNutt's essay, however, does not provide a more precise consideration of how the webs of power relations in which we all exist shape our worldviews and hinder or help their re-formation.

Thus, in one generation, pentecostals have gone from scientific illiteracy to engagement with some of the issues, at least within the broader

24. Lawrence McHargue, "The Christian and Natural Science," in Palmer, ed., *Elements of a Christian Worldview*, 147–77; quotation, 171.

context of evangelical theology. They have also come to ask larger questions about the scientific method and about how the advances of science inform our late modern worldview. And they have begun to see the human condition as enmeshed with the various orders of creation, so that human health partly depends on medical science, and human culture and politics partly depend on natural processes.

Still, as open as pentecostals are to engaging current issues in the sciences, they have done so mainly on the modernist assumptions of their evangelical mentors and dialogue partners instead of being motivated by their own pneumatological commitments. What would happen if they were to understand scientific inquiry within a pneumatological framework? How might the contemporary discussion in the theology of nature be enriched by a more robust theology of creation from a pneumatological perspective?

7.2 Mapping Creation: Toward a Pneumatological Semiotic

This section pursues the above questions about a pneumatological framework along two lines. First it explores the biblical materials suggestive of understanding the orders of creation as the handiwork of the Spirit of God, then it inquires into the experiential and epistemological issue of how these biblical insights regarding a pneumatological theology of creation can be empirically confirmed. One of the more fruitful lines of response to these matters is analysis of the semiotic process, the human activity of sign interpretation. Most helpful, especially with an eye toward the theology of nature and of creation this chapter aspires to, is the North American philosophical tradition, particularly the triadic semiotic of Charles Sanders Peirce and, building on Peirce, the metaphysics of experience of Donald Gelpi.

7.2.1 *The Spirit and the Orders of Creation*. In our environmentally conscious age, an increasing number of biblical interpreters are calling attention to the "Creator Spirit," the Spirit as being intimately involved with the orders of creation.[25] The Christian Testament's association of the groanings of creation with the eschatological work of the Spirit (Rom.

---

25. E.g., *PPP* 2:244, 437; 3:288; Wolfhart Pannenberg, "The Doctrine of the Spirit and the Task of a Theology of Nature," in Pannenberg, *Toward a Theology of Nature: Essays on Science and Faith*, ed. Ted Peters (Louisville: Westminster John Knox, 1993), ch. 5; Robert Faricy, *Wind and Sea Obey Him: Approaches to a Theology of Nature* (Westminster, MD: Christian Classics, 1988), ch. 2; Raniero Cantalamessa, *Come, Creator Spirit: Meditations on the Veni Creator*, trans. Denis and Marlene Barrett (Collegeville, MN: Liturgical Press, 2003); and Denis Edwards, *Breath of Life: A Theology of the Creator Spirit* (Maryknoll, NY: Orbis, 2004).

8:22–23) can only be understood against the Hebrew Bible's depictions of creation as the theater of the Spirit's presence and activity. Not only does the Spirit transform deserts into fertile fields and forests (Isa. 32:15); all creatures—donkeys, birds, goats, lions, fish, and so on—are nourished by the breath of Yahweh, apart from which "they die and return to their dust. When you send forth your spirit, they are created; and you renew the face of the ground" (Ps. 104:29–30; cf. Job 34:14–15). And when the psalmist also says, "By the word of the LORD the heavens were made, and all their host by the breath of his mouth" (Ps. 33:6), he is clearly echoing the Priestly author's account of the creation of the world by the *ruah* ("wind" or "breath") of God sweeping over the waters and the word of God speaking things into existence (Gen. 1:2–3).

Yet the *ruah* of God does not make a solitary appearance at the beginning of the creation narrative; *ruah* is also present at its culmination, with the formation of *ha adam*. Only when the Lord God breathed into *ha adam* did *ha adam* become a living being (Gen. 2:7). The Spirit's appearance on both ends of the creation narrative justifies rereading the creation story within an explicitly pneumatological framework.[26] In this perspective, a few observations can be made toward a pneumatological theology of creation that bridges the Genesis narrative with the science-religion dialogue of the late modern world.

First, the *ruah* of God blowing across the primordial world and the breath of life given to *ha adam* provide insight into the interrelationality of the Spirit and the orders of creation. The Spirit is not contradictory to nature, as modernity would have it; rather, the Spirit infuses the world. The vivifying breath of God provides the ontological conditions not only for the relationality of the spiritual and the material dimensions of reality but also for the relationality of human beings as male and female (1:27) and of human beings with the natural world, with each other in community, and with the divine. Is this not suggestive for the more recent attempts to overcome the dualism between spirit and nature, long assumed in scientific circles?[27]

Second, even as the life breath given to *ha adam* empowers *ha adam* to be a responsive creature, capable of being addressed by the divine and of taking responsibility for the orders of creation (1:26), so also the wind of God blowing across the primordial waters enables creation to respond to the divine command. In fact, the breath of God vivifies the

26. See Amos Yong, "*Ruach*, the Primordial Waters, and the Breath of Life: Emergence Theory and the Creation Narratives in Pneumatological Perspective," in *Pneumatology: Exploring the Work of the Holy Spirit in Contemporary Perspectives*, ed. Michael Welker (forthcoming).

27. Thus the work of the John Templeton Foundation. See also Kevin Sharpe, *Sleuthing the Divine: The Nexus of Science and Spirit* (Minneapolis: Fortress, 2000).

orders of creation and empowers them as creative agents in their own right. In some cases, the divine commands given in a passive voice are followed by specific divine actions of making (1:7, 16, 21, 25). But in other cases, God creates by saying (emphases mine): "Let the earth *put forth* vegetation: plants *yielding* seed, and fruit trees . . . that *bear* fruit" (1:11); "Let the waters *bring forth* swarms of living creatures" (1:20); and "Let the earth *bring forth* living creatures of every kind" (1:24). In the first and third case (but not the second), God's command is followed by "And it was so," before indicating God's response and activity. Further, on the third day, the dry land is allowed to appear, and God then proceeds only to call it Earth (1:9–10), and the earth itself is said explicitly to bring forth vegetation (plants, fruits, and trees). A case can be made that these hints from the Priestly author are fully consistent with the nuanced accounts of contemporary science.[28]

Third, not only does creation respond to the divine; God also responds in turn and interacts with the orders of creation. God sees, evaluates, and pronounces: at the end of each day—long before the appearance of human beings—what appears is good. In this sense, as Miroslav Volf puts it, creation is "an end in itself," having a value independent of human beings.[29] This demands a nonanthropocentric view of the orders of creation, including an environmental and ecological ethic of care for the earth on its own terms and not just for the benefit of human habitation.

Finally and perhaps most significantly for the contemporary science-religion dialogue, the *ruah* of God sweeping across the primordial waters infuses the orders of creation with a teleological dynamic, so that creation is best understood in terms of processes directed toward the eschatological intentions of God. Here we must be careful, given the many wrong turns and dead ends coughed up by the evolutionary process (e.g., the extinction of so many species of animals, not to mention the incalculably long periods of time before the appearance of life forms in the universe). Yet is not the evolutionary struggle also implicit in the "formless void and darkness" that covered the face of the deep (1:2)? Is it not precisely in and through this formlessness that the wind of God separates out, divides, and particularizes the orders of creation so as to bring forth complexity out of chaos? The cosmological, geological, and biological orders of creation emerge as increasingly complex systems of organization, each intrinsically connected to the others. Might the

28. E.g., Ted Peters and Martinez Hewlett, *Evolution from Creation to New Creation: Conflict, Conversation, and Convergence* (Nashville: Abingdon, 2003).

29. See Miroslav Volf, *Work in the Spirit: Toward a Theology of Work* (New York: Oxford University Press, 1991), 141–48 (on the theology of creation), esp. 144–45.

presence and activity of the *ruah* of God illuminate some of the topics much debated in the present science-religion dialogue: the teleological processes of emergence and the anthropic principle; the holistic interactivity and causal relations between systems and their constituent parts; and the interrelationality and interactivity of the mental and material domains of the world?

The challenge for Christian theology, however, is to translate these convictions into public discourse accessible to those without the community of faith and to provide for some means to clarify the validity of these interconnections besides just saying, "The Bible says so." Here we return to the task of doing theology in the public square, in this case, in dialogue with the sciences. Although mathematical proof can never be the goal of theological argument, neither is fideism an acceptable option. All this talk about the Spirit and the orders of creation—do they come together only in the figments of the exegetical imagination? My claim, however, is that all truth is God's truth and therefore communicable universally and verifiable in other tongues. How, then, can a pneumatological theology of creation proceed, especially when (at least historically) other voices, in particular the voices of the sciences, have made counterclaims? Do we not need a mediating discourse that allows for translation between the language of science and that of theology? For these particular needs, what we are calling for is a mutual context, a context as wide as the creation itself and amenable to the languages of the natural world, of the sciences, and of theology. Such would be a metaphysics, along with an interpretive account that justifies its articulation. Among various alternatives, the metaphysics of experience developed by Donald Gelpi in dialogue with the North American philosophical tradition provides one sure way forward. Its justification is the semiotic of C. S. Peirce.

7.2.2 Interpreting Creation: The Triadic Semiotic of Peirce. Charles Sanders Peirce (1839–1914) was a mathematician, logician, scientist, and philosopher extraordinaire whose work is gaining appreciation in our time.[30] Whereas I have previously availed myself of his ideas in developing what I then called a symbolics of nature,[31] I wish to appropriate Peircean insights toward what I here call a semiotic of the orders of creation. Despite the explosion of Peirce scholarship, few thinkers have taken his insights in the direction of a theology of creation in dialogue

---

30. Witness the founding of the Peirce Society and its quarterly journal, *The Transactions of the Charles S. Peirce Society.* For an overview of Peirce, see Amos Yong, "The Demise of Foundationalism and the Retention of Truth: What Evangelicals Can Learn from C. S. Peirce," *CSR* 29, no. 3 (Spring 2000): 563–88.

31. See Amos Yong, *Spirit–Word–Community: Theological Hermeneutics in Trinitarian Perspective* (Burlington, VT: Ashgate, 2002), ch. 6.2.

with the sciences. Yet Peirce's scientific methodology, theory of signs (semiotic), and triadic metaphysics beg for such a synthesis. And although my exposition must be extremely selective and fitted only to the argument being developed, it can be helpful not only to pentecostals but also to Christians looking for a way forward in the late modern world. First some comments on Peirce's method.

In an early essay, "The Fixation of Belief" (1877), Peirce identified four ways human beings come to establish their beliefs: tenacity, authority, taste, and shared methodical inquiry.[32] The first secures a kind of epistemic certainty, but does so by being a form of fideism that insulates one's beliefs from questioning. The second also provides assurance for one's beliefs, but through reliance upon external authorities and only at the risk of dogmatism, hierarchicalism, and parochialism. The third either acquiesces to the prevailing zeitgeist (fashion of the times) and finds certitude in the majority opinion or traffics in a kind of a priori form of deductive reasoning as being (allegedly) most pleasing to the human quest for knowledge; but times change (hence Kuhn talked about the shifting nature of paradigms), and a priori rationalism has bred divergent metaphysical visions unchecked by inductive testing. Although religious beliefs are indeed derived legitimately from any of these three ways (especially the second), they can only be adjudicated or clarified through the fourth approach, shared systematic inquiry, exemplified in the scientific method. This last way is the most promising way to fix one's beliefs. Peirce's methodical inquiry, however, is far from any kind of positivistic or dogmatic scientism. Rather, it is fallibilistic in being open to confirmation, falsification, or revision, as dictated by our engagement with, or experience of, reality, not only regarding its conclusions but also regarding itself as a method of fixing beliefs.

What led Peirce to this kind of provisionalism as a method of scientific inquiry? The response to this question leads us to the heart of Peirce's philosophy: his theory of signs, or semiotic.[33] Although considered a cofounder of contemporary semiotic theory with Ferdinand de Saussure

---

32. See *CP* 5:358–87.

33. Because of the unfinished and occasional nature of Peirce's semiotic writings and the vigor of the debates among Peirce scholars about its various aspects, it is best to consult broad overviews committed to laying out the theory as lucidly as possible. Most helpful for this purpose are Douglas Greenlee, *Peirce's Concept of Sign* (The Hague: Mouton, 1973); Max H. Fisch, "Peirce's General Theory of Signs," in *Peirce, Semeiotic, and Pragmatism*, eds. Kenneth Laine Ketner and C. J. W. Kloesel (Indianapolis: University of Indiana Press, 1986), ch. 17; David Savan, *An Introduction to C. S. Peirce's Full System of Semeiotic* (Toronto: Victoria College in the University of Toronto, 1988); and James Jakób Liszka, *A General Introduction to the Semeiotic of Charles Sanders Peirce* (Bloomington: Indiana University Press, 1996).

(1857–1913), Peirce's semiotic is distinguished from de Saussure's by its triadic structure.[34] De Saussure's claim to fame is his application of the traditional dyadic construct of the sign-object relation to linguistic theory. In this view, the sign divides into a signifier (a tangible thing) and what is signified (a conceptual meaning). Embedded in Saussurean semiotics are the perennial dualisms of philosophy: between the sign and the object of signification, between language and reality, and between thought and thing.

In contrast, Peirce defined signs as triadic sets of relations:

> A sign, or *representamen*, is something which stands to somebody for something in some respect or capacity. It addresses somebody, that is, creates in the mind of that person an equivalent sign, or perhaps a more developed sign. That sign which it creates I call the *interpretant* of the first sign. The sign stands for something, its *object*. It stands for that object, not in all respects, but in reference to a sort of idea, which I have sometimes called the *ground* of the representamen. (*CP* 2.228)

> Signs are divisible by three trichotomies; first, according as the sign itself is a mere quality, is an actual existent, or is a general law; secondly, according as the relation of the sign to its object consists in the sign's having some character in itself, or in some existential relation to that object, or in its relation to an interpretant; thirdly, according as its Interpretant represents it as a sign of possibility or as a sign of fact or a sign of reason. (*CP* 2.243)

> A *Sign*, or *Representamen*, is a First which stands in such a genuine triadic relation to a Second, called its *Object*, as to be capable of determining a Third, called its *Interpretant*, to assume the same triadic relation to its Object in which it stands itself to the same Object. (*CP* 2.274)

Using these texts as a springboard, let us unpack several basic features of Peirce's semiotic, keeping in mind our problematic of justifying a metaphysical framework sufficient for the science-religion dialogue (initially) and a pneumatological theology of creation (in the longer run).

Note, initially, the irreducibility of the triadic relation of representamen, object, and interpretant. Signs are not just things but relational functions. Smoke in the distance, for example, is a representamen, grounded in fire which creates in human minds any number of interpretants: "There is a forest fire caused by today's high heat"; or "Someone is lost"; or

---

34. Compare the two lead essays, W. Keith Percival, "Ferdinand de Saussure and the History of Semiotics," and Arthur Skidmore, "Peirce and Semiotics: An Introduction to Peirce's Theory of Signs," in *Semiotic Themes*, ed. Richard T. De George (Lawrence: University of Kansas Publications, 1981), 1–32 and 33–50 respectively.

"Someone is in danger!" The ground in this case is real enough, but is also a vague abstraction regarding the complex dynamics of the fire. This vagueness, however, can be clarified. Each of the interpretants, like all interpretants, either enables the prediction of certain kinds of behaviors or future events or serves as a guide for some course of action (or both). When these future events unfold and/or when the interpretants are so acted upon, each interpretant becomes another representamen grounded in the original interpretant—"Oh no, not a forest fire, just a farmer burning rubbish"; or "Boy scouts cooking salmon for lunch"; or "Yes, a boy is trapped on the third floor of the farmhouse!"—that produces further interpretants in the same or other interpreters, and so on. Observe what Peirce's triadic semiotic accomplishes in contrast to a dyadic construct. On the one hand, insofar as signs are grounded in their objects in some respect, their interpretants are constrained in those respects; thus interpretation cannot just be a subjective matter within human heads. On the other hand, insofar as signs produce interpretants in certain respects, not only can interpreters miss the respects with which the signs are communicating; in addition, all interpretants are necessarily vague in their various respects and thus demanding of further interpretation. Thus all interpretation, because it cannot just be an objective matter capable of definitive settlement, is fallible. In practice, certain things are decided upon in that their interpretants provide for settled courses of action. But given the qualitative open-endedness of the process of interpretation, one cannot predict when future events may call the "settled" interpretant into question. For these reasons, Peirce's semiotic avoids the fallacies of rationalisms that ignore the groundedness of ideas in real objects, and of empiricisms that ignore the open-endedness of interpretants in the signifying process. It emphasizes a contrite fallibilism over and against either a positivistic objectivism that fixes beliefs on the basis of presumed (but unreal) access to the objects of inquiry or a relativistic subjectivism that fixes beliefs on the basis of only social conventions. So, although it is true that "semiosis is in principle without absolute beginning, as well as without end,"[35] it is also true that relativism, skepticism, or nihilism is undercut, since Peirce's triadic semiotic establishes how human activity proceeds in engagement with the real world.

This leads to another important feature of Peirce's semiotic: his classification of signs. Here again we run into complex territory, given that Peirce identifies as many as sixty-six types of interpretants.[36] For our

35. Kelly A. Parker, *The Continuity of Peirce's Thought* (Nashville: Vanderbilt University Press, 1998), 149.

36. For Peirce's most succinct statements on the classes of signs, see "Division of Signs" (*CP* 2:227–73); and "The Icon, Index, and Symbol" (*CP* 2:274–308).

purposes, we will focus on the triad of icon-index-symbol. An icon is a sign with its own character that imitates, images, or resembles its object or exemplifies the qualities of its object. Maps, diagrams, and pulses are iconic signs. An index is a sign that is acted upon physically by its object. Fuel gauges, weather vanes, raps on doors, swelling, scents, and smoke are indexical signs. A symbol is a sign of a law, related to it by habit or by general rule. The (articulated) laws of physics, social conventions of language (e.g., words, sentences, books), and arguments toward conclusions are symbolic signs. The important element to note here is that human signifying activity, including language, is set within the broader framework of interpretation in general. Indeed, interpretation is central to creation's or nature's processes in Peirce's semiotic. Animals, for example, interpret pulses and scents, even as human beings can understand how these signs work for animals. Thus, all qualities, things, and experiences are signs of some kind, interpreted by other qualities, things, and experiences in certain respects. For this reason, Peirce mused that "the entire universe—not merely the universe of existents, but all that wider universe, embracing the universe of existents as a part, . . . all this universe is perfused with signs, if it is not composed exclusively of signs" (*CP* 5:448).[37]

Here we arrive at a third basic feature of Peirce's semiotic theory: its metaphysical connections. The language of First (representamen), Second (object), and Third (interpretant) calls attention to Peirce's reworking of Aristotle's, Kant's, and Hegel's categories. Peirce, however, created his own nomenclature and argued that any datum of reality could be understood finally in terms of the three categories of quality, fact, and law. *Firstness* is the pure possibility, the quality of anything in its immediacy, particularity, and suchness, independent from all interaction and thought. *Secondness* is actuality, the facticity of anything in its brutish opposition or resistance to other things. *Thirdness* is reality, the lawfulness, generality, and intelligibility of anything in its habits, tendencies, and dispositions as it meets the future. Hence the triadic relation of any sign exemplifies Peirce's metaphysics in that anything can be analyzed into its constituent parts (categories) but can be understood as a sign only in its triadic interrelatedness—that is, a representamen is what it is precisely in relationship to an object and an interpretant; remove either of the latter, and the representamen ceases to be that (the same goes for the other two elements of the sign).

37. See Felicia E. Kruse, "Peirce's Sign and the Process of Interpretation," in *Philosophy in Experience: American Philosophy in Transition*, ed. Richard E. Hart and Douglas Anderson (New York: Fordham University Press, 1997), 128–53.

But for our purposes, this metaphysical dimension of Peirce's semiotic is important for three other reasons. Initially, Peirce's category of Firstness as pure possibility provides for real novelty and spontaneity in the universe. Perhaps, from a pentecostal perspective, Firstness points to the realm of the Spirit's unpredictable activity, the impossible possibility of the world of the Spirit. Herein may be a metaphysical intuition regarding the Spirit's silence and hiddenness.

Secondarily, Peirce's category of Thirdness found a way to account for the reality of laws and universals that modern nominalism had dismissed. Modernist thinking had assumed the scholastic rejection of universals as no more than ideas at best or names at worst, partly because this seemed to legitimate the emerging scientific view of the world in purely material or physical terms. Peirce saw, however, that the scientific method assumed the reality of laws not only for the formation of hypotheses but also for their testing and experimentation. With this insight, Peirce's semiotic was able not only to correlate the human mind's interactions with the actualities of the physical world but also to align the mind's anticipations with the regularities (laws) of the orders of creation in practical ways.

Finally, Peirce's semiotic metaphysics (or metaphysical semiotic, if you prefer) provides an account for the causal interface between human mentality and the orders of creation.[38] Things become present to us through their signifying qualities, resistances, and lawful effects. The example, provided above, of smoke in the distance illustrates the congruence between mind and nature. A more artificial but no less real example of semiotic causation refers to the future determining the identity of the past, much as when an umpire calls a ball fair or foul after it lands. Certainly, the call can be debated—producing interpretants upon interpretants—even if these debates do not change the call. Hence what I call the eschatological character of semiosis as inquiry in the infinite long run which anticipates that reality will eventually reveal the truth behind all interpretants.

What gains have been made through the retrieval and appropriation of Peirce's semiotic theory, and what kind of help can we expect toward a pneumatological theology of creation? Most important is that its triadicity avoids the intractable dualisms that have plagued modern thinking on all fronts. Might not a triadic semiotic also be suggestive for crossing the disastrous chasm separating modern construals of mind and matter and of spirit and nature? Second, Peirce's triadic semiotic is realistic regarding the objects of interpretation. The importance of a realistic view of

---

38. See Joseph Ransdell, "Semiotic Causation: A Partial Explication," in *Proceedings of the C. S. Peirce Bicentennial International Congress*, ed. Kenneth L. Ketner (Lubbock: Texas Tech Press, 1981), 201–6; and Menno Hulswit, "Semeiotic and the Cement of the Universe: A Peircean Process Approach to Causation," *TCSPS* 37, no. 3 (2001): 339–63.

creation cannot be overstated for any theology of creation. Third, Peirce's semiotic also accounts for the pragmatic dimension of interpretation: we interpret to answer questions or to get things done. A pneumatological theology of creation is certainly concerned not only with theory but also with praxis. Fourth, the essentially triadic character of the sign relation means that human interpretation is an intersubjective and social process whereby interpretants are adjudicated for the achievement of various values in reality. It encourages shared communal inquiry: the more perspectives one has on any matter in question, the better grounds one has for arguing one interpretant to be superior to rival interpretants.[39] This is the best way to respond to the subjective dimension of interpretation, which emerges more as a factor of the causal process of semiotic interaction and less as a problem of individual perspectivism.

7.2.3 *Interpretation and a Metaphysics of Experience*. The groundwork has now been set to appreciate Donald Gelpi's metaphysics of experience and its capacity to contribute toward a pneumatological theology of creation. Almost from the beginning, Gelpi's project has been to develop an enculturated North American theology, and he has proceeded toward this end in dialogue with the North American philosophical tradition.[40] Insofar as the whole point of metaphysics is to provide a framework of explanation that can account for any known datum of experience, Gelpi's metaphysics of experience also aspires to universality. But having learned well from his North American philosophical dialogue partners, particularly from Peirce, Gelpi realizes that metaphysical speculation is not a purely rationalistic enterprise of deductive conclusions derived from a priori premises but a fallibilistic and communal form of inquiry guided by inductive testing and engagement with empirical reality. For this reason, he makes no apologies for locating his proposal within the North American philosophical context, even if he believes it to be sufficiently robust as a metaphysical hypothesis.

Also from the North American philosophical tradition—including William James's "stream of experience" and Alfred North Whitehead's "reformed subjectivist principle," which asserted that reality consists of nothing else but experiences of subjects[41]—Gelpi has discerned a root

39. See Mats Bergman, *Meaning and Mediation: Toward a Communicative Interpretation of Peirce's Theory of Signs* (Helsinki: University of Helsinki Press, 2000).

40. Gelpi summarizes his engagement with the North American philosophical tradition in Donald L. Gelpi, *The Varieties of Transcendental Experience: A Study in Constructive Postmodernism* (Collegeville, MN: Liturgical Press, 2000).

41. Donald L. Gelpi, *The Gracing of Human Experience: Rethinking the Relationship between Nature and Grace* (Collegeville, MN: Liturgical Press, 2001), esp. 276–77. Whitehead came to his "reformed subjectivist principle" after he moved from Cambridge University in England to Harvard University in 1924.

metaphor appropriate to his metaphysical vision: experience. Fully realizing that "experience" is a "weasel word" laden with unwanted baggage and rife with popular misuse, Gelpi nevertheless deems it important enough to rehabilitate for his own purposes.[42] I have elsewhere argued, on the basis of the development of Gelpi's own writing and thinking, however, that his project has from the beginning been driven by the attempt to think through his charismatic experience of the Spirit as a Roman Catholic Jesuit religious.[43] Indeed, his entire theology of conversion, so valuable for our own soteriology earlier (§2.2.3), is part and parcel of what he calls foundational pneumatology, the attempt to articulate how Christians can and should relate to and experience God. Gelpi rightly saw that a metaphysical account was required for this. Not to articulate a metaphysics leaves one working with unquestioned metaphysical assumptions at best or presuming faulty metaphysical ideas antithetical to one's experience at worst. Further, for the overall pentecostal purposes of this volume, the capacity to interpret strange tongues or to give public testimony to our own personal experiences assumes some theory of the whole (a metaphysics) that defeats any incommensurability thesis denying the possibility of truly communicating across languages, cultures, and even religious traditions. Finally, for our discussion of the science-religion interface in this chapter, neglecting metaphysical issues leaves the door open to the metaphysical naturalism or materialism so prevalent among those working in the natural and social sciences. So the question is not whether or if metaphysics, but whose or what kind of metaphysics.

James and Whitehead helped Gelpi embrace a process view of reality, but the former's tendency to psychologism (reducing ontological matters to psychological states of mind) and the latter's dipolar nominalism (dividing reality into objective actual occasions and subjective elements of mind incapable of explaining the reality of laws or habits) led him back to Peirce. Although Peirce did not call his own a metaphysics of experience, Gelpi suggests that Peirce's triadic vision is not only consistent with, and anticipatory of, Whitehead's philosophy of organism but also able to preserve all the virtues of the Whiteheadian philosophy without its liabilities.[44] Gelpi therefore rearticulates Peirce's basic categories—quality, fact, and law—as relational and elemental forms of

42. On "experience" as a "weasel word," see Donald Gelpi, *The Turn to Experience in Contemporary Theology* (New York: Paulist, 1994), 1–3.

43. See Amos Yong, "In Search of Foundations: The *Oeuvre* of Donald L. Gelpi, SJ, and Its Significance for Pentecostal Theology and Philosophy," *JPT* 11, no. 1 (2002): 3–26, esp. 23–26.

44. The most succinct and recent statement of Gelpi's metaphysics of experience is in Gelpi, *The Gracing of Human Experience*, ch. 8.

feelings at the heart of reality's processes, with higher life forms such as human beings consisting of evaluative feelings (qualities), decisional feelings (facts), and tendencies/habits (laws or generalities). Gelpi argues that these moves render the proposed metaphysics of experience logically consistent, applicable to all things one is attempting to account for, adequate (there is nothing known that it cannot account for), and coherent with other dimensions of our experience (including religious experience in general and Christian experience in particular).

Any metaphysical hypothesis worth its salt should meet these requirements. Space constraints prohibit me from explicating Gelpi's accomplishment on all of these points (but see §7.3.1), but I substantially agree with Gelpi that his metaphysics of experience avoids the most damaging fallacies that have plagued rival metaphysical hypotheses. For starters, its triadic character overcomes all of the dualisms of the philosophical tradition. Plato's unchanging ideas and changing phenomena, for example, undergird other misleading notions, such as the gnostic devaluation of the material world and the Kantian noumena-phenomena dualism. Whereas Peirce's categories of Firstness and Secondness account for Plato's ideas and phenomena, Thirdness means that reality is dynamic, always becoming something else, as its laws and habits mediate the transformation of the present into the future. Similarly, the Cartesian mind-body problematic, imbued as it is with medieval nominalism, is resolved in a triadic metaphysics that defines nature's processes in semiotic terms, on the one hand, and sees human cognition as a higher-level manifestation of the category of law, on the other. Finally, Aristotelian substance dualism is replaced with a dynamic view of reality shaped by real laws and habits. Essentialism, the idea that things have definite and immutable identities, is rejected insofar as essences become the hows of experience (qualities that make things present to us, which we then reify and arrange alphabetically in dictionaries), which are continuously evolving according to their accumulation of habits and tendencies, rather than whats (facts that resist or oppose us).

In addition to overcoming the traditional dualisms of philosophy, a metaphysics of experience provides for a more reliable process of inquiry over the one-sidedness characteristic of previous approaches. Classical approaches were divided between the rationalists, on the one side, and the empiricists, on the other. The Kantian revolution adopted the former in a radical turn to the subject (since all knowledge is mediated through the forms of the mind) whereas the sciences purported to be driven just by the facts. Peirce's Thirdness defended the intelligibility of reality even as Secondness secured the place of facts external to any human mind whatsoever. But insofar as representamens yield interpretants regarding certain respects of their objects (and not in the entirety of their objects), to that degree human knowledge proceeds according to inferential hypotheses, deductive clarifications, and inductive confirmation or falsification and back again (Peirce's version of the hermeneutical circle). Further, in contrast to Kant's turn to the subject, Peirce's triadic semiotic called for a "turn to the community"—a turn brought to fruition by his friend and colleague Josiah Royce[45]—wherein truth is attained, in the potentially infinite long run, through a shared process of inquiry. In this way, solipsistic subjectivism is traded in for intersubjective engagement with the world.

This leads, lastly for our purposes, to a metaphysics of experience as capable of avoiding the ontological fallacies of idealism and (especially naïve) realism considered on their own terms. Reality is much richer when considered in experiential terms of qualities, facts, and laws or of values, decisions, and habits. But mind is not absent from a triadically structured universe either. A metaphysics of experience considers what is ultimately real in dynamic and relational terms. Both idealistic and realistic accounts assume a subject-object distinction overturned in a triadic framework. If experiences are the ultimately real things, then objects of experience lie within, not without, experience—hence also the objects of signs lie within, not without, the semiotic triad—and subjects and objects are mutually subsistent or in-existent. If this is the case, then mind is not opposed to nature, nor is spirit opposed to matter. Does not this kind of triadic, social, and realistic metaphysics of experience thereby chart one path toward a pneumatological theology of creation?

7.3 Engaging Creation: Life in the Spirit

The hypothesis explored in this final section of the book can be plainly stated: if pneumatology leads us beyond binitarianism toward trinitarianism, does not a triadic metaphysics, by analogy, overcome all dualism toward a dynamic, social, and interrelational view of creation as a whole? Insofar as Peirce's philosophy insists that the meaning of any claim is to be discerned in the habits and activities such a claim generates, I will test

45. For the import of Royce, see ibid., ch. 5; and Gelpi, *The Varieties of Transcendental Experience*, ch. 11. Royce's communal and social view of interpretation is most extensively developed in Josiah Royce, *The Problem of Christianity*, ed. Frank M. Oppenheim, SJ (Washington, DC: Catholic University of America Press, 2001), part 2; and *Metaphysics*, ed. William Ernest Hocking, Richard Hocking, and Frank Oppenheim (Albany: State University of New York Press, 1998), part 1.

this theological hypothesis by inquiring into the creaturely experiences of the divine (in further dialogue with Gelpi), of revelation and truth, and of the orders of creation. Throughout, our concern remains that posed by the science-religion problematic sketched in the first section of this chapter. Put summarily, we need to make good on theological claims in our late modern Western, secular, and scientific context. Given the metaphysics of experience outlined in the preceding, what can a pneumatological theology of creation say about our experiences of God, of revelation, and of the world in this context?

7.3.1 *Experiencing God: The Spirit, the Charisms, and the Orders of Creation*. The challenge for theology in the late modern world, with its scientific assumptions about the closed nature of the universe, is to make sense of the claim that human beings can experience the divine. In one sense, Gelpi's metaphysics seeks to address exactly this question by "rethinking the relationship between nature and grace." Insofar as Peirce's triadic and semiotic metaphysics overcomes the dualisms of the philosophical tradition, it also enables a reconsideration of the God-world relationship.

Standing in faith and seeking understanding, Gelpi begins with the conviction that God is most clearly identified with creation in the incarnational and pentecostal events. Proceeding then to apply Peirce's categories to the biblical revelation (remember Gelpi's goal of developing an enculturated North American theology), Gelpi suggests that "the different 'winds,' or 'spirits,' described in the Bible are the laws that give experience purpose and direction" and "the 'Holy Breath' of Jesus is a life-force functioning in the midst of other vectoral feelings that shape experience. The history of the Breath's influence upon human experience can be described; its future consequences anticipated."[46] In one sense, Gelpi's project for the last twenty years and more has been to elaborate on the philosophical and theological implications of this line of thinking.

In brief, within a triadic, social, and realistic metaphysical framework, Gelpi suggests that human beings experience the Spirit of God in at least the following ways.[47] First, the Spirit's presence and activity transmute (set in a new framework) every other dimension of human experience, be it the affections, the intellect, the moral, or the interpersonal. Second, divine grace is mediated through the concrete realities of the sacraments, the communion of saints, or whatever other events are chosen by God. Third, the charisms reflect the increased sensitivity, receptivity,

---

46. Donald L. Gelpi, *Experiencing God: A Theology of Human Emergence* (New York: Paulist, 1978), 135–36.

47. See Gelpi, *The Gracing of Human Experience*, esp. 355–59.

and docility of the human person to interpret the habitual activities of the Spirit. Fourth, the Spirit enables human freedom by gifting human experience with the genuine opportunity to collaborate with the divine offer of grace; there can never be a simple dualistic opposition between divine and human willing in a triadic metaphysical framework. Finally, the Spirit personalizes human beings more and more fully (through the conversion process), orienting human experience toward the full assimilation of the image and life of Christ in their own lives. In these ways, Gelpi's pneumatology and his theology of conversion (see §2.2.3) find public expression within a metaphysical framework more conducive to late modern thinking. More important, this framework itself provides the needed public language to make twenty-first-century sense of the dynamic, holistic, and multidimensional soteriology and the ecumenical, sacramental, and charismatic ecclesiology for which this volume argues.

Here it is appropriate to build on Gelpi's insights toward a "charismology," or theology of the charismatic gifts of the Spirit. Most pentecostal treatments have focused on exegetical and experiential explications of Saint Paul's listing of the nine *charismata* (1 Cor. 12:4–11). Within the philosophical and pneumatological theology-of-creation framework in this chapter, however, pentecostal thinking about the charisms of the Spirit needs to be broadened in various ways. First, the problematic early modern distinction between "natural" and "supernatural" should be abandoned when one talks about the *charismata*, precisely because of the fallacious dualisms these imply.[48] If other gifts of the Spirit resist this kind of dichotomy—for example, the five "office gifts" identified in the Letter to the Ephesians (4:11) or the eight "personality gifts" enumerated by Paul in Romans (12:6–8)—then why not the charismatic gifts of the Spirit? On the one hand, a triadic metaphysics allows us to overcome the dualism altogether. On the other hand, it also helps us avoid the pantheistic identification of the Creator and the orders of creation because it preserves their distinctiveness (even as Peirce's Thirdness does not sublate Firstness and Secondness, as in Hegel's philosophy, but instead exists relationally with them). This helps us to reconceive of the spiritual gifts beyond the impasse of either "natural" or "supernatural." In this case, Paul's lists of charisms are not exhaustive of the Spirit's gifts to and through human beings.[49]

---

48. See Walter Hollenweger, "*Creator Spiritus*: The Challenge of Pentecostal Experience to Pentecostal Theology," *Theology* 81 (1978): 32–40; and Jürgen Moltmann, *The Spirit of Life: A Universal Affirmation*, trans. Margaret Kohl (Minneapolis: Fortress, 1992), ch. 9.

49. See *PPP* 2:206, 405, along with the "Mühleim Theses on Community and Charism," *PPP* 1:104–8.

This means, second, that the manifestation of the *charismata* is simply a more obvious sign of the interpenetration of the divine and the orders of creation. The incarnation is the most obvious event through which this mystery of the togetherness of the divine and the human is revealed. For Christians, the Bible is the word of God even as it contains the words of human beings. From a pentecostal perspective, the movement of the Spirit enables speaking in strange tongues, but only as the Spirit gives utterance (Acts 2:4). By analogical extension, why would the charismatic gifts be any different, and not be either merely transcendent or merely immanent?

Third, in this case, the *charismata* can be cultivated and developed. Though gracious endowments of the Spirit, they are not necessarily arbitrary. Walking in and after the Spirit sharpens our capacity to discern and imitate the Spirit's ways. Being mentored or discipled by those more mature in the ways of the Spirit will teach us to interpret the movements of the divine Breath. Contrary to popular belief, the more in tune we are with the Spirit, the more infused our lives will be with the Spirit's charismatic presence, even if we cease to marvel as much about it.

Fourth, cultivation of the gifts should not be for self-aggrandizement but for the edification of others. The *charismata* are for the common good (1 Cor. 12:7b)—for unifying the body of Christ; for enabling the gospel witness; for meeting human needs; for insight into the human condition and for guiding human action; for empowering human speech to name, to expose, to speak the truth—and herald the coming kingdom of God. Although "the gifts and the calling of God are irrevocable" (Rom. 11:29), the gifts belong not to their particular human vessel bearers but to those who receive the edification of the Spirit through them and to the Spirit, "who allots to each one individually just as the Spirit chooses" (1 Cor. 12:11).

Finally, the charismatic gifts need to be discerned in all circumstances. We experience the Spirit not only in the ecclesial context but in and through the various orders of creation, especially in the complex layers of human interaction.[50] Thus we must be discerning of the values, decisions, and tendencies (to use Gelpi's categories) present in and to our experiences. Life in the Spirit requires discerning the Holy Spirit from the various spirits of this world. The life, death, and resurrection of Jesus the Christ is the supreme Christian norm for such discernment, since the Spirit is no less than the Spirit of Jesus. Jesus is the man for others, who loved them and gave himself for them, whose deeds were signs of the eschatological kingdom, and whose virtues were etched in the memory of the earliest disciples and embodied in them as "fruits" by the working of the Spirit

---

50. See Volf, *Work in the Spirit*, 111–13.

of Jesus—in these and other ways, we discern the Spirit's comings and goings in the community of faith. If, whenever the prophets speak, the congregation has to determine afresh whether these new words are of the Lord (1 Cor. 14:29), then this is true also for every moment dedicated to life in the Spirit.

7.3.2 *Experiencing Revelation: Tracking the Spirit in the Late Modern World.* The preceding reflections open up a set of interrelated questions pertinent to a pneumatological theology of creation. If the Spirit is to be found in some way within the orders of creation, does this not eliminate any special, supernatural, or miraculous actions of God in the world? How, then, can we conceive of divine revelation? Does theology reduce to anthropology, and if so, are theological claims about human experiences instead of about the divine?

These questions came to the fore during the early modern period because of scientific advances. Modern responses divided between liberals and conservatives. The former sought to ground theological claims on universal human experiences, whereas the latter founded theology on the revealed and inerrant truths of Scripture. Pentecostals have waded into theological waters following their fundamentalist and evangelical cousins and, in most cases, uncritically assumed their categories. Most pointed has been the debate over the nature of the Bible's inerrancy. Is it absolute (in which case, limited to the original autographs), perspectival (in which case, scientific and historical references are true from the various perspectives and contexts of the ancient biblical authors, as in their telling of the "rising of the sun"), accommodative (i.e., in human terms), and so forth?[51] Less controversial but still important is the question of the inspiration of Scripture. Did it come about through divine dictation, through the illumination of the biblical authors' powers of perception, through special intuition or insight, or (the most prevalent current response) through some kind of "verbal" means whereby the Spirit of God directed both the thoughts and the words of the human authors?[52] And at the most general level, what about divine revelation? Surely such is historically manifest in Jesus and preserved in the scriptural witness. But pentecostals have also been of two minds about the nature of ongoing revelation by the Spirit: can new revelation be given, and if so, should not this revelation be at least consistent with, and not contradictory to, the Bible?

Preliminarily, a pneumatological theology of revelation would locate the doctrine of inerrancy in its modernist context with its dualistic

51. E.g., Norman L. Geisler, ed., *Inerrancy* (Grand Rapids: Zondervan, 1980).
52. E.g., Millard J. Erickson, *Christian Theology*, 3 vols. (Grand Rapids: Baker, 1983–1985), 1:206–7.

assumptions, rationalistic optimism, and *sola scriptura* foundationalism. Even in this context, naïve understandings of inerrancy and *sola scriptura* were quickly qualified—for example, inerrancy was limited to the original autographs of Scripture, Scripture has never been alone in a literal sense, and the doctrines of inerrancy and *sola scriptura* were not found in Scripture except deductively—and soon understood to be as much doctrines about God (and divine truthfulness and faithfulness) and about conservative Protestantism defining its norm of authority (against the infallibility of the pope and the experientialism of liberal theology) as about the Bible. With the unraveling of modernity, the explanatory power and theoretical usefulness of the idea of inerrancy (along with papal infallibility and experiential foundationalism) have come under question. But might there be helpful ways of reconstructing this idea in our late modern situation if, with the help of Peirce's triadic semiotic, conservative evangelical theologians understood the doctrine of inerrancy as a hypothesis about biblical propositions to be confirmed by ongoing inquiry extended infinitely (eschatologically), on the one hand, or as a narrative about Christian living whose operational consequences are tested pragmatically, on the other? From a classical Pentecostal perspective, then, this means that the authority of Scripture rests on its illuminating and transforming power by the Spirit.

(Similarly, the classical Pentecostal doctrine of tongues as the initial physical evidence of the baptism in the Holy Spirit derives from a modernist framework where "evidence" is opposed to "myth." One can argue toward initial evidence from those assumptions or even from Lindbeck's theory of doctrine.[53] But if classical Pentecostals are concerned to retain the doctrine in order to preserve our "distinctive testimony" and experience, it is more important to develop our pneumatological imagination instead, the task of this book. Preserving initial evidence without a robust pneumatological theology is to harp on the letter of a dead law; reviving our legal institutions will itself rejuvenate the law. We need more of the Spirit, and the distinctive pentecostal witness will come.)

Further, a pneumatological theology of revelation would affirm the inspired nature of the scriptural witness (2 Tim. 3:16). It is precisely the letter that kills, but the Spirit who gives life (2 Cor. 3:6). Here the triadic semiotic of Peirce illuminates the processes through which the word of

---

53. E.g., Donald A. Johns, "Some New Directions in the Hermeneutics of Classical Pentecostalism's Doctrine of Initial Evidence," in *Initial Evidence: Historical and Biblical Perspectives on the Pentecostal Doctrine of Spirit Baptism*, ed. Gary B. McGee (Peabody, MA: Hendrickson, 1991), 145–67; Joel Shuman, "Toward a Cultural-Linguistic Account of the Pentecostal Doctrine of the Baptism in the Holy Spirit," *PNEUMA* 19 (1997): 207–23; and Koo Dong Yun, *Baptism in the Holy Spirit: An Ecumenical Theology of Spirit Baptism* (Lanham, MD: University Press of America, 2003).

God is discerned as normative Scripture. In this view, what is revelatory is received (interpreted) by the community of faith through a dynamic process. The wisdom of the ancients, the encounter of the people with God, the laments of those exiled, the speech of the prophets, the incarnation, the Pentecost experience, the apostolic teachings[54]—in each case, these accounts are deemed by the community of faith to be inspired of the Spirit insofar as the people of God are empowered, healed, and transformed in this encounter. Semiosis confirms the canonical process, doctrinal development, and strategies of enculturation and contextualization whereby past realities are defined in new light over time.

Now that some of these traditional concerns have been addressed, what else needs to be emphasized about the distinctiveness of a pneumatological approach to the doctrine of revelation? First, revelation is transcendental: the Spirit breaks through into the human condition from beyond ourselves. Second, revelation is historical: the Spirit is poured out on all flesh, not suspended in the ethereal heavens. Third, revelation is contextual: the Spirit is concerned with real lives, real history, and real societies. Fourth, revelation is personal: we encounter the person of Jesus as the way, the truth, and the life, and the Spirit of Jesus as one who leads us into interpersonal and intersubjective relationship. Fifth, revelation is transformational: the word of God is living and active by the Spirit to accomplish God's will in us instead of just telling us about something "out there." Sixth, revelation is communal: we encounter the Spirit sacramentally (used in our pentecostal, loose sense) in various ways, and we discern the Spirit's sacramental presence and activity communally. Seventh, revelation is a verb, not a noun: through Scripture, the Holy Spirit evokes a new realm of possibilities and invites us as the church to inhabit this world. Eighth, revelation is progressive and dynamic: the gift of the Spirit calls us to respond, to act, and to interpret, and we are enabled to do so. Ninth, revelation is marked by love: the Spirit of truth is the love of God "poured into our hearts" (Rom. 5:5), leaving us with an unmistakable criterion for discernment. Tenth, revelation is received by humble faith seeking understanding: this gift of the Spirit, who bears witness in our hearts and keeps us in the truth through word and sacraments, cannot be presumed; we must be teachable, not incorrigible. Eleventh, revelation is propositional: words and sentences are the brute facts through which divine communication is

---

54. I hereby incorporate the broad spectrum of the Christian tradition's understanding of revelation; see Avery Dulles, *Models of Revelation* (Garden City, NY: Image, 1985); Wolfhart Pannenberg, ed., *Revelation as History*, trans. David Granskou (London: Macmillan, 1968); and T. J. Gorringe, *Discerning Spirit: A Theology of Revelation* (London: SCM; Philadelphia: Trinity Press International, 1970).

narrated and by which divine intentions resist our manipulative (fallen) interpretations. Finally, revelation is eschatological, the truth we long for: the Spirit is the down payment of the glory to be revealed, when "we will be like him, for we will see him as he is" (1 John 3:2).

So, although biblical propositions can be taken at face value—in fact, this is precisely how most pentecostals read Scripture at the devotional and existential levels—Bible reading is not about head knowledge; rather, it is about being able to speak the truth (to bear witness, to give testimony, to make confession) and to inhabit the truth (to embody, to experience, to actualize). And this, I submit, is what life in the Spirit is finally all about. Oral Roberts's cliché-ish "Expect a miracle today" is not about supernaturalism but about being open to the new, unexpected, and surprising things of the Spirit, who turns the world upside down (cf. Acts 17:6), who breaks the established habits of sin and replaces them with the living realities of Christ, and who opens us up to the transcendental, uncanny, and eschatological in-breaking of the kingdom.

7.3.3 *Experiencing Creation: Toward a Pneumatological Theology of the Environment*. Life in the Spirit is ultimately about life in this world, our world, God's world. It is about encountering God sacramentally and semiotically in one another and in the various orders of creation. On the one hand, we do not just make up the world: it will resist our domination. On the other hand, we have the responsibility of contributing to the world: we become what we will be through engagement with it.

The pneumatological approach we are applying here toward a theology of creation shows promise for an environment ethic.[55] And pentecostals are slowly developing a theologically informed response to our interaction with, and responsibility for, the orders of creation. We have already seen what the Spirit churches of Zimbabwe are doing with their "earth-keeping theology" (§1.3.1). Harold Hunter asks us to consider why we pray for healing but address neither the environmental and ecological factors that cause sickness nor the practical obligation to reduce, reuse, and recycle.[56] Agustinus Dermawan blames our lack of attention to this issue on our otherworldliness and pessimism and looks for resources to address this situation in the correlations between the "Creator Spirit"

55. Pentecostal Veli-Matti Kärkkäinen calls attention to the richness of recent pneumatological thinking focused on "ecological theology" in *Pneumatology: The Holy Spirit in Ecumenical, International, and Contextual Perspective* (Grand Rapids: Baker, 2002), 159–74. See also Grace M. Jantzen, "Healing Our Brokenness: The Spirit and Creation," in *Readings in Ecology and Feminist Theology*, ed. Mary Heather MacKinnon and Moni McIntyre (Kansas City, MO: Sheed & Ward, 1995), 284–98.

56. Harold D. Hunter, "Pentecostal Healing for God's Sick Creation?" *S&C* 2, no. 2 (2000): 145–67; and Jean-Jacques Suurmond, "Christ King: A Charismatic Appeal for an Ecological Lifestyle," *PNEUMA* 10, no. 1 (1988): 26–35.

of the Hebrew Bible and the relational concept of the Indonesian *Ibu Pertiwi*, or "mother earth."[57]

The pneumatological vision of Isaiah the prophet links the charismatically anointed Messiah with the healing and reconciliation of creation's destroying forces (Isa. 11:1–9; 32:16–20).[58] Hence the Spirit is poured out upon *all* flesh, including the wolf and the lamb, the leopard and the kid, the cow and the bear, the lion and the ox, all of whom are included in the blessings of God promised under the covenant with Noah (Gen. 9:8–17). The redemption of the creation is the work of the Spirit, and we have our roles to play in this process. Even the destruction promised for the earth will be accomplished only in and through the purifying fire of God (2 Pet. 3:10–12), but this is no less than the Spirit, whose cleansing work was inaugurated two thousand years ago with the appearance of cloven tongues of fire (Acts 2:3a). Hence not just the bride but the Spirit also says, "Come," and invites our contribution to the eschatological fountain of life (Rev. 22:17).

Peter Scott's work on a pneumatological theology of the environment is suggestive for us along this same line of thought.[59] In particular, Scott locates what we call here the theology of creation within a social and political framework—rightly so, given the interrelated multidimensionality of human life. Thus the fellowship of the Spirit is not limited to the human arena but applies even to the human interface with the natural realms, the common realm of creation. The goal is the recognition and enabling of the free space of the Spirit that nurtures fellowship, difference, and peace: "The means to fellowship is provided through those practices which enhance the mutual orientation of the agents of the common realm towards one another."[60]

How, then, might we summarize the central elements of a pneumatological theology of creation? Most important, the spiritual and the material realms are intertwined both ontologically and epistemologically. Regarding the former, the Spirit both hovers over the waters of creation and gives the breath of life: the human is intimately and intricately connected with the orders of creation. Hence our obligation to love our neighbor as ourselves can be extended here to the world that God called good. Regarding the latter, the heavens and the earth declare the glory

57. See Agustinus Dermawan, "The Spirit in Creation and Environmental Stewardship: A Preliminary Pentecostal Response toward Ecological Theology," *AJPS* 6, no. 2 (2003): 199–217.

58. See Karl Löning and Erich Zenger, *To Begin with, God Created . . . : Biblical Theologies of Creation*, trans. Omar Kaste (Collegeville, MN: Liturgical Press, 2000), ch. 14.

59. Peter Scott, *A Political Theology of Nature* (Cambridge: Cambridge University Press, 2003), esp. ch. 8.

60. Ibid., 202.

of God (Ps. 19:1). We need to read the signs of creation not to tell the future but so we can heal our present for our future.

Second, the Spirit does not simply shape the orders of creation; the Spirit is shaping them in anticipation of the eschatological reign of God. Insofar as the new Jerusalem comes down "out of heaven from God" toward the earth (Rev. 21:10), and insofar as our eschatological reality will include the resurrection (instead of the rotting) of our bodies, we see that the goods God created will ultimately be redeemed as well. The salvation of the cosmos (§2.2.1) demands our sociopolitical conversion (§2.2.3) and the witness of the entire *ecclesia* of God (individuals make little headway on their own; §3.2) if we wish to participate in the Spirit's redemption of creation's orders.

Finally, the triadic, social, and semiotic metaphysics of experience developed in this chapter suggests concrete ways in which we can participate in this redemptive process. Our responsibility is to discern (interpret) the complex web of ourselves and our environments; to be sensitive to how our environments correct our courses of activity; to be proactive in seeing hypotheses for their care, circumspect in deducing the consequences of our plans, and diligent in inducing the results of our actions toward the common good of the various orders of creation. Given the scientific capacities available to us late moderns, we sin against the orders of creation, against our neighbors (and ourselves), and against God should we not rise to meet the environmental challenges of our time. So here again we find ourselves calling upon the power and charismatic giftings of the Spirit to enable us to bear the good news to the ends of the heavens and the earth.[61]

This concluding chapter has had three interrelated and culminating objectives. First, it identifies the outpouring of the Spirit in the most comprehensive sense of touching not only all living creatures but also the natural orders of creation, the heavens and earth included; this calls for, motivates, and engenders a basic pneumatological theology of creation. Second, it engages the challenges posed to theology by modern science; it does so not only in terms of the results of the sciences but (more so) in terms of the methodology and epistemology of science. This has provided the opportunity to test the horizons of what is called here the pneumatological imagination to see if it might be able to engage the science-religion dialogue and debate. Third, this exercise has carried us from the realm of philosophy of science to metascience, or

---

61. This connection between the salvation of the cosmos and the charisms of the Spirit is detailed in Donald L. Gelpi, *The Firstborn of Many: A Christology for Converting Christians*, vol. 1, *To Hope in Jesus Christ* (Milwaukee: Marquette University Press, 2001), ch. 16.

metaphysics: a view of the whole. This was crucial for establishing the plausibility of the pentecostal claim to encounter the Spirit of God in our late modern world. My hypothesis is that the triadic, social, realistic, and semiotic metaphysics of experience developed here has provided a viable framework for interpreting creation, the scientific enterprise, and God for our late modern environment. Its nondualism, relationalism, holism, dynamism, experientialism, communalism, and fallibilism echo themes and motifs seen time and again in our attempts to articulate a pneumatological soteriology, ecclesiology, and theology. Have we thereby succeeded in articulating a plausible Christian theology for the late modern world from pentecostal and pneumatological perspectives?

Epilogue

We have come to a resting place in our attempt to discern the untraceable winds of the Spirit. Starting with pentecostalism on the ground, we were led to ask soteriological, ecclesiological, ecumenical, theological, interreligious, intercultural, and scientific/philosophical/environmental questions. We were guided throughout in our reading of Scripture by the Lukan lens, steadied in our theological reflection by Jesus, the Christ and inaugurator of the kingdom, and driven in our speculation by the Spirit (it is hoped!), who has been poured out upon all flesh. My not-so-modest aspiration was to think through pentecostal experience of the Spirit as far as possible toward the reformulation of Christian theology in our late modern world.

In hindsight, however, I must be modest in assessing our success. My thoughts have been identified as provisional throughout, partly because of my fallible nature, partly because I can never fully catch up with my/our experience, and partly because my desire to track the Spirit will always elude me. No doubt, many conclusions proposed here are already dated even as I finish this sentence, and the few valid points leave much unsaid, given my many limitations. I hope that you, my readers—God bless your perseverance through this—can help correct my perspective and deepen my reflections. If either has happened or will happen for you, I consider this labor of love a success for the future of Christian theology.

This said, is the project, then, a failure? Was an attempt to do theology in the world context doomed from the start, given the particularities of any individual's limited location and perspective? But what other kind of theology could I do if indeed theology is reflection on the good news of Jesus Christ? Good news is meant to be told not just to a few but to all the world. Is this not the impossible task of having to bear witness to the gospel to every creature, every culture, and every tongue? Yes, this is nothing less than the impossible possibility: impossible because of the finitude of my particularity but perhaps possible because of the Spirit who has been poured out on all flesh, who not only gives the gift of speech (in this case, writing) but also the miracle of hearing (in this case, reading) and understanding . . .

Scripture Index

Romans

1 Corinthians

Name Index

Subject Index